GEORGE WASHINGTON

GEORGE WASHINGTON
Gentleman Warrior

Stephen Brumwell

New York • London

Quercus

New York • London

© 2012 by Stephen Brumwell
Maps © 2012 by William Donohoe
First published in the United States by Quercus in 2013

ISBN 978-1-62365-845-8

Library of Congress Control Number: 2013937907

Distributed in the United States and Canada by
Hachette Book Group
237 Park Avenue
New York, NY 10017

Manufactured in the United States

10 9 8 7 6 5 4 3 2 1

www.quercus.com

For Laura, Milly, and Ivan

Contents

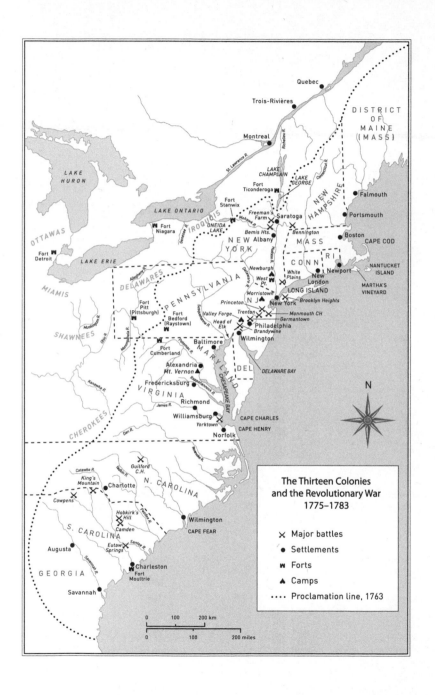

Quebec

Trois-Rivières

Montreal

DISTRICT OF MAINE (MASS)

LAKE HURON

LAKE CHAMPLAIN

LAKE GEORGE

St. Lawrence R.

Richelieu R.

Connecticut R.

Fort Ticonderoga

Falmouth

NEW HAMPSHIRE

Fort Stanwix

Portsmouth

LAKE ONTARIO

Freeman's Farm

Saratoga

Mohawk R.

Genesee R.

Fort Niagara

IROQUOIS

ONEIDA LAKE

Bemis Hts.

Bennington

Boston

CAPE COD

OTTAWAS

NEW YORK

Albany

MASS

R.I.

Hudson R.

Fort Detroit

LAKE ERIE

DELAWARES

Allegheny R.

CONN.

Newburgh

White Plains

West Pt.

New London

Newport

NANTUCKET ISLAND

MARTHA'S VINEYARD

Delaware R.

MIAMIS

PENNSYLVANIA

Morristown

LONG ISLAND

Princeton

N.J.

New York

Brooklyn Heights

Muskingum R.

Ohio R.

Monongahela R.

SHAWNEES

Fort Pitt (Pittsburgh)

Fort Bedford (Raystown)

Susquehanna R.

Valley Forge

Trenton

Head of Elk

Monmouth CH

Germantown

Philadelphia

Brandywine

Wilmington

Kanawha R.

Fort Cumberland

Potomac R.

Baltimore

MARYLAND

DEL.

DELAWARE BAY

Alexandria

Mt. Vernon

CHESAPEAKE BAY

Rappahannock R.

Fredericksburg

VIRGINIA

Richmond

James R.

Williamsburg

Yorktown

CAPE CHARLES

CAPE HENRY

Norfolk

Dan R.

CHEROKEES

Roanoke R.

Guilford C.H.

King's Mountain

Catawba R.

Yadkin R.

Charlotte

N. CAROLINA

N

Cowpens

Hobkirk's Hill

Pee Dee R.

Wilmington

S. CAROLINA

Camden

CAPE FEAR

Augusta

Eutaw Springs

Santee R.

Savannah R.

GEORGIA

Charleston

Fort Moultrie

Savannah

The Thirteen Colonies and the Revolutionary War 1775–1783

✕ Major battles

● Settlements

♜ Forts

▲ Camps

•••• Proclamation line, 1763

0   100   200 km

0   100   200 miles

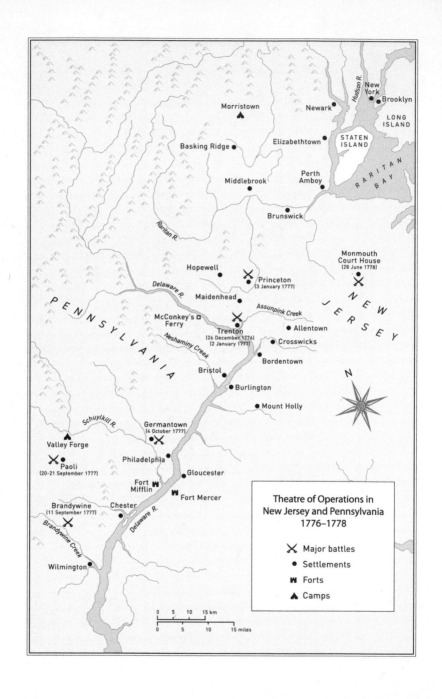

Theatre of Operations in
New Jersey and Pennsylvania
1776–1778

✕ Major battles
● Settlements
♦ Forts
▲ Camps

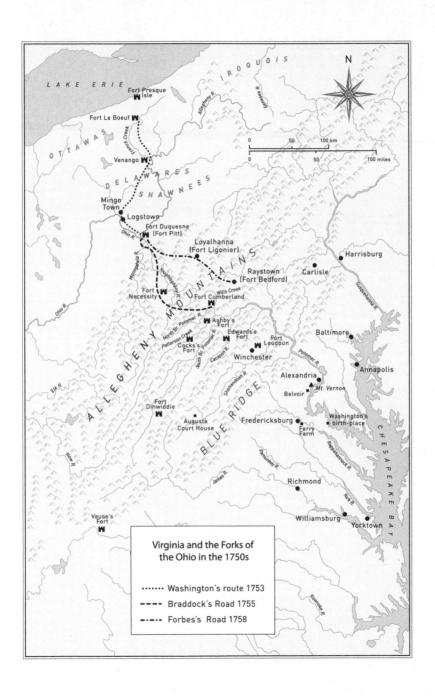

Virginia and the Forks of
the Ohio in the 1750s

········ Washington's route 1753

– – – Braddock's Road 1755

–·–·– Forbes's Road 1758

List of Illustrations

George Washington, by Charles Willson Peale, 1772. © Washington University, St. Louis / The Bridgeman Art Library

Lawrence Washington, by anonymous artist, c. 1740-50. © Courtesy of Mount Vernon Ladies' Association

Sarah 'Sally' Cary Fairfax, by Duncan Smith, 1916, after anonymous artist. © Virginia Historical Society, Richmond, Virginia / The Bridgeman Art Library

Captain Robert Orme, by Sir Joshua Reynolds, 1756. © The National Gallery, London / Scala, Florence

John Campbell, Fourth Earl of Loudoun, by Allan Ramsay, 1754. © Fort Ligonier

Battle of Princeton on 3rd January 1777, by William Mercer, c. 1786. © Philadelphia History Museum at the Atwater Kent / Courtesy of Historical Society of Pennsylvania Collection / The Bridgeman Art Library

The Battle of Germantown, 4th October 1777, by Xavier della Gatta, 1782. © Valley Forge Historical Society / The Bridgeman Art Library

George Washington at Princeton, by Charles Willson Peale, 1779. © Pennsylvania Academy of the Fine Arts, Philadelphia / The Bridgeman Art Library

General Nathanael Greene, by Charles Willson Peale, 1783. © Private Collection / Peter Newark Pictures / The Bridgeman Art Library

General Henry Knox, by Charles Willson Peale, 1783. © The City of Philadelphia

General Sir William Howe, mezzotint published by John Morris, c. 1777. © Anne S. K. Brown Military Collection

General Sir Henry Clinton, by John Smart, 1777. © National Army Museum, London / The Bridgeman Art Library

Charles Cornwallis, 1st Marquis Cornwallis, by Thomas Gainsborough, 1783. © Private Collection / Peter Newark American Pictures / The Bridgeman Art Library

General Horatio Gates at Saratoga, by James Peale, c. 1799. © Private Collection / Peter Newark American Pictures / The Bridgeman Art Library

Joseph Brant, Chief of the Mohawks, by George Romney, c. 1776. © National Gallery of Canada, Ottawa, Ontario, Canada / The Bridgeman Art Library

Washington at the Battle of Monmouth, 28 June 1778, by H. Charles McBarron Jr. © Private Collection / Peter Newark American Pictures / The Bridgeman Art Library

Self Portrait, by Major John André, 1780. © Yale University Art Gallery

The Surrender of Lord Cornwallis at Yorktown, October 19, 1781, by John Trumbull, 1787-1828. © Yale University Art Gallery / Art Resource, New York / Scala, Florence

The Surrender at Yorktown, October 19, 1781, by Louis Nicolas van Blarenberghe, 1785. © Chateau de Versailles, France / Giraudon / The Bridgeman Art Library

George Washington, by Gilbert Stuart, 1796. © Museum of the City of New York / Corbis

Washington Reviewing the Western Army at Fort Cumberland, Maryland, attributed to Frederick Kemmelmeyer, after 1794. © Metropolitan Museum of Art, New York / Giraudon / The Bridgeman Art Library

George Washington, by John Trumbull, 1780. © The Metropolitan Museum of Art / Art Resource / Scala, Florence

Introduction

During the late summer of 1777, Major Patrick Ferguson was, by common consent, the best marksman in the formidable British army bent upon breaking the back of American rebellion against King George III. Early on the morning of September 11, while observing the rebel forces arrayed in a defensive position along Brandywine Creek, southwest of the revolutionaries' capital of Philadelphia, Ferguson identified a tempting pair of targets. Some 100 yards off, in clear sight, were two horsemen. One wore the flamboyant uniform of a French hussar officer. The other, who rode a fine bay, was far more soberly dressed in a dark coat and an unusually large and high cocked hat. Like Ferguson himself, both riders were plainly engaged in reconnoitering their enemy's dispositions.

Against individual targets, 100 yards was long range for the muzzle-loading smooth bore muskets carried by most of the soldiers assembling along either side of the creek. Yet the major was not squinting down the barrel of a simple "firelock," but over the sights of a sophisticated breech-loading rifle of his own invention. Its seven-grooved bore could spin a ball with far greater accuracy than a common musket and over a longer distance. A year before, at the Royal Military Academy at Woolwich, London, Ferguson had demonstrated that fact before a panel of skeptical high-ranking officers, firing off four shots a minute to pepper a target set *200* yards away:[1] the riders he now contemplated were sitting ducks.

The dark-clad horseman was obviously a general officer, the dashing hussar his aide-de-camp. The hussar turned back, but his companion lingered. Moving out from the trees that sheltered him and a score of his corps of riflemen, Ferguson shouted a warning. The rider stopped, looked, and then calmly continued about his business. The major called again, this time drawing a bead upon the heedless horseman. The distance between them was, as Ferguson reported, one at which during even the most rapid firing he had "seldom missed a piece of paper," and he "could have lodged a half a dozen of balls in or about him" before he could ride out of range. But something stopped him from squeezing the trigger. Ferguson was an officer and a gentleman. As he conceded with unconcealed admiration, his proposed target was conducting himself with such coolness that to have shot him in the back would have seemed an unsporting, "unpleasant" action. And so the major let him trot off unmolested.

Later that same day the rival armies clashed in earnest. After a stubborn fight, British discipline prevailed, pushing back the rebels and increasing the threat to Philadelphia. Ferguson, who had been badly wounded in the right hand during the fighting, spoke with a doctor busy treating the wounded of both sides. From the surgeon's recent conversation with a group of enemy officers, it seemed that the two distinctively clad riders Ferguson had seen earlier were none other than General George Washington, the commander in chief of the revolutionaries' Continental Army, and the French officer attending him that day. As Ferguson freely acknowledged, he was "not sorry" to have remained oblivious of their identity.[2]

Had he known what the future held, both for him personally and for the cause in which he soldiered, the gallant major may have thought—and acted—differently. And if ever a single shot could have changed the course of history, an unwavering ball sped from Ferguson's rifle would surely have done so.

"I am a warrior." These were the uncompromising words that George Washington chose to describe himself in May 1779, at the height of the Revolutionary War. Washington was addressing the "Chief Men" of the Delaware nation of Indians, and his language was calculated to strike a chord with listeners who were themselves first and foremost tribal fighters—warriors in the purest sense. Yet even allowing for Washington's deliberate use of the rhetoric and vocabulary of Indian diplomacy, his self-characterization is telling. In 1779, George Washington *was* a warrior, "the commander in chief of all the armies in the United States of America," as he put it. In his message, Washington made a point of distancing himself from the revolutionary movement's political leaders while at the same time emphasizing what he shared with the Delawares: there were some matters about which he would not speak, "because they belong to Congress, and not to us warriors."[3]

Washington had established his martial credentials a quarter of a century before, during another war, in which he had fought alongside the British against the French and their Indian allies, who then included the Delawares. The military reputation that the young Washington forged during four years of fighting on the frontiers of Virginia and Pennsylvania underpinned his subsequent selection as commander in chief of the fledgling Continental Army in 1775, when Britain's North American empire was sundered by rebellion. It was likewise Washington's role as the revolutionaries' foremost soldier throughout the long, bloody, and bitter War of American Independence that bestowed the prestige that ensured his selection as first president of the new United States of America in 1789. Indeed, in January 1782, before that war had formally ended, the largest circulating newspaper in Europe, the *London Chronicle*, was already convinced that Washington had done enough as the military champion of American liberty to be "received by posterity as one of the most illustrious characters of the age in which he lived."[4]

While Washington's international reputation was, to a very large extent, the direct result of his exploits as a pugnacious fighting man, this aspect of his character is today curiously neglected: instead, he is seen as the calm, dignified leader providing the ballast that kept the revolutionary cause steady. There is, of course, much truth in this picture, but it is only part of the story. When Major Patrick Ferguson viewed Washington over the sights of his rifle at Brandywine in 1777, he clearly recognized a kindred spirit, possessing the key qualities expected of an eighteenth-century officer: bound by an unswerving code of honor, Washington was not simply a "gentleman," but a warrior who instinctively led his men from the front. In 1778, a British officer who had served with Washington twenty years earlier during the "French and Indian War" remained convinced that the man who now commanded the Continental Army was, above all else, motivated by a hunger for glory on the battlefield. In a widely read newspaper article, he bluntly observed: "His ruling passion is military fame."[5]

Washington's martial side—so obvious to those soldiers who fought alongside and against him—has been underplayed for several reasons. First, Americans of Washington's own generation, like their British contemporaries, held a deep-seated dislike of professional soldiers: this ingrained antipathy was rooted in fears of the threat posed by a strong standing army and the uses to which such a permanent force could be put by a power-hungry and unscrupulous military dictator. Soldiers were fundamentally unpopular: once they had won their battles and the patriotic spasms of public acclaim had subsided, the old antimilitary prejudices swiftly returned. In peacetime, armies were pared to the bone; such soldiers as remained in service were expected, like Rudyard Kipling's "Tommy," to maintain a low profile until they were needed again.

Given such suspicions, it suited Washington's countrymen to see him as a patriotic *amateur* soldier, a peaceful farmer who, like the Republican Roman hero Cincinnatus, returned to his plow once the war was won. The fact that George Washington took pains to disassociate himself from any suggestion that he might assume the mantle of military dictator, wielding his experience, prestige, and corps of battle-hardened veterans like a latter-day Oliver Cromwell—a gentleman farmer turned general who neglected to resume his plowing—does not mean that he lacked the inclinations of a thoroughly *professional* officer while in command of his troops.

Second, Washington's military reputation is dominated by his enduring image as the cautious "Fabian" general of the Revolutionary War's darkest days: averse to risk, he followed the strategy of the Roman commander Fabius Cunctator when faced by the Carthaginians, carefully avoiding confrontation and hoarding his scanty manpower until the chance to attack was too propitious and tempting to resist. This view of Washington was already ingrained during the war's early years: in its survey of the key events of 1777, the popular British *Annual Register* observed that Washington's conduct justified "that appellation, which is now pretty generally applied to him, of the American Fabius."[6] However, while often obliged to adopt a defensive stance, throughout his military career Washington's instincts were those of the warrior anxious to prove himself on the battlefield, and, when granted an outlet, his aggression was readily apparent. This aspect of Washington's generalship and character has been acknowledged by historians;[7] yet less attention has been given to the background influences that not only fired his "ruling passion" but ensured that it would be channeled more effectively within the strict bounds of gentlemanly behavior.

Third, and no less significantly, for a military leader of such undeniable front-rank importance, George Washington was singularly unfortunate in the artists who sought to capture his likeness as a soldier. Almost without exception, they portrayed an essentially passive Washington rather than the man of action that he undoubtedly was. This limitation is especially true of the work of the prolific Charles Willson Peale, who painted Washington seven times between 1772 and 1787 without, it can be argued, ever capturing his true character. Peale's work is instantly recognizable, not least because he had the knack of making all his subjects look strangely alike: from the portly Boston gunner Brigadier General Henry Knox to the scrawny French volunteer Marie-Joseph, Marquis de Lafayette, Peale's sitters share the same almond-shaped eyes, the same relaxed posture.

Peale's shortcomings are all the more regrettable because he knew Washington well and had actually fought under his command during the crucial Trenton-Princeton campaign of 1776–77. The work widely regarded as Peale's best portrait of Washington was painted in 1779 and depicts the commander of the Continental Army at Princeton, with Hessian standards captured days earlier at Trenton strewn at his feet. But even here the overriding mood is languid: rather than urging on his men to the attack, as eyewitness evidence testifies that he did, Washington is posed casually—legs crossed, right hand on hip, left lying upon a cannon barrel. Much later, in 1792, another Continental Army veteran, John Trumbull, chose to paint Washington on the eve of his Princeton triumph. The Connecticut-born Trumbull, who abandoned the military struggle in 1777 to concentrate upon recording the Revolution's pivotal military and political episodes in a series of huge canvases, was immensely proud of his full-length portrait of his old commander, considering it to be not only the best study of George Washington that he had painted, but the best of *any* picture to show him "in his heroic and military character." Despite this claim, as with Peale's interpretation, all is dignified calm; while a charger plunges and fighting rages in the background, its subject does nothing more vigorous than extend an arm clutching a half-closed telescope.[8]

It is interesting to speculate how the contemporary English artist Sir Joshua Reynolds, who excelled in painting dramatic, dynamic, and innovative portraits of soldiers and sailors, would have tackled Washington in his prime: given the iconic status his talent bequeathed to relatively minor players like the British cavalry leader Colonel Banastre Tarleton, Reynolds would surely have captured something at least of Washington's steely resolution and fiery spirit.

Washington's generation of fellow *Americans* also produced artists who could have done equal justice to his true character. Before Washington acquired global fame, the Pennsylvanian Benjamin West had already revolutionized "history" painting with his 1770 depiction of the death of the leading British military hero of the Seven Years' War, Major General James Wolfe. That, and other works, led to West's appointment as "history painter" to King George III himself, permanent residence in London, and the prestigious presidency of the Royal Academy. But it was West's fellow Academician the Massachusetts-born John Singleton Copley who pushed his artistic revolution further, injecting true drama into military portraits and such scenes as *The Death of Major Pierson*. Copley, like West, was sympathetic to the cause of his rebellious countrymen, but, as an American artist working in London, he, too, was obliged to focus upon subjects unlikely to jar with the sentiments of patriotic Britons; hence his *Pierson*, while set during the American Revolutionary War, celebrated a British victory, one scored over the French on the Channel Island of Jersey. Given their delicate professional positions, Copley and West alike were obliged to express their true sympathies through analogy or veiled symbolism, rather than full-blooded pro-American treatments of key events and personalities.[9]

Whatever else Americans won in 1783, it was not the battle of the brushes, and Washington's image as a soldier has suffered ever since. Washington was equally unlucky in the portraiture of his postwar presidential days. This was not due to any limitations on the part of the era's leading portraitist, Gilbert Stuart; far from it. Stuart was a gifted artist and a perfectionist to boot. As Charles Willson Peale's son Rembrandt recalled in 1859, both he and Stuart painted Washington's portrait in the autumn of 1795. Stuart's effort, known as the *Vaughan* portrait, won public admiration, but he was dissatisfied with the result and persuaded Washington to sit for him again in the spring of 1796. The resulting "head," the so-called *Athenaeum* portrait, was destined to become perhaps the best-known likeness of Washington. Unfortunately for posterity, as Stuart recalled, "When I painted him he had just had a set of false teeth inserted, which accounts for the constrained expression so noticeable about the mouth and lower part of the face."[10]

In fact, Washington had lost all but one of his teeth by 1789, obliging him to resort to a set of ingenious but clumsy dentures: the upper jaw of this "dental apparatus" was carved entirely from the tusk of a "sea-horse," or hippopotamus; the lower, made from the same material, was studded with human teeth. Created by John Greenwood of New York, himself a Revolutionary War veteran, it was, in the words of his grandson, "an uncouth and awkward affair" that pushed Washington's lower lip forward.[11] Washington was wearing these dentures when Stuart painted his initial *Vaughan* version. Yet for all its shortcomings, Greenwood's "dental apparatus" was superior to the replacement set, likewise crafted from "sea-horse" ivory, that Washington wore briefly in 1796, at the very time he sat for Stuart's even more popular and influential *Athenaeum* portrait. Indeed, in the last year of his life Washington wrote to Greenwood, assuring him: "I shall always prefer your services to that of any other, in the line of your present profession."[12]

Stuart's unsparing realism not only captured the full indignity of those badly fitting false teeth but once again depicted an essentially static Washington, the solemn peacetime statesman with nothing left of the restless warrior spirit that had won him his prominence in the first place. Stuart readily acknowledged that Jean-Antoine Houdon's bust of Washington, modeled from a life mask in 1785 in preparation for a full-length marble statue and before Washington lost his teeth, did not "suffer" from the "defect" in appearance revealed in his own painting.[13] Ironically, however, it was Stuart's image—which managed to be both a strikingly accurate record of his sitter in early 1796, while woefully misrepresenting his typical looks—that immediately eclipsed all previous portraits of Washington and was perpetuated in subsequent depictions of him.[14] So successful was Stuart's *Athenaeum* head that he even reproduced it upon a full-length portrait purporting to show Washington twenty years earlier, as he watched the British evacuating Boston in 1776.[15]

Unsurprisingly, therefore, it is the prematurely aged, sedate, and "fatherly" Washington of Stuart's acclaimed 1795 and 1796 portraits that modern-day Americans know best: from the dust jackets of countless books, from the colossal presidential lineup at Mount Rushmore, from postage stamps, and above all, from the dollar bills in their wallets.

This book is about the George Washington that the artists so signally failed to capture, the feisty young frontier officer and the tough forty-something commander of the Continental Army, not the venerated elder statesman of the Republic, champing self-consciously on his hippo teeth. It examines Washington's long and varied military career, tracing his evolution as a soldier and his changing attitude toward the waging of war. A central narrative anchored upon Washington's own experience is combined with an analysis of the background influences that shaped his conduct as an officer; ironically, these indicate that Washington's reliance upon English models of "gentlemanly" behavior and on British military organization were crucial in forging the army that won American independence and underpinned his own emergence as the most celebrated man of his age.

As the literature relating to George Washington's life and times is vast and ever expanding, the evidence considered here is necessarily selective. However, an effort has been made to consult a broad spectrum of published and archival material, ranging from the assessments of modern biographers and historians to the writings of Washington and his contemporaries. In particular, the massive project to publish Washington's correspondence, begun by the University of Virginia Press on the bicentenary of the Declaration of American Independence in 1976 and still ongoing, has proved immensely valuable, not simply by presenting accurate texts of the documents themselves, but through extensive editorial notes.

Aside from a brief sketch of his early life and military services in the French and Indian War, compiled to assist with a projected biography by his former aide-de-camp, Lieutenant Colonel David Humphreys, nothing resembling an autobiography was ever written by Washington.[16] That short memoir and other isolated instances when Washington revisited key episodes of his career—for instance, the Yorktown campaign of 1781—suggest that whatever insights such a work might have yielded into his notoriously "private" personality, its value as an historical narrative would likely have been compromised by a failing memory and a reluctance to face all the facts.[17]

By contrast, many others whose lives interacted with Washington's, particularly during the Revolutionary War, wrote memoirs in later life, and considerable use has been made of them here. Such reminiscences, often written decades after the events, must be used with caution, especially when distorted by hindsight or a self-serving agenda. Yet even works with such flaws can still preserve credible evidence. For example, when James Wilkinson published his *Memoirs of My Own Times* in 1816, his reputation had been blackened by persistent accusations of treasonable intrigue with Spain. Yet whatever his subsequent failings, Wilkinson had seen extensive service during the American War of Independence. His coherent narrative of the momentous Trenton-Princeton campaign of 1776–77 sheds much light on an episode for which the surviving contemporaneous sources are frustratingly patchy.

Similarly, a lengthy interval between events and their recording does not mean that such memoirs should automatically be discounted as unreliable. Elisha Bostwick was age eighty-three when he finally chronicled his services in the Continental Army nearly sixty years earlier. Despite all that had happened since, Bostwick had clearly never forgotten much of what he had seen in 1775 and 1776. As he observed: "Upon a retrospective view of the scenes of my past life, none are so clear and bright in my memory as those transactions of the Revolutionary War which I was a witness to and in which I took a part." At the Battle of White Plains, on October 28, 1776, when Bostwick was a lieutenant in the 7th Connecticut Regiment, he saw a British cannonball smash its way through four men standing nearby: in 1833, he could still recall the soldiers' names and the horrific nature of their individual wounds, adding: "Oh! What a sight that was to see, within a distance of six rods those men with their legs and arms and guns and packs all in a heap." That such a shocking shambles should remain etched upon a man's memory is unsurprising, but Bostwick retained an equally clear recollection of another, very different episode. After the Battle of Princeton on January 3, 1777, when he was escorting British prisoners to Peekskill in the Hudson Valley, his party bedded down in a barn. At "about midnight when all was still," one of the prisoners, a Scottish Highlander, stood and sung a ballad that Bostwick remembered as "The Gypsy Laddie." Looking back at the close of his own life, Bostwick wrote: "The tune was of a plaintive cast and I always retained it and sung it to my children, but that must die with me."[18] Old Elisha need not have worried: the haunting song he heard that night in 1777, also known as "The Raggle Taggle Gypsies," is as popular today as it ever was, providing a link between Washington's world and our own.

George Washington's active military experience fell into two distinct phases separated by a long interlude in which he retired from soldiering to follow the life of a gentleman farmer and politician. During the first phase, Washington was a soldier of the king, often fighting alongside units of the British Army but failing in his quest to secure a Crown commission in a regular regiment; during the second, he led the armed struggle against the same military institution that had apparently spurned him, seeking to exploit all that he had earlier learned of its strengths and weaknesses. This book reflects that pattern, giving due weight to both phases. It argues that whatever else he might have been—surveyor, farmer, politician, elder statesman—and despite appearances, George Washington was first and foremost a soldier; his colossal status rested upon the twin pillars of his character, the gentleman and the warrior.

Note: To ease readability, in quoted material all eighteenth-century spellings, capitalizations, and abbreviations have been modernized. Where necessary, punctuation has been slightly amended, taking care to preserve the precise meaning of the quotation.

1

FINDING A PATH

George Washington's American roots were planted in the wake of the bitter civil wars that racked the British Isles during the mid-seventeenth century. This confrontation between Crown and Parliament, between "Cavaliers" and "Roundheads," was the modern world's first "revolution": in 1649, it cost the stubborn Charles I his head and led to the establishment of a short-lived republic, or Commonwealth, under his nemesis, the formidable Lord Protector, Oliver Cromwell.

This era of protracted bloodshed, dislocation, and upheaval saw sporadic emigration across the Atlantic to England's existing North American outposts—the colonies composing New England, strung along Massachusetts Bay, and to the south, Virginia and Maryland on the Chesapeake. The fact that both of George Washington's great-grandfathers settled in Virginia in the decade before the restoration of Charles II in 1660 has led to the suggestion that they were part of a distinctive "Cavalier" migration to that colony, involving loyal supporters of the ousted Stuarts who were out of step with the triumphant Cromwellian regime and keen to rebuild their fortunes among like-minded exiles overseas.[1]

It is by no means certain that George Washington's ancestors fit the "Cavalier" profile. On the maternal side, considerable confusion clouds the fundamental political allegiance of William Ball, who reached Virginia in 1657, the year before Cromwell's death, and settled in Lancaster County.[2] By 1677, he held the rank of major in the county militia, a responsibility that suggests previous military experience. But while genealogists maintain that William fought for the Royalists at the pivotal English Civil War battles of Marston Moor in 1644 and Naseby in the following year, this is hard to reconcile with their accompanying claim that he had soldiered "under Fairfax." If this was true, then William's loyalties must have been radically different from what tradition maintains: Sir Thomas Fairfax was the outstanding *Parliamentarian* general of the civil wars, beating Prince Rupert at Marston Moor and commanding the New Model Army that crushed King Charles at Naseby.

The Royalist credentials of John Washington are slightly stronger, although he was scarcely some swashbuckling bravo. By a remarkable coincidence, like William Ball, he, too, arrived in Virginia in 1657, coming over as a ship's mate. John had been obliged to go to sea some years earlier after his father, the Reverend Lawrence Washington, was expelled from his living in the pro-Roundhead eastern county of Essex, allegedly for drunkenness, a trait for which the puritanical Parliamentarians had little tolerance. The reverend's disgrace entailed a sharp drop in wealth and status for the family, but in Virginia John set about restoring both.[3]

John Washington was perhaps twenty-five years old when he first made landfall in what was already known as "the Old Dominion." That term reflected Virginia's status as England's first American colony, established by a band of adventurers at Jamestown back in 1607, thirteen years before the more sober Pilgrim Fathers made landfall and founded Plymouth Colony to the north.

In the half century since its foundation, Virginia had experienced mixed fortunes. A last-ditch attempt by the local Powhatan Indians to eject the invaders in 1622 had almost succeeded in wiping out the colonists, while diseases along the unhealthy James River, where the first settlement had been established, had exerted a slower, but no less damaging, attrition. Despite such hazards, and the barrier to natural growth posed by an overwhelmingly male population, the colony had survived, and by the time Washington's English ancestors arrived, it was becoming a more stable society, based upon a single, lucrative cash crop: tobacco.

Both Virginia's expanding population and the increasing profitability of the tobacco harvest resulted from the same factor, a steady influx of unfree laborers. These were not yet the black African slaves with whom Virginia was to become so closely associated, but poor whites, indentured servants who received their sea passage from England in exchange for several years of unpaid toil for tobacco planters before finally earning their freedom and the chance to farm land of their own. During the course of the seventeenth century, it has been estimated, more than three-quarters of the 120,000 English emigrants to the Chesapeake Bay colonies of Virginia and its neighbor Maryland, which was founded in 1634, were bound servants.[4]

English emigration reached a peak between 1630 and 1660, the period within which Washington's forebears set foot in Virginia. Significantly, neither of them were indentured servants, but free men, members of the minor gentry or solidly respectable yeoman class, with enough capital to invest in their own ventures. Settling at midcentury, both John Washington and William Ball also reached the Old Dominion after it had weathered its stormy infancy and offered opportunity to men of substance and ambition. Free immigrants like them would dominate the future economic and social life of the Chesapeake, founding dynasties that yielded the region's political leadership.

Thanks to a good marriage to Anne Pope, John Washington prospered in a modest fashion. Exploiting the opportunities offered by the New World, he became a justice of the peace and also acquired responsibilities in local government and the military. It was as a colonel of militia that John Washington became embroiled in a controversial episode that would resonate into the lifetime of his great-grandson.

Although the last embers of Powhatan resistance had been stamped out during a brutal war fought between 1644 and 1646, the steady expansion of settlement inevitably sparked fresh friction with neighboring tribes. In 1675, a party of militia sent to chastise Doeg Indians who had killed a settler in a dispute over straying hogs ended up slaying fourteen friendly Susquehannocks by mistake. As tit-for-tat violence escalated, Colonel John Washington was placed in command of militia from Rappahannock and ordered to bring the Susquehannocks to heel.

Joining forces with Maryland militia, Washington's men blockaded a Susquehannock stronghold on the northern bank of the Potomac at Piscataway Creek. Five Indian chiefs emerged to parley with the besiegers. They denied responsibility for recent killings of colonists, blaming the bloodshed on Seneca warriors raiding from the north. But the Virginians remained unconvinced: several Susquehannocks had been apprehended close to where settlers had been murdered and were found in incriminating possession of the victims' clothing. In consequence, the five chiefs were summarily executed, clubbed to death in cold blood. Whether this retribution was exacted by Colonel Washington and his Virginians or the Marylanders remains unclear; when the killings drew the wrath of Virginia's governor, Sir William Berkeley, each party blamed the other. Whatever his precise role in that brutal episode, John Washington's ruthlessness and his notorious hunger for Indian land were remembered by the Susquehannocks themselves and perpetuated in the grim soubriquet they apparently gave to him: "Caunotocarious"—variously rendered as "town taker," or the more sinister "devourer of villages."[5]

By his death in 1677, the unscrupulous but determined John Washington had been able to accumulate a respectable estate of 5,700 acres, leaving most of it to his eldest son, Lawrence. As an attorney, Lawrence handled the interests of London merchants trading with Virginia's tobacco producers. He also continued his father's efforts to embed the family within Virginia's establishment, marrying Mildred Warner, whose father was one of the King's Council, which advised the colony's royally appointed governor. But Lawrence lacked John's restless energy and insatiable appetite for land: when he died in 1698, aged just thirty-nine, he had augmented his inheritance by barely a few hundred acres. Lawrence also left a widow and three children, John, Mildred, and Augustine.

The second son, Augustine, who was just three when his father died, was to become George Washington's father. Given his ranking in the family pecking order, Augustine's share of the Washington fortune was small. Yet he, too, lost no time in building upon it. In 1715, he married Jane Butler, whose own inheritance gave them another 1,700 acres of land. Augustine gradually bolstered this core, buying a farm on the south bank of the Potomac River, between Bridges Creek and Popes Creek, and later building a house there. Erected at a cost of 5,000 pounds of tobacco, it was a substantial brick-built mansion that emulated the far more imposing homes of Virginia's great planters.

Like his father, Augustine prospered in an unspectacular fashion, methodically acquiring property and the status that went with it: he built a gristmill on Popes Creek and became a justice of the peace, church warden, and sheriff. And he added more land, including a 2,500-acre tract farther up the Potomac, where Little Hunting Creek emptied into the broad, sluggish river. This was bought from his sister, Mildred, and had been her inheritance. Quite literally, Augustine had other irons in the fire: he was active in the development of iron ore and smelting. He and Jane had three children— Lawrence, Augustine, and Jane—and they seemed set for a happy and prosperous future together. But in May 1730, when Augustine was thirty-five, he returned from a business trip to England to learn that his wife had been dead for six months.

Now a widower with three children on his hands and a home and business to oversee, Augustine acted swiftly in finding Jane's replacement. His choice, Mary Ball, was the only child of Joseph Ball—the son of Major William Ball—and the much younger Mary Johnson. Mary Ball's father had died at the age of sixty-one, when she was only three. Like the first Washingtons in Virginia, the Balls had prospered in a slow but steady way, and Joseph was able to leave his daughter 400 acres of land, plus three slaves and some livestock. A final bequest—"the feathers in the kitchen loft to be put into a bed"—is a reminder of the humble aspirations of Virginians below the strata of the wealthiest planters.[6] Mary's mother married again, was widowed once more, and died when Mary was just twelve, leaving her orphaned but in possession of yet more land and property. Allied to her role as helpmeet, this made her a worthwhile catch for Augustine Washington.

In March 1731, the couple married. Augustine was thirty-six, Mary thirteen years younger. Within a year, on February 11, 1732 (or February 22, according to the Gregorian calendar adopted by Britain in 1752), a son was born to them in the house on Popes Creek. He was named George, just like the king in London.

The Virginia into which George Washington was born was very different from the colony his great-grandfathers had encountered during the 1650s. The "Old Dominion" was now the most venerable of no fewer than thirteen British colonies ranged along North America's eastern seaboard, from Nova Scotia down to South Carolina; they would be joined by a fourteenth, Georgia, in 1733. By midcentury their combined population numbered about one and a half million and was rising rapidly. Britain was not the only colonial power on the continent: France had settlements in Canada and Louisiana, while Spanish Florida bordered Georgia. Both components of New France together contained barely 70,000 people, and all of Spanish North America—including the Mexican borderlands—mustered perhaps 10,000 settlers; in population terms, these territories were therefore insignificant when set alongside the English-speaking colonies, yet they belonged to traditionally hostile powers and posed obstacles to expansion. And, of course, the vast interior west of the Appalachian Mountains was still inhabited by aboriginal Indian tribes; by the arrival of Washington's ancestors, epidemic illnesses and catastrophic warfare had already winnowed their populations to just 10 percent of what they had been before first contact with European fishermen, but while willing enough to exploit the incomers as trading partners, the survivors were determined to keep their remaining hunting grounds.

Populous and thriving, by the 1730s, Britain's older established colonies had already matured into increasingly sophisticated societies, capable of governing themselves with a minimum of interference from London, some 3,000 miles in distance, and three months away by round-trip. These provinces formed the core of what was already being styled the "British Empire" and were prized for their valuable raw materials and the growing markets they offered for the Mother Country's own manufactured goods. Despite the value placed upon colonial trade, at the time of Washington's birth Whitehall's authority was far from overriding. Most colonies, including Virginia, had a royally appointed governor; as the monarch's local representative, he was intended to enjoy viceregal status and wield appropriate power. Within each colony, the governor's chief support was the legislative and executive council, a body of about twelve eminent appointees who were expected to orchestrate political support for Crown policies. From London's perspective, the governor and his loyal council would work together to dominate colonial politics, whipping the locally elected "assemblies" into line. The reality was very different.

Taking their lead from events across the Atlantic, where the "Glorious Revolution" of 1688–89 had seen the authoritarian James II ejected, and the more biddable Dutchman William of Orange invited by Parliament to take his place as King William III, the lower houses of assembly had emerged as the dominant force in provincial politics, eclipsing the governor and his council. Closely linked to the rise of these parliament-like assemblies was the formation of distinct colonial elites who craved political power to match their increasing wealth and social prominence. By the late seventeenth century, the older colonies like Virginia were already home to major landowners who identified their fortunes with the success and prestige of their colony. Such gentry, whose influence was bolstered by an intricate network of intermarriage, monopolized political life. They alone were rich enough to offer the free food and drink required to buy the votes of the white freeholders who elected representatives to assemblies like Virginia's House of Burgesses.

By 1732, another dramatic change had occurred within Virginian society. The original workforce of indentured servants—who for all the risks and hardships they faced had come to the Chesapeake through personal choice—had been largely replaced by another composed overwhelmingly of involuntary laborers.

During the late seventeenth century, an economic upturn in England had slowed the flow of servants seeking to better their prospects in Virginia or Maryland. After 1718, Britain's new policy of transporting reprieved felons to the American colonies, in particular the Chesapeake, went some way to meeting the tobacco planters' continuing demands for unpaid manpower. Lesser criminals were required to labor for seven years before becoming free; in the case of felons convicted of crimes carrying the death penalty, fourteen years or even a life term might be applied. Those who came home early risked the gallows. By 1775, when war between Britain and her American colonies brought the one-way traffic to an abrupt end, an estimated 50,000 convicted criminals had been sent across the Atlantic, accounting for a quarter of all British immigrants.[7]

Ranging from hardened professional footpads and burglars lucky to escape the noose to starving children snared for petty thievery, this unwanted influx prompted howls of protest from the colonial elites, who blamed the convicts for an imported crime wave. Indeed, to the Pennsylvanian journalist Benjamin Franklin this "deluge of wickedness" upon Virginia, Maryland, and his own colony epitomized the "sovereign contempt" with which the "Mother Country" was capable of viewing its American "children." Writing in 1751 under the suggestive pseudonym "Americanus," Franklin advised his fellow colonists to retaliate by exporting "rattle-snakes for felons."[8]

Despite the outcry they provoked, these batches of English "transports" were insignificant when set beside the incoming waves of African slaves. Just a few hundred strong in 1650, a century later slaves numbered some 150,000, accounting for 40 percent of the Chesapeake's population. Subjected to a harsh work regime and brutal punishments and with precious little prospect of ultimate freedom, black slaves were increasingly regarded as inhuman brutes by their masters. This racist stance was adopted to justify an institution that flew in the face of the freedoms that Englishmen had fought so hard to win for themselves; bolstered by a dread of servile revolt, it also helped to promote solidarity between the Chesapeake's planters and a growing band of poor whites whose failure to achieve material success left them disgruntled and potentially rebellious.[9] In Virginia, even the lowliest former convict knew only too well that life could be much, much worse. George Washington was to grow up within a society in which the contrast between "liberty" and "slavery" could not have been starker.

Before long, young George was joined by a sister, Betty, and a brother, Samuel. But life in the Old Dominion remained precarious, particularly on the sultry, low-lying Tidewater, where river-borne fevers helped to keep the headstone carvers and grave diggers busy. Before he was three, George's half sister Jane was dead. In 1735, Augustine Washington moved his family to his new estate fronting the Potomac at Little Hunting Creek. There, in the home that would later become known as Mount Vernon, two more brothers were born: John Augustine, or "Jack," in 1736, and Charles a year later.

George's half brothers, Lawrence and Augustine junior, were both far older than he and away at school in England, where their father had also been educated. Lawrence returned home in 1738, by now a worldly-wise gentleman of twenty. George idolized him, and, for all the great difference in their ages, they became firm friends. Later that year, Augustine acquired another tract of land, this time on the Rappahannock River some two miles from the expanding village of Fredericksburg. Moving once again, he ensconced his growing brood in a two-story wooden building, named Ferry Farm from the nearby river crossing.

In the following year, war erupted between Britain and her old imperial rival, Spain. The conflict would be remembered by the strange name of "The War of Jenkins's Ear" after the English sea captain whose mutilation at the hands of vindictive Spanish coast guards provided a convenient excuse for hostilities. Coming after a generation of peace and dangling the alluring prospect of pilfering the Spanish Empire, the war was popular in Britain and its American possessions alike. The conflict promptly produced a hero for the

British public: by his daring capture of Spain's imperial outpost at Porto Bello in November 1739, Vice Admiral Edward Vernon generated a wave of patriotic fervor that saw him celebrated in poems and plays and on plates and punchbowls.[10]

Across the Atlantic, eleven colonies from Massachusetts to North Carolina contributed enough recruits to fill a sprawling four-battalion formation eventually totaling more than 4,000 men. Most, although by no means all, of the rank and file in this so-called American Regiment were volunteers; in Virginia, which contributed four companies, justices of the peace were authorized to conscript those able-bodied men who lacked employment, sweeping up vagrants, former indentured servants, and others considered undesirable and expendable. While the field and staff officers, along with one lieutenant per company, were to be British and appointed from London, all the other officers, including the captains, would be Americans. A total of eighty-eight blank king's commissions were sent across the Atlantic to be awarded to such "men of interest in their country" as the colonial governors deemed worthy.[11]

There were not enough of the coveted royal commissions to meet the demand, but Lawrence Washington mustered sufficient influence to secure the captaincy of one of the Virginian companies. Unorthodox in size and composition, the "American Regiment" was nonetheless a regular British Army unit, and Lawrence's commission was signed by King George II himself.[12] The regiment's proud continental title was also significant: it reflected an unprecedented display of cooperation, not simply between the American colonists and Great Britain, but between the individual colonies themselves.

Colonel William Blakeney, the English officer sent across the Atlantic to supervise the regiment's enlistment, was clearly impressed by the enthusiasm for the expedition that he encountered in New York. But the colonel also noticed a colonial trait that hinted at tensions to come: "From the highest to the lowest, the inhabitants of these provinces seem to set a great value on themselves, and think a regard is due to them, especially in the assistance they are able to give the Mother Country on such occasions." He added a warning: "and, as they are a growing power, should they be disappointed in what is promised them, and which they expect, future occasions of the like nature may suffer for it."[13]

The expedition's first target was the city of Cartagena, on the coast of what is now Colombia. Mustering at Jamaica in the autumn of 1740 under the command of the famed Vice Admiral Vernon and his army colleague Brigadier General Thomas Wentworth, the formidable Anglo-American armada reached Cartagena in the following spring. There, it initially made some headway but swiftly lost all momentum in the teeth of a combination of factors: unexpectedly determined Spanish resistance, friction between the naval and army commanders, and, above all, the Caribbean's array of lethal diseases. The unacclimatized invaders suffered appallingly. By the time it was finally called off in 1742, the expedition had cost the lives of more than 10,000 of the 14,000 soldiers ultimately involved. Just a fraction of them were killed in action, with the majority felled by malaria, yellow fever, or dysentery. Losses among the American Regiment were correspondingly high: for some of the colonies, nine out of ten of those who had set off with such high expectations of glory and booty never came home.[14]

One man who lived to tell the tale was Captain Lawrence Washington. His survival, when so many others died, probably owed much to his appointment to command the men of his regiment serving as marines, and berthing aboard Admiral Vernon's flagship, the eighty-gun HMS *Princess Carolina*.[15] As Vernon's crew had been on station in the Caribbean for more than a year and were already "seasoned" to its diseases, *Princess Carolina* offered a healthier environment than the troopships fresh from England and North America and the filthy camps established onshore.

Writing to his father from Jamaica in May 1741, as the survivors of the bungled Cartagena expedition regrouped for a strike against Cuba, Lawrence gave some hint of his experiences, observing: "War is horrid in fact, but much more so in our imagination."[16] Yet the hard facts of the Caribbean campaign were horrific enough. It is possible that Captain Washington had described them in previous letters home, of which he had "writ many" without any reply; or perhaps he made a conscious decision to spare his family an account of the ghastly sights he surely witnessed as Cartagena's harbor grew noisome with the floating bodies of the dead thrown overboard from the hospital ships, "affording prey to carrion crows and sharks, which tore them in pieces without interruption." This grisly detail was recalled by another eyewitness, Tobias Smollett, who served as a surgeon's mate aboard the fleet and drew upon his experiences at Cartagena in both his 1748 novel *Roderick Random* and in a factual account published in 1756.[17]

In his surviving letter, Lawrence Washington likewise failed to mention an episode early in the siege of Cartagena when he had participated in a hazardous amphibious assault. Unaware of this incident, George Washington's biographers have concluded that his half brother never experienced combat during the campaign. In fact, Lawrence helped to lead troops in a celebrated feat of arms: given his influence as a role model for young George, this is surely significant. Once again, Smollett provides the missing information, describing the skirmish in his nonfiction narrative of the campaign. On March 17, 1741, the army officers had sought Admiral Vernon's assistance in destroying a troublesome battery guarding the harbor, known as the Barradera. As Smollett reported:

> In compliance with this request, a detachment of 300 sailors, supported by a body of soldiers that still remained on board of the fleet, were conveyed thither at night in boats, under the command of Captains Boscawen, Watson, Coats, Washington, Mr. Murray, and Lieutenant Forrest, who attacked the battery with great valor, repulsed the enemy, and spiked up the cannon.[18]

Admiral Vernon, who claimed to have hatched the plan himself, praised the attack on March 18 as a "bold, resolute and well-executed enterprise," although the only officers he named in his dispatch to the governor of Jamaica were his own sailors; already at loggerheads with General Wentworth, he had no wish to glorify soldiers, "our gentlemen of parade."[19]

In his influential published account of the siege, Vernon's chief engineer, Captain Charles Knowles, agreed that the Barradera assault was "as bold, and surprising an enterprise, as is to be met with," although he, too, failed to include Lawrence Washington among the officers who led it. This omission may have been deliberate, as Knowles was clearly prejudiced against the American Regiment. From the very outset the Americans were despised, he wrote. While the troops from England were "raw and undisciplined," the Americans were even worse; many of the soldiers were Irish and therefore suspected of being "Papists" like the Spaniards, while even their officers were held in scorn, "composed of blacksmiths, tailors, shoemakers, and all the banditti that country [America] affords."[20]

The perceptive Smollett took a more balanced view of the American Regiment's potential. During the bloody and futile attempt to storm the fortress of St. Lazarus on April 9, 1741, he recalled, the Americans had been placed in the rear of the assault troops, relegated to carrying scaling ladders and woolpacks to fill up the fort's ditch. When the attack stalled, the Americans refused to bring their burdens forward. However, as Smollett added, "though they would not advance as pioneers, many of them took up the firelocks which they found on the field, and, mixing among the troops, behaved very bravely." In Smollett's considered view, the expedition's failure was not attributable to any lack of courage among the ordinary soldiers and sailors but resulted from "a low, ridiculous, and pernicious jealousy" between the navy and army officers, and especially the commanders. General Wentworth was "wholly defective in part of experience, confidence and resolution." As for Admiral Vernon, Smollett raged, he was "of weak understanding, strong prejudices, boundless arrogance, and over-boiling passions."[21]

Unlike those veterans who returned embittered by their experience of the whole botched venture, Lawrence Washington viewed Vernon in a more benevolent light. His close contact with the admiral, from whom, as George remembered "he had received many distinguished marks of patronage and favor," explains the veneration in which he held him, which endured despite the expedition's dismal outcome.[22]

Lawrence's yarns of fighting the "Dons" on the Spanish Main no doubt fired the imagination of his devoted half brother. They must have provided a welcome distraction from young George's homely existence, a world still largely bounded by mundane horizons and limited expectations. Very little is known of George's childhood, a void that allowed early hagiographers like Parson Weems to let their imaginations run wild and spin improbable tales intended to establish his saintly character. Despite the enduring legend, there is no evidence that six-year-old George ever confessed to wantonly taking an ax to one of his father's prized cherry trees.[23]

From the ages of about seven to eleven, George was probably tutored at home at Ferry Farm, and he then attended a school at nearby Fredericksburg. He certainly learned the rudiments of reading and writing, but spelling remained a problem for the rest of his life. This weakness in letters, which was shared by his poorly educated mother, was counterbalanced by a marked aptitude for figures, inclining him toward trigonometry and a precocious interest in surveying.

Augustine Washington died on April 12, 1743. He was forty-eight—a fair age for a Washington. By then he had accumulated more than 10,000 acres, split into at least seven tracts. None of Augustine's children were neglected in his will, but Lawrence, as the eldest son, naturally received the largest share, including the plantation on Little Hunting Creek. Renaming the property Mount Vernon in honor of his revered patron, Lawrence undertook major rebuilding. He commemorated this work by laying a carved cornerstone that proudly recalled his recent services as an officer of the king. Its design featured a heart, Lawrence's initials, and a pair of halberds; these were the ax-like pole arms carried by sergeants in the British Army and an unmistakable expression of the householder's martial credentials.[24]

While Lawrence upgraded Mount Vernon, eleven-year-old George, the third son and by a second marriage, had to be content with Ferry Farm and a share of the household slaves and other possessions. Ultimately, George's own inheritance made little difference, as his mother did not relinquish it to him when he came of age. Disinclined to remarry, Mary Ball Washington stayed put at Ferry Farm for another eighteen years after her son's twenty-first birthday, running the property down through poor management. Self-willed, selfish, and apparently utterly indifferent to her son's growing fame, she was a bane. Despite the best efforts of later apologists to cast her in a more sympathetic light, it is clear that George Washington's mother was a stultifying presence, one who not only denied him a happy and loving childhood but irked him far into his adult years.

For George, the grief resulting from the unexpected death of his father was compounded by the implications for his own future. Above all, it quashed any hopes that he, too, would enjoy the benefits of an English gentleman's education and the opportunity to experience the fabled Mother Country at first hand. It was a bitter disappointment, a blow that would have a lasting impact. Meanwhile, George continued his schooling locally: his surviving exercise books show that, while much attention was devoted to the practicalities of life among the Virginian gentry—copying out the most common legal documents, for example—some effort was also made to convey the social skills expected of his class. When he was aged about twelve, George carefully transcribed a document that was destined to influence him for the rest of his life. *Rules of Civility and Decent Behavior in Company and Conversation* was a handbook on manners for the aspiring gentleman, listing 110 maxims that laid down the ground rules of etiquette. Besides blunt injunctions against spitting into the fire, crushing fleas in company, and blowing one's nose at the table, the *Rules of Civility* offered advice on the tricky art of interacting with others, whatever their social rank. Throughout there was a strong emphasis on decorum and self-control. For example, Rule 1 read: "Every action done in company, ought to be with some sign of respect, to those that are present"; while Rule 40 cautioned: "Strive not with your superiors in argument but always, submit your judgment to others with modesty." Imbibed by Washington at an impressionable age, the *Rules of Civility* offered crucial guidance, providing a firm foundation for his future conduct.[25]

George was soon given an opportunity to put such guidelines to the test. With his father gone, the dashing Lawrence now played an even greater part in his life, as both a friend and a mentor. Once in full possession of Mount Vernon, Lawrence swiftly married Anne Fairfax, the daughter of Colonel William Fairfax, whose impressive mansion, Belvoir, was just four miles away. This was a development of immense significance for George, granting him access to the very highest level of Virginian society. At Belvoir and Mount Vernon alike, the awkward youngster began to acquire some of the finer social graces expected of a gentleman, while enjoying welcome respites from his mother's baleful company at Ferry Farm. In addition, like Lawrence Washington, the English-born Colonel Fairfax was a combat veteran. As a teenager during the War of the Spanish Succession, he'd served in *both* the Royal Navy and British Army under his cousins, Captain Robert Fairfax and Colonel Martin Bladen; increasingly adopting the role of surrogate father, he, too, offered a source of wartime anecdotes calculated to kindle a precocious interest in soldiering.[26]

The importance of Belvoir for George's prospects was greatly enhanced in 1747, when he was fifteen, with the arrival from England of Thomas, Lord Fairfax, the colonel's cousin. A former cavalryman, this hard-riding, fox-hunting, misogynistic aristocrat was proprietor of Virginia's Northern Neck. Inheritance of a royal grant, given back in 1649 by the exiled Charles II to one of his staunch supporters, John Culpeper, had made Fairfax the effective overlord of a great wedge of land totaling more than 5 million acres, sandwiched between the Potomac and Rappahannock Rivers, and stretching back almost 200 miles from Chesapeake Bay to their headwaters in the Blue Ridge Mountains.

Denied the English education experienced by his half brothers Lawrence and Augustine, at Belvoir George Washington encountered the next-best thing, mixing with its English-born residents, receiving their advice, and observing at first hand the refined Old World manners and elegant material culture that long-established Virginian dynasties still aspired to. In this rarefied enclave, it is possible that George may have deliberately imitated the speech patterns of his mentors, Colonel and Lord Fairfax, cultivating an English accent.[27]

Lord Fairfax's patronage soon provided George with a crucial professional opportunity and his first taste of a new and exciting environment. In March 1748, when a surveying party was sent into his Lordship's western domains as part of an ongoing initiative to nail down the boundaries of frontier land that was being sporadically and illegally settled, George was invited to go along. By then the sixteen-year-old had applied himself so diligently to his mathematical texts that he was already capable of running simple surveys and could look to a lucrative career as a land surveyor.

Two years earlier, when George was fourteen, there had been talk of a very different future, as a midshipman in Britain's Royal Navy. As Washington much later recalled, he came close to becoming a sailor of the king: the scheme, which was championed by Lawrence, and which perhaps owed something to his admiration for Admiral Vernon, had progressed to the point where George's baggage was ready for his departure; it only foundered at the last moment because his contrary mother, on the advice of her brother Joseph, suddenly turned against it with a passion.

While George made the 1748 trip as a traveling companion to George William, the son of Colonel Fairfax, it nonetheless provided a chance to learn more about surveying at first hand from a team of acknowledged experts. George's journal of the month-long expedition, which ranged beyond the Blue Ridge Mountains to the Shenandoah Valley, is the earliest surviving record of his candid thoughts and reactions.[28] His impressions are revealing, reflecting what was to be an enduring obsession with the vast North American interior, and especially the potential that it offered for financial exploitation. In the Shenandoah Valley, for example, George was struck by the "most beautiful groves of sugar trees . . . and richness of the land."

It was all very different from Ferry Farm or Mount Vernon. After one long day out with the surveyors, George stayed at the home of Captain Isaac Pennington, over the Blue Ridge. Still attuned to Tidewater notions of comfort and cleanliness, George stripped himself as usual before getting into bed, only to find that it was "nothing but a little straw matted together without sheets or anything else but only one thread bare blanket with double its weight of vermin such as lice, fleas etc."

On March 23, arriving some forty-five miles to the northwest at Colonel Thomas Cresap's fortified trading post at the mouth of the Potomac's South Branch, Washington and his companions came face-to-face with another, far more exciting, feature of frontier life. Cresap's post lay on a well-worn tribal trail, and they were "agreeably surprised at the sight of thirty odd Indians coming from war." Washington's first glimpse of "undomesticated" Indians amid their own natural environment clearly intrigued him, inspiring a detailed and unusually spirited description in his otherwise humdrum diary. A gift of liquor encouraged the Indians to perform an enthusiastic and striking "war dance." Forming a large circle around a great fire, George wrote, "the best dancer jumps up as one awaked out of a sleep and runs and jumps about the ring in a most comical manner." While the others followed his lead, the musicians began to play, beating time on a drum made from a pot half full of water with a deerskin stretched across it, and shaking a gourd "with some shot in it to rattle and a piece of an horses tail tied to it to make it look fine."

Some days later George and his companions encountered a very different group of frontier folk, "a great company of people—men, women and children" who followed them through the woods as they went about their surveying, proving more irritating than entertaining. These Germans, who had drifted down from Pennsylvania, were squatting on his Lordship's lands and were anxious at the prospect of being evicted from their homesteads.

Such non-English settlers were a new phenomenon in the 1740s, the spearhead of a fresh influx of immigrants from Europe who mostly bypassed the long-inhabited coastal settlements in search of land and freedom on their hazardous frontier fringes. Besides the Germans encountered by Washington's party, the backcountry of Virginia, North Carolina, and Pennsylvania was also attracting the so-called Scotch-Irish from Ulster, tough folk well suited to their dangerous new surroundings. Taken together, this incursion was slowly changing the ethnic balance of the hitherto overwhelmingly "English" colonies. To Washington and his companions, the German incomers were no less alien than the aboriginal warriors of the interior. Indeed, he believed them to be "as ignorant a set of people as the Indians. They would never speak English but when spoken to they all speak Dutch [*sic*]."

For much of the trip the party camped out in all weathers, dining on the wild turkeys they shot. Young George was roughing it in the wilderness and enjoying the experience. On April 8, after negotiating rugged, mountainous terrain, they camped in the woods "near a wild meadow." George wrote: "After we had pitched our tent and made a very large fire we pulled out our knapsack in order to recruit ourselves. Every [one] was his own cook. Our spits was forked sticks. Our plates was a large chip. As for dishes we had none." Having tasted, and relished, the wild frontier that would go far to shape his emerging character, George returned safe to Mount Vernon on April 13, 1748.

Later that same year, the impressionable teenager first met a young woman who was to exert an equally dramatic influence upon him. His friend George William Fairfax married the vivacious Sarah Cary and brought her home to Belvoir. Known as Sally, she was two years older than George Washington. From that time until almost the end of his life, Sally Fairfax was destined to enjoy a special place in George's affections. Although the loss of virtually all the correspondence that passed between them complicates the issue, as will be seen, the few surviving letters suggest strongly that Sally held a powerful and lasting attraction for George and that he swiftly fell deeply in love with her.[29]

George now pursued his interest in surveying to support himself and to accumulate more land of his own. By 1749, aged just seventeen, he was running professional surveys and over the coming three years conducted some 190, nearly all of them involving new grants on the frontiers of Lord Fairfax's Northern Neck domain. Here once again the Fairfax factor was to prove vital for George Washington's prospects: not only was surveying a profitable profession in its own right, yielding a higher annual income than that enjoyed by most Virginian planters or tradesmen, but it provided excellent opportunities for him to acquire prime tracts of land ahead of rivals. In his short spell of active surveying, it has been estimated that George earned something approaching £400; equating eighteenth-century sums to modern values is notoriously difficult, but in an age when a skilled artisan with a family to support might hope for an annual wage of £35, this clearly amounted to a tidy sum. In the same three-year period, by either purchase or grant, he acquired 2,315 acres of good-quality land in the Lower Shenandoah Valley, equaling that held by the far older Lawrence at Mount Vernon.

George took a break from surveying in September 1751 when he accompanied his beloved half brother to the island of Barbados, in hopes that the Caribbean climate would ease his increasingly troubling cough. It is likely that Lawrence Washington was suffering from one of the era's great killers: tuberculosis, or "consumption." In May 1749, he had been excused from attending Virginia's House of Burgesses, where he represented Fairfax County, "for the recovery of his health" and that summer sailed for England in search of a cure. When Lawrence returned with no improvement to his condition, it was resolved that he would try the warmer climate of Barbados instead and that George should go with him.

This was George Washington's one and only sea voyage, and it left a strong impression upon him. His journal of the trip to Barbados, which survives only in tattered fragments, notes the porpoises, which sported alongside the ship and which were often gaffed and served up for supper, and the changing weather conditions.

Washington swiftly acquired a smattering of nautical jargon, and his journal is full of abbreviations suggesting that a life before the mast might not have been such a bad idea after all.

The Washington brothers arrived at the island's leading settlement of Bridgetown in early November 1751, to be welcomed by the prominent merchant and planter Major Gedney Clarke, whose sister Deborah was married to Colonel William Fairfax. Yet again the Fairfax connection had its uses, introducing the new arrivals to such genteel society as Barbados boasted. It was Major Clarke who recommended a doctor to examine Lawrence; his diagnosis was encouraging, giving hopes of a cure. That same day, November 5, George and Lawrence rode out to seek lodgings for their stay. It was the cool of the evening, and, as George enthused in his journal, they were "perfectly enraptured with the beautiful prospects, which every side presented to our view."[30]

Such tranquil vistas were deceptive. Barbados was Britain's second-oldest Caribbean colony, established back in 1627. Sugar was the dominant crop, its intensive cultivation driven by a growing taste for tea and coffee in Great Britain and her North American possessions alike and by the widespread popularity of powerful rum distilled from molasses. But like the tobacco that soothed pipe smokers throughout Britain's empire, this sweetness came from the bitter experience of enslaved Africans. By the early 1750s, black slaves outnumbered the island's white population by more than three to one, leaving the planters in perpetual fear of an uprising. As a Virginian who had grown up surrounded by tobacco plantations, Washington was already familiar with the institution of slavery. Yet the Barbados version was notoriously harsh. Slaves toiled for long hours in the cane fields under a broiling sun. It was backbreaking work, and they were only kept to it by the lash and by a far more savage array of punishments for runaways and troublemakers. If George Washington noticed these brutalities, he failed to mention them in what survives of his journal, although, with his keen interest in military matters, he did remark on the island's fortifications; on November 13, 1751, he dined at Bridgetown's fort, tallying up the thirty-six guns mounted within the ramparts and another fifty-one in batteries outside.[31]

Just days later, George was "strongly attacked with the smallpox," a disease that took a heavy toll on his contemporaries, and particularly the young. Decades later, when he was among the most famous Americans of his generation, Benjamin Franklin still grieved for his son, "a fine boy of four years old" who had succumbed to smallpox in 1736. Franklin regretted bitterly that he had never inoculated his little boy, a risky procedure to be sure, but better than leaving him totally defenseless against the disease.[32] Smallpox survivors were often left disfigured with deeply pitted complexions—the "pox-fretten" faces that feature so often in newspaper advertisements describing runaway servants, deserters, and other miscreants. Washington was unusually lucky: in exchange for nothing more than a few shallow scars on his nose, he gained lifetime immunity from one of the era's worst scourges.

But Lawrence's persistent cough only worsened. After four months on Barbados, while George headed home to Virginia, he sailed on alone to Bermuda in hopes its climate would work a cure. That, too, was a futile effort: the invalid returned to his beloved Mount Vernon and died there in June 1752, still in his early thirties. Another Washington had found an early grave, and George had lost a much-loved friend and mentor.

Following Lawrence's death, George gradually abandoned the profession of surveying. Not even the great expanse of the Northern Neck was limitless, and the same Fairfax power that had given such a boost to George's career barred him from carving out an extensive territory of his own like surveyors elsewhere on Virginia's frontier. Surveying was a practical skill that Washington would never forget, and one that he would occasionally return to, but it was no longer the focus for his ambition: that turned increasingly to soldiering.

Undoubtedly encouraged by Lawrence's example and his tales of Caribbean campaigning, George actively sought a military position for himself by following his half brother's lead. Lawrence Washington's status as a bona fide combat veteran had gained him the

post of adjutant general for Virginia, which involved responsibility
for overseeing the efficiency of the colony's militia, composed of
those freeholders expected to turn out and fight in a military crisis; his deputy was George Muse, an Englishman who had settled
in Virginia and a fellow survivor of the ill-fated American Regiment's stint in the Caribbean. As Virginia's sporadic Indian wars
of the previous century were now a distant memory and there
had been no external threats to the colony since then, by the mid-
eighteenth century its militia had long since lost its true role; aside
from "patrols" intended to monitor and intimidate the slaves and
bound servants, it functioned more as a social club than a fighting
force to be reckoned with.[33]

The militia adjutancy was nonetheless prestigious and offered
a useful financial return for a minimum of effort. Learning in the
spring of 1752 that the office was to be split up into districts, George
asked Virginia's lieutenant governor, Robert Dinwiddie, to consider
him for the adjutancy of the familiar Northern Neck. Instead, on
December 13, he was commissioned adjutant for Southern Virginia, an office that carried the honorary rank of major, and yielded
a handsome annual salary of £100. Allied to his Fairfax connections and accumulating landholdings, this enhanced status gave
another sign that, as he entered his twenties, George Washington
was a young man of ambition, keen to make a name for himself. His
chance to do so came soon enough.

At the very time that George was lobbying Robert Dinwiddie
for his militia adjutancy, the governor was becoming increasingly
concerned about growing French interest in the Ohio Valley, a
region that Britain and France both claimed as their own. Tensions
there arose from mutual concerns: the French feared that an English presence on the Ohio, or, as they styled it, "La Belle Rivière,"
would hammer a wedge between New France's two distinct and
far-flung territories, Canada and Louisiana, so they determined to
safeguard communications between them by constructing a cordon of forts. For their part, the English worried that the French
thereby sought to hem them behind the daunting natural barrier

of the Appalachians and exclude them from the valuable fur trade with the Ohio's Indian inhabitants. While courting them as economic partners, both European powers underplayed the fact that these same tribes regarded the contested area as their own homeland and had no intention of budging.

The Ohio's native peoples—Shawnees, Delawares, and also Iroquois migrants known as "Mingos"—were fiercely independent. During the previous half century these Indians had been attracted to the depopulated Ohio both by its abundant game and because it offered a refuge from imperialism—not simply the imported European variety, but also that espoused by the Iroquois Confederacy. Spanning what is now Upstate New York, the Six Nations of the Iroquois regarded the Ohio region as a fiefdom, seeking to control its inhabitants through intimidation and the presence of their own envoys. By the early 1750s, however, Iroquois influence was waning, while the Ohio villagers increasingly exploited their strategically important location to trade with the French and British colonists alike.[34]

Given the ongoing rivalry between Britain and France, which had already generated three major wars between 1689 and 1748, a further clash was viewed as inevitable. The likelihood that friction in the Ohio Valley would spark the next conflict was increased in 1752, when the arrival of a new governor-general of Canada, Ange de Menneville, Marquis de Duquesne, heralded the onset of a more deliberate and aggressive policy of French expansion into the contested region.[35]

In the spring of 1753, Duquesne dispatched a force of 2,000 men, under Pierre de La Malgue, sieur de Marin, to build a chain of forts linking Lake Erie with the Forks of the Ohio, where the Monongahela and Allegheny Rivers join that waterway, and where modern Pittsburgh stands. By May, a first fort had been constructed at the Presque Isle portage, while a road was pushed south to another strongpoint at Fort Le Boeuf, on a branch of French Creek. With a fortified trading post already established farther south, at Venango, it required only a fort at the Forks themselves to complete the system.

Monitoring this encroachment upon what was ostensibly Virginian territory, Governor Dinwiddie reported his concerns to the Board of Trade, the body officially responsible for colonial affairs in London. Besides his position as a British official obliged to resist French expansionism, Dinwiddie had other, more selfish reasons for seeking action: in his late fifties and with decades of experience as a British imperial administrator, he was a leading member of a group of land speculators, the Ohio Company, that aimed to erect a fort of their own at the Forks of the Ohio as a hub for trade and settlement.

The Crown's response, received by Dinwiddie on October 22, 1753, outlined the stance to be adopted for the future: if any person, Indian or white, erected a fort within the province of Virginia, Dinwiddie should require them to depart in peace; if that approach failed and such "unlawful and unjustifiable designs" continued, the interlopers must be driven off "by force of arms." On no account should Dinwiddie become "the aggressor" by using troops outside "the undoubted limits of His Majesty's province."[36]

Learning that Dinwiddie intended to warn the French, Major Washington rode to Williamsburg and volunteered to carry the letter. Dinwiddie lost no time in accepting his offer. It was the beginning of a relationship that would prove crucial for propelling George Washington on his chosen path as a soldier. The tall young Virginian and the stubby, aging Scot made an odd pair, yet they shared a determination to resist French encroachments at all costs. On October 30, Dinwiddie commissioned Washington to place himself in the midst of the escalating imperial rivalry and deliver a summons "to the commandant of the French forces on the Ohio." Besides handing over Dinwiddie's letter, Washington would also be responsible for calling together those local Indian leaders who were believed to be sympathetic toward Britain and securing their help. Not least, he was to gather intelligence regarding the French dispositions and intentions.[37]

All this would involve a grueling round-trip across punishing terrain in the depths of winter, roaming for hundreds of miles within territory claimed by King George's inveterate enemies. Although lacking any diplomatic or military experience, the twenty-one-year-old Washington was physically well suited to the challenges ahead. No description of his appearance in 1753 survives, but he cannot have looked very different six years later when a letter attributed to his close friend George Mercer described him as "being straight as an Indian" and "measuring 6 feet 2 inches in his stockings," which meant that he was literally head and shoulders above most of his male contemporaries. His impressive height was balanced by a rangy and powerful physique, "padded with well developed muscles." Broad shouldered and "neat waisted," Washington had large hands and long legs, his strong thighs well fitted for gripping horse-flesh; indeed, he was "a splendid horseman."[38] The Ohio trip would draw upon all his reserves of strength and stamina.

Washington left Williamsburg on October 31, the very day he received Dinwiddie's orders.[39] On his way west he recruited a small, motley escort. At Fredericksburg on November 1, he was joined by a Dutchman, Jacob Van Braam, a former soldier who had recently advertised himself as a teacher of French and would serve as Washington's interpreter in that language. After gathering supplies and horses, another fortnight's travel by a newly constructed road brought the pair to the Ohio Company's trading post at Wills Creek, on the boundary of Virginia and Maryland, where the Potomac nudged the foothills of the Alleghenies. There they picked up the renowned frontiersman and explorer Christopher Gist. Aged about forty-seven, the tough and resourceful Gist was the party's essential guide and expert on Indian affairs. Another four experienced woodsmen were hired as "servitors."

Washington's band set out the next day, November 15, but their progress into the wilderness was hindered by the "excessive rains and vast quantity of snow that had fallen." It took them a week to reach the cabin of the Scottish gunsmith and Indian trader John Fraser at Turtle Creek, some ten miles from the Forks of the Ohio. Washington soon viewed the Forks themselves with his surveyor's eye, considering the site "extremely well situated for a fort," enjoying "absolute command" of both the Monongahela and Allegheny Rivers. In Washington's opinion, it was certainly a far better location than that already earmarked by the Ohio Company, two miles below the Forks. There they called upon Shingas, a pro-British chief of the Delawares, inviting him to attend a council to be held at Logstown, a key Indian trading village of the Ohio Valley, situated fourteen miles farther off.

When they reached Logstown on November 24, Washington discovered that the "Half-King," one of the most important of the Indians that Dinwiddie had instructed him to meet, was away at his hunting cabin. The Half-King was Tanaghrisson, an adopted Seneca who had been appointed by the Iroquois League to uphold its dwindling authority on the Ohio. As his title made clear, Tanaghrisson's personal authority was limited. As soon as he arrived the next evening, Washington invited him and the locally based interpreter John Davison to his tent. Washington was keen to hear the Half-King's own account of his journey to the French fort at Presque Isle in September 1753 and his dealings with the commandant there, the sieur de Marin.

Along with other representatives of the Ohio tribes, on that occasion Tanaghrisson had delivered a forceful warning against French expansion. In the version reported to Washington, he had not minced his words, articulating concerns common to many Indian tribes:

> *Fathers, both you and the English are white. We live in a country between, therefore the land does not belong either to one or the other; but the Great Being above allowed it to be a place of residence for us; so Fathers, I desire you to withdraw, as I have done our brothers the English, for I will keep you at arm's length.*

The Indians would "stand by" whoever paid most heed to their words. But, as the Half-King recalled, the hard-bitten Marin had rejected his claims and threats with contempt, making a threat of his own: "If people will be ruled by me they may expect kindness but not else."

The next day, November 26, 1753, the great council that Washington had convened was held in the Long House at Logstown. On behalf of Governor Dinwiddie, their "brother," he called upon the "Sachems of the Six Nations," Virginia's esteemed "friends and allies," to inform them of his mission and to seek their help in fulfilling it: he needed "young men to provide provisions for us on our way, and to be a safeguard against those French Indians, that have taken up the hatchet against us." After considering Washington's words, Tanaghrisson rose and, speaking for all, voiced his feelings of brotherhood. Washington would get his escort, but he must wait while the proper preparations were made: the ceremonial "speech belts" of prized wampum beads previously given by the French must be collected, so that they could be returned to them, while it was also imperative that Washington's escort should include representatives of all the key nations of the region—Mingos, Shawnees, and Delawares.

Washington was impatient to push on but, as Tanaghrisson was insistent, "found it impossible to get off without insulting them in the most egregious manner" and so reluctantly agreed to stay. Although a novice in wilderness diplomacy, Washington already knew enough to appreciate that the "returning of wampum, was the abolishing of agreements; and giving this up was shaking off all dependence upon the French." It was now, or in following weeks, as Washington later recalled, that he was "named by the Half-King . . . and the tribes of nations with whom he treated—Caunotaucarious (in English) the Town taker." As already seen, this was the name reportedly given to his great-grandfather, John Washington, by the Susquehannocks some seventy-five years earlier. Like the Senecas, by whom Tanaghrisson had been adopted, the Susquehannocks were an Iroquoian people, so it's certainly not impossible that the title could have been remembered and transmitted orally down the generations. Another possibility is that Washington drew upon his family's traditions and deliberately resurrected the name himself in a bid to impress the Half-King, and the other Indians he met that winter, with his own warrior heritage.[40]

On November 28, Tanaghrisson returned as promised, now accompanied by Monacatoocha, a pro-English Oneida also known as "Scarouady"; another representative of the Six Nations in the Ohio Country, his warrior status was delineated by tattoos—a tomahawk on his chest and a bow and arrow on each cheek.[41] Along with two other sachems, the Half-King and Monacatoocha now wanted to know exactly what business they were to be going upon. It was a question Washington had long anticipated, and his carefully rehearsed answers "allayed their curiosity a little."

Monacatoocha also conveyed fresh and alarming intelligence of French designs on the Ohio. He had recently heard that the French had summoned all the Mingos and Delawares to Venango, explaining that they had intended to be down the river that autumn and only the onset of winter had stopped them; they would move in the spring, and in still greater numbers. The Indians should not meddle, unless they wished that great force to fall upon *them*. According to Monacatoocha's informant, the French were prepared to fight the English for three years. If the end of that time brought stalemate, the Europeans would join forces to "cut off" the Indians and carve up their lands among themselves. This menacing speech had been delivered by Captain Philippe Thomas de Joncaire, the French commandant at Venango—Washington's next destination.

Chafing at all the frustrating delays but acknowledging the need for them, Washington resumed his journey only on November 30. An Indian assembly the night before had resolved that just three of the chiefs, along with one of their best hunters, would escort his party onward: a greater number would rouse French suspicions, bringing the risk of bad treatment, they reasoned. When Washington's little band left Logstown, it was accompanied by the Half-King Tanaghrisson, the Cayuga Jeskakake, an Iroquois chief named White Thunder, and a Seneca called Guyasuta, or "Hunter."

They reached Venango on December 4, after a trip of more than seventy miles, meeting nothing remarkable on the way save

for more hard weather. Seeing the white flag of the Bourbons flying from a house, Washington approached without hesitation to
find the commandant. Captain Joncaire advised Washington that,
as there was a general officer at the next post up the line, Fort
Le Boeuf, he would need to journey there for an answer to Dinwiddie's letter. Meanwhile, Joncaire and his fellow officers treated
Washington with the courtesy that the age expected from one gentleman to another, but with blunt frankness: yes, they intended
nothing less than to take full possession of the Ohio, and, by God,
they would do so. As the wine flowed more freely, they boasted
that, while it was true that the English could raise two men for
every one of theirs, Washington's countrymen were too lethargic
to thwart French plans.

A veteran soldier of New France, and vastly experienced in
Indian affairs, Captain Joncaire was old enough to be Washington's father; yet he clearly warmed to the self-confident and vigorous young Virginian: by his very presence at Venango, Washington
had shown he was a kindred spirit, ready to risk the hazards of the
wilderness and not to be confused with those who railed against
French plans from the safety of the council chambers and taverns of
Williamsburg and Philadelphia.

On December 5, heavy rain prevented Washington's party from
moving onward. The wily Joncaire exploited this hiatus to summon
Tanaghrisson, whom Washington had been keen to keep out of
his company. When the Indians came into his presence, Joncaire
deployed all his charm, wondering that they could be so near without coming to visit him. Gifts were offered, and alcohol disappeared
so fast that, as Washington noted, "they were soon rendered incapable of the business they came about."

The next morning, and none the worse for wear, the Half-
King asked Washington to stay and hear what he had to say to the
French. True to his pledge, when he met Joncaire, Tanaghrisson formally handed over the French speech belt, but the captain refused
to receive it: like Dinwiddie's summons, it must be delivered to the
senior commander at the next fort.

When Washington's party continued north on December 7, it was accompanied by "Monsieur La Force," the commissary of stores, whose mastery of Indian languages gave him immense influence among the tribes, and three other soldiers. This stage of their journey, covering about sixty miles, took four days: they were delayed by driving rain and snow and the swamps they were obliged to negotiate because French Creek was swollen so high and rapid that it was "impassable either by fording or rafting." Even under these trying circumstances Washington viewed the ground with an eye to its future exploitation: "We passed over much good land since we left Venango, and through several extensive and very rich meadows, one of which was near 4 miles in length, and considerably wide in some places," he noted.

They reached Fort Le Boeuf on the December 11 and once again received a cordial reception. Washington presented his credentials and Dinwiddie's letter to the commandant, Captain Jacques Legardeur, sieur de Saint-Pierre. Washington was clearly impressed: a Knight of the Military Order of St. Louis, Saint-Pierre was "an elderly gentleman" with "much the air of a soldier." Washington's assessment was accurate: Saint-Pierre came from an old, established Canadian military dynasty, and his own active service went back to 1732. A noted explorer of the west, he had fought against the formidable Chickasaws of the Mississippi Valley from 1737 to 1740, and the no less fearsome Mohawk allies of the English on the New York frontier during the War of the Austrian Succession.[42] Saint-Pierre postponed consideration of Dinwiddie's letter until the commandant at Fort Presque Isle, Louis Le Gardeur de Repentigny, could be summoned to look over it with him. When they had done so, Washington and his interpreter Van Braam were called in to check their translation.

On December 13, Saint-Pierre held a council of war, and its deliberations gave Washington a chance to stroll around the fort and make a remarkably detailed report of its dimensions and armament: there were four projecting bastions, each mounting two six-pounder cannon; another four-pounder was set before the gate, ready to repulse any break-in. According to the best estimate he could obtain, the garrison consisted of about 100 men, plus officers. Washington also ordered his followers to make a careful tally of the canoes intended to ferry the French to the Forks with the spring. There were "50 of birch bark, and 170 of pine," not to mention many others roughly "blocked out" ready for finishing.

It was not until the evening of December 14 that Washington finally received Saint-Pierre's answer to Dinwiddie's summons: that was a matter for the governor of Canada, the commandant said, who would be better able "to set forth the evidence and the reality of the rights of the King, my master, to the lands situated along the Belle Rivière, and to contest the pretensions of the King of Great Britain thereto." Dinwiddie's letter would therefore be forwarded to him, with Saint-Pierre guided by the marquis's response. Meanwhile, he assured Dinwiddie that he had no intention of withdrawing. He wrote: "I am here by the orders of my General, and I entreat you, Sir, not to doubt for a moment that I have a firm resolution to follow them with all the exactness and determination which can be expected of the best officer." He added: "I have made it a particular duty to receive Mr. Washington with the distinction owing to your dignity, his position, and his own great merit."[43]

For all his elaborate courtesy, and the "plentiful store of liquor, provisions etc." that he put into Washington's canoe for the return journey, the canny Saint-Pierre "was plotting every scheme that the Devil and man could invent, to set our Indians at variance with us, to prevent their going 'til after our departure." As Washington anxiously recorded: "I can't say that ever in my life I suffered so much anxiety as I did in this affair."

On December 16, despite a last French effort to persuade the Half-King to stay through the "power of liquor," Washington badgered the chief to leave with him. Clutching his polite but uncompromising rejection of Dinwiddie's request, Washington made the return journey from Fort Le Boeuf in appalling weather, first by canoe, then overland. The going was harder than ever, with the passage down the corkscrewing course of French Creek "tedious and very fatiguing"; several times it seemed their canoe would be holed on rocks, while they were often obliged to get out and toil in the icy water to heave it over the shoals. Where the creek was frozen solid, they were forced to portage, or manhandle, their canoe for a quarter of a mile across a neck of land.

Exhausted, they reached Venango only on December 22. From there, Washington intended to continue by land, riding the horses sent ahead with three of the "servitors." But White Thunder "had hurt himself much, and was sick and unable to walk," obliging Tanaghrisson to ferry him onward by canoe. Fearing that once he had set off, Joncaire would use all his wiles to win over the Indians, Washington cautioned against such "flattery" and "fine speeches." Tanaghrisson assured him he was immune to French advances.

The party's horses were now "so weak and feeble" from their exertions that they could not carry anything but essential baggage, and Washington proceeded on foot. As the snow fell more heavily than ever, the packhorses grew weaker and slower by the day. Washington remained keen to deliver his report to Dinwiddie without delay, and on Boxing Day he left the baggage to follow as best it could and pushed on through the woods with the hardy and reliable Christopher Gist. Both men were wrapped up in Indian-style "matchcoats," with packs on their backs and guns in their hands.

Now moving through lands prowled by pro-French Indians, they faced fresh hazards. Near the ominously named Murdering Town, a warrior took a potshot at them from just fifteen yards off. Thankfully, he was no sharpshooter. Neither Washington nor Gist was harmed, and they collared the Indian as he struggled to reload his gun. Incensed, Gist wanted to kill the would-be assassin on the spot, but Washington intervened, and he was turned loose. Anticipating pursuit from more hostiles, the pair now pushed on through the night without stopping, traveling on the next day until it was dark. They were bought up short by the Ohio (today's Allegheny), which, despite the intense cold, was only partially frozen. To cross over, Washington and Gist cobbled together a ramshackle raft. With just one "poor hatchet" between them, that took a day's work.

Jumping aboard their craft, they were barely halfway across when it jammed fast in the ice. As Washington was using his setting pole to jerk the raft free, the current threw a floe against it with such force that he was tumbled off into the deep, freezing water. Grabbing onto the raft, he clawed his way out. Unable to reach shore, Washington and his companion spent the night on an island, chilled and soaked. It was now colder than ever, and Gist was badly frostbitten. But despite his ducking, Washington miraculously remained unscathed. The next morning, the ice was thick enough for them to reach dry land, and they headed for Fraser's cabin.

There they encountered evidence that the anticipated frontier war was already beginning. They met a band of friendly Indians who had abandoned their raid to the south after discovering a massacred family of seven, the scalped bodies of adults and children alike strewn about and gnawed by hogs. Signs indicated that the killers were Ottawas, a tribe from beyond the Great Lakes known for strong French affiliations and a taste for human flesh. In coming years, such grim vignettes would become depressingly familiar along the exposed Pennsylvanian and Virginian frontiers.

Washington and Gist continued on their way on January 1, 1754, and by January 6 were back at Wills Creek, "after as fatiguing a journey as it is possible to conceive," chiefly owing to the unrelenting "cold wet weather, which occasioned very uncomfortable lodgings." It was all a contrast to the hospitality and congenial company of Belvoir, where, despite his professed desire to see Dinwiddie without delay, the weather-beaten Washington broke his journey to take a day of "necessary rest" among his Fairfax friends.

Reaching Williamsburg on January 16, Washington presented Dinwiddie with the French commandant's response, amplified by his own verbal account of events and his rough journal of "the most remarkable occurrences that happened to me." Washington's report and the detailed map that he drew to accompany it confirmed Dinwiddie's belief that the French threat to the Ohio was no mere chimera. To bolster his case, Dinwiddie quickly decided to print Washington's journal. Transcribed from his field notes inside twenty-four hours, this was subsequently published as a pamphlet in Williamsburg and London and, in the fashion of the age, reprinted entire or in part by magazines and newspapers on both sides of the Atlantic.[44] Reaction to its contents was mixed: while the Ohio Company's backers took comfort from Washington's confirmation of French designs upon that region, others suspected a cynical ploy to promote the company's interests.

Regardless of its reception, the widespread dissemination of Washington's Ohio journal brought him a first taste of international fame. Here was a genuine tale of danger and hardship among exotic "savages" to rival any novel. At just twenty-two, Washington had been catapulted from an obscure officer of the colonial militia to a bold adventurer whose name resonated with power brokers in London and Paris.

2

HEARING THE
BULLETS WHISTLE

In token of its approval for his recent excursion into the Ohio Country, Virginia's assembly awarded Washington £50, a sum, as he later grouched, that did nothing to recognize the hardships and dangers endured but merely covered his expenses.[1] The evidence in Washington's journal gave Governor Dinwiddie the ammunition he needed to contest French ambitions: at his urging, but only after much wrangling, the House of Burgesses voted £10,000 to raise a force of 300 volunteers to uphold Virginia's rights on the Ohio.

To help fill the six companies of what would become the Virginia Regiment, Dinwiddie lured recruits with promises of a share in 200,000 acres of land on the frontier they would be contesting. As a first step, 100 men from Frederick and Augusta Counties were to be placed under Major Washington's command. After training and equipping his detachment at Alexandria, Washington was to lose no time in marching for the Forks of the Ohio, where a small advance party of Virginians under Captain William Trent was already building a fort.[2] The urgent need for action was reinforced by reports from friendly Indians that the French were now heading there in overwhelming force.

While eager to join the offensive, given his youth and lack of military experience, Washington was reluctant to assume the responsibility of overall command. The rank of colonel and commander in chief of the Virginia Regiment instead went to Joshua

Fry, with Washington placed under him as lieutenant colonel. An Oxford-educated professor of mathematics in his early fifties, Fry was no more qualified for military command than Washington but was reckoned steady and reliable by Dinwiddie. The regiment's other officers were a polyglot bunch, born in North America, Great Britain, Holland, Sweden, and even France. They included men like George Mercer, who shared Washington's own Virginian roots, and more recent arrivals from Europe, such as the Scottish medical men Adam Stephen and James Craik; in the coming months of hard campaigning, these three, among others, would forge long-standing friendships with their young lieutenant colonel.

Recruits for the Virginia Regiment were not easy to come by. From Alexandria, Washington reported to Dinwiddie that such men as had enlisted were mostly the flotsam and jetsam of colonial society, "loose, idle persons that are quite destitute of house and home." Many also lacked coats on their backs, and even shoes on their feet, and, with no sign of a regimental paymaster, it was impossible to advance them the money to buy proper outfits. The recruits were nonetheless keen to acquire uniforms, and Washington was adamant that these should be red; even the "coarsest" local cloth would do. As he explained to Dinwiddie, the Indians would be "struck with" this martial display as "red with them is compared to blood and is looked upon as the distinguishing marks of warriors and great men." By contrast, Washington believed that the dowdy gray-white uniforms of the French common soldiers presented "a shabby and ragged appearance" that earned the Indians' contempt.[3] Dinwiddie, too, was persuaded: like his half brother Lawrence before him, George Washington embarked upon his first combat command wearing the blood-red coat that had been the trademark of the British soldier for more than a century.

Despite all the nagging logistical problems—which gave a foretaste of those that would dog him as commander of the Continental Army during the Revolutionary War—on April 2, 1754, Lieutenant Colonel Washington marched for the Forks with such men as he had already enlisted, about 160 in all, without waiting for Colonel Fry.[4] After several hard weeks on the trail, news came in that the French had already pounced. Trent's deputy, Ensign Edward Ward, and the thirty-odd men pushed ahead to dig in at the Forks had been sent packing upon the arrival of the long-anticipated enemy force on April 17. This had struck from Venango in overwhelming strength. According to reports, there were "upwards of one thousand men, eighteen pieces of artillery, and large stores of provisions and other necessaries" under Captain Claude Pierre Pécaudy, sieur de Contrecoeur, all ferried in "a fleet of 360 canoes and bateaux";[5] these were the very craft that Washington had seen laid up around Fort Le Boeuf that winter. Although the size of the French force was exaggerated, it was formidable enough to convince Ward and his puny command to surrender their post before a single shot was fired. Content with achieving his objective, Contrecoeur allowed the Virginians to retire unmolested.

Marching on to Wills Creek, familiar as the jumping-off point for his recent trek into the Ohio Country, Washington called a council of war to consider how best to respond to this crisis; such consultations were standard procedure within eighteenth-century armies and navies, and Washington would convene many more during his military career. Amid all the gloom there was one ray of hope: although the French had taken the Forks with contemptuous ease, their appearance had drawn a defiant response from the indignant "Half-King," Tanaghrisson. He sent Washington emissaries bearing the customary wampum belt as proof of his sincerity. They explained that the Half-King and his warriors were eager to fight the French and only waited upon Washington's assistance to strike.

Sensing that Virginian, and therefore British, prestige was at stake, Washington decided to advance to the Ohio Company storehouse at Redstone Creek, less than forty miles from the Forks. He assured Dinwiddie of his intention to construct a road to Redstone "sufficiently good for the heaviest artillery" and then hold out there until reinforcements arrived, ready to uphold his country's rights "to the last remains of life." Using his "inherited" Indian name,

"Conotocarious," Washington had also responded to Tanaghrisson's speech, anticipating joint action against the "treacherous" French.[6]

Given the odds stacked against Washington's force, this was a remarkably bold response. In addition, and acting entirely on his own initiative, Washington sent dispatches to the lieutenant governors of Virginia's northern neighbors, Pennsylvania and Maryland, soliciting their aid in the common cause. His letter to Maryland's Horatio Sharpe, who Washington believed to be "solicitous for the public weal and warm in this interesting cause," included a dramatic rallying cry worthy of Shakespeare's warrior-king Henry V. Indeed, he wrote, the news from the Forks "should rouse from the lethargy we have fallen into, the heroic spirit of every free-born Englishman to assert the rights and privileges of our king" and rescue "from the invasions of a usurping enemy, our Majesty's property, his dignity, and lands."[7]

As Washington knew all too well, the mountainous and densely forested terrain, which rose in a series of rampart-like ridges, posed a daunting barrier to military operations; his advance from Wills Creek was predictably slow, with a maximum pace of four miles a day. Yet the rough road inched inexorably forward, until, some twenty miles from Redstone, Washington was forced to halt by the rain-swollen waters of the Youghiogheny River. As he waited for these to subside, reports arrived that the French had now begun constructing their own fort at the Forks and were being reinforced.

Meanwhile Washington was fuming at news that he and his fellow officers in the Virginia Regiment were to receive less pay than British regular soldiers. Here was a prime example of colonial Americans being treated like inferior beings. "Why should the lives of Virginians be worth less than Britons?" he complained to Dinwiddie. Only the prospect of imminent action had prevented his officers from resigning their commissions in disgust. Washington himself, for whom personal honor and "reputation" would always be paramount, initially refused all pay, preferring to soldier on as a "volunteer."[8]

Dinwiddie now sent word that Colonel Fry was on his way with the much-needed reinforcements. As the level of the Youghiogheny had dropped, however, Washington resolved to resume his march for Redstone rather than await his tardy commanding officer. It was a clear sign of the young Washington's hunger for military distinction—whatever the risks. He had not gone far before he received another message from the Half-King: this warned that the French intended to attack the first English they encountered, reaffirmed his own allegiance, and pledged that he and his fellow chiefs would meet Washington for a conference in five days' time.[9]

Surmounting the last great barrier of Laurel Hill, Washington's little force descended until, on May 24, it reached a natural clearing within the blanketing forest—the Great Meadows. By scouring stray bushes from the lush grassland, Washington created what he described as "a charming field for an encounter." But his probing scouts could find no sign of an enemy to fight there.[10]

Christopher Gist, Washington's trusty companion on his Ohio diplomatic mission, arrived on May 27 with intelligence that fifty Frenchmen were heading that way, asking for the Half-King. Washington responded by sending out seventy-five men—about half of his force—to find them. Before their return, an Iroquois runner named Silver Heels came in with news that the Half-King was encamped six miles off. There was more: the chief had followed the tracks of two men to a well-hidden hollow, where he believed that the entire French party lay concealed.[11]

Despite misgivings that he was being duped into abandoning his camp, Washington divided his remaining force once again. Now at the head of about forty men, he followed Silver Heels to what he hoped would be a rendezvous with the Half-King. It was raining steadily, and as the night was "as dark as pitch" and the path barely wide enough to march single file, they often strayed and stumbled over one another. At sunrise on May 28, 1754, they reached the Indian camp. There, they found Tanaghrisson and a dozen warriors, all keen to smite the French; they included Monacatoocha, the Oneida sachem whom Washington had met on his diplomatic mission into the Ohio Country. The two parties moved off, with the Indians scouting ahead. A pair of warriors returned with news that some thirty French lay half a mile from the track, encamped within a rocky glen.

The Virginians and their Indian allies approached stealthily, resolving to surround the enemy and then "fall on them together," but before the cordon was complete, they were discovered. According to Washington's contemporaneous journal, it was only after the French raised the alarm and sprinted for their muskets that he gave the fateful order to open fire. He subsequently denied reports that the French had sought to avoid bloodshed by shouting an appeal for his party "not to fire." Whatever the precise sequence of events, Washington's own journal, and likewise his reports to Dinwiddie, leave no doubt that he approached the glen with hostile intent, and was planning a surprise attack when the French reacted.[12]

A brisk firefight followed. Caught in a crossfire from above, the French began to drop. After fifteen minutes the survivors broke and ran. With all escape barred, they tried to surrender. Washington moved forward to accept their submission, only to stand in dumbfounded horror as his Indian allies dashed forward to tomahawk and scalp the fallen, dead and wounded alike. It was only "with great difficulty" that Washington persuaded Tanaghrisson and his warriors to halt the slaughter. Such ferocity, while shocking to the uninitiated, was part and parcel of American frontier warfare, where enemies were for killing and vengeance to be exacted: indeed, the Half-King had insisted upon "scalping them all, as it was their way of fighting [and] . . . those people had killed, boiled and eat[en] his father."

Before Washington managed to stop the butchery, ten Frenchmen lay dead, including their young commander, Joseph Coulon, sieur de Jumonville. In a symbolic, yet all-too-physical rejection of French power, he had been dispatched by Tanaghrisson himself. Standing over the wounded ensign, the Half-King observed: "You are not yet dead, my father." He promptly finished the job, smashing

Jumonville's skull with his hatchet, then reportedly scooping out his brains and "washing his hands" with them.[13]

The score or so of Frenchmen who escaped the carnage desperately craved the protection of Washington's Virginians. To add to the confusion, their surviving officers were frantically protesting and waving papers under Washington's nose: they were on a diplomatic mission to locate the English and warn them away from their king's rightful domains, and look, here were their credentials. By instigating his unprovoked ambush, they accused, Washington had committed the heinous crime of murdering ambassadors.

Despite the obvious parallels with his own recent mission into the Ohio Country, Washington maintained that such claims of diplomatic immunity were no more than a belated smoke screen, sent up to blur the reality: had the boot been on the other foot, with the French succeeding in surprising *him*, they would have dropped all such pretense as soon as they had his men in their sights. Reflecting upon the episode in his journal, he wrote: "they came secretly, and sought after the most hidden retreats, more like deserters than ambassadors." In his report to Dinwiddie, Washington told how his own officers all agreed that the Frenchmen "were sent as spies rather than any thing else," and they were therefore being shifted to Williamsburg as prisoners. Tanaghrisson likewise held no illusions about their objectives, concluding that they had "bad hearts."[14]

Yet, knowingly or not, Washington had gone too far. Although Dinwiddie had failed to drum home the fact, his orders from London made it clear that, while Anglo-French hostilities on the Ohio were all too likely, the imperial rivals were still officially at peace, and so the British must avoid being branded as aggressors: actual fighting was only permissible if the French were informed that they were trespassing and then refused to withdraw.[15] Washington had given Jumonville no such opportunity.

First reports of the affair, brought in by the tireless Gist, reached Williamsburg on June 12. The following day, the *Virginia Gazette* welcomed this "total defeat of a party of French." The "well-timed success," which was attributed to Washington's "vigilance and bravery," had "riveted" the Indians to Virginia's cause, the newspaper crowed.[16] That canny Scot, Governor Dinwiddie, was more cautious. Sensing an impending international storm, he sought to sidestep his own responsibility as the man who had ordered Washington out on his hazardous enterprise. He claimed that the Half-King and his warriors were the prime movers: they had instigated the "little skirmish," so the Virginians were no more than their "auxiliaries," and acting on the defensive.[17]

Beyond the Old Dominion, the episode was viewed differently. As the nineteenth-century historian Francis Parkman observed in his classic history of the French and Indian War, *Montcalm and Wolfe*, "this obscure skirmish began the war that set the world on fire."[18] In doing so, it put North America's history on a trajectory that few, least of all Lieutenant Colonel George Washington, could have predicted.

On May 31, 1754, in the wake of the short but shocking explosion of violence within what became known as "Jumonville's Glen," George Washington wrote to his brother Jack describing his baptism of fire: he had heard the "bullets whistle" for the first time and believed there was "something charming in the sound."[19] The letter subsequently found its way across the Atlantic and into the pages of the popular monthly *London Magazine*, where it was perused by none other than King George II. That curmudgeonly old monarch, who had led his own British and Hanoverian troops against the French at the Battle of Dettingen in 1743 and who as a young cavalry officer had survived the far greater bloodbath of Oudenarde under John Churchill, Duke of Marlborough, in 1708, quipped that the Virginian would not consider that sound quite so charming once he had heard it more often.[20] In fact, it was a noise that Washington was destined to become reacquainted with all too soon.

Washington's letter to Dinwiddie, written after the Jumonville fight, had concluded on a pessimistic, if stoic, note. He expected the enemy to retaliate in overwhelming force at any moment. Come what may, they must be resisted, or the Indians would desert. Washington initially fell back to his old position at the Great Meadows.

There he ordered his men to build a small circular stockade of split logs, subsequently extended on two sides by low banks and shallow, knee-deep ditches: this was the aptly named "Fort Necessity." Conspicuously sited in the center of the lush expanse of grass, the rudimentary post was overlooked by hills, while woodland and scrub encroached to within 100 yards, enabling attackers to creep under cover to within comfortable musket range. Tanaghrisson was clearly unimpressed, later dismissing the fort as "that little thing upon the meadow."[21] He had been joined there by other Indians, mainly women and children, who feared French retribution for their menfolk's role in the defeat of Jumonville's party. Warriors were all too few, although the Half-King assured Washington that they would be coming.

Washington now learned that the death of Joshua Fry in a riding accident had led to his own appointment as colonel of the Virginia Regiment, a heavy responsibility for an inexperienced twenty-two-year-old. But a colonial commission, however exalted, meant little when set beside one signed by King George himself. That fact was soon made abundantly clear to Washington when, in mid-June, some 300 reinforcements arrived from the east. Most of them were badly needed drafts for his own regiment, but about 100 were regulars of an independent company from South Carolina commanded by Captain James Mackay. The Scottish-born Mackay had been a British officer since 1737, seeing service on the Georgia frontier during the previous war; as a holder of the king's commission, he was unwilling to take orders from a colonial officer, so his company remained a command distinct from Washington's regiment, "independent" in every sense. In standing on his dignity, Mackay anticipated London's official line on the relative seniority of regular and colonial officers: soon after, Secretary at War Henry Fox wrote to one of Mackay's colleagues, Captain Paul Demeré, stating: "no officer who has the honor to bear the King's Commission can be required, or ought, to act under the orders of a person who does not . . . without His Majesty's particular order for so doing." This blanket directive was soon after modified, but in a fashion that offered no comfort to Colonel Washington: when Crown and colonially appointed officers of the same rank served together, the regular would take command, even if the provincial officer's commission was of "elder date"; even worse, provincial general and field officers would have "no rank" alongside their Crown-appointed counterparts. This meant that any provincial officer of the rank of major or above would be junior to a regular captain.[22]

On a personal level, Washington and Mackay liked and respected each other as officers and gentlemen, but tensions inevitably arose between the professional soldiers and the amateurs. Mackay's regulars were unwilling to toil on Washington's road toward Fort Duquesne without the extra pay that they customarily received for such pick-and-shovel work. Washington was incensed, and when he moved westward once more, Mackay and his redcoats remained behind at Fort Necessity.

Washington's own progress soon came to a halt at Gist's trading station, where a conference opened on June 18 in hopes of rallying local Indians to the British cause. Despite the presence of the experienced George Croghan, the Indian agent for Pennsylvania, during three days of speeches it became increasingly clear that the Mingos, or Ohio Valley Iroquois, were under the Confederacy's orders to remain neutral in the Anglo-French contest; and for all their continuing protestations of friendship, the local Shawnees and Delawares were veering toward the French.[23] After the conference broke up, scarcely a handful of warriors stood by Washington. Even the Half-King, Tanaghrisson, decamped to Fort Necessity and, when summoned to return, demurred with lame excuses.

As Washington's own support dwindled, news arrived that the French at the Forks were now stronger than ever. An Indian reported that a force of 1,200, a third of them tribal warriors drawn from as far afield at the Great Lakes and the St. Lawrence Valley, the rest Franco-Canadian troops and militia, were on the warpath to avenge Ensign Jumonville. The party actually numbered about 700, yet this still gave them a significant edge over the 400 or so with Washington, of whom scores were sickly. It was not simply a question of numbers. Unlike Washington's command, the force heading toward him was composed of skilled guerrilla fighters. For the Indians, war was a way of life, its techniques of concealment and ambush readily adapted from hunting. The Canadian militiamen were also far more formidable opponents than their amateur status suggested: in contrast to the disparate English colonies, where the militia had long since lost its cutting edge, the tightly controlled and militarized society of New France ensured that its able-bodied menfolk became highly effective irregulars, fine marksmen who were as adept at paddling canoes as marching on snowshoes, capable of campaigning in all seasons across the most rugged terrain. Moreover, they were now led on by an officer with a strong personal motivation to avenge Jumonville: his elder brother, Captain Louis Coulon de Villiers.

In response, Washington quickly fortified Gist's storehouse with a sketchy stockade, recalled his road builders, and appealed for Mackay's aid. The captain responded to the crisis, and another council of war was convened. As their men had less than a week's rations and their supply lines were already dangerously stretched, the Virginian and the Scot agreed to fall back the thirteen miles to Fort Necessity. Even so, it took three days to manhandle the nine swivel guns—simple, wheelless cannon capable of being mounted on wooden fortifications—across the punishing mountainous terrain to the Great Meadows.

When Washington arrived at the stockade, the Half-King bluntly advised him to keep going east. But the Virginians were too tired from hauling their swivels to move any farther, and there were heartening rumors that more reinforcements were drawing near. Unconvinced, Tanaghrisson and his remaining Mingos now melted into the forest, never to return. As Indian agent Conrad Weiser noted in his journal, the Half-King had become exasperated by Washington's domineering attitude toward his Indian allies; although "a good-natured man," he was inexperienced, always "driving them on to fight" while ignoring their sage advice.[24] Indeed, the bold front maintained by Washington in an effort to win the respect of the tribes had backfired badly: his determination to stay put and slug it out with the far larger force heading his way, so hazarding his entire command, was the antithesis of Indian warfare, where fighting was typically avoided if the odds were unfavorable. Further evidence of his own reckless quest for glory, this decision ignored the specific advice of Dinwiddie, who had cautioned Washington to avoid making "any hazardous attempts against a too numerous enemy" and was clearly troubled by his advance to Redstone without awaiting the expected reinforcements.[25]

At first light on July 3, 1754, an excited party of scouts jogged into Washington's camp at the Great Meadows, dragging a wounded sentry with them. A "heavy, numerous body" of the enemy were just four miles off, they reported; all—whites and Indians alike— were stripped for action in the summer heat. By 11 a.m. the enemy was at hand.[26] To Washington's delight, the French were out in the open, apparently eager for a conventional firefight. Shouting and whooping, they opened fire from about 600 yards away—too far off to inflict any casualties. Washington drew up his men outside their unfinished entrenchments, waiting for the enemy to come within effective range. Filtering into woods just 60 yards off, the French and Indians fired again. They were now well within killing distance, and at Washington's order his men fell back. Some of the Virginians retreated with undue haste, a fault attributed to the cowardly example of their commanding officer, Washington's lieutenant colonel, George Muse.[27] Their withdrawal left Washington and the South Carolina Independent Company dangerously isolated; although the enemy failed to exploit this opportunity, Muse's brief loss of nerve was to haunt him for the rest of his days.

Back behind their shallow earthworks, the defenders returned fire with muskets and swivel guns. The vulnerability of Washington's position was now readily apparent. All too soon, bullets began slapping into the fort and its defenders, fired by men maximizing every scrap of cover and whose position was betrayed only by their muzzle flashes and gunsmoke: within easy musket range of the surrounding woods and hills, Fort Necessity was less a refuge than a deathtrap.

As the hours dragged on, the desultory fusillade began to take its toll. Late afternoon brought misery of another kind. A rainstorm drenched the meadows, swiftly turning the defenders' trenches into muddy streams and soaking much of their ammunition. Besides Mackay's regulars, few carried bayonets, so a determined sortie with cold steel was not an option: in any event, the enemy's Indians and militia would never stand to meet the shock of such a frontal assault but simply slip aside and shoot down their assailants from cover. Lashed by the enemy and the elements alike, the dejected defenders turned to their rum kegs for solace.

With darkness, the enemy's fire finally slackened. In the ensuing silence a Frenchman called across the sodden grass with an invitation to parley. Washington sensed a trap. Given their obvious advantages, why would the French want to talk unless this was a ploy to enable their negotiator to spy out his deployments? The Dutchman Captain Van Braam was ordered to shout a refusal. But the response indicated that the French were themselves willing to receive an emissary from the fort, so Van Braam was sent out under cover of a flag of truce. By now a third of the defenders were dead or wounded, the rest demoralized at the grim prospects before them or too drunk to care. At the start of the fight, the French had deliberately killed all the defenders' horses and cattle and even their dogs: with no means to carry off the swivel guns, retreat was not an option; without meat on the hoof, neither was a continued defense.

The French apparently held all the cards. Washington was therefore pleasantly surprised by Villiers's lenient terms: if the garrison surrendered, they would be allowed to go free. Inside the tiny stockade, by the light of a spluttering candle, Van Braam haltingly translated the clauses on the rain-blotted paper for Washington and Mackay. Both officers had some minor quibbles, but Villiers quickly addressed them. It was agreed that they must deliver up the prisoners taken with Jumonville and leave two captains, Van Braam and a Scotsman, Robert Stobo, behind as hostages. In exchange, they would be granted the coveted "honors of war," marching off with drums beating, and carrying their weapons and ammunition and even one of their swivel guns. Such surprising generosity should have raised suspicions. Neither Mackay nor Washington expressed any, and both signed the capitulation, the king's officer writing his name above the Virginian's.

In fact, the French commander's preamble contained the true explanation for his leniency. This stated: "Our intention has never been to trouble the peace and good harmony which reigns between two friendly princes, but only to avenge the assassination which has been done to one of our officers, the bearer of a summons." That same crucial word, *l'assassinat,* appeared again in the main document.

This open admission that the English had murdered an official French emissary subsequently caused an international storm. In his own defense, Washington maintained that Van Braam—whose acquaintance with English was also far from perfect—had mistranslated the crucial French words as "the death" or "the loss" of Jumonville. In reality, the point was less important than it seemed. What mattered was that at the time of the incident, Britain and France were still officially at peace: it followed therefore that Jumonville had been killed unlawfully.

The next morning, Washington and his hungry, bedraggled, and hung-over force marched out of their muddy trenches, carrying their wounded with them. Ironically, given the future significance of that date for Washington and his countrymen, it was July 4. Despite the capitulation terms, they were systematically plundered by the "savages." Exhausted and disheartened, the garrison plodded just three miles before encamping once more. There Washington left them, riding on to Williamsburg to deliver his personal report of the disaster.

The word is not too strong to describe a mission that had failed at all levels and for which Washington himself bore a large share of responsibility. At twenty-two, he was too young, naïve, and inexperienced for the command. His humiliating defeat and the plummeting decline in British prestige that immediately resulted swiftly drove those Ohio Indians who remained undecided into the French camp.

In personal terms, however, these same events only enhanced Washington's reputation as a man of honor in the eyes of his countrymen. At Fort Necessity he had demonstrated a bravery in the face of heavy odds that endeared him to his fellow Virginians, not least because the colonial press, quoting Washington's and Mackay's own report, inflated wildly the losses they had inflicted upon their attackers. On September 15, the House of Burgesses registered its approval by formally thanking Washington and the other officers for their bravery at Fort Necessity.[28] Two names were conspicuous by their absence: the hapless Van Braam, whose flawed translation of the capitulation terms was briefly blamed for the furor over Jumonville's "assassination," and the wretched Muse. The Huguenot ensign William La Péronie, who would have been the obvious choice to translate the surrender terms on July 3 had he not been seriously wounded at the time, went to Williamsburg in early September to seek compensation for possessions lost at Fort Necessity. While there, he heard that Muse had not only confessed his own cowardice but compounded his dishonorable conduct by telling many of the councillors and burgesses that the rest of the officers were "as bad as he." La Péronie had even been quizzed whether it was true that Muse had challenged Washington to a duel. The "chevalier" had answered that Muse would rather go to hell, "for had he had such [a] thing declared, that was his sure road." If he had crossed Muse's path himself, La Péronie assured Washington, he would have answered his impudence with his horse whip.[29]

In international diplomatic terms, the "Jumonville Affair" and its aftermath at Fort Necessity had branded the British as aggressors and Washington as an assassin. The French mood of righteous indignation was bolstered by their possession of Washington's own journal of events during the early summer of 1754, which had been lost amid the confused evacuation of Fort Necessity and picked up by the victors. As part of the ongoing propaganda war against

Britain, this was eventually published in Paris in 1756, along with other documents intended to support the French version of events.[30]

Before then, the journal's contents had already stirred the wrath of none other than New France's governor general, the Marquis de Duquesne. On September 8, 1754, he could barely control his rage when he wrote of it to Captain Contrecoeur, commanding at the Forks of the Ohio. The marquis castigated Washington as "the most impertinent of men," who had lied "a great deal in order to justify the assassination of Sieur de Jumonville, which has recoiled upon him, and which he was stupid enough to admit in his capitulation." Duquesne concluded on a note of wishful thinking: "There is nothing more unworthy, lower, or even blacker than the opinions and the way of thinking of this Washington! It would have been a pleasure to read his outrageous journal to him right under his nose."[31]

At Williamsburg, where Washington arrived on July 17, 1754, Governor Dinwiddie quickly tried to slough off responsibility for the consequences of his brisk young protégé's latest actions. Just as he had sought to avoid personal blame for the killing of Jumonville, he now shifted culpability for the defeat at Fort Necessity; this setback had resulted from a failure to obey his own orders to halt any offensive until all the available forces had been concentrated, he argued.[32] In an attempt to redress the situation, Dinwiddie and his council now aimed to do just that, ordering Washington to unite with Colonel James Innes, who would lead a fresh strike across the Allegheny Mountains. Thoroughly disillusioned by his recent experiences, Washington protested that Virginia's forces were totally inadequate for the job required of them, not simply numerically, but in terms of supplies, equipment, and pay. Dinwiddie's initiative promptly stalled, and the French remained unchallenged in the Ohio Valley, their position now anchored upon Fort Duquesne at the Forks.

Washington's bloody scrimmages had broadcast what the politicians in London and Paris already knew only too well: that the next major military confrontation between the old enemies was merely a matter of time. In a reversal of the conventional pattern, where hostilities in Europe generated shock waves that eventually triggered colonial sideshows across the Atlantic, this time North American events ignited wider conflict. Accordingly, both powers soon took action to strengthen their forces on that continent, now set to become a significant theater of operations in its own right.

As a first step, Great Britain pledged more cash and arms for colonial defense. In addition, Maryland's governor, Horatio Sharpe, received a royal commission as lieutenant colonel to command all troops recruited locally "to oppose the hostile attempts committed by the French in different parts of His Majesty's Dominions."[33] This was just a stopgap measure. To the politicians back in London, Washington's recent performance had simply reinforced the prejudice against "amateur" colonials. One British veteran, the royal governor of Virginia and ambassador in Paris, William Anne, Earl of Albemarle, acknowledged that, while Washington and many other colonials possessed "courage and resolution," they lacked "knowledge or experience" of real soldiering; in consequence, there could be "no dependence on them." If the job was to be done properly, it would be necessary to send professional soldiers from the Old Country, "to discipline the militia, and to lead them on."[34]

In November, the British Army's captain-general, William Augustus, Duke of Cumberland, authorized the dispatch of two regiments of redcoats from Ireland, the 44th and the 48th Foot, and the raising of two more in the colonies themselves. These regulars were intended to provide the disciplined kernel of manpower around which an ambitious new strategy aimed at crushing French ambitions in North America, and "to secure, for the future, His Majesty's subjects and allies in the just possession of their respective lands and territories," could be based.[35] The first step would be to drive the French from their posts on the Ohio and to secure that region for Britain with a strong fort. That done, it would be necessary to dislodge the enemy from Niagara and establish a post there that would make the British masters of Lake Ontario, so cutting communications between Canada on the St. Lawrence and Louisiana on the Mississippi. Secondary objectives were the French forts at Crown Point, at the southern end of Lake Champlain and menacing the colony of New York, and at Beauséjour, which posed a similar threat to Britain's northernmost colony, Nova Scotia.

For Washington, the closing months of 1754 brought fresh disappointment. Rumors that the Virginia Regiment was to be placed on the British regular establishment (that is, officially adopted as a British Army unit)—raising the prospect that Washington might receive the coveted king's commission as colonel—were cruelly dashed. Instead, the regiment was to be split up into independent companies: that meant there would be no officers ranking higher than captain, and they would of course be junior to regulars of the same rank. Accustomed to exercising command and unwilling to accept demotion from colonel, Washington promptly resigned his commission in indignation and rode home.

Governor Sharpe, along with his counterparts Dinwiddie and Arthur Dobbs in neighboring Virginia and North Carolina, now hoped to launch a winter assault against Fort Duquesne. Washington, whose experience and knowledge of the terrain was considered invaluable for such an operation, was urged to accept command of a company, an offer sweetened by assurances that he would not have to take orders from anyone he had previously commanded and would keep the honorary title of "colonel."

Replying to Sharpe's aide, William Fitzhugh, from Belvoir on November 15, Washington spurned this offer with contempt, drawing attention to the services he had already rendered, hazards for which he had received the official thanks of Virginia. The hollow honor of a colonel's title left him especially irate: "If you think me capable of holding a commission that has neither rank or emolument annexed to it," he wrote, "you must entertain a very contemptible opinion of my weakness, and believe me to be more empty than the commission itself." For all that, Washington made it clear that a future military appointment was certainly not out of the question, stating unequivocally: "My inclinations are strongly bent to arms."[36]

Momentarily putting his abiding martial ambitions to one side, Washington now turned to domestic matters. As his mother remained stubbornly ensconced at Ferry Farm, which he should by rights have inherited on his twenty-first birthday, Washington looked elsewhere for a home of his own. Mount Vernon was currently empty: Lawrence Washington's daughter Sarah, who had been left the estate in his will, died in 1754; this made George himself heir to the estate in succession to Lawrence's widow. As she had remarried soon after Lawrence's death and moved away, George took her place. That December, he became squire of Mount Vernon, renting the estate, which included eighteen slaves, for an annual fee of 15,000 pounds of tobacco.

All thoughts of developing Mount Vernon were soon put on hold by the arrival of news that revived hopes of a military career under terms that even the touchy Washington was willing to consider. Although the proposed colonial expedition against Fort Duquesne had come to nothing, in February 1755, advance elements of the expected force of British regulars, commanded by Major General Edward Braddock, arrived in Virginia's Hampton Roads. Aged sixty, Braddock had gained his first commission at fifteen. Despite this lengthy military career, his experience of combat was minimal. Braddock had been selected for the job as a faithful political adherent of Cumberland and for his abilities as an administrator and disciplinarian. Braddock's orders from Cumberland were to assemble a substantial force of regulars and provincials and, as the first step in the ambitious strategy already agreed, to lead them against Fort Duquesne.

Quickly sensing a new opportunity, Washington lost no time in writing to congratulate the general on his arrival. This gambit had the desired effect: Washington's readiness to serve, along with his established reputation and knowledge, swiftly drew an invitation to join Braddock's "family" of personal staff. The letter came from the general's senior aide-de-camp, Captain Robert Orme of the prestigious Coldstream Guards, who added a most flattering comment: "I shall think myself very happy to form an acquaintance with a person so universally esteemed."[37] The urbane, dashing, and sophisticated Orme, whose appearance when Washington knew him was captured in a splendid portrait by Joshua Reynolds, was exactly the kind of company that the young Virginian aspired to and epitomized his notions of martial glory. Washington emphasized his willingness to serve under Braddock as a volunteer, deploying a little flattery of his own: his zeal to join the expedition was only increased by what he knew of Braddock's "great, good character," and by his earnest desire to "attain a small degree of knowledge in the Military Art" under his command. Because Washington's own business affairs required his attendance and would suffer in his absence, he asked the general's further indulgence while he settled them and promised to call on him as soon as he reached Alexandria.[38] They met there in late March 1755, and it was agreed that Washington should officially join the army at its base camp at Fort Cumberland, a new strongpoint built on the Maryland side of the Potomac near the old Ohio Company warehouse at Wills Creek.

Washington ensured that men of influence knew of his latest deed in Virginia's defense. He broadcast his decision to serve—"without expectation of reward or prospect of attaining a command"—in letters to three of the colony's key figures: John Robinson, the speaker of the House of Burgesses, which was frequently at loggerheads with Governor Dinwiddie; to Carter Burwell, the chairman of the Military Committee; and to the prominent landowner William Byrd III of Westover. As this selfless act would inevitably involve heavy expenses, Washington also wondered whether Virginia might see fit to give him another modest award of £50 in recompense for his personal losses during the previous campaign.[39]

It was not only Virginia's power brokers whom Washington sought to impress by his return to military service in April 1755. At the end of the month, while en route to join Braddock's army, and with the prospect of fresh dangers looming ever closer, Washington halted at his Bullskin plantation to write to Sally Fairfax. He expressed the fervent hope that she would help to ease the hardships of the campaign by corresponding with him. None of his friends, he added, were "able to convey more real delight" than Sally, to whom he stood "indebted for so many obligations." It was only the first of several unavailing appeals he would send to Belvoir in coming months.[40]

On May 1, Washington caught up with Braddock and his staff at Frederick; the general had been there for more than a week, attempting to organize transport and supplies for his expedition. Two days later, when they arrived at the tiny township of Winchester, the general's frustrations only intensified. Dinwiddie had promised that a powerful band of Cherokees and Catawbas from the Carolinas would be awaiting him there, but they were nowhere to be seen. Dinwiddie had sent a "proper person," Christopher Gist's Indian trader son, Nathaniel, to conduct the southern warriors to Virginia. Some 300 had actually started north, but, to Braddock's mortification, after a few days' march they were "diverted" by Gist's estranged business partner Richard Pearis, who plied them with liquor and persuaded them to view Gist as an impostor without authority. Braddock was left wondering why Virginia, and not the governments of North and South Carolina—the "natural allies" of the Cherokees and Catawbas—had handled such an important affair in the first place.[41]

Increasingly disillusioned by the failure of the colonies to deliver the support and resources that he had expected, Braddock and his "family" of staff reached Wills Creek on May 10. That same day, Washington was formally appointed as Braddock's third aide-de-camp, ranking after Orme and Captain Roger Morris of the 48th Foot.

During May, Braddock gradually concentrated his army of about 2,000 men, some three-quarters of them regulars from the 44th and 48th Regiments, and the independent companies of New York and South Carolina. The two redcoat battalions from Ireland had been brought up to strength by intensive recruiting within America, enjoying rich pickings among the Chesapeake's under class of indentured servants; according to a soldier in the 48th Foot, they included unfortunates "that had been kidnapped in England and brought over here and sold to the planters."[42] The balance of Braddock's army consisted of locally raised "provincials," enlisted from volunteers. These were mostly recruited by Virginia, whose companies now wore coats of "blue turned up with red," with small contingents from Maryland and North Carolina.[43]

In addition, Braddock's force was accompanied by an impressive "train" of twenty-nine cannon, howitzers, and mortars manned by men of the Royal Artillery. This gleaming brass ordnance was very different from the crude iron swivel guns usually seen on the frontier, reflecting recent technological advances that would continue to characterize artillery throughout Washington's career as a soldier and for long after. The twelve- and six-pounder guns (so designated by the weight of the shot they fired) and the eight-inch howitzers (classified from the diameter of their shells) were all mounted on field carriages fitted with limbers (detachable wheeled frames with attachment poles), to enable them to be drawn easily by teams of horses. The guns were equipped with the recently introduced elevating screw, which greatly improved accuracy. In skilled hands, such weapons were capable of surprisingly rapid fire: according to James Wood, a Royal Artillery volunteer during the War of the Austrian Succession, at a contest between the Austrian and British artillery in May 1747, he and his colleagues "fired a short 6-pounder ten times in a minute." This seemingly incredible feat was made possible by the use of "quick-firing" ammunition, with the projectile and charge "fixed" together. Such speed came at the cost of safety, as it allowed no time for the gun barrel to be carefully sponged of any smoldering embers that might ignite the next round prematurely: at a review in the following year, Wood reported how "the gunner in ramming up the charge of one of the short sixes, it went off and blew off the arm that rammed home and the end of the ramrod struck a foot soldier in the head and killed him on the spot and wounded several others." A more realistic rate of fire was two to three rounds a minute, keeping pace with the infantry's musketry. Such guns could fire either solid shot or, for close-range work, canister: this was a tin case filled with musket balls that spread its contents on leaving the muzzle, like a giant shotgun. Designed to fire at higher elevation, the short-barreled howitzers were becoming increasingly popular: they could fire canister but more typically employed a hollow shell filled with gunpowder that exploded, scattering shards of metal once its fuse had burned down. Mounted on flat wooden beds, the stumpy cohorn mortars were simpler weapons, designed solely for lobbing shells during siege operations.[44]

Whether Braddock's powerful artillery would ever see action remained a moot point that May, as the expedition showed no sign of leaving Fort Cumberland. Washington had been there for just five days when he received the general's orders to ride back to Virginia's Tidewater and collect £4,000 for the army's use from the Crown agent John Hunter at Hampton Roads. Directing Hunter to forward a further £10,000 to Fort Cumberland inside two months, Washington was to return with the first consignment of bullion without delay.[45] Braddock had entrusted his new aide with a heavy responsibility and an irksome journey across drought-hit countryside. From Winchester, Washington sent a special express messenger warning Hunter to meet him at Williamsburg with the cash. By May 22, Washington was at Claiborne's Ferry on the Pamunkey River; there he encountered a courier from Governor Dinwiddie with the perplexing news that Hunter was away on business in the north. Thankfully, Hunter's partner in Williamsburg was able to assemble virtually all of the vital £4,000. Back at Winchester, where he arrived on May 27, Washington had expected to meet a troop of Virginian Light Horse to shepherd him and the gold safely to Fort Cumberland. Instead, he was obliged to make do with a less dashing escort of local militia.[46]

When he rejoined Braddock on May 30, Washington found the general more furious than ever at the colonies' continued failure to deliver the promised wagons, horses, and supplies upon which his campaign depended. With the notable exception of the Pennsylvanian Benjamin Franklin, who had produced the expected vehicles, teams, and drivers, Braddock's wrath encompassed virtually the entire colonial population, high and low, and not just the contractors actually responsible for the breaches of faith. This irked the proud Virginian Washington, who complained that Braddock looked "upon the country . . . as void of both honor and honesty." He and the general had become embroiled in frequent disputes on the subject, "maintained with warmth on both sides."[47]

Yet the relationship between the British general and his young American aide was clearly far more cordial than such wrangling suggests. Many years later, when himself an aging man, Washington gave a surprisingly balanced picture of the general: "His attachments were warm—his enmities were strong—and having no disguise about him, both appeared in full force. He was generous and disinterested—but plain and blunt in his manner even to rudeness," Washington recalled.[48]

As the expedition's acknowledged expert on North American frontier warfare, Washington was keen to impress Braddock with the need to adapt his European techniques to the irregular bushfighting he could expect to encounter at the hands of the "Canadian French and their Indians." According to Washington's recollection, the bluff general and his cronies were so predisposed toward "regularity and discipline" that they held their enemies in "absolute contempt."[49]

This was too harsh. In fact, while still at Alexandria, Braddock had issued orders intended to relieve his men of all unnecessary equipment—their heavy buff leather shoulder and waist belts and their useless swords—and to swap their thick woolen waistcoats and breeches for lighter garments made from tough "Osnabrig" cloth. In addition, the regulation system of drill, by which a battalion of British infantry was split up to deliver its firepower in a complex sequence of numbered "platoons," was simplified so that each of the ten companies could become a "firing" in its own right under the command of its own familiar officers. Perhaps most significantly, at a council of war at Fort Cumberland, Braddock gained his officers' approval for proposals to secure the army while it was on the march and encamped. This would be achieved by sending out "small parties very well upon the flanks, in the front, and in the rear, to prevent any surprise which the nature of the country made them very liable to."[50]

Such precautions would be badly needed. One thing was already clear: not only would the expedition lack aid from the formidable southern Indians, but it could anticipate little support from the local tribes of the Ohio. Already disenchanted by the events of the previous summer at Fort Necessity, they were further alienated by Braddock's arrogance and indifference toward them and their interests. The general's attitude was recalled with bitterness by Shingas, the same Delaware sachem who had met Washington at the Logstown council in November 1753. In company with representatives of the Shawnees and Mingos, "King Shingas" had approached Braddock to discover his plans for the Ohio Country once the French had been ousted. Braddock had replied bluntly that "the English should inhabit and inherit the land." When Shingas then asked "whether the Indians that were friends to the English might not be permitted to live and trade among the English and have hunting ground sufficient to support themselves," Braddock was blunter still, stating "that no savage should inherit the land." After the general refused to change his uncompromising stance, Shingas and the other chiefs responded "that if they might not have liberty to live on the land they would not fight for it." Only a handful of Mingos, including Washington's old acquaintances Monacatoocha, White Thunder, and Silver Heels, stayed on to scout for the army.[51]

While the fuming Braddock impatiently awaited essential supplies from Winchester, a detachment of about 600 men under his efficient but irascible deputy quartermaster general, Sir John St. Clair, was pushed forward to clear a path for the main army and establish an advanced supply depot. They found the going even harder than anticipated. One redcoat of the 48th Foot reported that it was necessary to halt every hundred yards to "mend" the road, sometimes blasting rocks to make it viable for the "great quantity of wagons." They slogged doggedly onward "over rocks and mountains almost unpassable," fueled on a wilderness diet of rattlesnake, bear, and deer.[52]

By June 5, after six days of strenuous road building and two days of rest, St. Clair's contingent had reached no farther than the Little Meadows, just twenty-two miles west of Fort Cumberland. Meanwhile the stalled "grand Army" still at the base camp was growing sickly as "the bloody flux"—dysentery—began to take a grip, as it inevitably did in crowded, static encampments. In addition, intelligence from Pennsylvania that the French were sending reinforcements to the Ohio from Canada led Washington to believe that Braddock's army would "have more to do than go up the hills to come down again."[53]

During this enforced lull, Washington took the opportunity to renew his own campaign to engage the correspondence of Sally Fairfax, sending off his third appeal since leaving Mount Vernon. He had actually seen Sally in May while en route to Williamsburg to collect Braddock's gold. On that occasion, while Sally had expressed a desire to be informed of Washington's safe return to camp, she had asked that any letter should be sent to an "acquaintance," rather than to her in person. Washington had taken that "as a gentle rebuke and polite manner of forbidding my corresponding with you." This inference, which was borne out by the fact that Washington had "hitherto found it impracticable to engage one moment" of Sally's attention, did little to quash his hopes of a correspondence that would, as he wrote, "remove my suspicions, enliven my spirits, and make me happier than the day is long."[54]

Washington was nothing if not persistent in his approaches to the married Sally, who seems to have deliberately withheld her own letters to avoid encouraging his attentions. Despite much speculation, there is no evidence that their relationship was ever consummated physically.[55] Given the close-knit world of the Virginian gentry, in which the merest whiff of scandal would have been detected and commented upon by letter writers and diarists, an affair is certainly unlikely. However, in terms of Sally's role as a powerful motivating force for the young Washington, the sexual issue is irrelevant: indeed, his attitude toward her resembled that of a medieval knight-errant, a courtly lover keen to win some token of favor through conspicuous deeds of bravery.

Leaving in staggered divisions, the rump of Braddock's army finally moved out from Fort Cumberland between June 7 and June 10, 1755. Its progress was glacial, sometimes covering just two miles a day across the mountainous terrain. After it became obvious that the army was hobbled by its dependence upon heavy wagons, a council of war resolved to cut back on wheeled transport and increase the use of packhorses to carry supplies. Officers, including Washington, cheerfully gave up their own baggage horses for "His Majesty's service."[56]

Yet the army's rate of advance remained unacceptably slow. On June 16, after halting at the Little Meadows, Braddock faced the fact that something more drastic needed to be done. He summoned yet another council of war but, before it met, sought Washington's candid opinion. On the previous day, Washington had been seized with violent fevers and headaches, so severe that he had been forced to dismount and accompany the army in a covered wagon. By Washington's own recollection, it was nonetheless he who suggested the plan that was swiftly adopted: a flying column formed from about 1,300 elite troops, accompanied by the minimum of artillery and ammunition wagons necessary for the job, should forge ahead. The balance of the army, under Colonel Thomas Dunbar of the 48th Foot, would follow with the heavy transport and the rest of the ordnance as soon as it could.[57]

The advance guard began its march on June 18. During the next five days Washington traveled onward by cart while his illness "continued without intermission." By June 23, when they reached the Great Crossing of the Youghiogheny River, Washington was so sick that he received "the General's positive commands" not to stir until he had recovered. Even then, only the doctors' warning that to push on would risk endangering his life, combined with Braddock's solemn word of honor that he would be brought up in time to join the final assault on Fort Duquesne, persuaded Washington to obey and to await the reserve troops.

While Washington sweated out his fever, Braddock's advance guard pushed on. By June 25, it had reached the Great Meadows, where Washington's command had surrendered almost a year before. The feeble fortifications had been leveled, but, as a British officer reported, the ground remained strewn with the bones of men who had died there. The next day, the troops encountered another ominous scene. Resting under a rocky hill where the enemy had encamped the night before, they examined trees stripped of bark, on which the Indians had used red paint to depict "the scalps and prisoners they had taken with them"; the French had contributed graffiti of their own, huffily described by Captain Orme as "threats and bravados with all kinds of scurrilous language."[58]

Such attempts at intimidation did nothing to halt the slow yet inexorable advance of Braddock's force. The sickly Washington was desperate to be in at the kill: writing to his friend Captain Orme on June 30, he confessed that he would rather lose £500 than miss the campaign's climactic battle. By July 2, when the rear division under Dunbar had almost reached the Great Meadows, Washington could describe himself as "tolerably well recovered." He attributed his improvement to a liberal dose of "Dr. James's Powders." Prescribed on Braddock's personal orders before they parted, this popular remedy had lived up to its reputation as the era's cure-all: within four days, as Washington informed his brother Jack, his fevers and other complaints had eased, and he had hopes of catching up with the general, now twenty-five miles ahead of him.[59]

Still too weak to mount his horse, Washington resumed his jolting journey by covered wagon along the rough track that Braddock's advance column had hacked deep into the backcountry. When he finally caught up with the army on July 8, the mood of the general and his men was buoyant, and with good reason. Since leaving Fort Cumberland they had negotiated more than 120 miles of primeval wilderness, laboriously hauling wagons and artillery over daunting mountain ranges and blazing a trail through dark, forbidding forest. It was an impressive logistical feat. Along the way, fear of Indian ambush had been ever present. Yet thanks to Braddock's careful dispositions, the dreaded enemy had done no more than scalp stragglers. Security along the way had been so intensive that on July 6, jittery scouts had gunned down one of their few tribal allies, the son of Monacatoocha, after mistaking him for a hostile warrior.[60] Such episodes were regrettable but had failed to halt the army's momentum. A formidable force of British redcoats and blue-coated American provincial troops, complete with artillery, was now poised within twelve miles of its objective, Fort Duquesne. Overwhelming victory surely lay within its grasp.

The next morning, July 9, 1755, the long column began its final, methodical approach. Washington now resumed his place as one of Braddock's three aides-de-camp. Although his fever had subsided, he remained far from well. Before mounting his horse, Washington was obliged to strap cushions to his saddle, presumably because his disordered bowels had brought on an agonizing attack of piles.

Remarkably, the army now drawing ever closer to the Forks of the Ohio included a veritable cluster of men whose destinies were to be intertwined with Washington's. The commander of Braddock's advance guard, Lieutenant Colonel Thomas Gage, would rise to head the British Army in North America during the opening phase of the Revolutionary War, opposing Washington at Boston. By then, two other redcoat officers present that day, Charles Lee of the 44th Foot and Horatio Gates of the New York Independent Company, had switched their allegiance to the revolutionary cause, becoming Washington's colleagues and, ultimately, his rivals. Daniel Morgan, a humble teenaged wagon driver in 1755, was one of Washington's most effective subordinates during the War of Independence, leading a corps of crack-shot riflemen against the British. For good measure, Morgan's first cousin and fellow teamster under Braddock was none other than Daniel Boone, destined for future fame as the quintessential American frontiersman.

Briton or American, cultivated gentleman or unlettered bullwhacker, every last man of Braddock's weary command knew that the campaign's final phase was fast approaching. In order to avoid a defile, which offered a prime site for a French and Indian ambush, Braddock resolved that his army should instead follow an alternative route involving a double crossing of the snaking Monongahela River. Though the river was shallow, its banks were steep and readily defendable, so the risk of attack there was real enough.

But by early afternoon, both crossings had been completed without incident. These hazards now safely behind them, Braddock's men breathed a collective sigh of relief and marched steadily onward into the silent forest.

This calm was deceptive. The French had no intention of relinquishing Fort Duquesne without a fight, although it had taken the inspired oratory of a tough young Canadian officer, Daniel de Beaujeu, to convince their skeptical Indian allies that even now all was not lost and that Braddock's seemingly unstoppable force could be confronted, halted, and beaten.

Stripped to the waist, Beaujeu loped off at the head of 850 men— French soldiers, Canadian militia, but mostly greased and painted tribal warriors—along the rough forest trail leading to the Monongahela. About six miles from the fort, they suddenly spotted the red uniforms of Braddock's advance guard some 200 yards off. Both sides stood, momentarily astonished. Gage's grenadiers were the first to react, presenting their muskets and sending several volleys crashing through the woods. The range was long for inaccurate smooth bore weapons, but a chance shot killed Beaujeu. Robbed of their charismatic leader, the French and Canadians hesitated and looked set to recoil before Braddock's juggernaut. But another experienced officer, Jean-Daniel Dumas, promptly stepped forward to steady them. The Indians meanwhile had fanned out into the open woods on either side of the track, concealed themselves behind trees, and commenced a withering fire upon Gage's exposed men. All the while, these warriors kept up their spine-tingling war whoops. It was a terrifying sound that none who survived that afternoon would forget.

With casualties mounting and unnerved by an enemy who remained unseen but who could be heard all too clearly, the advance guard fell back in disarray. It collided with the main body of Braddock's army, still marching up the forest track. The effect was catastrophic. In the words of Washington's report to Dinwiddie, the British regulars were "immediately struck with such a deadly panic, that nothing but confusion and disobedience of orders prevailed among them."[61] This harsh verdict is borne out by other eyewitness accounts, yet the redcoats' response is understandable: for soldiers trained for conventional European campaigning, there could be no more traumatic introduction to the bewildering and peculiarly savage conditions of American wilderness warfare. Indeed, for one of Braddock's veteran "old standers," Private Duncan Cameron of the 44th Foot, the Monongahela was the "most shocking" fight that he had ever experienced: as Cameron had already survived the harrowing siege of Cartagena in 1741, the intensive firefights at Dettingen in 1743 and Fontenoy in 1745, and the savage close-quarters combat at Culloden in the following year, his assessment is telling.[62]

As their disorder increased, so the regulars instinctively huddled together. Swathed in thick gunsmoke, they fired mechanically and blindly, shooting down their own hapless comrades. Victims of this "friendly fire" included many of Washington's fellow Virginians, who attempted to fight the Indians in their own fashion by breaking ranks and seeking cover behind trees. As Washington put it in a famous epitaph, *they* "behaved like men, and died like soldiers."[63] The Virginian troops killed that day included several officers who had served under Washington throughout the previous campaign: the Scot William Polson, the Frenchman William La Péronie, and the Swede Carolus Gustavus de Spiltdorf were among them.

Amid the chaos, Braddock's officers spared no pains to rally their men and fight back as best they could. Lieutenant Colonel Ralph Burton of the 48th Foot led about 100 of his regiment against a dominating hill to the right of the track, but when he was wounded the attack petered out.[64] In all, some sixty officers were killed or wounded. But while others fell fast all around him, Washington somehow escaped unscathed, despite four bullets through his coat and two horses shot beneath him.

Not content with rebuffing Braddock's army, the exultant French and Indians now sought to annihilate it, attempting to surround the fear-crazed troops bunched on the narrow track. By about 4 p.m., when Braddock himself was mortally wounded, his men could take no more. A formal retreat was ordered but swiftly became a frenzied rout. As Washington reported to Governor Dinwiddie, the traumatized survivors instantly broke in headlong flight, "like sheep before the hounds." The efforts of Washington and his brother officers to rally them were futile: as well to try stopping the rampaging "wild bears of the mountains," he wrote.

By now Washington was Braddock's only unwounded aide-de-camp. He placed the stricken general in a "small covered cart" and, accompanied by the last of the troops, managed to get him across the nearest ford of the Monongahela. When the bleeding Burton and some other officers succeeded in rallying about 100 survivors on high ground, described by Orme as a "very advantageous spot," Washington was sent to halt the fugitives already farther down the track. Crossing the river's second ford, he soon encountered Lieutenant Colonel Gage attempting to restore order there. As Washington rode back to the hill chosen for the rear guard's stand, he met Braddock and his escort coming toward him; as most of the demoralized troops had melted away, there had been no option but to follow them.[65]

Braddock's defeat had been total. Some two-thirds of his force were killed or wounded. The injured who could not be carried off were slaughtered and scalped where they lay. An unlucky handful were captured by the Indians, led off in triumph to Fort Duquesne, and ritually tortured to death by fire.[66] The survivors faced a harrowing retreat through the woods to reach Dunbar's reserve column, camped some forty miles off near the spot where Washington had bushwhacked Jumonville just over a year before.

Although drained by illness and reeling from all the exertions and anxieties of the past day, Washington was now charged by Braddock with the task of riding ahead to contact Dunbar, "to make arrangements for covering the retreat, and forwarding on provisions and refreshments to the retreating and wounded soldiery." That night's ordeal remained seared in Washington's memory. Decades later, he recalled how the sights and sounds he encountered could scarcely be described. Indeed, the piteous appeals of the wounded men who littered the route "were enough to pierce a heart of adamant."[67]

General Braddock died four days later, near Washington's old battleground at the Great Meadows. Washington, who received Braddock's sash and pistols as keepsakes, supervised the interment. The army then marched over the grave, to obliterate all sign of the burial and thus prevent Braddock's body becoming the object of a "savage triumph."[68]

Beyond doubt, Braddock's defeat was a disaster for British prestige. But despite all the shock and recriminations, George Washington emerged with an enhanced reputation. A year earlier, at Fort Necessity, he had presided over a demoralizing and politically embarrassing defeat from which it was hard to salvage anything more than a reputation for personal courage. At the Monongahela, Washington had participated in a far bloodier rout, only to become a genuine hero. As a mere aide-de-camp, this time Washington shouldered no share of blame for the disaster. On the contrary, he had behaved impeccably, and his conspicuous gallantry did not go unnoticed by the burgeoning Anglo-American press. From Philadelphia to London, newspaper readers once again encountered the name of George Washington.

Washington's well-publicized exploits, and not least his miraculous survival amid the mayhem that had claimed so many lives, suggested to some that the tall young Virginian was destined for greater things. Just five weeks after the battle, the Reverend Samuel Davies interrupted a sermon to draw attention to "that heroic youth, Colonel Washington, who I cannot but hope Providence has hitherto preserved in so signal a manner for some important service to his country."[69] Decades later, American newspaper editors would remind their readers of the reverend's prescience.

For many colonial Americans, "Braddock's Defeat" marked a watershed in their relationship with the Mother Country. During another five years of bloody warfare with New France and her Indian allies, British redcoats would more than redeem the reputation they had lost during that nightmarish afternoon near the Monongahela River. Nevertheless, the stubborn Braddock and his stiffly disciplined regulars were taken to characterize a hidebound and increasingly irrelevant Old World; the resilient Washington and his self-reliant Virginia "Blues" typified the New. However simplistic and misleading, in 1755, this message was widely believed. In 1775, it would resonate more strongly still.

3

DEFENDING THE FRONTIER

As the shocking news of Braddock's defeat spread through Britain's American colonies, Washington rode from Fort Cumberland to Mount Vernon and collapsed, exhausted, into bed. He had barely done so before a letter arrived from his neighbor, Colonel Fairfax, congratulating him on his deliverance. It included a postscript written by Sally, thanking heaven for Washington's safe return and gently chiding him for his "great unkindness in refusing us the pleasure of seeing you this night." If he did not call at Belvoir first thing next morning, then the Fairfaxes would come to him.[1] Given Washington's persistent but totally futile attempts to engage Sally Fairfax's correspondence during the Braddock campaign, her sudden show of interest must have been as vexing as it was flattering. Washington was now the hero of the moment and the toast of Virginian society, but his flirtation with the married Sally continued in its familiar pattern, delicious yet ultimately frustrating.

Far from tranquil Mount Vernon, on the exposed frontiers of Virginia and Pennsylvania, the consequences of the massacre on the Monongahela were all too soon apparent. As Washington recalled many years later, the "very avenue" that had been so laboriously hacked to the Forks of the Ohio by Braddock's army now offered a ready conduit for retaliatory raiders against the frontiers of Pennsylvania, but "more especially those of Virginia and Maryland."[2] The Shenandoah Valley, where Washington had first ventured as a young surveyor, now lay wide open to Indian war parties. Settlers who had established isolated farmsteads in the sixty-mile swathe of

forest between the town of Winchester and the advanced outpost of
Fort Cumberland bore the brunt of raids that left burned cabins and
scalped and mutilated bodies behind them and which spread terror
in a wave that sent refugees scuttling eastward.

In the midsummer of 1755, Britain's few regular soldiers on the
continent were either demoralized by their recent introduction to
frontier warfare under Braddock or based far to the north, in New
England, New York, and Nova Scotia. Virginia must look to its own
defense, and the colony's Assembly voted £40,000 to reconstitute
the Virginia Regiment on an enlarged strength of 1,000 men organized in sixteen companies, plus another 200 or so skilled woodsmen to serve as "rangers"; if insufficient recruits were forthcoming
within three months, the regiment would be completed by drafting
militiamen.

Given his public profile, which was now higher than ever thanks
to his exploits on the Monongahela, Washington was the obvious
choice to command the Virginian force. There can be little doubt
that Washington, ambitious for distinction and recognition, wanted
the job. While he had no intention of thrusting himself forward for
what promised to be a thankless task involving "insurmountable
obstacles" likely to cost him whatever reputation he had already
acquired, his correspondence makes it clear that he would feel duty
bound to accept such a responsibility if it were *offered* to him—
provided the terms were honorable, of course.[3]

On August 14, 1755, Governor Dinwiddie commissioned the
twenty-three-year-old Washington as both colonel of the Virginia
Regiment and commander in chief of all the forces to be raised for
the colony's protection. Washington had discretion to select his
own staff officers, to contract for all necessary supplies, and to act
defensively or offensively as he considered best. These were extensive powers, but they brought commensurate responsibilities that
would soon drive him to distraction. Washington had been ordered
to establish his headquarters at Winchester, "the nighest place of
rendezvous to the country which is exposed to the enemy." Recruits
were to assemble there and at Fredericksburg and Alexandria.[4]

From the outset, Washington's orders to his officers made it clear that his regiment would aspire to high standards of training and discipline. His major, Andrew Lewis, was urged to make sure that the muster rolls were called three times a day, with the recruits trained as often in "the new platoon way of exercising" that formed the cornerstone of the British Army's regulation drill for delivering volley fire. Significantly, they were also to undertake regular shooting practice at individual targets, "that they may acquire a dexterity in that kind of firing": this was to be a flexible unit, competent in "conventional" tactics, but also capable of "irregular" bush fighting. And in all things, Major Lewis was to ensure that "good regular discipline" was observed, in line with the established *Rules and Articles of War.*"[5]

In mid-September, Washington assumed his new command with a tour of inspection, riding from Winchester back to the familiar Fort Cumberland on Wills Creek. This strongpoint still held a residue of Virginian, Maryland, and North Carolinian troops from Braddock's campaign; it now became the base for the rump of the Virginia Regiment, under its lieutenant colonel, the fiery Adam Stephen. Upon his arrival at Fort Cumberland, Washington formally appointed his officers, drawing heavily upon fellow veterans of the previous year's fighting. Ever a stickler for appearances, Washington was determined that they should match his own exemplary sartorial standards. Like the Virginian companies that had served under Braddock, the colony's revived regiment wore coats of blue faced with red. Besides an ordinary soldier's uniform for rough work on detachment and scouts, each officer was to provide himself with a far more splendid "suit of regimentals" for duty in camp or garrison. This was to be "of good blue cloth; the coat to be faced and cuffed with scarlet, and trimmed with silver." A scarlet, silver-laced waistcoat, blue breeches, and, if possible, a silver-laced hat completed the ensemble.[6]

It was one thing to organize a Virginia Regiment on paper and to announce a corps of gaily uniformed officers, quite another to find the humble rank and file needed to fill its companies.

From the outset, the recruiting net was flung wide, falling far beyond the Old Dominion. For example, Captain Joshua Lewis was ordered to Annapolis in Maryland and to any other center of population in that colony where there was a prospect of drumming up men; his junior officers were to range even farther afield, trawling the "back parts" of both Maryland and Pennsylvania for manpower.[7]

From Fort Cumberland, Washington resumed his tour of inspection, dropping down through the Shenandoah Valley for some 120 miles to Fort Dinwiddie, a strongpoint on Jackson's River garrisoned by a company of his regiment under Captain Peter Hog. By early October he was back in Alexandria. In Washington's absence, the garrison at Fort Cumberland had come under increasing pressure from enemy raiders.

With recruitment sluggish, Lieutenant Colonel Stephen lacked the manpower to intercept Indian war parties that crossed the mountains, leaving the settlers below his post dangerously exposed. "It sits heavy upon me," he wrote, "to be obliged to let the enemy pass under our noses without ever putting them in bodily fear." So many hostiles were lurking around the fort that all contact with the inhabitants was cut off. As Stephen reported, "Nothing is to be seen or heard of, but desolation and murders heightened with all barbarous circumstances and unheard of instances of cruelty." The smoke from the burning farmsteads soon hung so thick that it screened the very mountains from the garrison's sight.[8]

Given the enemy's ability to bypass Fort Cumberland with impunity, it was soon clear to Washington that, far from establishing any outer defensive cordon to the west of the Allegheny Mountains, simply safeguarding the Shenandoah Valley itself would be challenge enough. This fact was underlined in early October, when Washington returned to his base at Winchester, just over the Blue Ridge Mountains and only seventy miles from peaceful Alexandria. There he soon encountered a scene of panic and confusion as shoals of terrified backcountry settlers sought sanctuary in the town. Washington offered to head the local militia against the Indians, but they were understandably unwilling to leave their own families undefended.[9]

Chaos bred defiance: as Washington informed Dinwiddie, his orders to requisition wagons for essential supplies had to be enforced at sword point and in the face of threats to blow his brains out. The frontier folk were fiercely independent and suspicious of authority; this was scarcely the kind of deference that a Tidewater gentleman like Washington expected. Even the men of his regiment were proving truculent, with desertion rife. Indeed, unless the Virginia assembly passed a military law with enough teeth to curb "the growing insolence of the soldiers, [and] the indolence, and inactivity of the officers," Washington warned that he would be obliged to give up his command.

Thoughts of resignation were soon forgotten, however, when fear-crazed messengers arrived, warning that whooping hostiles were now within just miles of Winchester itself. Washington finally managed to muster some forty militiamen and rangers and led them out into the forest. This tense patrol ended in farcical anticlimax: the hubbub that had triggered the reports stemmed from the antics of a trio of drunken Virginian light horsemen, "carousing," cursing, and firing off their pistols in the woods.[10]

Yet the hysteria was real enough and proof of the psychological potency of the French and Indian terror tactics: for every one of the seventy or so settlers reported killed or missing in the first wave of raiding, scores more were left displaced and traumatized. Even small bands of tribal warriors could wreak havoc out of all proportion to their numbers. As Washington emphasized time and again during his frontier command, in the wilderness the Indians held all the cards: cunning, vigilant, and able to live off the land, they were "no more to be conceived, than they are to be equaled by our people," he warned. Indeed, the only "match" for Indians were more of their own kind.[11]

Washington explained to his old friend Christopher Gist, who had been given a captain's commission to recruit a company of "active woodsmen" intended to go at least some way to meeting the shortfall of skilled forest fighters, that Indian allies were never "more wanted than at this time." But the disasters at Fort Necessity and on the Monongahela, which had dealt devastating blows to British and Virginian prestige, ensured that none came forward that autumn. Hearing rumors that Andrew Montour, a renowned Pennsylvanian scout, was marching against the French outpost of Venango at the head of 300 warriors, the desperate Washington tried to divert some of them to Fort Cumberland. Calling upon his experience of frontier diplomacy, he hoped that Montour would extend his hearty welcome to his old acquaintance Monacatoocha and others, assuring them how happy it would make him, "Conotocaurious," to take them by the hand and "treat them as brothers of our great King beyond the waters."[12]

Washington's gambit came to nothing. Meanwhile, and just a month into his command, he faced another, and no less galling, frustration. This chafed at Washington's most sensitive spot, his finely tuned sense of honor. The problem surfaced in late October, after Washington rejoined the core of his regiment at Fort Cumberland: although nominally supreme commander of Virginia's forces, he was now apparently outranked by John Dagworthy, a mere *captain* of Maryland troops.

Dagworthy headed just thirty men at Fort Cumberland, yet he claimed to possess something that Washington craved but still lacked: a commission from King George himself. Back in 1746, Dagworthy had gained a captaincy in provincial forces recruited for a projected expedition against Canada. That attack never took place, the troops were disbanded, and Dagworthy accepted a cash lump sum in lieu of his half pay as a retired officer. But in 1755, he was still citing his defunct commission to pull rank on officers holding colonial appointments, including Lieutenant Colonel Stephen.

It was a state of affairs that Washington found intolerable and which he resolved to redress through official channels. Meanwhile, he avoided an unseemly confrontation by the simple expedient of quitting Wills Creek as soon as possible. Pausing only long enough to order the companies of rangers under Captains William Cocks and John Ashby to construct two small bastioned stockades on Patterson Creek, intended to go some way to filling the undefended void between Forts Cumberland and Dinwiddie, Washington rode back to Winchester and then on to Williamsburg to enlist Governor Dinwiddie's backing against Dagworthy.[13]

Although exasperated that Washington and Stephen had let the situation arise in the first place, Dinwiddie was quick to appreciate the potentially disastrous implications of such wrangling. He reported the problem to Lieutenant Governor William Shirley of Massachusetts, who had become Britain's stop gap commander in chief in North America after Braddock's death. Dinwiddie feared that the insult to Virginia was grave enough to discourage the House of Burgesses from backing the war effort. The best solution, he felt, would be to award Virginia's highest-ranking officers temporary, or "brevet," commissions in the regular army so they could not be outranked by awkward juniors.[14]

While awaiting Shirley's adjudication, Washington was able to enjoy such modest social pleasures as Williamsburg offered; its round of balls provided a marked contrast to the hardships of the frontier zone some 150 miles off. Washington's hopes that royal commissions would soon be on their way were bolstered by reports that highly exaggerated accounts of the Virginians' exploits at Braddock's defeat were circulating in London. Already convinced that "strict order" was the very "life of military discipline," Washington was further heartened to learn that Virginia's Assembly had passed a bill authorizing stiffer punishments for men of the colony's regiment found guilty of serious offenses: previously, only treason carried the death penalty; now a soldier could also forfeit his life for mutiny, sedition, desertion, and striking a superior. Earlier that summer, Virginia's legislators had already approved draconian corporal punishment for those same crimes: while "not extending to life or members," this nonetheless permitted the same savage floggings of up to a thousand or more lashes that were inflicted upon the redcoats, earning them the grim nickname "bloody-backs." As

Washington put it to Lieutenant Colonel Stephen, "We now have it in our power to enforce obedience."[15]

By the autumn of 1755, the men of Washington's Virginia Regiment were already under what amounted to British Army discipline. Elsewhere in British North America, a very different regime prevailed: while theoretically facing the death penalty for the most serious military crimes, the provincial troops raised in New England served under far milder discipline, with corporal punishment limited to the biblical thirty-nine lashes.[16]

But as 1755 drew to a close, the Virginia Regiment could hardly afford to hang even the most hardened reprobate: with fewer than 500 men, it mustered below half of the official number voted by the Assembly. That autumn's recruiting drive had been a dismal failure: as Washington complained, several officers had been out for six weeks or even two months "without getting a man," instead frittering away their time "in all the gaiety of pleasurable mirth" with friends and relations. At the appointed rendezvous at Alexandria on December 4, he told Dinwiddie, ten recruiting officers produced just twenty men between them: if he had anything other than Virginian paper currency, which was shunned beyond the Old Dominion, he would send officers to "Pennsylvania and the borders of Carolina," where he was confident recruits could be found. The situation was so dire that Washington hoped that Virginian soldiers who had joined the regular 44th and 48th Regiments during the Braddock campaign, but had since deserted, might reenlist with him if they were granted indemnity.[17] But in slave-owning Virginia, even now certain recruits remained unacceptable. When Captain Hog reported the presence of "mulattos and negroes" in his company at Fort Dinwiddie, Washington was adamant that they should be barred from carrying arms, instead serving only as "pioneers or hatchetmen"—in other words, manual laborers.[18]

Fear of a slave revolt in the eastern Tidewater counties underpinned the Assembly's reluctance to order a major mobilization of Virginia's manpower to fight the war on the western frontier.[19] Lack of numbers dictated the strategy that Washington would adopt in

1756, and long after. In the New Year, he formally sought Dinwiddie's directions about whether to "prepare for taking the field—or guarding our frontiers in the spring," but in reality there was no alternative to a defensive stance. Even had the Virginia Regiment boasted its full complement of 1,000 men, any strike against Fort Duquesne was ruled out by a dearth of artillery and of skilled engineers capable of conducting a siege. With no prospect of an offensive, further steps were taken to shore up Virginia's shaky frontier; besides the two new forts on Patterson Creek, Washington had ordered Captain Thomas Waggoner and sixty men to build and garrison two more stockades on the South Branch of the Potomac. In addition, he began lobbying for Virginia's evacuation of Fort Cumberland and its replacement by another "strong fort" within the Old Dominion. In Washington's opinion, not only was Fort Cumberland poorly sited in defensive terms, but it presented an "eye sore" to Virginia—a veiled reference to the ongoing affront to Washington's authority posed by the stubborn Dagworthy.[20]

Meanwhile, Governor Dinwiddie awaited William Shirley's adjudication of that "great dispute." When Shirley's response finally arrived, it could scarcely have been more unsatisfactory for Washington: Governor Sharpe of Maryland had been appointed to settle the row with Dagworthy—his own colony's officer. Goaded beyond endurance, Washington now secured Dinwiddie's permission to approach Shirley in Boston and present him with a "memorial" from his officers for the Virginia Regiment to be accepted into the regular British Army. While Washington was preparing for his trip to Massachusetts, Shirley himself took action, instructing Sharpe to order Dagworthy to stop exercising command over the Virginians. However, as the question of his regiment's status remained unresolved, Washington decided to head north regardless and plead its case to Shirley in person. Washington had good reason to expect a sympathetic hearing. Not only had he met Shirley at Braddock's Alexandria conference in April 1755, but he had become friendly with the governor's son William, who served as the general's personal secretary and was slain at the Monongahela.

In early February 1756, in company with his aide Captain George Mercer and another close friend, the Scottish Highlander Robert Stewart, Washington set off on a round-trip of more than 1,000 miles to Boston. All three officers wore the brave blue, red-faced, and silver-laced uniform that Washington had specified, and they were accompanied by two liveried servants. This conspicuous display had a purpose of its own, helping to enhance George Washington's standing in colonies already growing familiar with his name and exploits.

The journey introduced Washington to British America's Middle and Northern Colonies, and to its three largest cities, all of them thriving urban centers without counterparts in the Old Dominion. His party traveled via Philadelphia; with about 18,000 inhabitants and 3,000 houses, it was then the largest city in the American colonies. Fronting the Delaware River, its formal grid of streets made straggling Williamsburg look like a glorified village. From there they rode on to New York, a city still jammed into the tip of the peninsula flanked by the Hudson and East Rivers, but already boasting a population of some 14,000. Leaving their horses at New London in Connecticut, Washington and his entourage took ship to Newport, Rhode Island, before continuing by water to Boston. With a population of 15,000, the busy port, balanced on its narrow "neck," was second only to Philadelphia in size and importance.[21]

En route, the thriving provincial press took flattering note of Washington's progress and of his mixed fortunes as a soldier. At his destination, the widely read *Boston Gazette* praised him as "a gentleman who has deservedly a high reputation for military skill, integrity, and valor; though success has not always attended his undertakings."[22] While such public recognition was surely gratifying, the long-awaited meeting with Shirley brought little satisfaction. Now that the Dagworthy conundrum had been resolved, the governor was surprised that Washington had even bothered to make the arduous trip north. All the same, he provided him with written confirmation that Dagworthy no longer held a royal commission and that Washington was his superior.[23] But Shirley was not empowered to upgrade the Virginia Regiment or any of its officers to regular status: Washington—like all other colonial field officers—would remain subservient to any redcoat captain. Even worse, before Washington's arrival, Shirley had already approved the appointment of Governor Sharpe as commander of all forces raised not only in Maryland, but also in South Carolina, Pennsylvania, *and* Virginia.[24]

Besides a hefty bill in expenses and gambling losses and a half-hearted dalliance with the well-heeled and long-faced heiress Mary Eliza Philipse, which was conducted intermittently as he passed through New York, Washington had little to show for his month's jaunt. More frustrated than ever, he was once again resolved to resign his commission.

Back in Virginia, Washington's mood was not improved by the first signs of what would become a mounting wave of criticism against the conduct of his regiment's officers. There were clearly some grounds for these gripes. In January, for example, a court of inquiry had found Ensign Leehaynsious De Keyser guilty of behaving in a "scandalous manner such as is unbecoming the character of an officer and a gentleman" after he cheated at cards. During a game of brag at Fort Cumberland, De Keyser had hidden the nine of diamonds under his thigh—"foul play" that was revealed when he rose from his chair and the card flopped to the floor.[25]

Washington capitalized on the ensign's disgrace to send an "Address" from Winchester that was read to the assembled officers of the seven companies at Fort Cumberland by Lieutenant Colonel Stephen. He wrote: "This timely warning of the effects of misbehavior will, I hope, be instrumental in animating the younger officers. . . . Remember, that it is the actions, and not the commission, that make the officer—and that there is more expected from him than the *title*." Besides indulging their pleasures, Washington added, his officers would do well to devote leisure time to professional study. Much information could be gleaned from reading military texts—for example, Humphrey Bland's *Treatise of Military Discipline*; first published in 1727 and already in its seventh edition by 1753, this was the era's most popular and influential English-language military manual. A standard primer for the young British Army officer of the mid-eighteenth century, Bland's book would be quarried by Washington for decades to come.[26]

Lieutenant Colonel Stephen believed that a regiment so top-heavy with officers could afford to shed several "without hurting the service." Resorting to vocabulary from his medical days, he was sure that a "purgation" would be positively beneficial, leaving behind the "men of spirit and honor," of whom "proper things" might be expected. While acknowledging that some of his officers had "the seeds of idleness very strongly ingrafted in their natures," Washington assured Dinwiddie of his own efforts, "both by threats and persuasive means . . . to discountenance gaming, drinking, swearing, and irregularities of every other kind." Regrettably, the problem had been aggravated by "that unhappy difference about the command" at Fort Cumberland, which had kept him from enforcing his orders in person.[27]

Given Washington's decision to walk away from a direct confrontation with Dagworthy, this was lame stuff. Virginia's speaker, John Robinson, had urged him to silence the critics once and for all by shifting his own headquarters forward to Fort Cumberland, so that he could oversee the situation personally. Determined to ride out the storm, Washington refused to budge. Replying to Robinson, he grew even more prickly and defensive, while again seeking to offload the blame onto the Maryland officer. Indeed, while Washington couldn't be answerable for the behavior of individuals, *his* intentions were pure. No one had acted more for Virginia's interests than he, and if anyone was responsible for the "many gross irregularities" at Fort Cumberland, it was Dagworthy. He assured Robinson: "It will give me the greatest pleasure to resign a command, which I solemnly declare I accepted against my will."[28]

For all this blustering, Washington soon changed his mind. Men of influence were quick to caution against anything as rash as resignation. Colonel Landon Carter sought to cool Washington's temper by assuring him that such criticism could not have come from anyone who knew him. But this reassurance was double edged: if Washington relinquished his command, Carter added, he and his friends would be hard pressed to justify his conduct. For Washington, as Carter cheerfully continued, surely death was preferable to such dishonor: better to share "Braddock's bed" than allow anything to tarnish those laurels that still lay in store for him. The final touch was an unsubtle thrust at Washington's chivalric soft spot. "A whole crowd of females" had tendered their wishes for his success, Carter reported, and were even now praying for his safety. The canny Carter must have known that gallant Washington, so hungry for acclaim, and for the admiration of young women like Sally Fairfax, could never have disappointed *them*.[29]

Besides such direct appeals to his sense of duty and honor, other factors gave Washington reason to reconsider his latest threat to resign. Governor Sharpe, it seemed, had a higher opinion of his abilities than he had imagined: in the event of any intercolonial westward offensive, Sharpe wanted Washington for the plum job of second in command. In addition, active steps were finally being taken to increase Washington's manpower: Dinwiddie anticipated that the House of Burgesses would vote funds to increase the Virginia Regiment to 2,000 men; if necessary, one in every twenty militiamen from all save five exposed frontier counties would be conscripted. This initially raised the alluring prospect of a powerful regiment of two battalions, each ten companies strong. In fact, it soon became clear that the total "number in pay"—if they could be raised at all, of course—would be just 1,500, with new recruits added to the existing sixteen companies to constitute a single, expanded regiment.[30] It was not an ideal solution, but it seemed that at least *something* was being done to augment Washington's resources.

Above all, Washington shelved all thoughts of resignation because of a fresh crisis on the frontier. The French and Indian raiders, who had been quiet over the winter, now resumed their assaults with a vengeance, striking with devastating effect against soldiers and settlers alike. On the evening of April 18, 1756, in a textbook decoy ambush, they inflicted a heavy blow on the garrison of one of the outposts between Winchester and Fort Cumberland, Fort Edwards on the Cacapon River. Three soldiers searching for stray horses had encountered hostiles close to the fort and raised the alarm. A party of about forty to fifty men under Captain John Fenton Mercer promptly sallied out to give chase. But the first Indians were merely bait. When Mercer and his men had been lured a mile and a half from the fort and were breathlessly "rising a mountain," the trap was sprung. Fired upon "very smartly," outnumbered two to one and in danger of being totally surrounded, after half an hour of heavy fighting, the surviving Virginians retreated while they still could. More than a third of them failed to get back to the stockade: Captain Mercer—a veteran of Fort Necessity and the brother of Washington's close friend George—was killed, along with Ensign Thomas Carter and fifteen men; another two came in wounded. It was, in Washington's words, "a very unlucky affair" and all the more galling because it was impossible to avenge: given the continuing lack of men, a council of war at Winchester reluctantly resolved against marching to the scene.[31]

Elsewhere, isolated settlers who refused to abandon their farmsteads fell prey to the raiders. In an episode that underlined Washington's helplessness and frustration, on April 22, a small war band of six Indians crossed the mountains within five miles of another stockade, Cunningham's Fort, surprising David Kelly and his family. Kelly was killed and scalped; his wife and six children hustled off as captives. One of Kelly's teenaged sons escaped and brought tidings of the raid to Winchester. As the *Pennsylvania Gazette* reported, Colonel Washington immediately sent off a detachment of thirty men. It was a futile gesture: they buried what was left of Kelly and found the raiders' tracks but could not "get up with them."[32]

The raid underlined the fundamental flaw in the defensive "chain of forts" strategy that Washington was reluctantly obliged to accept: isolated stockades and blockhouses were worthless beyond the limited zones that their paltry garrisons were prepared to patrol and were therefore unable to stop the infiltration of swift-moving Indian war parties. It also highlighted a phenomenon that only exacerbated the sufferings of the settlers. Like those who descended upon the Kellys, Indian raiders often killed potentially troublesome adult males, while sparing women and youngsters seen as more biddable and likely to be assimilated into the tribe. Such widespread adoption of white captives left raw wounds among settler communities: the dead could be decently buried and mourned; captives, whose fate remained uncertain, granted grieving kinfolk no such sense of closure. Unsurprisingly, the practice only intensified "Indian hating" among the beleaguered inhabitants of the "backcountry."[33]

The shock engendered by the upsurge of enemy activity had a major impact upon Washington and was the decisive factor in causing him to shelve his plans of relinquishing a command from which he could never expect to "reap either honor or benefit." As an emotional letter to Dinwiddie, written on the same day that the Indians descended upon Kelly and his brood, makes clear, he was deeply affected by the sufferings of the inhabitants and felt a personal responsibility for them. He pledged: "The supplicating tears of the women, and moving petitions from the men, melt me into such deadly sorrow, that I solemnly declare . . . I could offer myself a willing sacrifice to the butchering enemy, provided that would contribute to the people's ease."[34]

In lieu of recruits or Indian allies, the beleaguered Virginia Regiment was bolstered by militia summoned to Winchester from ten Tidewater counties. Some 1,200 militiamen answered the call, yet, from Washington's perspective, these undisciplined, costly, contrary, and unreliable amateur soldiers were more of a hindrance than a help. Many of them lacked firearms, yet all made inroads into his carefully hoarded stockpiles of supplies.

The new crisis subsided when the Indian raiders withdrew, but the frontier's defenders were soon fighting among themselves. Drunkenness and brawling prompted Washington to issue orders on May 1 threatening five hundred lashes, without benefit of court-martial, to "any soldier, who shall presume to quarrel or fight" and one hundred lashes for drunks. The militia faced no such sanctions, with predictable results. A week later, Washington noted, the militia detachment from Prince William County began to demonstrate "superlative insolence" toward his soldiers and officers. After a militiaman was sent to the guardhouse for abusing an officer of the Virginia Regiment, his own officer instigated a rescue bid, swearing that Washington's officers were all scoundrels, and he could "drive the whole corps before him." When one of them called his bluff, the militia officer took "fright" and publicly acknowledged his fault the following morning.[35]

Washington's exasperation at the shortcomings of the temporary militia, in particular their inferiority to regularly maintained troops, would only intensify in coming years. In May 1756, however, his complaints drew an increasingly unsympathetic response from Williamsburg. Even Washington's old patron and friend Colonel William Fairfax cautioned him to stop grumbling about a force that he had himself called upon, and instead seek to emulate those stoic Roman heroes who had happily overcome far greater "fatigues, murmurings, mutinies and defections" than he was ever likely to face.[36]

Once the alarm was over, most of the militia was sent home, save for about 500 from frontier counties who were posted to bolster garrisons until the Virginia Regiment could be brought up to strength by the expected drafts. The long-anticipated draft act was finally implemented during May, but the results were disappointing, not least because those selected by lot could avoid service by finding another man to take their place or by immediately paying a £10 fine. In consequence, as Dinwiddie reported, "the draughts in most of the counties paid fines rather than go to Winchester, [and] these fines were given to volunteers that enlisted and received the 10 pounds." In a pattern that would be repeated in future wars, the burden of Virginian military service fell most heavily on the poor and desperate: those drafts who could not afford to pay the fine—which amounted to a poor man's annual earnings—and substitutes unable to resist an offer of hard cash. The yield was unimpressive: of the 246 drafts brought into Winchester by June 25, several deserted, three were discharged as unfit for service, and another six were Quakers who refused to serve on religious grounds. In mid-July, the Virginia Regiment mustered just 591 men—not even half of the promised 1,500. As an act of Parliament had been passed to allow the British regulars to recruit indentured servants, provided their masters were compensated for the time they still had to serve, Washington hoped that the Virginia Regiment could do likewise. If so, the regiment could soon be completed, he believed, although Dinwiddie cautioned him "not to enlist any convicts who probably may be fractious, and bad examples to the others."[37]

British units like the bloodied 44th and 48th, and the newly authorized "Royal American Regiment" had enjoyed considerable success in seeking recruits among the servants of Pennsylvania and Maryland. By attempting to tap into the same pool of manpower, the Virginia Regiment was drawing ever closer to the British regular model. A muster roll for Washington's own company, listing eighty-six men present during August 1757, shows that only twenty-three—just over a quarter—were natives of Virginia. Of the rest, there were one each from New York, New Jersey, Maryland, Pennsylvania, Holland, and Germany; but the majority—fifty-six men, or 65 percent of the total—had been born in the British Isles. The percentage of native-born recruits for the regiment as a whole was higher, at 41 percent, but the preponderance of incomers remains striking, particularly compared with the Massachusetts provincials, where more than 80 percent of personnel had been born in that colony.[38]

Now that Dagworthy's pretensions had been curbed, there was nothing to stop Washington from joining the bulk of his regiment at Fort Cumberland and taking command in person. Yet he maintained his headquarters at Winchester. With the Blue Ridge now effectively Virginia's frontier, Washington argued, that town could become a rallying point for inhabitants who would otherwise flee. Emphasizing Winchester's suitability as a base for assembling reinforcements and supplies and for reacting against raids, Washington convinced Dinwiddie that a large and strong fort should be built there.[39]

When Washington paid another visit to Fort Cumberland in early July, however, his presence was immediately apparent through intensified discipline and training. On July 6, a general court-martial sentenced several deserters to severe floggings of a thousand lashes: they were to "receive as much of their punishment as the surgeon . . . shall judge they are able to bear." Next evening all the men except the new drafts were to practice the official "exercise," followed by a stint of unofficial "bush fighting." The following afternoon, the garrison fired at targets, then formed up into a single battalion to "go through the platoon exercise and evolution."[40]

After Washington rode back down to Winchester, Adam Stephen carried on his work with a will. Having caught two men in "the very act of desertion," he reported, they "wealed them 'til they pissed themselves and the spectators shed tears for them." Stephen hoped these bloody floggings would "answer the end of punishment," by providing a grim example calculated to deter others from going astray.[41] Through a series of regimental orders sent up from headquarters, Washington sought to instill the behavior expected of officers and gentlemen at second hand. These instructions, like the imposition of a regular-style regime of training and discipline, had a clear purpose. The ultimate object, as Washington emphasized in a proclamation printed in the *Virginia Gazette* on August 27, 1756, was to "show our willing obedience to the best of Kings" and through "unerring bravery" earn the royal favor and "a better establishment as a reward for our services"—in short, to be officially recognized as a "regular corps."[42]

Washington's brave words were undermined by an advertisement, on the very same page of that issue of the *Gazette*, seeking the apprehension of seventeen men of the Virginia Regiment who had deserted from the post at Maidstone, just south of the Potomac River. Interestingly, none of them were Virginians. Save for a Scot and an Irishman, all had been born across the Potomac in Maryland and were in their late teens or early twenties. Reporting such "great and scandalous desertions" to Dinwiddie, Washington blamed them on the "fatiguing service, low pay, and great hardships in which our men have been engaged."[43]

Criticism of Washington and his regiment now intensified. Rumors and gossip escalated into an effective propaganda campaign that harnessed the growing power of the press to broadcast its allegations as widely as possible. In an article that dominated the front page of the *Virginia Gazette* of September 3, 1756, an anonymous correspondent writing as "the Virginia-Centinel" lambasted the officers of the colony's regiment as a bunch of vice-ridden rakes who disparaged the noble efforts of the militia and skulked idle in their forts while the country around was ravaged by merciless raiders. It concluded by denying that the public could "receive much advantage from a regiment of such dastardly debauchees."[44]

Washington was not named in the article, but, as commander of the regiment, he was clearly deemed culpable for his subordinates' shortcomings. His friends were quick to reassure him. John Kirkpatrick wrote that the "self-evident falsities asserted by that witty writer of the Centinel, must condemn him in the judgment of every rational, reflecting being." Such an effort to "foment an ill spirit of slander, and propagate lies, to amuse the unthinking mob" did not reflect the views of the "whole thinking part of the legislative power." *They* still backed Washington and were satisfied with his "conduct for the preservation of the country." Like Kirkpatrick, another friend, William Ramsay, urged him to ignore the tirade: "Show your contempt of the scribbler by your silence," he advised.[45]

In fact, the broadside was about more than Washington and his touchy officers: harking back to the old antipathy toward standing armies, it voiced an ingrained distrust of paid professional soldiery and an admiration for a selfless amateur militia. Such opinions were only reinforced by Braddock's defeat and more recent humiliations on other fronts.

Indeed, while the frontiers of Virginia and Pennsylvania sustained hit-and-run raids during the spring and summer of 1756, far heavier fighting had already flared elsewhere. At first, things had gone surprisingly well. During the previous September, the disaster in the Ohio Country had been partially offset by Anglo-American successes to the north. A mixed force of British regulars and Massachusetts provincials had fulfilled its role under the original plan for the 1755 campaign and captured Fort Beauséjour in Nova Scotia. In addition, a French lunge from Canada against the New York frontier had been parried and rebuffed during a rambling and bloody engagement at the foot of Lake George. Colonial forces commanded by the Irish-born superintendent of the northern Indians, William Johnson, had acquitted themselves well during the sprawling fight, fending off a formidable combination of French regulars, Canadian militia, and their Indian allies. Losses among the enemy's officers had been heavy, with the slain including Captain Saint-Pierre, the aging veteran who had so impressed Washington with his soldierly bearing at Fort Le Boeuf in December 1753.[46]

Despite these badly needed and much-trumpeted victories, by late summer of 1756, when the "Virginia-Centinel" unleashed his attack, the initiative had swung back in favor of the Franco-Canadians. Under the command of a determined new governor general, Pierre de Rigaud, Marquis de Vaudreuil, and a competent field commander from France, Louis Joseph, Marquis de Montcalm, they had launched a lightning strike against the isolated post of Oswego on Lake Ontario, snapping up its demoralized garrison and cowing the remaining troops on the New York frontier.

That same season saw the arrival of Braddock's official replacement as Britain's commander in chief in North America, John Campbell, Earl of Loudoun. The earl and the reinforcements of redcoats that arrived with him came too late to stave off disaster at Oswego, but he lost no time in seeking to orchestrate a renewed war effort in which the colonies would be obliged to place their burgeoning resources behind the Mother Country. This was an objective that was to cause Loudoun intense frustration, and to further sour relations between Crown and colonies.[47]

For Washington, Loudoun's arrival promised a fresh source of patronage, particularly as the earl had also received the honorary title of governor of Virginia. It revived hopes of the military advancement, and the regular officer's commission, that Braddock would surely have provided had he lived. As a clear sign of his intentions, Washington's new Winchester strongpoint, which was constructed despite the ongoing clamor that he should shift his base forward to Fort Cumberland, was named Fort Loudoun in compliment to the incoming commander in chief.

During the autumn of 1756, Washington quit Winchester for long enough to make a fresh inspection of his extensive front line, which stretched from the Potomac down to the North Carolina border. This "very long and troublesome jaunt on the frontiers" gave him a taste of the hazards that his scattered detachments, based in isolated stockades and blockhouses, were daily facing in the field. Washington had ridden about 100 miles down the Shenandoah Valley to reach Augusta Court House when he received warning that Indians were roaming to the south. After pushing on to Vause's Fort, on the Roanoke River, where it was rumored that militia could be assembled to oppose the raiders, Washington, accompanied by just his servant and a guide, apparently escaped death by the skin of his teeth. As the trio rode down a rain-swept, forest-fringed road, they were spotted by hostiles lying in ambush. These warriors let them pass unmolested, saving their bullets for two horsemen who appeared from the other direction less than two hours later. This deliverance from almost "certain destruction," as Washington described it, must have seemed like another manifestation of the "Providence" or "Destiny" that had protected him at Fort Necessity and on the Monongahela. Expressing his conviction in the existence of some benevolent force controlling the fate of humans, Washington used both terms as readily as "God" or "Heaven." Indeed, while conforming to the conscientious churchgoing expected of the gentry in Anglican Virginia, there is no compelling evidence that Washington was deeply religious.[48]

Despite his close shave, after three weeks in the saddle Washington returned to Winchester without even having seen an enemy Indian. The report that the colonel sent to Williamsburg was nonetheless a bleak one: owing to "the bad regulation of the militia," the "wretched and unhappy" inhabitants of the "whole back-country" were convinced of their approaching ruin and streaming off toward the Southern Colonies. They had petitioned Washington for men of his regiment to protect them, but such a redeployment would leave Winchester vulnerable. Another observation implied criticism of Dinwiddie himself: some eleven Catawbas from the south—Indian allies that Washington had been desperate to attract ever since he accepted his command— had come into Winchester. More could have been had, Washington complained, if only "the proper means [had] been used, to send trusty guides to invite and conduct them to us."[49]

In hectoring the man who had first given him his command and who shared many of his own goals and frustrations, Washington went too far: his "unmannerly" criticisms earned a personal rebuke from Dinwiddie, who was rapidly losing patience with his headstrong and apparently ungrateful protégé. It was time to bring him to heel. Rather than accept Washington's recommendation that Fort Cumberland be evacuated and the frontier anchored upon the new Fort Loudoun, Dinwiddie and his council resolved that the contentious strongpoint on Wills Creek should not be abandoned, but rather reinforced. To that end, Washington was to march there immediately with most of the men he had assembled at Winchester.[50]

When Washington pointed out that such a move would strip Winchester bare, he was ordered to recall the garrisons of his smaller, outlying posts to make up the shortfall. He grudgingly agreed to go to Fort Cumberland, but a letter to one of his captains, in which he regretted "the fate of the poor, unhappy inhabitants left by this means exposed to every incursion of a merciless enemy," left no doubt of his feelings. Shortly before Christmas 1756, more than a year after assuming command of Virginia's forces, Washington finally established his headquarters at Fort Cumberland.[51]

Dinwiddie's decision had been influenced by a comment from Lord Loudoun himself, who agreed that reinforcing the most "advanced" outpost was the best way of baffling the raids. Assuming that Washington had already "executed his plan" to retire to Winchester, Loudoun registered his grave concern at such a move: it would not only have a "bad effect as to the Dominion" but would "not have a good appearance at home," he warned.[52]

Washington was mortified that Loudoun should "have imbibed prejudices so unfavorable" to his character.[53] In the New Year, he set about seeking to change Loudoun's opinion by sending him an analysis of the Old Dominion's war effort. In what he characterized as a "concise" letter, but which in fact rambled on at pamphlet length, he aimed to provide a "candid" account of Virginian affairs and more "particularly of the grievances which the Virginia Regiment has struggled against for almost three years."[54] As "a principal actor from the beginning of these disturbances," Washington considered himself well qualified to do so. In the pages that followed, he resurrected familiar themes: the ineffectiveness of the disorderly and tardy militia; the money that had been squandered by failing to pursue "regular schemes or plans of operation"; the misplaced reliance on a "pusillanimous" defensive strategy that earned the "contempt and derision" of the Indians; the futility of such a policy given the lack of manpower to defend an extensive frontier; and the unassailable logic of an offensive campaign to destroy the root of the problem.

In a passage that must have struck a chord with Loudoun, who had encountered determined resistance to his policies from elected assemblies across British America, Washington railed against Virginia's failure to impose effective "military laws and regulations." Instead, the Old Dominion had a mere "jumble of laws" that did nothing except render "command intricate and precarious," making it difficult to exercise authority without riling the "civil powers," who, "tenacious of liberty," were instantly suspicious of "all proceedings that are not strictly lawful," even when such innovations were justified by the circumstances.

Yet for all the obstacles placed in its way, Washington maintained that the Virginia Regiment had proved stalwart in the colony's defense. His beleaguered bluecoats had seen their fair share of action, fighting "more than twenty skirmishes" in which they had lost "near a hundred men killed and wounded." The regiment had long been "tantalized" by hopes of becoming a regular unit of the British Army while, if Braddock had lived, Washington himself would surely have met with "preferment equal to my wishes." He had long since reached the conclusion that it was impossible to continue in his present service "without loss of honor." Only Loudoun's appointment raised hopes that this dismal situation might change for the better. A passage that Washington wrote, but decided against including in his letter to Loudoun, reveals deeper personal bitterness. In this, he begged leave to add that his own "unwearied endeavors" were "inadequately rewarded." His orders were ambiguous, leaving him "like a wanderer in a wilderness," while he was held answerable for the consequences "without the privilege of defense!"[55]

Washington's most significant proposal was not presented directly to Loudoun but was saved for a covering letter addressed to his aide-de-camp, Captain James Cunningham. This suggested that Virginia, Pennsylvania, and Maryland should together raise 3,000 well-regulated men. They would be enough to secure the key "passes" between Fort Cumberland and the Ohio and take possession of that waterway. Supplied with a "middling" train of artillery, the same force could then conquer "the terror of these colonies"—Fort Duquesne itself.[56]

Hearing that Loudoun had summoned five lieutenant governors of the "Southern Colonies" to a meeting in Philadelphia to thrash out a plan of operations for 1757, Washington sought Dinwiddie's permission to attend in person. As Dinwiddie would be on hand and whatever was decided would be passed on to Washington anyway, the governor could see no good reason for the trip but, as the colonel was so insistent, gave him leave to go. By late February 1757, Washington was in Philadelphia once again, whiling away several weeks in gambling, dancing, and shopping before Loudoun arrived. While there, he took the opportunity to write a "memorial" to Loudoun on behalf of the officers of the Virginia

Regiment, formally requesting his patronage. This was couched in suitably deferential terms, but in a letter to Dinwiddie written some two weeks earlier, likewise seeking royal recognition for the regiment and its officers, Washington made no effort to conceal his mounting resentment at what seemed like a deliberate policy of discrimination against colonials.[57]

Washington listed the attributes that entitled the Virginia Regiment to regular status: its long and arduous service, rigorous training, proper uniforms, and, above all, the fact that it was raised to serve "during the King's or colony's pleasure," unlike other provincial units, which were seasonal formations, assembled "in the spring and dismissed in the Fall." The truth of all this prompted Washington to voice deep-seated frustrations, expressed in biting and sarcastic language:

We can't conceive, that being Americans should deprive us of the benefits of British subjects; nor lessen our claim to preferment. . . . Some boast of long service as a claim to promotion—meaning I suppose, the length of time they have pocketed a commission—I apprehend it is the service done, not the service engaged in, that merits reward; and that there is, as equitable a right to expect something for three years hard and bloody service, as for 10 spent at St. James's etc. where real service, or a field of battle never was seen.

For good measure, Washington took a swipe at Dinwiddie himself, complaining that it was the "general opinion" that the Virginia Regiment's services were "slighted" or had "not been properly represented to His Majesty." In its criticism of what Washington believed to be the British Empire's lopsided system of patronage, the letter has been convincingly identified as revealing a "significant development" in his "political identity and thinking," marking "a step toward republicanism and nationalism."[58]

In his long letter to Loudoun, Washington had tactfully glossed over his own role in the great controversy of 1754—the

"Jumonville affair." By an extraordinarily unlucky coincidence, at
the very moment that he was seeking to cement his credentials
with the commander in chief, that embarrassing episode was suddenly resurrected. A French book, which included a translation
of the rough journal of events that Washington had lost at Fort
Necessity, had been captured aboard an enemy ship. In March
1757, the proprietor of the *Pennsylvania Gazette* advertised his
intention to publish a translation within two months. That year,
English-language editions emerged in both Philadelphia and New
York, so reminding readers of events that Washington would have
preferred to forget.[59]

Lord Loudoun finally reached Philadelphia on March 14. His
strategic summit convened next day and lasted for a fortnight.[60] By
its end, all Washington's hopes had been dashed. There would be
no offensive against Fort Duquesne in 1757. In fact, as South Carolina was considered to be in greater danger than Virginia, some 400
of the Old Dominion's troops would be diverted there instead. As
part of the shake-up, however, Loudoun decreed that Fort Cumberland was henceforth to be garrisoned by Maryland, leaving Virginia
responsible for manning five forts within its own territory: Washington's headquarters would revert to Winchester after all. Nothing
came of Washington's plea that the Virginia Regiment be formally
attached to the British Army. Neither was there any prospect of the
king's commission that he had sought for himself.

Loudoun was an exceptionally busy man, mired in paperwork
and hobbled by instructions from London; the difficulties he faced
in securing supplies, manpower, and the cooperation of colonial
officials with little enthusiasm for the war were Washington's own
problems writ large. Under the circumstances, Washington's failure
to achieve his personal goals at Philadelphia was unsurprising. But
his approaches to Loudoun did not draw a total blank; his recommendations on behalf of fellow Virginians who were keen to serve
as regular officers received serious consideration at headquarters.
For example, it was through Colonel Washington's interest and recommendation to Loudoun's aide-de-camp, Captain Cunningham,

that William Henry Fairfax, the son of his esteemed Belvoir neighbor, gained an ensign's commission in the 28th Foot later that year.[61] Washington's conspicuous failure to secure a king's commission for *himself* may have been a reflection of his unwillingness to accept a drop in rank from colonel—and the fact that he was too useful in his present post. In addition, unlike "Billy" Fairfax and other colonial officers who secured regular rank, Washington never offered to purchase a commission, instead expecting one as a just reward for his efforts.[62]

On his return from Philadelphia, Washington revealed his disappointment in a letter to Richard Washington, the London merchant who supplied him with fashionable goods and to whom he had last written back in December 1755. Since then, Washington explained, he had become an "exile," posted "for twenty months past upon our cold and barren frontiers" and charged with protecting "from the cruel incursions of a crafty savage enemy a line of inhabitants of more than 350 miles extent with a force inadequate to the task." Returning to his favorite theme, Washington once again emphasized that an attack on Fort Duquesne, that notorious "hold of barbarians" who had become "a terror to three populous colonies," was the only cure for Virginia's woes: the continuing failure to launch such an assault was all the more galling because the prospect of a major offensive to the north by Lord Loudoun would distract French attention to that sector.[63]

Reluctant to take no for an answer, Washington wasted little time in presenting his pet scheme to Colonel John Stanwix, commanding the first battalion of the newly raised Royal American Regiment, who had been appointed by Loudoun as commander in chief of all the forces—regular and provincial alike—in Pennsylvania and the southern provinces. Based in Carlisle, Pennsylvania, with five companies of his battalion, the experienced Stanwix was now Washington's immediate superior. Escaped captives from the Ohio Country confirmed that just 300 men garrisoned Fort Duquesne, Washington informed him. Surely the opportunity to reduce Fort Duquesne was too good to be lost? "I do not conceive that the French are so strong in Canada as to reinforce this place, and defend themselves at home this campaign," he argued.[64]

Because the unusually large number of companies—and therefore officers—in the Virginia Regiment made it an expensive unit to pay, in May 1757, Governor Dinwiddie informed Washington that the Assembly had decided to slash its strength. It would now consist of ten companies rather than sixteen.[65] However, as each of these was to consist of 100 men and the regiment still only mustered about 650 rank and file, a sum not exceeding £30,000 had been earmarked to raise the manpower needed to bring it up to strength. Given the continuing unpopularity of military service, exactly how the recruits were to be found remained unclear, although the Assembly subsequently approved another draft, targeted even more specifically at the poorest and most vulnerable members of white Virginian society—men considered to be work-shy vagrants or who lacked the property qualifications to vote. This new attempt to swell the Virginia Regiment with reluctant conscripts rather than willing volunteers would create more problems than it solved.

In the same letter in which he announced the reorganization of the Virginia Regiment, Dinwiddie made another announcement redolent of future difficulties for Washington: as Charleston merchant Edmond Atkin had been appointed superintendent of Indian affairs for the Southern Colonies, Washington was to have no more dealings with Virginia's Indian allies. Expertise in managing relations with the Indians was badly needed. Some 150 Cherokees who had been gathered at Winchester by Major Andrew Lewis were already disgruntled and disillusioned by their treatment at the hands of the Old Dominion. Captain George Mercer warned that their loyalty was wavering owing to mismanagement: they complained that "the great men of Virginia were liars," in contrast to the French, who "treated them always like children, and gave them what goods they wanted."[66] But if Washington assumed that Atkin would relieve him of a burden, he was to be sorely disappointed: the new superintendent lacked the tact and diplomacy crucial for his post; by contrast, Atkin had the unfortunate knack of irritating and alienating those he was required to work with, Indians and whites alike.

Predictably enough, the draft bill passed in the spring of 1757 failed to solve Washington's manpower problems; the resentful draftees deserted in droves. Lenient treatment of the first to be apprehended merely encouraged others to abscond, so Washington determined to take harsher measures: on July 11, he wrote to Dinwiddie, pleading for a copy of the recently reactivated "mutiny and desertion bill," along with blank warrants to allow the sentences of courts-martial to be enforced. Just days later, he informed Colonel Stanwix that, of some 400 drafts, no fewer than 114 had promptly gone off. Some of them had been retaken, albeit only after a fight, and Washington had now built a lofty gallows, "near 40 feet high," on which he intended to "hang two or three . . . as an example to others."[67]

Washington meant what he said: writing to Dinwiddie from Fort Loudoun on August 3, he reported that two of those condemned, Ignatious Edwards and William Smith, had already been strung up. Both were, in Washington's opinion, beyond redemption: Edwards had deserted twice before, while Smith "was accounted one of the greatest villains upon the continent." Washington had actually warned Edwards in person that another lapse could not be forgiven; Edwards, described as a "great fiddler and dancer," may have gambled that his winning ways would save his neck. If so, he misjudged his colonel. Other, less heinous offenders escaped with a severe lashing.[68]

Such harsh sentences were mandatory only when colonial troops were actually serving alongside British regulars and fell under their *Articles of War*. By seeking to impose them upon his own provincial regiment, even though it was acting independently of the redcoats, Washington once again underlined his determination to transform his regiment into an elite unit worthy of joining the regular establishment. In the opinion of an officer who served alongside him in the following year, however, Washington's reputation as "a tolerably strict disciplinarian" came at the cost of his personal popularity: he was "not then much liked in the army" as his "system" jarred with "the impatient spirits of his headstrong countrymen, who are but little used to restraint."[69]

While Washington was whipping his men into shape, a fresh campaign was unfolding far from the Ohio. As Washington had anticipated, it involved a major assault upon Canada. In line with specific instructions from William Pitt, the new secretary of state for the Southern Department with responsibility for American affairs, Loudoun concentrated the bulk of his regulars at Halifax, Nova Scotia, poised for an amphibious thrust against the fortress of Louisbourg on Cape Breton Island. Loudoun had originally planned to strike first at Quebec, the capital of New France, but Pitt preferred Louisbourg. This interference from afar clearly unsettled the commander in chief, and when subsequent orders arrived granting him discretion over which objective to attack first, he now plumped for Louisbourg rather than Quebec. It was a disastrous choice. Stormy weather and the appearance of a superior French fleet in North American waters thwarted Loudoun's great expedition before a gun was even fired.

Anglo-American embarrassment at this misadventure was soon compounded by horror and rage after Montcalm exploited the conspicuous absence of Loudoun and the bulk of his troops, and the removal of any immediate danger to Quebec, to assault the lightly defended New York frontier. In August 1757, after a short siege, the marquis captured Fort William Henry at the foot of Lake George. The garrison, which, like Washington's command at Fort Necessity, surrendered upon condition of receiving the "honors of war," fell victim to France's tribal allies. Montcalm had secured his own military objective, yet these warriors deemed themselves cheated of the legitimate prizes—scalps, prisoners, and booty—for which *they* had fought. Perhaps 200 prisoners, including soldiers' wives and children, were killed before order was restored.[70]

The massacre, bad enough in reality but further exaggerated in gory newspaper reports on both sides of the Atlantic, had an even greater psychological impact, marking a low point in the war and in the reputation of Britain's soldiers and their leadership. Together with the total failure of Loudoun's Louisbourg expedition and his brusque, imperious treatment of the touchy colonial assemblies, this latest disaster left the earl facing mounting criticism, not only in America, but also in London. There, Loudoun's patron, the British Army's commander, the Duke of Cumberland, had likewise suffered a dramatic fall from grace after failing to preserve his father's prized continental territory of Hanover from the French. That defeat, allied with the emergence of a viable coalition ministry combining the financial gifts of Thomas Pelham-Holles, Duke of Newcastle, and the vigorous war leadership of Pitt, ushered in a radically new approach to the war in North America and ultimately sealed Loudoun's fate.

While Loudoun's strategy for 1757 was clearly flawed, placing too much emphasis upon a single front, his troubled tenure as commander in chief laid the foundations for ultimate victory over New France. The unglamorous but essential logistical infrastructure for a concerted war effort had laboriously been put in place; and far from ignoring the realities of local conditions that had contributed to Braddock's defeat, Loudoun had taken pains to train his redcoats to fight in the bewildering American woods, exploiting the hard-earned experience of irregulars like the tough New England ranger Robert Rogers, who had spent the past two years waging a vicious guerrilla conflict in the Champlain Valley.

The war's axis shifted northward during 1757, but the frontiers of Pennsylvania and Virginia continued to face sporadic raids by war parties fitted out at Fort Duquesne. In consequence, the Virginia Regiment's detachment to South Carolina was halved to 200 men. Including the new drafts, this gave Washington eight companies, or about 700 men, to protect Virginia's lengthy frontier. As ever, the regiment's manpower was insufficient for the job. In mid-June, when intelligence suggested that a large body of French and Indians, complete with artillery, were heading hotfoot for Fort Cumberland, a council of war at Fort Loudoun reluctantly resolved that the scarcity and dispersal of the troops ruled out any relief expedition.

Instead, vulnerable garrisons should be concentrated at Winchester, the enemy's next likely objective. Alerted by Washington, Colonel Stanwix prepared to march there at the head of his Royal Americans and as many Pennsylvanian provincials as could be assembled. The alarm proved false, and Stanwix never moved from Carlisle, but his response to the emergency highlighted the professional reputation that Washington had established: Stanwix—a veteran of half a century of regular service—readily deferred to the Virginian's local knowledge, trusting to his "judgment and experience in the operations in this country." Washington exploited his standing with Stanwix to drum home a favorite theme: the unreliability of the colonial militia. "No dependence is to be placed upon them," he warned. Indeed, militiamen were "obstinate and perverse" and too often egged on to disobedience by their own officers.[71]

While obliged to remain on the strategic defensive, Washington was keen to exploit any opportunity for low-level aggressive action. His instructions to his company commanders emphasized that, although their main objective was to protect the inhabitants, "and to keep them if possible easy and quiet," one-third of available manpower should be pushed out in "constant scouting parties" capable of intercepting raiders before they could strike: rather than simply waiting for the enemy, Washington's men were to seek them out. Once again, Washington stressed the need for his captains to "neglect no pains or diligence" in training their men and to devote some of their own leisure hours to studying the finer points of their chosen profession. The captains' instructions included a statement that underpinned Washington's own creed as a soldier: "Discipline is the soul of an army. It makes small numbers formidable, procures success to the weak, and esteem to all."[72]

That summer the viability of the small-scale patrols that Washington recommended was enhanced by the presence of significant numbers of Cherokees and Catawbas. The value of such warriors had been demonstrated when Lieutenant James Baker of the Virginia Regiment and some Cherokees penetrated about 100 miles beyond Fort Cumberland, then tracked and ambushed ten Frenchmen. The

skirmish epitomized the ferocity of frontier warfare. After opening fire, Baker and his allies rushed in with their tomahawks. They
killed three and took prisoner three others, all of them officers. Of
these, one was too badly wounded to march and was therefore slain
on the spot; another was "served in the same manner soon after"
in vengeance for the death of the Indians' leader, "the truly brave"
Swallow Warrior, and the wounding of his son. It was only after a
punishing march, during which they had no "morsel" to eat for four
days, that the party came in to Fort Cumberland with five scalps
and the surviving officer.[73]

Baker's raid gave a rare cause for celebration but had unforeseen consequences. When the French officer was brought down
to Winchester, some of Washington's officers invited him and
one of his Cherokee captors to join them for a convivial glass of
wine. Atkin, the Indian superintendent, took umbrage: he had
not yet had a chance to interrogate the prisoner and complained
to Washington. This provoked a feisty response from the Virginians: "as our officers and men risked their lives in [the] taking
of the prisoner, we are entitled to speak to him when we please,"
they informed their colonel. Indeed, whatever command Atkin
enjoyed over the Indians, he had none over *them*—"gentlemen
who from their station in life, their births and education ought to
be treated with respect."[74]

The squall blew over, but Atkin was soon at the center of a fresh
storm, which caused Washington far greater concern. As he knew
from hard-earned experience, allied Indians didn't fight for nothing: they required endless gifts and careful nurturing. Far from
managing matters at Winchester, in early July Atkin alienated the
Indians by jailing ten Cherokees and Mingos he suspected of spy-
ing. Not surprisingly, as the exasperated Washington reported to
Stanwix, this had "greatly alarmed" the prisoners' friends. They sent
runners to inform their people "that the English had fallen upon
their brethren." Irate warriors managed to force the release of the
prisoners; they refused to even talk to Atkin until Washington had
reassured them that a mistake had been made.[75]

All that was bad enough, but when Atkin left Winchester in mid-August, he took his deputy—Washington's old frontier companion Christopher Gist—and his Indian interpreter, Richard Smith, with him, along with the essential supply of presents, thereby exacerbating Washington's problems when more Cherokees turned up demanding the customary largess. The consequence, as Washington warned Dinwiddie, was that while the "warlike, formidable" Cherokees seemed to have a "natural, strong attachment" to the English, the treatment they had received was now inclining them toward the French, who were "making them vastly advantageous offers." The present system of managing Indian affairs risked losing allies who were crucial to the English colonies in general and to Virginia in particular.[76]

That summer, Washington's myriad frustrations—with Atkin, with deserters, and, above all, with the futility of the defensive policy he was forced to follow—fed into increasing tensions with Dinwiddie, by now a sick man and heading for retirement. Not least, Washington believed that his reputation was being unfairly traduced and that he had been condemned without the chance to defend it. Washington had been incensed by malicious gossip, passed on by one of his former captains, William Peachey, that the great scare of spring 1756, when the frontier reeled under the prospect of Indian attack, was simply a "scheme" by which he, as Virginia's commander in chief, hoped to enhance his own influence by extracting men and money from the gullible Assembly. He denied such slanders with a passion:

> *It is uncertain in what light my services may have appeared to Your Honor—But this I know, and it is the highest consolation I am capable of feeling; that no man that ever was employed in a public capacity has endeavored to discharge the trust reposed in him with greater honesty, and more zeal for the country's interest, than I have done: and if there is any person living, who can say with justice that I have offered any intentional wrong to the public, I will cheerfully submit to the most ignominious punishment that an injured people ought to inflict!*[77]

Dinwiddie knew nothing of such stories and advised Washington to ignore them. Looking back over their sometimes troubled four-year relationship, however, the long-suffering Scot was adamant that any blame for the recent breakdown lay with Washington: "My conduct to you from the beginning was always friendly," he wrote, "but you know I had great reason to suspect you of ingratitude." Dinwiddie had the king's leave to sail for England in November; he could only wish that his successor as incoming lieutenant governor would show Washington as much friendship as he had done.[78]

Washington's touchiness was exacerbated by his own declining health. Attempting the impossible had stretched him to the limit, mentally and physically. Under the continuous strain, even his formidable constitution began to crack. By August 1757, Washington was suffering from the "bloody flux," the graphically descriptive slang for the pre-twentieth-century soldier's all-too-frequent companion, dysentery. When fever ensued, his friend, regimental officer, and personal physician James Craik resorted to the era's customary response and bled him copiously: applied three times in two days, this drastic treatment not surprisingly left him weaker than ever and incapable of even walking. On November 9, it was Washington's close friend and aide-de-camp Robert Stewart who informed Dinwiddie that his colonel had reluctantly followed Dr. Craik's strong recommendation to seek a change of air and "some place where he can be kept quiet" as offering the best chance of recovery.[79]

That same day, with winter fast approaching and no improvement to his condition in sight, Washington quit his Winchester headquarters. He headed home to Mount Vernon, to recuperate or die.

4

TARNISHED VICTORY

Save for servants, Mount Vernon was empty and lonely. At nearby
Belvoir, Sally Fairfax was likewise almost alone. To Washington's
great grief, his staunch friend, patron, and surrogate father Colonel William Fairfax had died on September 2, 1757; Sally's husband,
George William, had traveled to England to deal with inheritance
matters. Sally knew nothing of Washington's presence just a few
miles away, and, with her husband absent, for reasons of decorum
he hesitated to even inform her of it.

It was only after he had been examined by a physician, the Reverend Charles Green of Alexandria, who forbade meat and recommended an insipid diet of "jellies and such kind of food," that
Washington finally took the plunge and wrote to Belvoir, seeking a
recipe book and the necessary ingredients. Whether Sally responded
to this pitiful appeal is not disclosed in the surviving correspondence. That any contact between them was kept to a minimum, and
by Sally's choice, is suggested by the message that Washington later
sent over to Belvoir along with a letter announcing George William Fairfax's safe arrival in London: this yearned wistfully for the
"favor" of a visit from her.[1]

The New Year brought little improvement to Washington's condition. When, in January 1758, he set out for Williamsburg to avail
himself of its wider medical knowledge, he fell so ill on the way that
he was obliged to turn back. As spring came on, Washington had
grounds to fear "an approaching decay" and that, like his beloved
half brother Lawrence, he faced a lingering cough-racked death by

consumption. Reporting to his immediate superior officer, Colonel Stanwix of the Royal Americans, Washington lamented that his ruined constitution had quashed any last "prospect of preferment in a military life"; under the circumstances, it was perhaps better that he should resign his command, making way for another, more capable person whose efforts might be crowned by greater success.[2]

Despite such pessimistic predictions, in early March 1758, Washington finally managed to complete the painful journey to Williamsburg. There, he consulted Virginia's most eminent physician, Dr. John Amson. His pronouncement that George was in no obvious danger acted like a powerful tonic upon him. Reprieved from an early grave, his thoughts now turned to the future in general, and to matrimony in particular.

Washington's infatuation with Sally Fairfax is clear evidence of his fondness for women. But Sally was unobtainable, and, as already noted, his approaches were confined to those of a knight-errant espousing an idealized "courtly love." That Washington *was* attracted to females on the earthlier level to be expected from a young man in his early twenties is strongly suggested by a lascivious letter from his close friend George Mercer, sent from South Carolina during the previous summer. Not only did Charleston's buildings compare unfavorably with Williamsburg's, but the local "fair ones" were also, in Mercer's opinion, "very far inferior to the beauties" of Virginia. The Carolina girls were wary of encouraging advances, fearing the "multiplicity of scandal" in their gossip-fueled society; in any event, Mercer was scarcely tempted to try his luck. Employing breathless language that surely indicates that this cannot have been the first time that he and his colonel had discussed such matters, Mercer observed: "Many of them are crooked and have a very bad air and not those enticing, heaving, throbbing, alluring letch, exciting, plump breasts common with our northern belles."[3]

On his way to consult Dr. Amson, Washington had called at White House in New Kent County, the home of the recently widowed Martha Dandridge Custis. Returning from Williamsburg with a clean bill of health, the reinvigorated Washington felt strong enough to start courting her in earnest. Whether the twenty-six-year-old widow of Daniel Parke Custis matched Mercer's physical criteria for Virginian womanhood is unclear from surviving portraits, but her other attractions were certainly ample enough: with an estate assessed at the best part of £24,000, she was one of the colony's wealthiest matches.

Through her family, Martha enjoyed connections that may have exerted further appeal for an ambitious young gentleman driven by notions of martial glory. Martha's uncle, William Dandridge, had served in the Royal Navy, and, like Captain Lawrence Washington, saw action during the ill-fated expedition to Cartagena. In addition, her late husband's grandfather, the Virginian-born Daniel Parke II, had climbed high within the British Army, and was present at one of the era's pivotal battles as aide-de-camp to none other than John Churchill, the legendary Duke of Marlborough. When Marlborough drubbed the French and Bavarians at Blenheim in 1704, it was Colonel Parke who had been granted the singular honor of delivering news of the victory to Queen Anne. When he finally arrived at Windsor Castle after an eight-day journey, Parke showed his monarch the duke's first unofficial announcement of his victory, famously scribbled to his wife Sarah on the back of a tavern bill, then gave her his own eyewitness account of events. The customary reward for the bearer of such momentous tidings was 500 guineas, but Parke artfully asked for his delighted monarch's miniature instead. The colonel's unorthodox request paid off handsomely: the queen's portrait came in a diamond-studded golden locket and was accompanied by *1,000* guineas. Despite this spectacular high point of distinction, Parke's subsequent career was dogged by disappointment, scandal, and tragedy. Hoping for appointment as royal governor of his native Virginia, to his intense chagrin Parke was instead posted to the far-flung, lawless and unhealthy Leeward Islands. There, his bitterness gave vent to debauchery: he reputedly proved so rapacious toward the islanders' wives and daughters that in 1710, on Antigua, their outraged menfolk lost patience, rioted, and lynched him. For all his brutal and ignominious end, Colonel Parke had nonetheless penetrated the privileged inner circles of Britain's military and imperial establishment. A reminder of that fact was a fine portrait of Parke in his dashing prime, red coated, bewigged, and flaunting his miniature of Queen Anne, which looked down on Washington when he came courting at White House; given his own repeated but fruitless attempts to infiltrate the ranks of the British Army, it must surely have stirred both interest and envy.[4]

The strapping and confident Washington clearly made a favorable impression upon the diminutive Martha, who was less than five feet tall. Within a month of first calling upon her, he apparently made a formal proposal of marriage and was accepted. Martha Custis was accompanied not only by a sizable fortune, but by two children. John and Martha, familiarly known as "Jacky" and "Patsy," were aged four and two: Washington's forthcoming marriage would bring with it a ready-made family and the responsibilities of a stepfather. Soon after resuming his command at Fort Loudoun, Winchester, in early April, Washington ordered what was in all likelihood his wedding suit. By the first ship bound for Virginia, Richard Washington in London was instructed to send enough "of the best superfine blue cotton velvet as will make a coat, waistcoat and breeches for a tall man with a fine silk button to suit it and all other necessary trimmings and linings together with garters for the breeches."[5]

By then the military situation, like Washington's own domestic prospects, had undergone a dramatic transformation. The new ministry in London, fronted by the energetic and charismatic Pitt, was determined to change Britain's dismal record in North America. Discredited by his failure to deliver a victorious offensive, Lord Loudoun was recalled in March 1758 and replaced by his fellow Scot, Major General James Abercromby. In essence, however, Pitt's strategy for the coming campaign followed a blueprint that Loudoun had already prepared in February, which sought to learn from the bitter lessons of the previous year.[6] Instead of one main thrust against New France, there would now be three: besides a fresh seaborne expedition bound for Louisbourg, another large army would proceed against Montreal and Quebec via the Champlain Valley; in addition, and as Washington had long urged to anyone willing to listen, there would be a new attempt to take Fort Duquesne and belatedly avenge Braddock's defeat.[7]

The renewed Ohio offensive was to be led by the fifty-year-old Brigadier General John Forbes, an experienced and tactful Scot who offered a striking contrast to the bluff and outspoken Braddock. His army, which, on paper at least, was almost three times the size of that assembled in 1755, would include a kernel of British regular troops. These redcoats were all newly raised: thirteen companies of Montgomery's Highlanders and four of the Royal Americans. Both of these units were unconventional by British Army standards: Montgomery's was overwhelmingly composed of Gaelic-speaking Scottish Highlanders, while the Royal Americans mustered a mixed bag of manpower, including many Germans recruited in Europe and Pennsylvania. The remaining two-thirds of Forbes's projected 6,000-strong force would be composed of provincials from Pennsylvania and Virginia, with smaller contingents from Maryland, North Carolina, and Delaware.

For the coming campaign, Virginia resolved to raise a second regiment, appointing the prominent planter William Byrd III, who had served as a volunteer aide to Loudoun, as its colonel. This decision to double the Old Dominion's manpower to 2,000, which flew in the face of its previous niggardly defense policy, resulted from Pitt's unexpected announcement that the costs involved in equipping and maintaining all American provincial forces would henceforth be met by His Britannic Majesty's government, with other expenses to be reimbursed in due course.[8] Virginia's resulting readiness to pay generous enlistment bounties in 1758 ensured that both of its regiments were brought up to strength with genuine volunteers rather than truculent conscripts. But while Pitt's openhandedness worked an immediate and positive impact upon colonial willingness to support the Mother Country's war effort, it had unforeseen consequences that would ultimately prove disastrous for British North America.

By April 1758, Washington's health was restored, and he clearly hoped to play a prominent part in the coming campaign. Congratulating Colonel Stanwix on his promotion to brigadier general, Washington asked him to mention his name to Forbes—not as one who sought further advancement, but rather as "a person who would gladly be distinguished in some measure from the *common run* of provincial officers," of whom he understood there was to be "a motley herd." Asking the same favor of his old friend Thomas Gage, who was now colonel of a newly formed regiment of light infantry, Washington felt the request was not unreasonable: after all, he had "been much longer in the service than any provincial officer in America."[9]

Washington's eagerness to serve was increased by another of Pitt's initiatives, aimed at soothing relations between British regulars and their colonial colleagues: this tackled the vexing problem of relative "rank" by stipulating that for the future all provincial officers—including majors, lieutenant colonels and full colonels—would only be subject to orders from regulars of their own grade or above.[10]

For a man like Washington, who had twice failed to exert his authority over men holding, or claiming to hold, a royal captain's commission, this was a crucial concession. A regular colonel would still outrank a colonial one, but that was a realistic ruling and accepted as such. For all the enduring stereotypes of bumbling port-soaked majors or smooth-cheeked foppish ensigns looking down their powdered noses at savvy colonials, the typical British officer rose through merit and hard service. Even though most commissions were bought for set fees, progression up the chain of seniority was only permitted if the candidate had experience to match the responsibility. By contrast, many provincial captains, particularly in New England, were simply "elected" by the men of the companies they would lead, a selection process often based on personal popularity rather than military capacity. Indeed, Washington himself had gained the coveted rank of major at the stroke of Governor Dinwiddie's pen for nothing more dangerous than agreeing to oversee militia musters; a regular officer might face fifteen or more years of hard and bloody service, rising from ensign to lieutenant and then captain under the gimlet eye of King George II before achieving equivalent status, if he ever did. It was only right and proper that when British and colonial officers of similar rank served together in America, the regular should take seniority.

During the spring of 1758, while Washington remained at Winchester, General Forbes established his headquarters at Philadelphia, slowly assembling the various components of his expedition. As Lord Loudoun's adjutant general in 1757, Forbes was a specialist in logistics, but, like Braddock before him, he was soon exasperated by the cynical double-dealing he encountered as he tried to amass the wagons and supplies needed to move his army westward.

Recruiting reliable Indian allies for the coming offensive was another headache. During his stint as Loudoun's right-hand man, Forbes had also been at the forefront of attempts to adapt the British Army for war in the American backwoods and well knew the value of tribal allies. Forbes was therefore delighted to learn that a powerful force of southern Indians—Cherokees and Catawbas—had converged upon Winchester to join his campaign. When Washington wrote to Brigadier Stanwix on April 10, some 500 warriors had already reached the little Shenandoah Valley town, mostly setting off to seek the enemy on the frontiers of Virginia and Maryland. More were on their way. Drawing upon hard experience, Washington warned that it would prove difficult to retain these warriors' services unless Forbes's campaign started promptly. If there were delays and the Indians went home, then no words could express how much they would be missed. In Washington's opinion, the security of Forbes's army as it marched against Fort Duquesne would depend upon the assistance of tribal allies, making their management "an affair of great importance," demanding "the closest attention of the commanding officer" himself.[11]

Forbes was unschooled in the etiquette of Indian diplomacy, but to his dismay and growing anger, neither of Britain's official Indian superintendents, Sir William Johnson and Edmond Atkin, or even their deputies, was willing to help manage these capricious warriors. True to form, the Cherokees demanded a steady supply of costly presents and provisions. Expecting Forbes's main army to muster and march immediately, they grew bored and drifted home as the weeks dragged by with no hint of an offensive. Struggling with paperwork in distant Philadelphia, Forbes could do nothing as the most formidable force of Indians yet assembled to aid a British army dwindled away to just a few score warriors.

Given Washington's experience of frontier warfare, Forbes counted upon him and his veteran Virginians to play a key role in the coming campaign. Back in March, on hearing rumors of Washington's resignation, Forbes had written to Virginia's acting governor, John Blair, expressing his disappointment at losing a soldier with "the character of a good and knowing officer in the back countries." Greatly flattered, Washington thanked Forbes heartily for this good opinion when he wrote to congratulate him "on the promising prospect of a glorious campaign." Forbes's faith in Washington and his men was bolstered by the verdict of his quartermaster general, that notoriously quarrelsome and picky survivor of Braddock's expedition, Sir John St. Clair. He had seen four companies of the 1st Virginia Regiment at Winchester, observing that, if the other six were as good, Forbes could "expect a great deal of service" from a unit that did honor to its colonel.[12]

St. Clair's assessment testifies to Washington's determined efforts to shape his regiment into an elite unit. His success in doing so had already been apparent in Charleston during the previous summer, where the two companies sent there under Adam Stephen and George Mercer had impressed the Royal Americans. According to Mercer, these regulars had expected "to see a parcel of ragged, disorderly fellows headed by officers of their own stamp (like the rest of the provincials they had seen)." Instead, they had encountered "men properly disposed who made a good and soldier-like appearance"; who were capable of performing "in every particular as well as could be expected from any troops"; and under officers who were clearly gentlemen, complete with sashes and gorgets to denote their rank, "genteel uniforms," and with swords properly hung and hats smartly cocked. By dint of such efficiency and élan, Washington's men had "lost that common appellation of provincials"; instead, they were distinguished by "the style and title of the detachment of the Virginia Regiment." As Lieutenant Colonel Stephen proudly reported to Washington, his men were both well disciplined and versatile, "and have this advantage of all other troops in America, that they know the parade as well as Prussians, and the fighting in a close country as well as Tartars."[13] Even allowing for some boasting by his subordinates, Washington had forged an unusually flexible and efficient formation, skilled in both regular and irregular warfare: this was precisely the versatility that Lord Loudoun had sought to instill within his own redcoat battalions.

At the start of the 1758 campaign, therefore, Washington's stock with Forbes stood high. But for reasons concerned less with strategy than with colonial politics he was soon to forfeit much of that goodwill. Forbes's original plan had envisaged advancing from Philadelphia via the Pennsylvanian settlements of Carlisle and Raystown to Fort Cumberland in Maryland. From there, his army would follow the existing road to Fort Duquesne, painstakingly created by Braddock's doomed command three years earlier. Even at this early stage, the mere fact that Forbes's troops would concentrate on Conococheague Creek, within Pennsylvanian territory, was enough to set Washington's Virginian hackles rising. On April 18, he wrote to St. Clair, warning that the Indians would take umbrage, as they had long been accustomed to resort to Winchester, leaving from and returning to Fort Loudoun there. This objection merely hinted at a far greater controversy to come, which would "cast its shadow" over Washington's role in the 1758 campaign.[14]

Brigadier General Forbes was seriously ill at the opening of his expedition, and became more so as it progressed; tormented by the all-too-prevalent "flux," it is possible that he was also suffering from stomach cancer. Like so many other Scots to be found on the Appalachian frontier during the 1750s—men like Adam Stephen and James Craik of the Virginia Regiment—Forbes had studied medicine before gaining his first commission, and he now took a grim professional pleasure in chronicling his own ailments. Battling sickness as much the enemy, he was obliged to orchestrate his campaign from the rear, entrusting frontline leadership to his second in command, the thirty-nine-year-old Lieutenant Colonel Henri Bouquet of the Royal American Regiment. Bouquet was an excellent choice for the job. Born in Switzerland, like many of his countrymen Bouquet learned his trade as a mercenary: before becoming an officer of King George II he had held commissions in the armies of Sardinia and the Dutch Republic. During the previous autumn Bouquet had commanded at Charleston, South Carolina, establishing a rapport with the officers of the two companies of Washington's regiment who had been sent there by Loudoun.

In keeping with Forbes's plan to safeguard his supply line and avoid lengthy wagon trains, Bouquet anchored the army's advance upon carefully fortified depots, established forty to fifty miles apart; the first of these was at Raystown, about 100 miles from Fort Duquesne, where the army's advance units, including half of the 1st Virginia Regiment under the experienced Lieutenant Colonel Stephen, concentrated in early summer. Unlike Braddock's command, which had enjoyed no such safety net, if by some mischance Forbes's army met with a check in the wilderness it would have fallback positions within reach, so preventing a local defeat from escalating into a headlong rout. Somewhat ironically, as Forbes himself acknowledged, this "protected advance" strategy was taken directly from a recent military manual, published in 1754 by a *French* officer, Lancelot, Comte Turpin de Crissé.[15]

Like Forbes, with whom he worked well, Bouquet was an unusually enlightened soldier, schooled in the traditions of European warfare but also keen to adapt to American conditions. When Colonels Washington and Byrd each proposed the radical step of dressing their men "after the Indian fashion" for the coming campaign, both the general and his second in command greeted their initiative with enthusiasm. As so few genuine Indians now remained with the army, white men equipped like "savages" could prove useful as scouts, Forbes told Bouquet, "for as you justly observe, the shadow may often be taken for the reality, and I must confess in this country, we must comply and learn the art of war, from enemy Indians or anything [sic] else who have seen the country and war carried on in it."[16]

Washington's readiness to field an entire regiment dressed like tribal warriors, swapping their regulation coats, breeches, and spatter-dashes for "Indian leggings," shirts, blankets, and even "breech-clouts" (loincloths), is intriguing, particularly given his previous insistence upon high standards of regimental dress and his personal penchant for fine clothing. That the same man who in 1754 had naïvely assumed that blood-red uniforms would impress Indians could now adopt such informal "Indian dress" for officers and men alike also reveals the impact of frontier warfare upon Washington's evolution as a soldier; by 1758, hard reality had supplanted romantic fancy. As Washington explained to Bouquet that July, "proceeding as light as any Indian in the woods" was "an unbecoming dress I confess for an officer, but convenience rather than show I think should be consulted."

When 200 of Washington's men arrived at Raystown under the veteran Major Lewis, all decked out Indian-fashion, Bouquet was delighted. He thanked Washington for "this extraordinary dispatch," whose "dress should be our pattern on this expedition."

As Bouquet prepared to march his troops across the forbidding, forested Allegheny Mountains, he was not simply concerned with appearances. During the first weeks of August, on the fields outside Raystown camp, he drilled his regulars and provincials in tactics intended to repel any attack upon his line of march in the woods. One unusually observant eyewitness, the Reverend Thomas Barton, noted that Bouquet arrayed his troops in four parallel columns, each of two men abreast and separated by about fifty yards. After marching for some distance in this formation, the troops shook out into one long, two-deep line, capable of keeping up "an incessant fire." This fusillade was followed by "a sham pursuit with shrieks and halloos in the Indian way" before the line rallied and reformed.

As Bouquet informed Forbes, such "a very long front" would stymie the standard French and Indian tactics, which invariably sought to outflank and surround the enemy.[17]

Washington was initially ordered to concentrate his men at Fort Cumberland and then start building a road northward to connect with Raystown. Because of the supply and transport problems that dogged the campaign, it was only in late June that Washington could begin his advance to Wills Creek, which he reached on July 3 with the remaining five companies of his own regiment. Colonel Byrd arrived four days later with eight companies of the 2nd Virginia Regiment and about fifty Indians he had brought from the Carolinas. Washington now contemplated surroundings that were familiar, if scarcely auspicious: it was from Wills Creek that he had embarked upon his fruitless diplomatic mission in 1753; from there that he had set off on two ill-fated attempts to seize the Forks of the Ohio in 1754 and 1755; and the rickety stockades of Fort Cumberland had often provoked controversy during the frustrating years of command since then.

As Washington awaited further orders, Forbes dropped what proved to be a bombshell for the Virginians. Acting on the advice of his engineers and of his cousin James Glen, the former lieutenant governor of South Carolina, the general announced that he had now changed his mind about the army's route to Fort Duquesne. Instead of doglegging down from Raystown to Fort Cumberland and then following the old Braddock Road, it would push directly westward across the Alleghenies to the Forks of the Ohio. Explaining his reasoning to William Pitt, Forbes emphasized that this would shorten his route, and "labor of cutting the road, [by] about 40 miles." Indeed, using Braddock's Road would save little work, as in the three years since it was first cut it had become swamped by the returning forest.[18]

Washington, Byrd and their fellow Virginians were aghast at this unexpected, last-minute change of plan. More than disinterested military factors lay behind their response. Ever the proud Virginian, Washington was outraged that his own colony now looked set to lose the monopoly of what would likely become the key post-war artery to the unexploited west, giving access to those rich and tempting lands that his expert surveyor's eye had assessed when he first penetrated the Ohio Country in 1753. The fact that the profits would be reaped by the Old Dominion's archrival Pennsylvania only salted the wound.

In coming weeks, Washington worked assiduously to convince Bouquet, and through him Forbes, that Braddock's Road remained the best route forward. The resulting rift between Washington and his commanders dealt a damaging blow to his reputation as a trustworthy officer worthy of the king's commission, and he had no one but himself to blame.

Although Washington lost no opportunity to champion the old road and disparage the new, for many weeks Bouquet refused to question his motives for doing so. Washington's track record as a brave, selfless officer gave no reason to suspect that he was acting for anything other than the good of His Majesty's service. Although he had been granted leave to travel to Winchester, where he was standing to represent Frederick County in the Assembly elections, Washington did not take it. This decision was influenced by rumors that "a body of light troops" would soon be pushed forward; keen as ever for a chance to pursue his quest for military glory, Washington lobbied Bouquet to employ both himself and his regiment.[19]

Indeed, on July 24 —the very same day that Washington topped the Winchester poll, bagging 309 of the 397 votes cast—Bouquet assured him that Forbes had mentioned several times how much he depended upon him and his Virginians and would lose no opportunity to exploit his experience and "knowledge of the country." Two days later, Bouquet informed Forbes of his confidence that Colonel Washington was "animated by a sincere zeal to contribute to the success of this expedition, and ready to march from whatever direction you may determine with the same eagerness." On the day after that, Bouquet wrote to Washington again, not doubting that the Virginian was "above all the influences of prejudices and ready

to go heartily where reason and judgment shall direct." In an effort
to clarify matters, "so that we all center in one and the same opinion," Bouquet proposed that he and Washington should meet midway between Fort Cumberland and Raystown on July 29. During
their discussion, however, the true reasons for Washington's implacable hostility toward the new road soon became all too clear to
the Swiss veteran. As he wearily told Forbes, "Most of these gentlemen do not know the difference between a party and an army, and
find everything easy which agrees with their ideas, jumping over all
difficulties."[20]

Any lingering doubt in the matter was removed by a letter that
Washington soon after wrote to an old friend from the Braddock
campaign, Forbes's aide-de-camp, Major Francis Halkett of the
44th Foot. This was an unsubtle attempt to use Halkett—a worthy,
if not especially bright staff officer—to sway Forbes against the
Raystown route. "If Colonel Bouquet succeeds in this point with
the General," Washington warned Halkett, "all is lost! All is lost
by Heavens!" There would be no victors' laurels to be gathered;
instead, the delays involved in straying off the "beaten path" and
negotiating a succession of daunting mountains would scupper
the entire campaign.[21]

This gambit was all the more reprehensible because on that very
same day, August 2, Washington sent Bouquet a minutely detailed
recapitulation of his case in favor of Braddock's Road, which concluded with a solemn declaration that all was proposed for the best
reasons, without "any private interest, or sinister views." But by now,
even the tolerant Forbes had reached the limits of his patience. On
August 9, apparently after stumbling across Washington's melodra-
matic note to the hapless Halkett, he wrote to Bouquet: "By a very
unguarded letter of Colonel Washington, that accidentally fell into
my hands, I am now at the bottom, of their [the Virginians'] scheme
against this new road, a scheme that I think was a shame for any
officer to be concerned in." Two days later, Forbes informed the
commander in chief, Major General Abercromby, that Washington
was the "leader and adviser" of the Virginians' "foolish suggestions."

This was hardly the kind of notice at British Army headquarters that Washington wanted.[22]

Not surprisingly, Washington's intrigues undermined Forbes's faith in him as an officer and cost him much of the credit he had accumulated as the expedition's expert on frontier warfare. In early September, when Forbes believed the time was right to march the remaining Virginians from Fort Cumberland to join the main army at Raystown camp, he mentioned to Bouquet that he "would consult Colonel Washington, although perhaps not follow his advice, as his behavior about the roads, was no ways like a soldier."[23]

In fact, Washington's "behavior" was even worse than his disappointed commanders believed. A few days earlier, he had sent a letter to his staunch friend John Robinson, the speaker of Virginia's House of Burgesses, which painted the campaign in the most pessimistic light. All hopes of winning glory were gone, he predicted, and only a miracle could produce "a happy issue." In Washington's opinion, the campaign's "miscarriage" resulted from the conduct of its leaders, who were "dupes," or perhaps "something worse," to "Pennsylvanian artifice." Rather than let such slights to Virginia pass unchallenged, he added, a "full representation of the matter" should go before the king. Washington even volunteered to present this in person: "I think without vanity I could set the conduct of this expedition in its true colors, having taken some pains, perhaps more than any other, to dive into the bottom of it." For good measure, Washington added a line lifted from a letter he had recently received from his former military secretary John Kirkpatrick bemoaning "the luckless fate of poor Virginia to fall a victim to the views of her crafty neighbors."[24]

The wrangling over the rival roads is significant, and not simply for what it reveals of the young Washington's stubbornness. For all his apparent desire to enter the imperial establishment by gaining a regular army commission and the approval of British commanders, at heart Washington remained a Virginian. His overriding loyalty to the colony of his birth epitomizes the reluctance of British North America's inhabitants to abandon local allegiances for the greater good. Little wonder that London-based commentators in the 1750s still used the "mother-child" metaphor to characterize the relationship between Britain and her colonies: all too often, from Whitehall's perspective, the colonists behaved like unruly offspring—selfish, jealous, and addicted to bickering among themselves. It seemed incredible that they could ever share a broader identity as Americans and work together.

During the late summer of 1758, Brigadier General Forbes had enough on his plate without having to adjudicate colonial rivalries. His own woes were exacerbated by troubling news from the north: although Major General Jeffery Amherst's army had clawed itself ashore on Cape Breton and commenced besieging the fortress of Louisbourg, the great force of redcoats and provincials led up the Hudson Valley by the commander in chief, James Abercromby, had been decisively defeated. On July 8, his frontal assault upon the French lines at Ticonderoga was bloodily repulsed; that disaster compounded another, two days earlier, when Abercromby's second in command, Brigadier General George Augustus Howe, was killed in a skirmish after landing at the head of Lake George. During his short time in America, the dashing Lord Howe, who was the eldest of three brothers destined to make a mark upon the continent's history, had achieved unprecedented popularity among the colonial population. Courteous and debonair, yet fearless, tough, and practical, Howe had personified the qualities of gentleman warrior that Washington himself held so dear. His untimely death, which robbed the Anglo-American cause of its most promising leader, was widely seen as a catastrophe, with Washington among the many who sincerely lamented "the loss of that brave and active nobleman."[25]

Despite these bleak tidings from the New York frontier and for all the frustrating setbacks that jinxed his own campaign—chronic supply problems, the "desertion" of his Indian allies, and, not least, his deplorable health—Forbes remained optimistic. The implacable Scot had planted other plans, and his army's methodical advance allowed them time to mature. In contrast to Braddock, who had given little weight to Indian diplomacy, Forbes appreciated that tribal support was crucial to the campaign's outcome. This was not simply cynical politicking. Sympathetic to the Ohio Indians' perspective, Forbes analyzed the underlying reasons for their disaffection. In a dispatch to Pitt, he identified problems destined to sour relations between whites and Indians long after the colonists had won their independence from Britain and the frontier had shifted far to the west. Forbes blamed the current pro-French disposition of the Shawnees and Delawares upon the abuses of "the saddest of mortals called Indian traders," and the "madness" of thrusting settlements into the Indians' hunting grounds.[26]

Forbes's hopes of luring these hostile nations to a peace conference now rested largely upon unlikely allies. The Quaker Israel Pemberton, who led the Friendly Association for Regaining and Preserving Peace with the Indians by Pacific Measures, had already given credence to that long-winded title by establishing contact with the Ohio tribes. Pemberton's initiative was bolstered by the courage and persuasiveness of a Moravian missionary, Christian Frederick Post. He embarked upon a hazardous journey among the Delawares, bearing invitations from Forbes and Governor William Denny of Pennsylvania for them to return to their former lands along Pennsylvania's Susquehanna River. Braving appalling dangers, the tenacious Post proved remarkably successful. While the French could only look on in vexation, he coaxed their key Indian allies into giving him a hearing, heeding his words of reconciliation, and agreeing to attend a great conference scheduled to be held at Easton, Pennsylvania, in October. With an increasingly realistic prospect of unpicking New France's Indian alliance network on the Ohio, Forbes was no longer so anxious to forge ahead. As he put it in a cryptic observation to Bouquet on August 9, "As we are now so late, we are yet too soon. This is a parable that I shall soon explain."[27]

Although most of the Cherokees had long since quit Forbes's army, clashing ominously with the frontier folk of northwest Virginia as they rambled home, his force retained the services of a small, but significant, contingent of warriors from other southern tribes. In late August about fifty Indians—Catawbas, Tuscaroras, and Nottoways—arrived at Raystown. As the Reverend Barton reported, these warriors craved vengeance: for the death of their English "brothers" under Braddock, whose bones they had seen scattered at the Monongahela, and for the Catawba chief Captain Bullen, freshly slain in an ambush near Fort Cumberland. As Washington informed Bouquet, the loss of Captain Bullen and another warrior killed alongside him, Captain French, was a heavy blow, as they "were very remarkable for their bravery, and attachment to our interest." Both were buried with military honors.[28]

As the summer dragged on and Washington's command at Fort Cumberland awaited orders to advance, other soldiers of the 1st Virginia Regiment encountered the enemy at closer quarters. One of them, Michael Scully, had a narrow escape after he was bushwhacked by Indians as he rounded up horses outside Raystown camp. As Adam Stephen reported to Washington, Scully—an Irishman and a former butcher—was confronted by two warriors who aimed their guns at him; luckily, the weather was wet and their powder damp, and both missed fire. One of the Indians ran forward wielding his tomahawk, but Scully shot him down when he was just four paces away. Scully felled another Indian with the butt of his musket but was instantly seized by a third, who wounded him twice in the head with a sword and slashed him across the face with his scalping knife. That Indian tried to take the Irishman's scalp, but "Scully being very strong" threw him down on top of the second Indian, "gave him a stroke with his gun" for good measure, then, imagining more of the enemy were coming up, ran into camp covered in wounds. For a forty-five-year-old described in the muster roll of Major Lewis's company as having "very large though clumsy limbs," it was an impressive performance. Equally noteworthy is Stephen's assumption that his colonel would *know* who Scully was; it testifies to Washington's keen interest in his men, and the importance of such paternalism for his regiment's fighting spirit.[29]

Scully's determined stand and his arrival in camp "in a bloody condition" was duly reported by Colonel Bouquet in a dispatch to Forbes and also featured in the Reverend Barton's diary, which noted anything of unusual interest.[30] Barton was curious to see Fort Cumberland and arrived there on the evening of September 6 to find Washington and Lieutenant Colonel George Mercer of the 2nd Virginia Regiment encamped with 850 of their men. Both officers treated Barton and his companions to "a very polite reception, and generous, hospitable, entertainment." On the morning of Sunday, September, 10, Barton preached a sermon, "by desire of Colonel Washington from Nehemiah 4-14."[31] Washington's choice of text is perhaps significant and, given the ongoing row over the roads, suggestive of his prevailing Virginian, rather than broader British, loyalties:

And I looked, and rose up, and said unto the nobles, and to the rulers, and to the rest of the people, Be not ye afraid of them: remember the Lord, which is great and terrible, and fight for your brethren, your sons, and your daughters, and your houses.

The next day, Washington unexpectedly received a "short, but very agreeable" letter that immediately pushed the fortunes of the Old Dominion and Fort Duquesne into the background. Dated September 1, it was from Sally Fairfax. Before the start of the campaign, and with a view to his impending marriage to Martha Custis, Washington had ordered an extensive remodeling of Mount Vernon. When George William Fairfax wrote to update Washington on the progress of the renovations, his wife Sally apparently took the opportunity to tease her old admirer about his brisk courtship; as Washington phrased it—in words that may repeat Sally's—"the animating prospect of possessing Mrs. Custis."

As usual, Sally's note has vanished, but she saved Washington's reply.[32] It makes for revealing reading. Written as Washington was once again poised to lead his men into danger, it indicates that, whatever else he had pledged to Martha Custis and for all the

painting and plastering at Mount Vernon, his heart still belonged
to Sally Fairfax. Washington professed himself a "votary to Love,"
but the object of his affections was not his intended bride. His
words leave no doubt of that:

> *I acknowledge that a lady is in the case—and further I confess,
> that this lady is known to you. Yes Madam, as well as she is
> to one, who is too sensible of her charms to deny the power,
> whose influence he feels and must ever submit to. I feel the
> force of her amiable beauties in the recollection of a thousand
> tender passages that I could wish to obliterate, 'til I am bid to
> revive them. . . . You have drawn me my dear Madam, or rather
> have I drawn myself, into an honest confession of a simple fact.
> Misconstrue not my meaning—'tis obvious—doubt it not, nor
> expose it.*

In her letter, Sally had declared that she was happy, leading Washington to make a curious confession for a man about to marry: "I
wish I was happy also."

The conclusion that Sally Fairfax, rather than Martha Custis,
remained the real object of Washington's affections in the summer
of 1758 is confirmed by his next letter to her.[33] This was written
in response to Sally's reply, again missing, to his latest testament
of love. Washington opened with a telling question: "Do we still
misunderstand the true meaning of each other's letters? I think it
must appear so, though I would feign hope the contrary as I cannot speak plainer without—but I'll say no more, and leave you to
guess the rest."

But what Washington went on to say, after updating Sally with
news of Forbes's campaign, was plain enough to anyone remotely
familiar with Joseph Addison's play *Cato*, a tragedy first performed
in London in 1713, and especially admired in British North America.
Rather than participating in the campaign against Fort Duquesne,
Washington wrote, he would consider his time "more agreeable
spent believe me, in playing a part in Cato . . . and myself doubly

happy in being the Juba to such a Marcia as you must make." As Marcia was Cato's daughter, and Juba the Numidian prince obliged to hide his love for her, the message was obvious.

The fortnight that separated Washington's two impassioned letters to Sally Fairfax must have found him in emotional turmoil; that same period proved a dramatic watershed for Forbes's campaign. During August the controversial road from Raystown had been pushed across the daunting barriers of Allegheny Mountain and Laurel Hill; by September 1, an advance guard of 1,500 men was constructing the next fortified depot on Loyalhanna Creek, fifty miles from Fort Duquesne.

Given the rugged terrain, this was steady progress; but it was too slow for some. Riding back into Raystown on the evening of September 10, the Reverend Barton encountered a depressing atmosphere: "The season is far advanced," he noted. "The leaves begin to fall, the forage to wither, and cold nights to approach. All these circumstances concur to damp our spirits, and make us uneasy." It required the physical presence of General Forbes to dispel the gloom. He finally arrived in camp on September 15, escorted by dashing light horsemen and stolid Highlanders. Forbes was, as Barton reported, "in a low state," so ill that he was slung in a contraption resembling a horse-borne sedan chair. Yet the appearance of the frail, sickly Scot worked wonders on his jaded army: he smiled at the crowds who turned out to greet him, and the troops seemed "inspired with fresh spirits," with every face now cheerful.[34]

Washington lost no time in writing to Forbes, passing on good wishes for his recovery; the general appreciated the sentiment, "being quite as feeble now as a child almost." For all his pain, Forbes had not lost his dark sense of humor: hearing that Colonel Byrd was also sick, he advised him to come to Raystown, "where I should hope to prove a better physician than he will probably meet with at Fort Cumberland." Byrd, another victim of dysentery, was too weak to move, but Washington visited the general, arriving in camp on the evening of September 16, accompanied by clattering troopers of Captain Stewart's light horse. He returned to Fort Cumberland next day with orders to march the Virginians into camp.

On September 21, Washington, Byrd, and the rest of their men finally joined Forbes's army. They found the general in somber mood, and with good reason: on the previous evening he had received disheartening news from Loyalhanna. In a rare lapse of judgment, Bouquet, the advance guard commander, had approved a proposal from the ambitious Major James Grant of Montgomery's Highlanders to lead a reconnaissance in force against Fort Duquesne. Besides reconnoitering that post, there was talk of retaliating against the "Indian rabble" that had launched irritating raids on Loyalhanna. Beyond that, Grant's mission was vague: as Bouquet told Forbes, the major's actions were to be "guided by the circumstances."[35]

Major Grant had left Loyalhanna on September 9 at the head of a picked detachment of about 800 regulars and provincials, including more than 150 men from Washington's 1st Virginia Regiment under Major Lewis and all the available Indians. Pausing at a forward entrenchment established by Washington's old antagonist John Dagworthy, now a lieutenant colonel, by the evening of September 13, Grant's troops were within striking distance of their objective. Present among the Virginians was young Ensign Thomas Gist, the son of Washington's wilderness guide Christopher Gist. He remembered that they had been ordered to wear their white shirts uppermost, so that they could easily identify each other in the dark. That ploy followed standard European practice for nighttime assaults, which were accordingly known as "camisards"; but now it had another unexpected and disconcerting effect. As they marched silently down toward the fort, each holding onto his leader's shirttail, the moonlight glittered on their musket barrels and played upon the pale, flapping shirts "in a movement" that, as Gist recalled, "made some of the soldiers observe that we looked more like ghosts."[36]

By sunrise on September 14, Major Grant had penetrated close to his target without detection but was flummoxed about what to do next. After burning some of the fort's outbuildings and apparently with the object of rallying his own scattered detachments, he proceeded to rouse the garrison and its tribal allies by ordering his drummers to beat and his bagpipers to play. During the bush fight that followed, Grant's divided command was soundly defeated and scattered in confusion. A stubborn stand by Captain Thomas Bullitt and fifty of his Virginians, who had been posted to guard the baggage horses and provisions, gave the survivors a chance to get away. Finally overwhelmed, Bullitt and the last of his men were forced into the Ohio River; the captain escaped, but many others drowned. The portly Grant, who like Forbes was a veteran of the last war in Flanders and one of his most experienced subordinates, refused to flee, declaring "his heart was broken and he could not survive the loss of that day." He was captured sitting despondently on a log.[37]

As a senior officer, Major Grant received scrupulously courteous treatment from his captors, reflecting the established international code of conduct between gentlemen. Other, less exalted prisoners were not so lucky. Thomas Gist, who was shot across the forehead and through the right hand before being captured by a Wyandot—or Huron—warrior, saw comrades forced to run from the edge of the woods to the fort. These "poor unhappy fellows" were pursued by Indians and met by others from the fort wielding tomahawks, knives, swords, and clubs. Screaming and yelling, the warriors "beat and drove" their victims "from one side of the cleared ground to the other, till the unhappy men could not stand; then they were tomahawked, scalped, and in short was [sic] massacred in the most barbarous manner that can be imagined."

In hellish scenes that recalled those enacted in the wake of Braddock's defeat three years earlier, a handful of prisoners were burned alive. To his "unspeakable grief and terror," Robert Kirkwood of Montgomery's Highlanders, who had been captured by Shawnees after being lamed by a blast of buckshot, witnessed five captives "burned in the most cruel manner." Kirkwood's account is corroborated by that of a twelve-year-old boy who escaped from

Fort Duquesne on December 2 after two years of captivity. He had seen "a prodigious quantity of wood" carried into the fort, which was used to burn "five of the prisoners they took at Major Grant's Defeat, on the Parade."[38]

Grant's raid was a bloody outing for Washington's regiment. In a letter to his friend and neighbor George William Fairfax—written on the very same day that he pledged undying love for Sally—Washington described it as "a heavy stroke." On the official casualty returns, of the 174 Virginians who participated, no fewer than 68 were marked down as killed or missing, presumed dead. It was widely conceded that the Virginians had fought bravely, and, although Washington played no part in the action, he took great pride in his men's sterling performance. "It is with infinite pleasure," he wrote to Fairfax, "I tell you that the Virginians, officers and men, distinguished themselves in the most eminent manner." General Forbes himself had complimented Washington publicly on his men's good behavior; combat had also forged bonds of comradeship between the Virginians and Highlanders, who were "become one people, shaking each other by the hand wherever they meet."[39]

In his letters home, Washington neglected to mention that Forbes had also taken the opportunity to castigate both him and Byrd for their blatantly partisan stance over the rival roads. Already exasperated by tidings of Grant's debacle, the general's temper was not improved when he learned of a letter penned by Lieutenant Colonel Stephen reporting opinion that the road from Loyalhanna to the Ohio was "now impracticable." Quite why Stephen had written such a thing Forbes was at a loss to know, but he assured Bouquet that Washington and Byrd would prefer it to be "true than otherways, seeing the other road (their favorite scheme) was not followed out." In confronting the colonels, Forbes had not minced his words:

> I told them plainly that, whatever they thought . . . in our
> prosecuting the present road, we had proceeded from the best

*intelligence that could be got for the good and convenience of
the army, without any views to oblige one province or another;
and added that those two gentlemen were the only people that
I had met with who had showed their weakness in their attachment to the province they belong to, by declaring so publicly in
favor of one road without their knowing anything of the other.*

Indeed, for all Washington's mutterings, Forbes had never heard
a Pennsylvanian say a word, good or bad, about the road. As for
himself—and for Bouquet, too—the "good of the service" was all
that mattered, with the jealousies and suspicions of the provinces
not worth "one single twopence."[40]

Despite this tongue-lashing, Washington was unrepentant and
remained convinced that Forbes had taken the wrong route. Writing to Virginia's new lieutenant governor, Francis Fauquier, on September 25, he reported, "Our affairs in general appear with a greater
gloom than ever." Washington could see no prospect of opening up
the rest of the new road that campaign, and therefore no "favorable
issue to the expedition." [41]

Not everyone shared such pessimism. Even the jarring blow of
Grant's defeat failed to discourage the resilient Forbes for long; as
anticipated, the fortified camp at Loyalhanna minimized the effects,
allowing the advance guard to hold its ground. Back at the sprawling Raystown complex, where the bulk of the army now waited to
move forward, camp life resumed its familiar routines of drill and
discipline. Amid all the continuing delays, boredom and homesick-
ness bred desertion. At a general court-martial held on September
24, eight provincials were found guilty of quitting their units. Serving alongside regulars, they were subject to the full force of military
law: three were sentenced to floggings ranging from five hundred
to nine hundred lashes; the others were to be shot. Forbes approved
the punishments, but of those marked down for death, four were
reprieved after their officers interceded for them: those spared
included John Hanna, a red-headed Irishman from the 1st Virginia
Regiment, on whose behalf Washington himself had spoken up.

John Doyle of the Pennsylvania Regiment would provide an example for the rest.[42]

On September 26, the Reverend Barton walked with Doyle to the place of execution. In eighteenth-century armies, punishment functioned as a grim, instructional theater. Doyle gave a bravura performance. As Barton reported with approval, he "behaved with uncommon resolution; exhorted his brother-soldiers to take example by his misfortunes; to live sober lives; to beware of bad company; to shun pretended friends, and loose wicked companions." Above all, he implored them never to desert. When he saw the six-strong firing squad, Doyle knelt down and stripped off his coat, inviting them to come close and aim for his heart. He shunned the proffered blindfold but looked his executioners, "who advanced so near that the muzzles of their guns were within a foot of his body," full in the eye. Here the drama departed from the script. At a signal from the sergeant major the executioners fired, but aimed so low that Doyle's "bowels fell out, his shirt and breeches were all on fire, and he tumbled upon his side, raised one arm 2 or 3 times, and soon expired." It was a "shocking spectacle" to all, and a "striking example" for Doyle's fellow soldiers—so shocking and striking, in fact, that Barton ended his journal abruptly at that precise point.[43]

Doyle's execution was intended to discourage desertion as the army prepared to resume its lumbering progress. In orders issued two days later, Forbes acknowledged that his men had already "gone through a great deal of fatigue," but as "the advance posts of the army [were] almost at the enemy's nose," he placed his confidence in their "alacrity and steadiness in carrying on the rest of the service that we may show our enemies the danger of rousing Britons fired and animated with love of their King and Country."[44]

Despite the primacy of his Virginian interests, Washington still nurtured some flicker of the broader British patriotism that Forbes sought to kindle. When the general appealed for advice on formations to be adopted when the army made the last lunge for its objective, Washington prepared a detailed response, giving his thoughts "on a line of march through a country covered with wood, and how [it] may be formed, in an instant, into an order of battle." His accompanying drawings, executed with all the precise penmanship of a trained surveyor, proposed a formation that maximized security on the march, while retaining enough flexibility to respond swiftly to attack. The scheme, which was accompanied by two meticulously detailed plans, was calculated for a short forced march, taking along field artillery but no cumbersome wagons. It envisaged a 4,000-strong force, spearheaded by a vanguard of 1,000 picked men organized in three divisions, followed by two brigades and a rear guard. On the march, the column would be covered by small flanking parties. If the enemy attacked from the front, some 600 men would screen the flanks while the elite vanguard fanned out to the right and left, taking cover behind trees and seeking to execute an aggressive pincer movement. Washington was confident that the enemy would find this "different from any thing they have ever yet experienced from us." Elements of the "order of battle," notably the reliance upon a long, thin line to outflank and encircle the enemy, reflected tactics that the innovative Bouquet had already tested at Raystown, although it's unclear whether he and Washington collaborated on them.[45]

The prospects for putting such theories to the test improved on October 14, when Washington received orders to march his Virginians to reinforce Bouquet. This move was prompted by news of a determined French descent upon Loyalhanna two days before. Aiming to capitalize on Grant's defeat and deliver a blow capable of halting Forbes's advance until the spring, the commander at Fort Duquesne, Captain François-Marie Le Marchand de Lignery, sent out a raiding party of 600 French and Indians under Captain Charles Philippe Aubry. They surprised the camp while Bouquet was away searching for an easier route over Laurel Hill; in his absence, the defense was orchestrated by the Pennsylvanian Colonel James Burd. Despite outnumbering their assailants, Burd's men got the worst of a three-hour-long fight and were forced back behind the camp's stout stockades. They eventually rebuffed the assault, thanks to the firepower of their artillery, but nonetheless sustained heavier casualties than the raiders and lost their priceless draught horses. Bouquet and Forbes were both deeply troubled by an episode in which the enemy showed such apparent contempt for the odds against them.[46]

By October 23, Washington and his men had covered the fifty miles to Loyalhanna, a post soon renamed Fort Ligonier in honor of the British Army's commander in chief and Forbes's patron, Sir John Ligonier. This "sudden" march from Raystown gave Washington the opportunity of assessing the controversial connecting road for himself, and the experience only confirmed his dire predictions: "I can truly say that it is indescribably bad," he wrote to Governor Fauquier. Indeed, only the providential discovery of an alternative pass over Laurel Hill had enabled the wheeled transport to get through. General Forbes and his escort caught up on November 2. As Washington now recognized, with the bulk of the army pushed forward to Loyalhanna, the campaign's crisis was fast approaching; on November 5, he conceded to Fauquier that the time for harping upon difficulties was now past.[47]

The very next day, however, Washington was casting doubts on the viability of any further advance. That evening, following an interrupted conversation with Bouquet, he sent him his "crude thoughts" on that head. Washington's letter highlighted the risks involved in moving against Fort Duquesne with no guarantee of adequate supplies and of the potentially disastrous consequences of a clash in the woods. A renewed offensive would consume provisions needed to garrison Loyalhanna, he argued, perhaps leading to the abandonment of that post and its artillery. As for a battle, even if the enemy was routed, recent experience suggested that the Anglo-Americans' own losses would be "perhaps triple." If it was certain that the enemy's defeat would prompt an immediate evacuation of their fort, or if adequate supplies could be stockpiled, then they shouldn't hesitate to advance—"but one or the other of these we ought to be assured of," Washington warned.[48]

Washington's bleak analysis articulated the concerns of other senior officers. On Saturday, November 11, Forbes summoned a council of war including Bouquet, St. Clair, and all his colonels. The case against a further advance, which included those reasons already emphasized by Washington, carried the day. The council concluded: "The risks being so obviously greater than the advantages, there is no doubt as to the sole course that prudence dictates."[49]

Forbes's campaign seemed set to end ignominiously at Loyal-hanna after all. But a chance event the next day, November 12, changed everything. Seeking to repeat their success of a month before, the French at the Forks sent a strong party to reconnoi-ter Forbes's camp and rustle his livestock. The general countered with a force of 500 men, including Washington and his Virgin-ians. According to a report published soon after in the *Pennsyl-vania Gazette*, Washington "fell in with a number of the enemy" about three miles from Loyalhanna, attacked them, and took three prisoners—"an Indian man and woman, and one Johnson, an En-glishman (who, it is said, was carried off by the Indians some time ago from Lancaster County)." Hearing the firing, Lieutenant Col-onel Mercer went to Washington's aid. Approaching at dusk, and seeing the two captured Indians, Mercer's men mistook their fellow Virginians for the enemy; Washington's made the same mistake, upon which "unhappily a few shot were exchanged." Recounting this episode some thirty years later, Washington remembered things rather differently, being adamant that he had gone to help Mercer. In Washington's recollection, the encounter was also far deadlier and more traumatic than the cursory newspaper cover-age suggested; indeed, it had placed his life "in as much jeopardy as it had ever been before or since." The uncontrolled spasm of "friendly fire" was checked only by Washington's personal inter-vention. Using his sword to knock up the leveled muskets, he "never was in more imminent danger by being between two fires." Captain Bullitt, the hero of Grant's Defeat, later claimed that *he* stopped the firefight, which had resulted from Colonel Washing-ton's mistake. Whatever the cause, Washington did not exaggerate the risks: Forbes reported two officers and almost forty men killed or missing.[50]

The capture of the renegade Johnson offered compensation. In exchange for his life, he gave vital intelligence, revealing that Fort Duquesne was virtually bereft of Indian support. There were several reasons for this swift erosion of tribal manpower. Glutted with glory and plunder won in their destruction of Major Grant's command, western warriors from the Great Lakes had promptly left for their distant villages, taking their captives with them; these included young Ensign Gist, who set out with his Wyandot captors on 15 September, loaded with "about fifty pound of plunder . . . got chiefly from the Highlanders"; the party only reached their village near Detroit after trekking and paddling for almost a month.[51]

In addition, the Indian conference at Easton, engineered by the dedicated Pemberton and Post and attended by representatives of the Six Nations, the Delawares and Shawnees, had convinced the wavering Ohio tribes that their best interests now lay with the British, not the French. Last, but not least, the capture of Fort Frontenac on Lake Ontario by a force detached from Abercromby's mauled Lake George army in August under Colonel John Bradstreet shut off the supply of Indian trade goods from Canada via the St. Lawrence River; France's influence among the tribes had always hinged more upon economic reality than sentimental attachment, so such shortfalls in everything from vermilion face paint to gunpowder mattered. Washington's New York friend Joseph Chew reported this "glorious stroke" while nursing a hangover, "having sat up late last night and finished several bottles to the health of Colonel Bradstreet and his army."[52] Taken together, these three factors stripped Captain Lignery of Indian support. Armed with this intelligence, instead of digging in at Loyalhanna for the winter, Forbes resolved to push on and seize his objective.

The final advance was made by 2,500 "picked men," accompanied by just "a light-train of artillery" and unencumbered with baggage or even tents. This select force was divided into three brigades. Washington, who had been forgiven his earlier subterfuge, commanded the 3rd Brigade. It was composed of his own 1st Virginia Regiment, plus artificers, North Carolinians, Marylanders, and

"Lower County" troops from Delaware, some 720 in all. Although nominated the 3rd Brigade, Washington's actually formed the army's 1st Division. With Bouquet and Colonel Montgomery commanding the other two brigades, Washington was the only provincial officer to be given such heavy responsibility: at long last, he was receiving the kind of recognition that he believed his efforts deserved.[53]

As Forbes's army edged closer to its objective, so the threat of ambush increased. For the final fifty-mile phase of the advance, therefore, it was agreed that fortified camps should be established at far shorter intervals than before, just a few days' march apart. Some 500 Pennsylvanians were sent on ahead of Washington's brigade to construct the first secure base; this spearhead force was commanded by Colonel John Armstrong, an experienced frontier fighter renowned for leading a long-distance raid that had torched the Delaware town of Kittanning on the Allegheny River above Fort Duquesne in September 1756.

Equipped with felling axes, Washington's brigade was to hack a rough road along the trail that Armstrong's men had blazed. On November 15, in bone-chilling cold and steady rain, his artificers began to hew their way through the dripping forest. Driving their cattle with them, Washington's men advanced some six miles before making camp on Chestnut Ridge. Reporting his progress to Forbes, even now Washington couldn't resist reminding the general of the advantages of the old Braddock Road: it was "in the first place good, and in the next, fresh," so offering the best communication between the "Middle Colonies" and Fort Duquesne should the army be fortunate enough to take it.[54]

Negotiating tough terrain in depressing, wintry weather, the army's progress was painfully slow. Despite laboring "from light 'til light," Washington's exhausted brigade covered only another six miles before it was necessary to halt again. From his temporary camp on November 17, Washington sent Forbes a letter that provides further evidence of his strong paternalism toward the men of his regiment. Sergeant William Grant had been confined at Loyalhanna on a charge of behaving insolently toward two officers of the 2nd Pennsylvania Regiment. The sergeant was tried by a general court-martial, but, as the sentence was not known when the 1st Virginia Regiment marched out, Washington hoped that Forbes would look into the matter "and forward him if it is found consistent . . . as he is a very fine fellow, and as desirous of coming on as I am to have him do so."[55] Given his own attitude toward Pennsylvanians, Washington may have approved of his sergeant's response when Ensign Edward Biddle and Lieutenant Jacob Kearns interfered while he was arguing with a sutler over a bill for rum, threatening to send him "to the Devil that instant": Grant had presented his musket at the ensign and then threatened to blow the lieutenant's brains out. Given the provocation, and as the night was too dark for Grant to identify the pair as officers, he was acquitted.[56]

By late morning on November 18, Washington's men had reached the base already established by Armstrong, known as "New Camp." While his brigade halted to slaughter bullocks and dress their rations, axmen started work to clear the next stage of the route. Washington moved on, now taking the lead from Armstrong, who stayed behind to hold the camp with his Pennsylvanians. A rapid march covering ten to twelve miles brought Washington to Turtle Creek. There, during November 20, he built a second fortification, "Washington's Camp." Besides the men of his own brigade, Washington now commanded elements of the other two, about 1,500 men altogether—his largest field command prior to the outbreak of the Revolutionary War.

While Montgomery's brigade cut the road connecting the first two camps, Washington's worked to clear the path to the third and final base. Known as "Bouquet's Camp" and some ten miles from Fort Duquesne, it would provide the jumping-off point for the assault. By November 23, Forbes and all three of his brigades were assembled there. Now so close to his prize, Forbes had no intention of stumbling into the kind of chance encounter that had wrecked Braddock's campaign. Next day he gave orders for his army's final march, employing a formation intended to allow a swift and effective response to attack. Despite claims by historians that this followed the plans recently drawn up by Washington, it clearly owed more to the drills devised and practiced by Bouquet back at Raystown camp; indeed, weeks after receiving Washington's suggestions, Forbes was still undecided about the best formation to adopt and urged Bouquet to "have something cut and dry" to propose.[57]

Rather than marching one behind the other in the single column proposed by Washington, the three brigades were ordered to advance abreast, with each split into four parallel columns, like the prongs of a fork. By shortening their lines of march, these could rapidly deploy into an extensive firing line that the enemy would struggle to overlap. In addition, there were flanking parties of the "best gunmen," while "Indians and light horse" probed in front and drums beat at the head of each column to avoid confusion; this exact formation is illustrated in a drawing among Forbes's papers in the National Archives of Scotland, Edinburgh. Paper plans were one thing, moving men through the dark and disorienting forest quite another: despite all the elaborate precautions, as one officer reported, when they moved forward, "it was a matter of vast difficulty to keep the narrow columns from intersecting."[58]

In the event, Forbes's brigades never faced the ultimate test of combat in the woods. Nor were his gunners obliged to bombard Fort Duquesne with shot and shell. Rather than stand their ground, the garrison demolished the fortifications, then withdrew to the north in hopes of returning to fight again when the odds were better. On November 24, as they shivered at Bouquet's Camp, Forbes's troops heard the thud of a distant explosion. That evening their Indian scouts reported a great pall of smoke hanging over the Forks; a few hours later they claimed that the French had gone after burning everything; light troops sent to investigate confirmed their reports.[59]

When Forbes and his army reached the Forks on the morning of November 25, 1758, they found charred and smoking ruins.

It was a dismal scene, made ghastly by the unburied bodies of Major Grant's men slain more than two months before, which still strewed the ground around for miles about, "so many monuments to French inhumanity." They were given a decent burial, along with the skulls and bones of Braddock's soldiers, killed in 1755 and left lying above ground ever since like some backwoods Golgotha.[60]

Forbes, who had joined the advance in his horse-borne litter and who was now sicker than ever, renamed the abandoned strongpoint Fort Pitt in honor of the minister who'd sent him there. For all its sense of anticlimax, the conquest marked the end of three years of warfare on the Virginian frontier and was widely recognized as a remarkable achievement. Reporting the destruction of that "terrible fort . . . that nest of pirates which has so long harbored the murderers and destructors of our poor people," Henri Bouquet had no doubt where the credit lay: "After God the success of this expedition is entirely due to the General," he wrote. Forbes had engineered the Treaty of Easton, which "knocked the French in the head"; he had secured "all his posts . . . giving nothing to chance"; and, not least, he had refused to yield "to the urging instances for taking Braddock's Road, which would have been our destruction." Washington was chief among those who had lobbied for that route, but he too acknowledged Forbes's achievement. In a letter to Governor Fauquier, he paid tribute to the indefatigable Scot's "great merit"; many years later he remembered his old commander as "a brave and good officer."[61]

With winter fast closing in, it was resolved to install a garrison at Fort Pitt, including part of Washington's long-suffering Virginia Regiment under Colonel Hugh Mercer of the Pennsylvanians; like Forbes and so many other soldiers fighting for the Ohio Country, Mercer was a Scot who had begun his career in medicine. Now a loyal subject of King George, he had once been a rebel in the Jacobite army of Bonnie Prince Charlie. Mercer had come to America in the wake of the Young Pretender's bloody defeat at Culloden in 1746. Ten years later, he had distinguished himself as a captain of Pennsylvanian troops during Colonel Armstrong's celebrated attack on Kittanning. A former insurgent, in time Hugh Mercer would become one again.[62]

Washington himself had no intention of wintering in the wilderness. The eradication of Fort Duquesne had restored peace to Virginia's frontiers, "which was the principal inducement to his taking arms" in the first place. In addition, the ailments that plagued him during the previous autumn and winter had returned. His health, which "had been declining for many months . . . occasioned by an inveterate disorder in his bowels," now grew so poor that he decided to resign his command, and this time in earnest.[63]

Before riding back to Virginia, Washington's last regimental duty was to organize clothing and supplies for his men left behind at Fort Pitt. That done, the twenty-six-year-old formally resigned his colonel's commission. On New Year's Eve, the officers of the Virginia Regiment implored Washington to reconsider his decision and lead them on for another campaign that would surely bring the entire American war to a victorious conclusion. Their "humble address" testified to Washington's popularity and to the esprit de corps he had instilled within his regiment. They expressed sadness at the "loss of such an excellent commander, such a sincere friend, and so affable a companion." If anything, the loss to their "unhappy country" was even greater than their own: when it came to military experience, allied to "patriotism, courage and conduct," Washington was irreplaceable and uniquely qualified to uphold "the military character of Virginia."[64]

Washington was clearly touched by his officers' sentiments. On January 10, 1759, he replied that their affectionate and public declaration of approval for his conduct in command of Virginia's troops was "an honor that will constitute the greatest happiness of my life, and afford in my latest hours the most pleasing reflections."[65]

But Washington did not intend to change his mind. Four days earlier he had married Martha Custis, turning his back on the military career that he'd always craved and had pursued during four hard, frustrating, and sometimes bloody years. Now a family man, Washington traded his dreams of martial distinction for the reality of peaceful domesticity as a gentleman planter. Writing from Mount Vernon some months later, he assured his longtime London correspondent, the merchant Richard Washington: "I have quit a military life, and shortly shall be fixed at this place with an agreeable partner."[66]

In 1759, there was nothing to suggest that George Washington's decision to exchange his sword for a plowshare would not be final.

5

BETWEEN THE WARS

On his twenty-seventh birthday, February 22, 1759, George Washington assumed his seat in Virginia's House of Burgesses. Four days later, he stood in the chamber to receive the formal thanks of the House "for his faithful services to His Majesty, and this colony, and for his brave and steady behavior, from the first encroachments and hostilities of the French and their Indians, to his resignation, after the happy reduction of Fort Duquesne."[1]

This public acknowledgment of Washington's efforts as a soldier over the previous five years must surely have given him considerable satisfaction: while he had failed to secure the British officer's commission that he craved and had enjoyed precious little opportunity to slake his lust for glory on the battlefield, his hard years of military service had not gone unrecognized.

In 1759, as his devoted biographer Douglas Southall Freeman maintained, Washington was "Virginia's most distinguished soldier," and this immense prestige had a profound impact upon his prospects *within* the Old Dominion. Indeed, Washington's soldiering had propelled him from obscure planter augmenting the income from his run-down Rappahannock farm with his earnings as a local surveyor to one of the most respected men in Virginia, consulted by the colony's leadership. Colonel Washington's growing renown as defender of Virginia's frontier had clearly contributed to his decisive victory in the previous summer's Assembly elections, although the £40 he spent to treat thirsty voters to 160 gallons of beer, rum, wine, punch, and cider no doubt helped.[2]

Washington's wartime reputation landed him the greatest prize of all: the standing and confidence to court and marry a woman who was reputedly the wealthiest widow in Virginia. When he wed Martha Custis it is highly likely that Washington was still in love with Sally Fairfax, the unattainable wife of his friend and neighbor. From that point forward, however, he seemingly suppressed those feelings and focused wholeheartedly upon his bride and the new family she brought with her.

Among the socially privileged ranks of Anglo-American society in the mid-eighteenth century, financial considerations mattered in marriage. But there was a growing assumption that such unions should also be "companionate," based upon a genuine affinity that might ripen into love. Soon after her husband's death, Martha Washington destroyed virtually all of the private correspondence between them, so the precise nature of their relationship is difficult to establish. Yet such evidence as survives suggests that it conformed to the "companionate" model and was characterized by genuine intimacy: after sixteen years of marriage, as he contemplated the daunting task of commanding Congress's Continental Army against Britain, Washington assured his wife of his "unalterable affection" for her. The fact that the Washingtons had no children of their own need not indicate a lack of passion; it is possible that Martha's last delivery had left her unable to conceive; as likely, although this, too, is conjecture, "the Father of his Country" was sterile.[3]

Without doubt, marriage immediately transformed Washington's prospects, catapulting him into the front rank of Virginia's planters. In addition to his existing holdings of 5,000 acres worked by 49 slaves, the Custis connection brought another 17,000 acres, 300 more slaves, and a handsome townhouse in Williamsburg, altogether assessed at £23,000.[4] In terms of Washington's personal fortune and status, therefore, despite the many frustrations and disappointments he had experienced, his decision to follow the lead of his half brother Lawrence and thrust himself forward for a military career had undoubtedly been the right one.

As the tribute paid him by his regimental officers and the thanks of his fellow Burgesses both made clear, Washington had gained special credit for his determination in seeing the job through from start to finish. Had he retired in 1757, amid the prevailing mood of wrangling, war weariness and defeatism, the story might have been very different, with all his previous efforts squandered. As it was, Washington resigned in the wake of an unexpected and much-trumpeted victory when Virginia's readiness to support the war effort had been transformed by Pitt's generosity: in the ensuing mood of euphoria, all the old gripes about Washington's shortcomings as commander of Virginia's forces were forgotten.

While there is no doubt that in 1759 Washington's standing in Virginia was higher than ever, it is nonetheless true that his celebrity beyond the Old Dominion fell far short of the expectations raised by his high profile in 1754–55. As the war against New France moved toward its climax, the Anglo-Americans had other heroes, both dead and alive, to occupy the limelight. Among the martyrs was Lord Howe, "the darling" of the colonists, killed at Ticonderoga in 1758. Those still living included another young brigadier general, James Wolfe, who had emerged as the popular hero of the victorious siege of Louisbourg that same summer. Howe and Wolfe were both British, of course, but even Freeman's claim that Washington deserved recognition "as the most conspicuous native-born American provincial who had followed a career of arms" is debatable: by early 1759, if newspaper coverage is any indicator, that title belonged more rightfully to a rough and daring New England frontiersman of humble Scotch-Irish parentage, the ranger Major Robert Rogers.[5]

In 1759, Washington apparently turned his back on a military career for good. Nowhere in his writings did he mull over what he had learned during the years since he'd volunteered to carry Lieutenant Governor Dinwiddie's summons into the Ohio Country; perhaps, as a new life stretched before him, such reflections seemed irrelevant. But given what the future held for Washington, it is worth considering the long-term significance of his experiences during that time.[6]

As a veteran officer, Washington now knew that war was not all "charming," whistling bullets. Soldiers were more likely to die from dysentery or smallpox than the enemy's lead or steel, while Fort Duquesne had fallen to the methodical chock of felling axes, not shrieking war cries and crashing cannon fire. With hard experience, boldness had given way to caution, manifested in a growing willingness to seek the opinion of others through formal councils of war. Courage and leadership on the battlefield mattered, to be sure, but victory also hinged upon other, less glamorous, factors: discipline, training, planning, logistics, and, not least, the maintenance of harmonious relationships between frontline soldiers and rear-echelon civilians. Though he failed to acknowledge the fact at the time, in all of these areas Washington's personal experience of command bequeathed invaluable lessons.

As colonel of the original Virginia Regiment, Washington gradually created a formation that was, by 1758, as well trained and disciplined as any in the provincial service and, judging by its combat record, worthy of acceptance into the regular British Army. For Washington, the antithesis of his own trustworthy regiment was the unruly and unreliable colonial militia; this preference for the long-service professional soldier and disdain for the short-term amateur—which overturned his countrymen's ingrained prejudice against "standing armies"—would continue to dominate his attitude toward the waging of war.

While basing his own standards of military perfection upon those established by the British Army, Washington knew that even the red-coated professionals were not invincible: he had seen them run at Braddock's defeat, their proverbial discipline eventually dissolved by an alien environment and unfamiliar enemy. Hence, from the outset, his own bluecoats were drilled in regular *and* irregular tactics; and, in common with the most forward-thinking officers like Henri Bouquet, Washington sought to devise realistic military formations capable of coping with wilderness conditions.

As commander of his own regiment, Washington had absorbed key lessons in leadership, learning how to motivate officers and men, gaining their respect while maintaining the distance required by rank. He had acquired familiarity with the nuts and bolts of practical soldiering, watching the dense paragraphs of Humphrey Bland's *Treatise of Military Discipline* transformed into the reality of files, platoons, and companies drilling and sweating on the parade ground. Washington had not flinched from the responsibility of imposing discipline, depriving miscreants of the skin off their backs and, upon occasion, of their lives.

From his experience of serving under Generals Braddock and Forbes, Washington had also gained an insight into the mindset of two contrasting British commanders, the first bullish and authoritarian, the second tactful and patient, but no less determined in pursuit of his objectives. For all their differences in temperament, both men had faced the challenge of organizing an army and the logistical nightmare of pushing it across the interior wilderness. Although the final outcome of their campaigns was very different, Braddock and Forbes had each surmounted immense difficulties to come within striking distance of their objective.

Perhaps the most important lessons of all arose from Washington's own mistakes. Woefully inexperienced but keen to win a name for himself, in 1754 he had displayed a rashness that looked set to cost him his life and reputation when he stood and fought against the odds at Fort Necessity. After 1755, while in command of the troops defending Virginia's frontiers, Washington showed poor judgment in spending far too long away from his men; they had endured danger and hardship while he pursued his own selfish career objectives, enjoying the comforts of Williamsburg, Philadelphia, and Boston. In Washington's absence, morale and discipline had suffered, justifying some of the "Virginia-Centinel's" barbed criticisms.

During that same period, Washington regularly clashed with his civilian superior, Lieutenant Governor Dinwiddie, deploying his own political patrons, the powerful Fairfaxes and the Assembly's speaker, John Robinson, as allies to outflank him; through this sniping, Washington eventually alienated the long-suffering royal official who had launched his career and shared many of his objectives. Under the command of Forbes, Washington was guilty of further indiscretion, disloyalty, and factionalism; he was lucky to be given a chance to redeem himself. Yet it is significant that Washington seized that opportunity and salvaged his reputation as an officer and gentleman; as will be seen, unlike many young men in his position he *learned* from his errors, making it difficult to overemphasize the importance of those same years in shaping his character.

In early April 1759, Washington left Williamsburg for Mount Vernon along with his bride, his stepchildren, Jacky and Patsy, and their servants and baggage. In preparation for married life Washington had added an extra storey to the original building. It remained sparsely furnished and simply decorated; it would be Martha's task as Mount Vernon's new mistress to transform it into a stylish and comfortable home. Meanwhile, Washington devoted himself to the role of gentleman farmer, taking an unusually keen interest in his plantations and their productivity. While the sprawling Custis domains on the York River were entrusted to a competent overseer, Washington assumed personal responsibility for the five farms, encompassing about 4,000 acres, that composed the Mount Vernon estate. In doing so, he undertook a range of duties as demanding as those expected of a regimental colonel on active service.[7]

Like his soldiering, Washington learned his farming on the job. Keen to preserve the land and its fertility, he experimented with alternatives to the Virginian staple crop of tobacco. In his efforts to do so, he ordered the latest books from London, works distilling the techniques that were driving England's "agricultural revolution." Drawing upon them, he was prepared to dabble and diversify. By 1765, Washington was also cultivating hemp, wheat, and corn. Although his hemp and flax proved unprofitable, production of the other crops—which could be sold on the domestic market, so avoiding costly shipping fees and commissions for London agents—rose over the next three to four years.

While Washington pored over his seed catalogs, the war against New France ground on. During 1758, the Anglo-Americans had gained the initiative, but the conflict was far from won. For example, although John Forbes had captured the Forks of the Ohio, the French still held hopes of retaking them. In the spring of 1759, Captain Lignery remained at Venango, where he massed reinforcements for projected counterattacks on Loyalhanna and Fort Pitt; by early July, he commanded some 700 Frenchmen and many more Indians. As it happened, this powerful force was diverted north to Niagara after intelligence arrived that a British army was en route to attack that crucial fort. In late July, Lignery arrived to find Niagara already besieged by the Anglo-Americans and a strong contingent of Iroquois, who had finally been persuaded to abandon their long-standing neutrality. The results of this shift were immediately apparent. Despite dwindling influence within the Ohio Country, in their own backyard on the New York frontier, the Six Nations remained a force to be reckoned with, and all but a handful of Lignery's tribal allies promptly abandoned him rather than clash with them. When he attempted to break through the siege lines at La Belle Famille, his force was halted by British firepower, then hounded into flight by Six Nations warriors. Fort Niagara surrendered the next day, so marking the real end of Bourbon influence on the Ohio; after burning their contentious forts at Venango, Le Boeuf, and Presque Isle, the French withdrew westward to Detroit.[8]

That September, as Washington's good friend George Mercer reported, the victors were busy securing their gains with a "very respectable" new fort at "Pittsburgh," built of brick and capable of withstanding bombardment and holding a formidable garrison.[9] The region's Indians, the same Delawares, Shawnees, and Mingos who had recently ravaged the frontiers of Virginia and Pennsylvania, now seemed reconciled to the new regime. As another of Washington's former officers, Robert Stewart, informed him, they were inclined "to enter into and cultivate a strict and permanent friendship with us," meekly delivering up the captives they had taken in years of raiding. This change of heart was just as well: both the Delawares and the Shawnees were more numerous and powerful than previously imagined, even after the war casualties they'd suffered.

According to Stewart, these same Indians held Washington above all others responsible for their losses: "Both those nations are greatly incensed against you, who they call the Great Knife and look on you to be author of their greatest misfortunes," he reported.[10]

Coming from fellow warriors, Washington's latest appellation was a compliment of sorts, no less menacing than "Devourer of Towns." Very similar terms—"Big Knives" and "Long Knives"—were employed by the Ohio Indians as a catchall name for Virginians; this suggests that Washington, through his long stint of frontier service, had come to personify the Old Dominion's war effort not only in the eyes of his fellow Virginians, but for Indians, too. The name also testifies to Washington's unusually close acquaintance with the region's tribes, stretching back to his diplomatic mission in 1753.

As Stewart realized, for all their apparent tranquility, the Ohio Indians remained a dangerous enemy if angered. This fact had been clear to General Forbes. In February 1759, as he lay dying in Philadelphia, he summoned his dwindling strength to warn the new commander in chief, Jeffery Amherst, of the importance of treating the Indians fairly and with respect. Forbes, who was by now reduced to a "most shocking and deplorable" sight, believed that Indian affairs were not generally understood, while those with the necessary expertise—men like Sir William Johnson, Britain's superintendent of the northern Indians—used it for their own selfish ends. Forbes pleaded: "I beg in the mean time that you will not think triflingly of the Indians or their friendship; when I venture to assure you that twenty Indians are capable of laying half this province waste, of which I have been an eye witness."[11]

Amherst would have done well to heed Forbes's advice, but in 1759 he was preoccupied with the ongoing conquest of Canada. Besides Niagara, by August his troops had captured the Champlain Valley fortresses of Ticonderoga and Crown Point. The most significant—and famous—success came in September, when a detached force, under the command of the fiery young Major General Wolfe, seized Quebec. The decisive battle before the walls of the city on September 13 cost Wolfe his life, adding poignancy to an unexpected victory that sparked unprecedented celebrations on both sides of the Atlantic and providing a dramatic emotional highpoint for what became known as the *annus mirabilis*.

Unlike Amherst's forces, which included thousands of provincials, Wolfe's Quebec army had been composed almost entirely of veteran redcoats. Nominally British units, they also mustered a significant minority of officers and rank and file recruited in America, including both men born in the colonies and recent immigrants. For example, the 48th Foot had received an influx of local manpower both before and after its blooding under Braddock; returns compiled in 1757 show that some 12 percent of its rank and file were "Natives of America"; the number of men recruited on that continent among former indentured servants and transports from Britain would undoubtedly have been higher. The 48th's lieutenant colonel in 1759 remained Ralph Burton, who had been wounded in command of the regiment while fighting alongside Washington on the Monongahela. Another survivor of Braddock's defeat, and a former ensign in the Virginia Regiment who went on to distinguish himself at Louisbourg and Quebec as a lieutenant in the Royal American Regiment, was Alexander Stephen, the brother of Washington's tough right-hand man, Adam Stephen.[12]

Both the joint British-American nature of Wolfe's victory and its cost in human terms were brought home to Mount Vernon by the fate of William Henry Fairfax, for whom Washington had helped to secure an ensign's commission in the 28th Foot. Young "Billy" came through the siege of Louisbourg unhurt but was mortally wounded at Quebec during the climactic battle on the Plains of Abraham; Wolfe had been leading Billy's regiment in a bayonet charge when he received his own fatal injuries. There was a sad footnote in 1761, when the fifty guineas that Washington had loaned Billy three years earlier toward his expenses were repaid by his brother, Bryan.[13]

At the close of the *annus mirabilis*, patriotic Britons on both sides of the Atlantic were drawn more closely together than ever before, anticipating a glorious future for a mighty Protestant empire.[14] Blood shed by men like Billy Fairfax and James Wolfe had helped to cement the bond. The spirit of joint endeavor and shared sacrifice was epitomized by the decision of the colony of Massachusetts Bay to vote £250 to pay for a monument to young Lord Howe in Westminster Abbey. It was unveiled on July 14, 1762, in testimony, as its inscription stated, of "his services and military virtues" and of the affection he had inspired among the officers and soldiers of Massachusetts. Work on the monument was supervised by the late Lord Howe's younger brother Richard, now Fourth Viscount Howe, who'd distinguished himself for his fighting spirit as a captain in the Royal Navy. Deeply touched, "Black Dick" Howe intended to erect an obelisk as a reciprocal gesture of affection for his dead sibling and of gratitude to those Americans who cherished his memory; this was no less dear to another hard-fighting brother, Colonel William Howe, who had led Wolfe's light infantry in a daring commando-style assault up the cliffs above Quebec on the memorable September 13, 1759. In coming years, as military opponents of George Washington, both Richard and William Howe were destined to play as important a role in British-American affairs as their much-lamented brother, George Augustus.[15]

By the time Lord Howe's monument was finished, the sense of transatlantic unity and promise had only strengthened as Anglo-American armies completed the methodical conquest of Canada in 1760 and then proceeded to snap up Bourbon possessions in the Caribbean, taking the rich French sugar island of Martinique in early 1762 and, after Spain belatedly entered the conflict, capturing the fabulously wealthy port of Havana that same summer. All these conquests prompted fresh celebrations in British North America; they seemed prescient of a new era of prosperity for the colonies within an expanded British Empire and under a benevolent young king, George III, who had ascended to the throne upon his grandfather's death in 1760.

Given these stirring times and the reports from all battle fronts that filled pages of newspapers like the *Virginia Gazette*, it is perhaps unsurprising to find hints that Washington had not completely forgotten his own dreams of military glory. His enduring interests were reflected in an invoice he sent to the London merchant Robert Cary on September 20, 1759 ordering busts to embellish Mount Vernon. These could not have been any more martial: two great captains of antiquity, Alexander the Great and Julius Caesar, and four commanders who had made their names in Washington's own century—Charles XII of Sweden; Frederick the Great of Prussia; John Churchill, Duke of Marlborough; and Marlborough's fellow victor at Blenheim, Prince Eugene of Savoy. In addition, and continuing his distinctly warlike approach to interior decorating, Washington requested "2 furious wild beasts of any kind," posed "as if approaching each other and eager to engage." Washington's military tastes were clearly untypical: while Cary was able to supply a pair of suitably belligerent lions, which remain in place at Mount Vernon, there were no busts available in the sizes required by Washington of any of the six military heroes. Poets, and philosophers, both ancient and modern, could be supplied instead, but Colonel Washington wasn't interested in *them*; apparently, only soldiers reflected the warrior image he sought to project.[16]

Washington's duties in Virginia's House of Burgesses also brought reminders of a conflict in which he had recently fought. In November 1759, he served on a committee that considered the petitions of men of his old regiment who had now fallen on hard times. Christopher West had enlisted in the Virginia Regiment in September 1754 and was captured by the Indians in February 1756. After two years of captivity in Canada, he had been sent from Quebec to England to be exchanged for a French prisoner. At long last, "after many hardships," West managed to rejoin his regiment and now sought compensation for his "lost time." On Washington's recommendations, the House agreed to allow West £32 to cover his pay during his captivity, with any further arrears to be settled by the regiment's paymaster. Another petitioner must have struck an even stronger chord with Washington: in November 1758, Daniel McNeil had been wounded in a skirmish with the enemy at Fort Ligonier—probably the Loyalhanna "friendly fire" incident in which Washington had come so close to losing his life. McNeil's injuries left him incapable of supporting his wife and three small children. After Washington and his fellow burgess Francis Lightfoot Lee examined his claim, it was resolved to grant him an immediate payment of £10, plus £5 per year for future subsistence.[17]

Although he had retired from active service, Washington's experience continued to make him a valued pundit on Virginia's military affairs. In 1760, a fresh Indian war had erupted, this time with the powerful Cherokees, whose growing alienation had been clear ever since they'd forsaken the Forbes expedition. That spring, Cherokee gunmen blockaded a fort built within their territory on the Little Tennessee River; yet another outpost named after the unlucky Lord Loudoun, it was garrisoned by men of the South Carolina Independent Companies and provincial troops from the same colony. When Lieutenant Governor William Bull of South Carolina appealed for help, Virginia's Assembly voted to complete its regiment to 1,000 men under Colonel William Byrd and mount a relief expedition. Washington was notified too late to attend the crucial vote, and the absence of his expertise was mourned by Major Robert Stewart. In his opinion, Washington's advice would probably have prevented "an expedition that a thousand circumstances concur in rendering impracticable." Stewart believed it was madness to send raw, new-raised troops into the mountainous country of the "warlike and formidable" Cherokees, who in "their numbers and mode of warfare have so vast a superiority."[18]

Stewart's doubts were shared by his former commander. Besides the Virginian contingent, a force of regulars under Washington's old comrade of the Forbes campaign, Colonel Archibald Montgomery, had marched to the relief of Fort Loudoun. Writing to a London correspondent, Washington believed that, while the French were now "so well drubbed" that there seemed little doubt that the conquest of Canada would be completed that summer, the Cherokees were a different matter. Healthy and in high spirits when they left Charleston, Montgomery's men had already "penetrated into the heart of their country," but their commander needed to be wary, as he had "a crafty subtle enemy to deal with that may give him most trouble when he least expects it."[19]

Both Stewart and Washington were correct in their analysis. On August 9, 1760, with no prospect of help in sight, the starving garrison of Fort Loudoun was obliged to surrender. Montgomery's force had fended off a Cherokee ambush near the settlement of Etchoe on June 27 but, with scores of wounded to care for, lacked the transport to push onward with enough supplies to complete its mission; Byrd's command moved so sluggishly that it was still inside Virginian territory when the fort fell.

Amherst subdued the heartland of Canada as easily as Washington had predicted, but it took another expedition to bring the defiant Cherokees to heel. This was commanded by none other than James Grant, the same officer who had been overwhelmed and captured outside Fort Duquesne in September 1758. Exchanged in time to join Montgomery's expedition, Grant now knew the Cherokees and their daunting mountains and had no intention of underestimating either. Like Forbes before him, Grant was sympathetic to the Indians, informing Amherst: "If both sides were heard . . . the Indians have been the worst used." Most of the Cherokees regretted recent killings and would gladly make peace if possible, Grant added.[20] But Amherst was unconvinced by such claims: the Cherokees must be severely punished before there could be any talk of peace. Grant was obliged to obey. His 1761 punitive campaign, which ravaged the Cherokees' towns, was a model of its kind, using packhorses to penetrate the tribe's mountainous homeland and deploying seasoned veterans who were no longer unnerved by war whoops. Grant's advance was screened by a small but highly effective corps of scouts: these were an unusual mixture of northern and southern Indians— Mohawks and Mahicans, Catawbas and Chickasaws—leavened with white rangers and volunteers from the regulars.[21]

Grant's motley scouts were led by Captain Quintin Kennedy of the 17th Foot, who had been wounded at Braddock's defeat as an ensign in the 44th and had since made a name for himself as one of the British Army's leading practitioners of American bush fighting.

Kennedy's corps included yet another survivor of Braddock's campaign, the Iroquois warrior Silver Heels, who had alerted Washington to the presence of Ensign Jumonville's party in 1754. Having helped him to ignite a global war, Silver Heels had seen far more of the ensuing conflict than Washington. Striking up a friendship with the ambitious and energetic Kennedy, Silver Heels had followed him to war on the New York frontier and then against the Cherokees in the Carolinas. There his experiences highlighted the cultural differences between the tribal allies. On May 6, 1761, when Grant's expedition reached Fort Ninety Six, eight Chickasaws came into camp and performed the war dance. A British officer, Captain Christopher French of the 22nd Foot, reported how "one of them observed that Silver Heels a Seneca Mohawk Indian who came with us from New York was a looker on, [and they] desired he would dance, which after some difficulty [on] account of his not being understood by them, he did." After the Cherokees were subdued by Grant's deliberate scorched-earth strategy, Silver Heels joined Kennedy on the expedition sent from the mainland against Martinique. Kennedy commanded the four companies of rangers that spearheaded the successful assault on the island in January 1762. Having escaped numerous hazards since 1755, like many other British veterans Kennedy swiftly succumbed to the West Indian climate; but Silver Heels survived and accompanied the slaves and other plunder that the captain had sent back to New York.[22]

Just as colonial Americans seemed increasingly "British" in identity as the war entered its final, victorious phase, for their part, some Old Country soldiers reciprocated by relating ever more closely with the people they had been sent to protect. They consciously adopted the "American" label to distinguish themselves from officers serving in Germany, who were believed to receive greater recognition; this gave an interesting twist to George Washington's persistent gripe that colonial officers received second-class treatment compared with Britons.

Writing from London in October 1760, where he had been sent with Major General Amherst's dispatches announcing the final conquest of Canada, Major Isaac Barré revealed an affiliation with the Americans that was destined to grow far stronger in coming years. Barré, who had served as Wolfe's adjutant general at Quebec and was shot in the face during the firefight on the Plains of Abraham, bitterly informed Amherst that "any seam or scar" received in Germany was "called a mark of honor, when the same in a poor American is either unnoticed or supposed to be got by inoculation."[23] Two years later, when the British were besieging Havana, another Quebec veteran, Lieutenant Colonel Henry Fletcher of the 35th Foot, told his sister that, while officers who had "stayed at home in peace and quietness" had monopolized the promotion list, those on active service had been shamefully shoved aside: "You will no doubt call us a parcel of growling Americans," Fletcher wrote, adding that they had good cause to be so.[24]

This intriguing "Americanization" was also apparent in the tactics adopted by the British Army. By the Caribbean campaigns of 1762, the veteran redcoats were employing unconventional techniques that would have shocked Braddock. Enemy strongpoints on mountainous Martinique had fallen to fluid and headlong assaults by light infantry, grenadiers, and rangers, plus a handful of Indian warriors like Silver Heels. The general who assumed command of the victorious Martinique army for the attack on Havana observed: "They have conquered in a few days, the strongest country you ever saw, in the American way, running or with the Indian whoop." As that "growling American," Colonel Fletcher of the 35th, put it in another letter home, these highly aggressive tactics had worked wonders in intimidating the opposition: "Our North American manner of attacking the enemy equally surprised as well as frightened them to such a degree that none of them . . . could be prevailed upon, either to attack or defend."[25]

When the Seven Years' War was brought to a close at the Peace of Paris in 1763, Britons on both sides of the Atlantic contemplated a new era of greatness. Just twelve years later, they were locked in a bitter and bloody civil war. Ironically, the seeds of that conflict sprouted from the sheer scale and decisiveness of Britain's victory.

Unlike previous Anglo-French struggles, which had typically ended with a restoration of the prewar situation, the Seven Years' War caused seismic shifts in the balance of power. Ministers in distant London now faced the challenge of administering vast new American territories: on the mainland alone they had acquired Canada and all other French claims east of the Mississippi. Before the definitive treaty was signed, France had already transferred Louisiana west of the Mississippi to Spain, thereby relinquishing its remaining American territory. Meanwhile, in partial exchange for Havana, Spain ceded Florida to Britain.

The maintenance and administration of this greatly expanded North American empire would require money and manpower. Before these new costs were even considered, there was the question of paying the reckoning for the war that had just been won. At its beginning, Britain's national debt stood at nearly £75 million; by 1763, it had rocketed to almost £123 million, with interest at £4.5 million a year—and this at a time when the annual national budget was just £8 million. With taxation far higher in Britain than in America, it seemed only fair to British policy makers that the colonists in whose interests the war had been fought should help to shoulder the burden. This assumption misread the mood and mindset of Americans who had long since grown accustomed to ruling themselves through their own elected assemblies, bodies like Virginia's House of Burgesses. Americans were not represented in Parliament, so why should they pay the taxes it sought to impose upon them? Indeed, to do so would deprive them of their prized *English* liberties; over the coming decade, sporadic British efforts to tax the colonies would be interpreted by many Americans as a sinister ministerial plot aimed at achieving nothing less.[26]

There were other baleful legacies to Britain's overwhelming victory in 1763. The humiliations heaped upon a humbled France ensured that revenge against her old enemy would henceforth become the primary objective of her foreign policy. More immediately, the eradication of French power on the North American continent played a part in fomenting another dangerous Indian war, far more widespread than the conflict with the Cherokees.

As the tribes of the interior were no longer needed as allies against the old enemy, Major General Amherst sought to cut costs by ending the customary policy of providing them with ammunition and other gifts. Deeply offended by what they regarded as a gross show of contempt and convinced by a flow of white settlers across the Appalachians that the promises made at the Treaty of Easton back in 1758 were meaningless, a formidable Indian confederacy, embracing the Ohio and western tribes, struck back with a devastating coordinated assault. Small posts recently taken from the French, like Venango and Presque Isle, were engulfed, leaving larger strongpoints—Forts Niagara and Pitt and the stockaded settlement at Detroit—marooned under Indian blockade. Raids lapped against the frontiers of Virginia and Pennsylvania, prompting an exodus of settlers that recalled the grim years 1755 to 1758.[27]

This Indian war of independence, traditionally named after the Ottawa leader Pontiac, erupted when Amherst was least able to quell it. Most of the veteran regulars responsible for conquering New France had been sent to the Caribbean, where they died in the thousands from tropical disease. Those survivors of the siege of Havana who trickled back to New York were but a pitiful remnant of the once-formidable "American Army." The desperate Amherst managed to gather some 400 Highlanders—all that now remained of Montgomery's regiment and two battalions of the 42nd, or Royal Highland Regiment—and to place them under the command of Washington's old commander, Colonel Henri Bouquet, with orders to relieve Fort Pitt.

Obliged to retrace the road he'd followed during Forbes's campaign, by early afternoon on August 5, Bouquet had marched his convoy of packhorses as far as Bushy Run, about twenty-five miles from his objective. Here, he was attacked by a strong force of Indians: local Delawares, Shawnees, and Mingos joined by Wyandots, Miamis, and Ottawas from the west.

Alerted by the Indians' tracks and fires, Bouquet had arrayed his command in a hollow square. This defensive formation kept the enemy at bay, but with casualties mounting and little water to be had, by evening his situation looked bleak. The next day, the Indians renewed their assault, fighting with a determination that impressed their enemies. Bouquet proved equal to the crisis. By deliberately weakening part of his perimeter, he lured the Indians forward into a devastating trap, meeting them with close-range volleys followed by a counterattack that allowed his regulars to ply their bayonets. According to Private Robert Kirkwood of Montgomery's Highlanders, at this the Indians "set to their heels and were never after able to rally again."[28]

Bouquet's close-run victory enabled him to push on to Fort Pitt and was widely celebrated as proof that the Indians, who had beaten Braddock and Grant nearby, "and expected to have served Colonel Bouquet in the same manner," were no longer invincible. The outcome owed much to the resilience of Bouquet's veterans and to his own presence of mind: since 1758, he had clearly continued to devote thought to the tactical demands of the wilderness. Writing to congratulate him on his success, one of his officers, Captain Harry Gordon, observed, "You have many times talked of the disposition you put in practice, as preferring it, and I made no doubt the consequence would show the justice of your thoughts."[29]

Bushy Run did not end the Indian war. The conflict dragged for another year before the momentum of the tribes' offensive slackened in the face of growing disunity and a systematic advance against the villages along the Muskingum River, west of Fort Pitt, commanded by the indefatigable Bouquet. Yet "Pontiac's War" wrecked Amherst's reputation as the conqueror of Canada; he was replaced as commander in chief in North America by Washington's friend and yet another veteran of Braddock's defeat, Major General Thomas Gage.

The unexpected Indian war had prompted much comment and alarm in London. In October 1763, in a belated attempt to defuse tensions between whites and Indians, a proclamation was issued.

Renewing the pledge made at the Treaty of Easton five years earlier, this banned white settlement west of the Appalachians, reserving that territory for the Indians "for the present." Intended to appease and reassure the tribes, the proclamation had the opposite effect on the colonists, not least George Washington.

From his first teenaged forays beyond the Blue Ridge Mountains, Washington had been drawn by the trans-Appalachian west and its rich potential for exploitation. By 1763, for all his own extensive acreage at Mount Vernon and the Custis plantations, Washington's hunger for western land was stronger than ever, and he remained receptive to any initiative that might add more. This interest was stimulated by economic problems: at the very time Washington was working to maximize the productivity of his farms, he was facing an increasingly frustrating relationship with the English merchants who acted as agents in selling his tobacco and who bought and imported the luxury items that were virtually unobtainable in the American colonies.

Both George and Martha Washington were reluctant to scrimp on the fashionable English clothes and furniture fitting for their station or on regular entertaining. The Virginian custom of unstinting hospitality ensured that there were often guests for dinner at Mount Vernon. There were parties, card games, dancing, and such balls and theater performances as Williamsburg or Alexandria could offer, but, above all, fox hunting. An accomplished horseman, Washington was as devoted to following the hounds as any English country squire. His diaries are full of descriptions of hunting, cornering, and killing foxes across the Northern Neck. For example, in January 1769, he was out hunting with his Fairfax County neighbors on five successive days. Washington was equally fanatical about preserving the purity of his pack of hounds, noting with despair the "promiscuity" of bitches such as "Countess," who broke free from her kennel and mated once with Washington's own spaniel and twice with "a small foist looking yellow cur" before her escape was discovered.[30]

The Washingtons' lavish lifestyle and George's policy of upgrading and expanding his estates and then buying more slaves to work the extra acres, came at a price. In early 1764, he received a jolt when Robert Cary and Company informed him that he was no less than £1,811.1.1 in their debt. Washington was ruefully obliged to admit that the merchant's figures were right: the harsh reality was that Mount Vernon tobacco fetched lower prices than that grown by his neighbors. Time and again, Washington complained that he was underpaid for his tobacco and overcharged for the imported goods, which were often of inferior quality or damaged during their passage across the Atlantic. Just as Washington was convinced that provincial officers had failed to receive their just rewards, so it now seemed that the colonists were being treated as second-class citizens of the British Empire, palmed off with outmoded and shoddy merchandise. Every chipped piece of china, every ill-fitting pair of breeches, every barrel of beer that had already been drunk down to the dregs by thirsty sailors on the voyage from England contributed to a growing sense of resentment.

Washington's readiness to experiment with alternatives to tobacco offered one possible solution to the financial dilemma; but, given his long-standing interests, land speculation was far more alluring. Washington was willing to seek land wherever it could be found, and not just in the west. In the wake of the 1763 peace, he made two trips to the Dismal Swamp, which straddled Virginia's border with North Carolina, an area that appeared to offer potential for drainage and development. Washington's account of his trip to the region that October provides a detailed record of a swamp that was a geological oddity, lying above the surrounding land.[31] Along with several partners Washington formed a company to drain and develop the area. The next year, 1764, slaves were sent to start work, but returns were modest.

In June 1763, Washington joined eighteen other speculators from Virginia and Maryland in a far more ambitious venture called the Mississippi Company: this aimed to take out an option on a vast swathe of land—2.5 million acres—recently conquered from the French. Yet before the company members could even file their petition, their hopes were dashed by that October's royal proclamation.

That same legislation blocked another ploy by which Washington hoped to acquire western lands. Ever since 1759, the recently retired Washington and other officers of the Virginia Regiment had petitioned for their share in the 200,000 acres of bounty land promised by Governor Dinwiddie to stimulate recruitment back in 1754; like the Mississippi Company, this initiative was sunk by the new ban upon trans-Appalachian settlement. While it failed to halt the flow of white settlers across the mountains, the proclamation was more effective in blocking the efforts of major speculators like Washington, who required clear title to land before they could sell it.[32]

But Washington remained undeterred, viewing the 1763 proclamation as a "temporary expedient to quiet the minds of the Indians." To be ready to act when that barrier fell and to preempt other speculators, in 1767 he proposed a partnership to another Virginian veteran, Captain William Crawford; according to local tradition, Washington had known Crawford since they were schoolboys in Fredericksburg. Together they would survey and patent prime tracts around Pittsburgh and farther down the Ohio. Washington told Crawford that anyone who "neglects the present opportunity of hunting out good lands and in some measure marking and distinguishing them for their own . . . will never regain it." Crawford, who was on the spot, would identify the best locations, while it was Washington's role to secure them as soon as possible, covering the costs of surveying and patenting. Tracts would be divided up between them. Washington urged Crawford to proceed in all secrecy, both to avoid broadcasting his dismissive attitude toward the proclamation and to keep competitors in the dark.[33]

The opportunity that men like Washington had been waiting for came in November 1768, when the Iroquois formally relinquished their claim to an extensive territory, including what would become Kentucky. Seeking to guarantee the integrity of their tribal heartlands, the Iroquois had surrendered land that was not theirs to give. While the so-called Treaty of Fort Stanwix was never ratified by Britain and was angrily repudiated by the Shawnees and other tribes of the Ohio Valley for whom Kentucky was a prized hunting

ground, it stimulated a land grab that effectively pushed the dividing line between whites and Indians far westward to the Ohio River;
over the next quarter century the Shawnees and a growing band of
tribal allies would fight tenaciously to defend that new frontier.[34]

Encouraged by the bulging of the hated Proclamation Line, in
the following year Washington formally renewed his claim to a
colonel's share of the long-promised bounty lands—the just due of
those who had "toiled, and bled" for Virginia. Washington hoped
for a single large reserve within which each qualified veteran could
pick the best lands he could find. Instead, Fauquier's successor as
Virginia's lieutenant governor, Norborne Berkeley, Lord Botetourt,
and his council required claimants to make their selection from
twenty distinct parcels of land. In response to this, Washington
called meetings of the veterans and persuaded them to appoint his
partner Captain Crawford to act as surveyor for all.[35]

In autumn 1770, in company with another veteran of the Virginia
Regiment's campaigns, his friend Dr. James Craik, Washington set
out to supervise the surveys, traveling to the Great Kanawha River,
a tributary of the Ohio below Pittsburgh. The trek took him past
places evocative of memories: the Great Meadows, where he had
been obliged to capitulate in 1754 and the site of Braddock's massacre a year later. He also met Thomas Gist, the son of his faithful
guide Christopher, who as an ensign in the Virginia Regiment had
been captured by the Hurons at Grant's Defeat. Yet Washington's
detailed journal remained focused on the future potential of these
lands, not their past significance; he was more concerned with soil
and timber than recollections of near-death encounters. For example, in his diary for October 13, 1770, Washington wrote: "When we
came down the hill to the plantation of Mr. Thomas Gist, the land
appeared charming; that which lay level being as rich and black as
anything could possibly be."[36]

Only occasionally did Washington note the intrusion of the past
upon the present. On October 28, he encountered "an old acquaintance," one of the Indians who had accompanied him on his diplomatic mission to the French forts in 1753. Seneca chief "Kiashuta,"

or "Guyasuta," was apparently delighted to see Washington once again, even though he had fought against the British during the French and Indian War and the ensuing Indian rebellion associated with Pontiac; indeed, before that outbreak, Guyasuta had moved among the discontented tribes seeking to forge a truly pan-Indian confederacy; had he succeeded, the outcome of "Pontiac's War"— and the course of North American history—might have been very different. To Washington, however, Guyasuta the visionary Indian diplomat remained the "Hunter": he now lived up to his name by supplying his guests with a "quarter of very fine buffalo."[37]

It was Washington who allotted the bounty lands among the veterans, officers, and soldiers alike. When his own field officer's share was added to that bought from men too poor to help finance the surveys or too skeptical to risk a commitment, Washington had amassed some 24,000 acres; with land eventually acquired under other bounty provisions included within the 1763 proclamation, which invited war veterans to settle in Florida, Canada, and other territories wrested from the Bourbons, this total rose to more than 35,000 acres. His policy of selecting the very best land—"the cream of the country," as he later called it—for himself and his crony Craik attracted criticism from fellow veterans.[38]

Washington responded by emphasizing that it was only through *his* determination that they had been given the chance to claim their bounty lands at all. One veteran who felt that he had been denied his rightful quota was Major George Muse, the same man who as Washington's lieutenant colonel at Fort Necessity had been stigmatized as a coward. Muse's "impertinent letter" has regrettably been lost, but Washington's angry response reveals his lasting contempt for an officer who had failed to match his own standards of gentlemanly conduct. He wrote:

> *I am not accustomed to receive such from any man, nor would have taken the same language from you personally, without letting you feel some marks of my resentment. . . . For though I understand you were drunk when you did it, yet give me leave*

to tell you, that drunkenness is no excuse for rudeness; and that,
but for your stupidity and sottishness you might have known,
by attending to the public gazettes . . . that you had your full
quantity of ten thousand acres of land allowed you . . . do you
think your superlative merit entitles you to greater indulgences
than others? . . . All my concern is that I ever engaged in behalf
of so ungrateful and dirty a fellow as you are.[39]

Washington's uncharacteristically withering dismissal of the wretched Muse suggests that his own military service and the high reputation that he had established continued to matter to him. This may help to explain why, in May 1772, he chose to pose for his first and what would presumably be his last formal portrait dressed not as the gentleman farmer he was, but as the officer of the Virginia Regiment that he had once been.

The resulting portrait of Washington, the first of seven to be painted by Charles Willson Peale, reveals an amiable-looking forty-year-old, confident of his status and apparently unconcerned about concealing the paunch now straining the buttons of the waistcoat he had worn in his twenties. In fact, as Peale could testify, the approach of middle age had done nothing to diminish Washington's phenomenal strength. During his stay at Mount Vernon, the artist recalled how he and some other young men were stripped to their shirtsleeves and engaged in the sport of tossing a heavy iron bar. Without deigning to even remove his coat, Washington sauntered over, hefted the bar, and flipped it way beyond the farthest mark.[40]

Peale's portrait includes telling details; they offer evidence that Washington's selection of his old uniform was deliberate rather than whimsical and intended to recall specific aspects of his military career. For example, the faded crimson sash across his chest had once belonged to Braddock and was given to him as a keepsake by the dying general after the disastrous engagement from which Washington had miraculously emerged unscathed and with such credit. From the pocket of his waistcoat juts a folded paper marked "Order of March," a carefully observed detail commemorating

Washington's responsibilities as brigadier under Forbes in 1758. Washington's gorget—the small crescent-shaped badge of rank worn at the throat by eighteenth-century officers—bears the rampant lion and unicorn of the royal arms. This hint of lingering allegiance to Britain's monarchy is intriguing. In 1772, the very act of donning his old regimentals must have evoked mixed memories of Washington's days as guardian of the Virginian frontier, stirring both pride in his achievements and a residual anger at the slights he had endured. He could not have known that in just three years he would be in uniform once again, this time fighting to protect Virginian and American liberties from British tyranny.[41]

In fact, when he posed for Peale's portrait, Washington had already acknowledged that armed resistance to imperial policies was not unthinkable. As noted, during the 1760s, Washington's existing sense that the British establishment had failed to recognize his abilities was compounded by fresh grievances relating to his treatment at the hands of voracious London merchants and by the legislation that consistently hamstrung his ventures into land speculation. While Washington was clearly irked by what he regarded as British discrimination against colonials, during that same decade, as British taxation policies provoked vociferous colonial reaction, he scarcely gained the reputation of a radical revolutionary. In the House of Burgesses, where he represented his own Fairfax County from 1765, he typically took a backseat in the debate over what was increasingly seen as a ministerial conspiracy to strip Americans of their hard-won English liberties. Through Washington's personal correspondence, however, it is possible to trace his growing disillusionment with imperial policies, a hardening in his attitude and, ultimately, an acceptance that war with Britain was inevitable.

In September 1765, Washington gave a dispassionate assessment of the effect of that year's Stamp Act upon trade between Britain and her colonies. Rising to oppose Prime Minister George Grenville's measure in a forceful speech in Parliament, the Quebec veteran Isaac Barré had used the opportunity to defend the much-maligned British Americans, describing them as "Sons of Liberty." Barré, like the former war leader William Pitt, was hailed as a "friend" of the colonists; when his words were reported in American newspapers, they were swiftly embraced as a proud title by the most determined opponents of British taxation.[42] Washington was not yet among them. While certainly believing the act, which aimed to impose a tax upon paper, to be "ill judged," Washington distanced himself from "the speculative part of the colonists, who look upon this unconstitutional method of taxation as a direful attack upon their liberties, and loudly exclaim against the violation." However, as he assured his wife's uncle, Francis Dandridge, people were already beginning to realize that they could live without those "many luxuries which we lavish our substance to Great Britain for." Turning to the "necessaries of life," for the most part they could be found within the colonies themselves. This was scarcely firebrand rhetoric, but it nonetheless demonstrated a willingness to begin cutting the apron strings that still tethered colonial "children" psychologically to the "Mother Country."[43]

As the controversy dragged on and ministers in London came and went, imposing legislation in fits and starts, British attempts to generate American revenue encountered peaks of colonial resistance, matched by deceptively tranquil troughs when economic conditions in America improved and discontent subsided. This suggests that, for many colonials, opposition to British policies was fueled by economic as much as by ideological factors. Yet the underlying issue, the perceived threat to liberty, endured; during the second half of the 1760s, the political stance of Washington, who was as interested as anyone in financial realities, slowly shifted.

By 1769, when the next concerted wave of British taxation policy, the Townshend Duties of 1767, prompted colonial resistance through nonimportation pacts, Washington's position had altered significantly from four years earlier. By now he was contemplating armed resistance against "our lordly masters in Great Britain," who seemed bent upon depriving Americans of their freedoms. But while Washington believed that "no man should scruple, or hesitate a moment to use a-ms [arms] in defense of so valuable a blessing" as liberty, he was still emphasizing that this "should be the last resource; the dernier resort." Addresses to the king and Parliament had been tried and failed, yet it remained to be seen whether economic warfare targeting British trade and manufactures would bring ministers to a proper awareness of Americans' rights and privileges.[44]

In May 1769, Washington was present when the House of Burgesses resolved that it alone had the right to tax Virginians. After Lieutenant Governor Botetourt responded by dissolving the defiant Assembly, Washington was among those burgesses who promptly adjourned to a local tavern and signed an agreement pledging to embargo all taxed items from Britain. Like many men of his class, however, Washington took a dim view of unrestrained mob action against British policies. He was unmoved by the "Boston Massacre" of March 1770, in which several members of a crowd were shot dead by the British soldiers they were baiting, and appalled by the destruction of property resulting from the "Boston Tea Party" in late 1773, when Bostonians disguised as Mohawks dumped a consignment of cut-rate East India Company tea into their harbor. Yet he was even more vehemently opposed to the punitive measures, which smacked of despotism, that the exasperated British promptly imposed in retaliation. These so-called Coercive Acts, which closed the port of Boston to all commerce, stripped the Massachusetts assembly of its powers to appoint the governor's council, and saw the return of redcoats who had been removed amid the tension following the "Boston Massacre," were widely interpreted as an all-out attack upon colonial rights and proved the real turning point for men like George Washington.[45]

By the summer of 1774, Washington was reconciled to the inevitability of war with Britain. Writing to Bryan Fairfax, the brother of his friend George William Fairfax, Washington believed that the time for petitions was now over: "Does it not appear, as clear as the sun in its meridian brightness, that there is a regular, systematic plan formed to fix the right and practice of taxation upon us?" he asked. Surely, the attack upon the liberty and property of the Bostonians mounted

by the Coercive, or "Intolerable," Acts was proof of that. Such tyrannical measures left no doubt that the ministry in London would stick
at nothing to carry its point. For Washington, the only response was
now clear: "Ought we not, then, to put our virtue and fortitude to the
severest test?" It was another rhetorical question.[46]

Washington's words reveal his alignment with other Americans,
mostly from his own privileged background, who had imbibed the
ideology evolved by a diverse but distinct body of English political
writers during the second quarter of the eighteenth century. Col-
lectively called the "Country Party," these reform-minded thinkers
among the landed gentry argued that the hallowed English constitution was endangered by the "corrupt" politics of the age, personified
by the long-serving "prime minister," Sir Robert Walpole; their writings provided a lens through which English and American radicals
scrutinized the policies of subsequent British ministries, seeing the
same dire tendencies that had ruined the virtuous Roman Republic, despite the best efforts of public-minded patriots like Cato, the
hero of Joseph Addison's much-admired play. Key "Country Party"
texts warning against impending tyranny included John Trenchard
and Thomas Gordon's *Cato's Letters* and *The Independent Whig* and
Henry St. John, Lord Viscount Bolingbroke's periodical *The Crafts-
man*. These works, and many more of a similar bent, could be found
in the extensive library of Daniel Parke Custis, which Washington
inherited upon marrying his widow, Martha Custis, in 1759; he had
already begun reading about English history and politics while still
a teenager.[47]

Ironically, the rarefied worldview of Englishmen who believed
that their hard-won liberties were in peril resonated most strongly
across the Atlantic among disgruntled Americans like Washington, bolstering suspicions of a calculated bid to strip them of
their property and so reduce them to "slavery." Just as Washington's English-born mentors at Belvoir had provided patterns for his
future conduct, so the writings of English political thinkers shaped
the way in which he perceived the worsening crisis between colonies and Mother Country.

What Washington and many other Americans were now contemplating was a fight in defense of their cherished freedoms. Viewed from London's perspective, such resistance would brand them as rebels. The last rebellion against the ruling Hanoverian regime, in 1745–46, had been crushed with signal savagery: on the battlefield of Culloden, in brutal punitive expeditions into the Scottish Highlands, and through a spate of executions. Twenty years later, the heads of men who had served in the Jacobite armies of Bonnie Prince Charlie and been hung, drawn, and quartered for treason were still spiked on Temple Bar overlooking Fleet Street, one of London's busiest thoroughfares. In the early hours of December 9, 1766, that year's *Annual Register* reported, a furtive sportsman "was observed to watch his opportunity of discharging musket-balls from a steel cross-bow, at the two remaining heads upon Temple Bar." His targets belonged to Francis Townley and George Fletcher, who were among officers of the Manchester Regiment executed on Kennington Common on August 2, 1746.[48] In 1775, there was nothing to suggest that a new crop of American rebels would not share their fate.

One man who knew about rebellion from hard personal experience, the former Jacobite Hugh Mercer, had relocated from Pennsylvania to Virginia in 1771. Mercer's move south came at Washington's suggestion, and he settled near Mount Vernon at Fredericksburg. The two veterans forged a strong friendship, and both were members of the town's Freemasons' lodge. Mercer's daughter Anne married Robert Patton; their great-great-grandson would become that quintessential American warrior, General George Patton.[49]

Another British-born veteran of the French and Indian War, Horatio Gates, came to Virginia soon after Mercer, in 1772. Gates was a former regular army officer who had captained a New York independent company at Braddock's defeat and had been wounded there. He subsequently served as brigade-major to Brigadier General Stanwix at Fort Pitt in 1759. Two years later, when Stanwix's replacement, Robert Monckton, was appointed major general to command the expedition against Martinique, he took Gates along as his aide-de-camp. Following the capitulation of the island's key cita-del of Fort Royal in February 1762, Gates was awarded the honor of carrying the victory dispatches to London. Despite this mark of dis-tinction, which brought promotion to major, after the peace, Gates's military career stagnated. Like Washington, Gates felt aggrieved at being denied the recognition that he believed his services merited, eventually choosing to make a new life in the Shenandoah Valley. There he soon established friendships with neighbors, including that seasoned veteran of the Virginia Regiment, Adam Stephen.[50]

From his Berkeley County plantation, "Traveler's Rest," Gates extended an offer of hospitality to another old comrade of the Brad-dock expedition, Charles Lee, who had come to Virginia in Feb-ruary 1774. Lee too was convinced that he had never received due recognition of his efforts and abilities from the British establish-ment. After the peace of 1763, Lee followed a rambling and varied military career that had taken him to a Poland torn apart by insur-rection, and as far afield as Moldavia, where he had fought with the Russians against the Ottoman Turks in a campaign that helped to convince him of the superiority of guerrilla warfare over more con-ventional strategies.[51]

An outspoken advocate of American liberty, in Virginia, Lee soon made his mark on the local political scene: he was in Williamsburg when the news arrived of London's draconian response to the Bos-ton Tea Party, and in conjunction with another radical, the brilliant young Virginian lawyer Thomas Jefferson, he helped to orchestrate an official day of fasting to express solidarity with the Bostonians. From the Old Dominion, Lee headed north to Philadelphia and New York. Drawing upon his extensive military experience, he published a pamphlet calculated to stiffen the resolve of Americans now bracing themselves for war with Britain. Lee assured them that they had nothing to fear from the redcoats—"debauched weavers 'prentices, the scum of the Irish Roman Catholics, who desert upon every occasion, and a few Scots, who are not strong enough to carry packs"; though "expert in all the tricks of the parade," such troops were "totally unfit for real service." In his estimation, the "yeomanry of America" would prove more than a match for the regulars: in just a few months, by concentrating on the basics, such militia could be transformed into a "most formidable infantry." Lee believed that the Americans had another crucial advantage on their side: unlike "the peasantry of other countries," they were familiar with firearms from infancy and consequently "expert in the use of them." Gates warned Lee to moderate his "zeal in the noble cause" while adding that he was himself willing to risk his life "to preserve the liberty of the western world." Like Gates and Mercer before him, Lee settled in Virginia and was likewise destined to play a leading role as the political crisis intensified into a military conflict.[52]

During 1774, even as war looked ever more likely, Washington had other concerns. Besides overseeing the steady expansion of Mount Vernon, which acquired a new wing, he was entrusted with the melancholy responsibility of selling off the familiar furniture and furnishings of the far grander mansion at Belvoir. The Fairfaxes—George William and his wife, Sally—had decided to make a new home in England; they never came back. For Washington, their departure marked a break with the past: it was at Belvoir, as a gangling teenager, that he had begun to acquire the polish of the finished gentleman; it was there he had listened to Colonel Fairfax's inspirational tales of European warfare—and fallen in love with Sally: in different ways, both had exerted a profound influence upon his first career as a soldier.

There was also the still-unresolved matter of the war bounties, both those resulting from Dinwiddie's 1754 announcement regarding the Ohio lands and those promised by the British government under the 1763 proclamation. When he finally learned, in early 1774, that Lord Hillsborough, the secretary of state for the American colonies, had ruled that only *regular* soldiers were eligible to apply for the 1763 bounties, it seemed yet another example of anti-American prejudice: echoing the words of the angry letter that he had written to Dinwiddie on behalf of his Virginia Regiment in 1757, he observed: "I conceive the services of a provincial officer as worthy of reward as a regular one, and can only be withheld from him with injustice." As such a ruling rested upon equal measures of "malice, absurdity, and error," he could see no reason to be bound by it.[53]

In any case, events were now moving with a momentum that suggested such imperial decrees would soon be redundant. That August, Washington returned to Philadelphia as one of Virginia's seven delegates to the First Continental Congress, summoned to hammer out a pan-colonial response to the escalating dispute with Britain; attended by representatives from every colony save Georgia, this was a show of cooperation that would have been unthinkable during Washington's twenties, when Americans were notorious for their intercolonial squabbling.

The fifty-six delegates included men who had achieved prominence during the previous decade of periodic resistance to British legislation by openly challenging Parliament's right to levy taxation: in 1765, besides galvanizing Virginia's strident response to the Stamp Act, the backwoods lawyer Patrick Henry gained fame—and notoriety—with his warning that, just as Charles I had met his master in Oliver Cromwell, so he didn't doubt that "some good American would stand up, in favor of his country." Two years later, equally emotive language had been used by another of the delegates sent to Philadelphia in 1774. In a series of articles known as the "Letters of a Pennsylvania Farmer," John Dickinson had argued that craven submission to London's policies would complete "the tragedy of American liberty," leaving his countrymen no better than the downtrodden peasantry of France and Poland, "in wooden shoes and with uncombed hair." Other delegates, sharp legal minds John Adams of Massachusetts and John Jay of New York, were to undertake a still greater role in their country's affairs in coming years.

Even now, old ties exerted their pull. Resolving to form an "Association" imposing a boycott on British imports from December 1, 1774, delegates continued to describe themselves as "His Majesty's most loyal subjects." To enforce this pact, "Committees of Observation and Inspection" were to be formed in "every county, city, and town," picked by those men qualified to elect representatives in their own legislatures.[54] This was a crucial development: while the delegates sent to Philadelphia had been drawn overwhelmingly from the traditional leadership strata of landowners, merchants, and planters epitomized by gentry like Washington and the Congress's president, his fellow Virginian Peyton Randolph, the new committees reflected a far broader membership, giving humble artisans and farmers a heady taste of power and influence.

Washington said little enough during the six weeks of debates, although there is no doubting the strength of his private views. That September, while the Congress was still in session, he received a letter from Robert Mackenzie, who had served as a captain in the Virginia Regiment and was now a lieutenant in one of the British regiments recently sent to overawe the truculent populace of Massachusetts Bay. Back in 1760, when he first tried to transfer to the regulars, Mackenzie had written to Washington for a testimonial. His request was declined, courteously but firmly, because Washington felt such a reference should better come from Mackenzie's current colonel, William Byrd. Mackenzie had eventually succeeded in securing an ensign's commission in the 58th Foot, only to be captured by the French as his regiment was on passage to the siege of Havana in 1762. Since then, he had gained a lieutenancy in the 43rd Foot. It was in that capacity that Mackenzie sought to alert his former colonel to the dangerous extremism of the Boston radicals he now found himself billeted among; they were bent upon nothing less than "total independence," he warned, and needed to be reined in by "abler heads and better hearts." Indeed, their rebellious behavior and scandalous "attacks upon the best characters" in the colony had obliged General Gage to put Boston in "a formidable state of defense."[55]

Washington's reply showed that he now shared much in common with the very men that Mackenzie was bidding him to shun. Neither the leaders of Massachusetts Bay nor "any thinking man in all North America" were seeking independence from Britain, he wrote. On the contrary, it was the "ardent wish of the warmest advocates for liberty, that peace and tranquility, upon constitutional grounds, may be restored, and the horrors of civil discord prevented." That said, the colonies would never "submit to the loss of those valuable rights and privileges, which are essential to the happiness of every free state, and without which, life, liberty, and property are rendered totally insecure." If the ministry in London was determined "to push matters to extremity," Washington predicted, "more blood will be spilt . . . than history has ever yet furnished instances of in the annals of North America."[56]

That civil war grew more likely by the day. In Philadelphia, Washington made some telling purchases: a new sash and epaulettes for his uniform and a book by a veteran officer of the 48th Foot, Thomas Webb, entitled *A Military Treatise on the Appointments of the Army*.[57] When Washington returned from Philadelphia, he found Virginians busily preparing for impending war. The notoriously inefficient county militia was being reorganized into more rigorously drilled "independent companies"; as the Old Dominion's most illustrious soldier, "Colonel Washington" was in heavy demand to head them. By March of 1775, Washington had been invited to lead five companies, including that of his own Fairfax County—the first to be raised. That same month, a second Virginia Convention was summoned; this ordered that the colony should "be immediately put into a posture of defense." As war loomed ever closer, so the value placed upon Washington's experience rose correspondingly: his standing ensured that he was comfortably elected as a delegate to the Second Continental Congress, scheduled to open in Philadelphia on May 10, 1775. Some two weeks before then, news reached Mount Vernon that the anticipated rebellion against Britain had already erupted, with murderous clashes on April 19 between redcoats and militia at Lexington and Concord in the countryside surrounding Boston.

Writing to his close friend and former neighbor, George William Fairfax, who was now in England, Washington was adamant that the heavy losses inflicted upon the regulars as they were chivvied back into Boston should convince even the most hawkish British minister that, far from being cowards, Americans were willing to "fight for their liberties and property." It was indeed unhappy "to reflect, that a brother's sword has been sheathed in a brother's breast, and that, the once happy and peaceful plains of America are either to be drenched with blood, or inhabited by slaves." These were sad alternatives, he acknowledged: "But can a virtuous man hesitate in his choice?"[58]

Washington would answer his own question soon enough.

6

HIS EXCELLENCY
GENERAL WASHINGTON

In the wake of the bloodshed at Lexington and Concord, the Second Continental Congress in Philadelphia resolved that the New Englanders converging upon the chastened and beleaguered redcoat garrison of Boston should form the basis of a truly pan-colonial army. It was momentous decision, and it posed another: who should command it?

Contenders included Artemas Ward, commander in chief of the Massachusetts troops and already leading the thousands of amateur soldiers laying siege to Gage's army. Like Washington, Ward was a veteran of the French and Indian War; as a local man, he also enjoyed the backing of influential Yankees. Other delegates championed Charles Lee, the veteran British Army officer who had recently settled in Virginia and who boasted impressive credentials as a professional soldier.

Then there was George Washington. Not only was he still widely esteemed for the military and personal reputation that he had established during the 1750s, but his election was urged by some, especially the Massachusetts lawyer John Adams, for hard political reasons. If his own recollection is to be credited, Adams's oratory was instrumental in swaying his fellow congressmen toward Washington by arguing that the selection of a Virginian would help to dispel a common notion that New England was attempting to dominate the rest of the colonies, thus overcoming traditional provincial rivalries and forging a unified war effort against Britain. As Adams remembered putting it, Washington was:

> *a gentleman whose skill and experience as an officer, whose independent fortune, great talents and excellent universal character, would command the approbation of all America, and unite the cordial exertions of all the colonies better than any other person in the union.*[1]

According to the interpretation widely accepted by his biographers, Washington was surprised to be nominated: tormented by doubts of his ability to undertake the job, he accepted only with extreme reluctance and because his sense of duty outweighed his misgivings. In fact, there is considerable evidence that Washington was always a strong candidate and that he exploited opportunities in Philadelphia to bolster his chances, capitalizing upon his enduring reputation to take a prominent role as Congress planned its response to the outbreak of open warfare with Great Britain.[2]

Just five days into the session, on May 15, Washington was appointed to chair a committee to advise New Yorkers on how to respond if anticipated British reinforcements landed among them. The committee's recommendations—that they should only resist if attacked—prompted broader discussion within Congress about the respective merits of war and peace, of vigorous resistance versus reconciliation. Divisions between moderate and militant factions led to a compromise on May 25–26: congressional advice that New York should enlist 3,000 men to serve until December 31 was balanced by a further appeal to King George III. Known as the "Olive Branch Petition" and couched in restrained and respectful language, this voiced the delegates' hopes for a restoration of "harmony" between Crown and colonies. Yet for all its professions of loyalty and devotion, the petition included no hint of concessions by Congress, instead appealing to the king to prevent further bloodshed and repeal the legislation that had sparked trouble in the first place.[3]

In coming weeks, as such initiatives appeared increasingly futile, momentum gathered behind the concept of a truly "American Army," to be controlled by Congress. When a second committee was formed, to draft plans to distribute ammunition and military stores throughout the colonies, it was once again headed by Washington. On June 3, Congress voted to borrow £6,000 to purchase gunpowder for what was now being styled "the Continental Army." Another committee was appointed to estimate the cost of a year-long military campaign, with Washington once more called upon to chair it. Congress finally took the plunge on June 14, when it gave orders for the recruitment of ten companies of riflemen—six from Pennsylvania and two each from Virginia and Maryland—to reinforce the "American continental army" at Boston. A fourth committee was responsible for drafting the rules and regulations to govern these riflemen and all other troops to be raised by Congress: as before, Washington took the helm.

By chairing these key military committees at the very time when Congress was recognizing the need for a Continental Army and considering who should command it, Washington highlighted his qualifications for that job. His decision to attend Congress dressed in full military uniform underlined the same point in striking visual fashion.[4]

Working alongside key delegates from almost every colony, Washington impressed them at first hand not only with his military expertise, but with the other essential prerequisite for the post—his credentials as an officer and a gentleman of unimpeachable character. In addition, Washington looked and acted the part: according to Congressman Benjamin Rush, he had "so much martial dignity in his deportment that you would distinguish him to be a general and a soldier from among ten thousand people." Rush added proudly: "There is not a king in Europe that would not look like a valet de chambre by his side." Anticipating that Washington would make a favorable impression upon her, Abigail Adams discovered that the reality far exceeded expectations, informing her husband John that "the one half was not told me."

Struck by Washington's dignity and modesty, she observed that "the gentleman and soldier look agreeably blended in him."[5] By contrast, Artemas Ward had a distinctly lackluster military reputation and a homely appearance, prompting Charles Lee to dub him "the churchwarden." As for Lee himself, despite a sharp intelligence and unrivaled experience of soldiering in both America and Europe, he had an odd, even eccentric character: scrawny, beaky, and disheveled, he preferred the company of dogs to that of his fellow men. Crucially, Lee lacked a critical qualification for the top command: he was not a native-born American.

Whatever the reality of his role in swaying delegates in Washington's favor, on June 14 it was John Adams who nominated him, and the next day he was unanimously elected "to command all the Continental forces raised or to be raised for the defense of American liberty." On June 16, 1775 Washington formally accepted the post. In his address to Congress he acknowledged himself "truly sensible" of the "high honor" done to him but expressed "great distress from a consciousness that my abilities and military experience may not be equal to the extensive and important trust." However, as Congress desired it, he would exert all his powers "in their service and for the support of the glorious cause."[6]

Washington's personal correspondence reveals conflicting feelings virtually identical to those he had experienced twenty years before when contemplating command of Virginia's forces. In 1775, as in 1755, there's little doubt that Washington actually wanted the job, but that rather than thrusting himself forward with unseemly eagerness, he needed to be asked. As before, when the invitation came, Washington's determination to pursue his personal quest for honor, as expressed through public duty, left him no option but to accept.

A variety of evidence nonetheless shows that Washington's abiding hunger for recognition battled a genuine sense of trepidation at the magnitude of the task ahead. Soon after accepting the command, Washington tearfully informed his fellow Virginian Patrick Henry: "From the day I enter upon the command of the American armies, I date my fall, and the ruin of my reputation." In a letter to his wife, Martha—one of just three to have survived—Washington solemnly assured her that he had done all in his power to avoid the appointment, "But, as it has been a kind of destiny that has thrown me upon this service, I shall hope that my undertaking of it, is designed to answer some good purpose." He added that it was beyond his power to refuse "without exposing my character to such censures as would have reflected dishonor upon myself, and given pain to my friends."[7]

Before leaving Philadelphia for Boston, Washington received "instructions" from Congress for his "better direction." These authorized him to recruit an army as large as he thought fit, although it must be no more than double the enemy's force; this limitation was dictated by cost and the old suspicion of standing armies. Washington was subject to the wishes of Congress, but, as the man on the spot, had discretion to exercise his own initiative: as events unfolded, many decisions must inevitably be left to his "prudent and discreet management." Using his "best circumspection" and consulting with his council of war when appropriate, General Washington would discharge the "great trust" committed into his hands and thereby ensure "that the liberties of America receive no detriment."[8]

By emphasizing the importance of advisory councils, Washington's instructions reflected a tried and trusted feature of eighteenth-century warfare, one that he had already encountered while serving under British generals Braddock and Forbes and regularly employed during his own time in command of Virginia's frontier defenders. Washington's willingness to adopt this "collegiate" approach and to heed his subordinates' views would prove crucial for the survival of the revolutionaries' armed struggle by putting a brake on his own natural aggressiveness. Yet the council of war was a double-edged sword: too much reliance upon it could breed indecision in a commander, particularly as it had become customary to heed a majority vote. It was a rare general who overturned the consensus of his officers: when James Wolfe rejected his brigadiers' advice at Quebec in 1759 and went ahead with his own plan for a last-ditch attack on the city, he was very much the exception to the rule. Washington apparently interpreted his "instructions" as an obligation to comply with a council's prevailing opinion: it was only in early 1777, after receiving clarification from Congress, that he realized that a majority vote was not binding and that he had the right to overrule it.[9]

Heading north via New Jersey, Washington and his escort reached New York City on the afternoon of June 25. There he received an enthusiastic welcome from prominent local patriots accompanied by nine companies of smartly uniformed militia. The next day, the New York Provincial Congress delivered an address that left no doubt of how it interpreted Washington's role: while hailing him and his generals as champions of "the glorious struggle for American liberty," its members felt sure that, once the contest had been decided, "by that fondest wish of each American soul, an accommodation with our Mother Country," Washington would "cheerfully resign" his command "and reassume the character of our worthiest citizen."[10]

In his response, Washington sought to allay fears—implied, if not committed to paper—that he might be tempted to abuse his trust, using his powers to become a military dictator in the mold of a Caesar or Cromwell: "When we assumed the soldier," he declared, "we did not lay aside the citizen, and we shall most sincerely rejoice with you in that happy hour, when the establishment of American liberty on the most firm, and solid foundations, shall enable us to return to our private situations in the bosom of a free, peaceful, and happy country."[11]

Washington echoed the New Yorkers' hopes for the reestablishment of "peace and harmony between the Mother Country and the Colonies," but even as he wrote, the prospects for rapprochement were dwindling. On June 17—the day after he accepted command of the Continental Army—the conflict had escalated with a ferocious battle outside Boston.

Since the fighting at Lexington and Concord, the town's British garrison had been hemmed in by swarming New England militia.

Starved of fresh provisions and dominated by high ground within comfortable artillery range, the redcoats were in an increasingly precarious position. Never an aggressive commander, Lieutenant General Thomas Gage initially refused to sally out and seize the crucial heights on the Charlestown Peninsula and Dorchester Neck. Spurred on by the arrival of a trio of more combative major generals—William Howe, Henry Clinton, and John Burgoyne—Gage finally decided to act. Warned of Gage's intention to break out on June 18, General Ward forestalled him during the night of June 16–17 by constructing a redoubt on Breed's Hill on the Charlestown Peninsula.

Now facing bombardment, the British lashed out. The combat-hardened Howe was given 2,200 men and ordered to eject the rebels from their fresh earthworks. William Howe had missed the garrison's costly jaunt to Lexington and back, an experience that had led Hugh, Lord Percy, the intelligent and highly professional commander of the 5th Foot, to concede that whoever looked upon the rebels as "an irregular mob" would be "much mistaken." Indeed, his Lordship continued, they had "men among them who know very well what they are about," having served as rangers against the Indians and Canadians during the previous war.[12]

Underestimating the willingness of the Yankee militia to face regulars in a formal engagement, Howe launched most of his command in an unsubtle frontal assault up Breed's Hill. The first attack was repelled by devastating close-range musketry, obliging the shocked Howe to regroup and try again. Reinforced by another 400 troops from Boston, he led his shattered battalions back up the hill, sustaining further heavy casualties before the defenders ran out of ammunition and the surviving redcoats stormed in with the bayonet. The British had "won" the battle, but at crippling cost: a staggering 40 percent of them were killed or wounded; spattered with the blood of his men, Howe was miraculously unscathed. The physical damage of this "Battle of Bunker Hill" (as it was misnamed after an adjoining height), was real enough, its psychological impact greater still. The rebels had proved their mettle once again, making it clear to British generals that they were far from despicable and that future attacks on fortified positions were likely to incur equally prohibitive losses.

The creditable performance of the New England militia in April and June 1775 reflected intensive drilling for a year or more prior to the first shots. For example, Jonathan Brigham, of Marlborough, Massachusetts, who fought at Lexington and Bunker Hill, joined his local company of minutemen in April 1774. This rapid-reaction force "met punctually through the year two days a week for the purpose of military exercise and improvement." Another Lexington veteran, Sylvanus Wood of Woburn, Massachusetts, had spent fifteen months training with his minuteman company before hostilities commenced, being "disciplined with activity" by a former British regular "who was in the fight on Abrahams Plains with the brave General Wolfe."[13] Not surprisingly, if somewhat ironically, this training regime followed official British Army drill: the published *1764 Regulations* prompted no fewer than twenty-six North American imprints between 1766 and 1780, with demand ominously peaking in 1774–75.[14] The Massachusetts minutemen of 1775 were therefore far better trained and motivated than most colonial militia, and their sterling performance surprised British officers accustomed to the unenthusiastic and inefficient New England provincials of the previous war.

But amid all the talk of British casualties another hard lesson of Bunker Hill was overlooked. The redcoats, many of them raw recruits, had marched over the riddled bodies of their comrades to seize their objective. These were not the feeble parade-ground soldiers so recently derided by Charles Lee. British regiments that fought at Bunker Hill took an enduring pride in having done so. Ten years later, the officers of the 43rd Foot presented a gold medal to Thomas Loftus, a humble private on June 17, 1775, "to perpetuate the memory" of his distinguished conduct on that day of carnage.[15] Often depicted by patriot propaganda as hapless minions of a tyrannical ministry, men like Loftus were no less determined to hazard their lives than the defenders of American liberty. It would be a bitter and bloody contest.

Washington arrived at Cambridge, outside Boston, on July 2, 1775, and established his headquarters there. The following day, he assumed command from Artemas Ward, who became the army's senior major general. The third-ranking general, appointed with Washington's blessing, was the maverick Englishman Charles Lee. There were two other major generals: Connecticut's Israel Putnam was a burly survivor of hair-raising exploits as a ranger during the French and Indian War who had garnered fresh fame for his leadership at Bunker Hill; Philip Schuyler of New York hailed from an old and wealthy Dutch family and was another veteran of the previous American war. Horatio Gates, Washington's fellow survivor of the Monongahela, was appointed to the staff post of adjutant general, with the rank of brigadier. Another eight brigadier generals were appointed for field service: they included Richard Montgomery of New York, yet another former British Army officer who'd helped to conquer New France; Nathanael Greene of Rhode Island, whose Quaker upbringing had done nothing to discourage a passion for soldiering; and John Sullivan, a lawyer from New Hampshire.

Washington's army was weaker than expected, at about 16,000 men. Rumor reckoned the British at 12,000; their real strength was barely half that, but they were solidly fortified and controlled the sea. It was unclear to Washington whether the redcoats would attempt to break out, staging another Bunker Hill–style assault on the besiegers' lines, or use their fleet to "carry their arms . . . to some other part of the continent." A third option—to "relinquish the dispute"—would never be accepted by the ministry in London "unless compelled" by force of arms.[16]

As commander in chief, Washington immediately set about the task of forging a viable and genuinely "American" army from the "mixed multitude of people . . . under very little discipline, order or government" that he had inherited. His General Orders issued on July 4 emphasized the need for unity among this motley crowd:

They are now the troops of the United Provinces of North America; and it is hoped that all distinctions of colonies will

be laid aside; so that one and the same spirit may animate the
whole, and the only contest be, who shall render, on this great
and trying occasion, the most essential service to the great and
common cause in which we are all engaged.

The army's ability to uphold that cause would hinge upon two qualities that Washington had demanded of his Virginia Regiment: "exact discipline" and "due subordination." Failure to address these "most essential points" would inevitably cause "hazard, disorder and confusion," leading to "shameful disappointment and disgrace."[17]

In his official report to John Hancock, the president of Congress, Washington delivered a positive verdict on the manpower he must work with. Despite the presence of too many "boys, deserters and negroes" among the troops of Massachusetts, he was pleased to find "materials for a good army," with "a great number of able-bodied men, active [and] zealous in the cause and of unquestionable courage." Writing more candidly to fellow Virginians, Washington was less flattering, characterizing the New Englanders as "an exceedingly dirty and nasty people." For all that, he felt the men would "fight very well"—*provided* they were led by good officers. Here was the real problem in Washington's opinion: contrary to newspaper reports, in general the Yankee officers were "the most indifferent kind of people" he had ever seen. Too many of them shared the "unaccountable kind of stupidity" shown by the ordinary soldiers. Plainly, they were not *gentlemen*. Because the officers were virtually "of the same kidney with the privates," they were reluctant to exercise their authority, preferring to "curry favor with the men" who had chosen them, and upon "whose smiles possibly they may think they may again rely." In consequence, Washington had "made a pretty good slam" among those officers who fell short of his own exacting standards and shown themselves unworthy of their commissions.[18]

This cull began within a week of Washington's arrival in camp. Confirming the verdict of a general court-martial on July 7, which sentenced Captain John Callender to be cashiered for cowardice, the commander in chief took the opportunity to warn of the "fatal consequences of such conduct," both to the army and to the cause it was defending. Officers must show a courageous example to their men. Those who did their duty "as brave and good officers" would earn "every mark of distinction and regard." Shirkers, by contrast, could expect punishment "with the utmost martial severity," irrespective of "connections, interest or intercessions." Callender had been accused of failing to bring forward his artillery piece at Bunker Hill by none other than General Putnam. Yet in his case at least, the judgment was dubious, the resulting opprobrium unjust. At his trial, Callender plausibly maintained that he had lacked ammunition of the correct caliber for his cannon; he subsequently cleared his name by reenlisting as a volunteer cadet in the artillery, fighting so bravely that he was reinstated as an officer within the year.[19]

While those considered unsuitable officer material were cashiered in disgrace, other men who had shown leadership potential received recognition. For example, William Lee, an orderly sergeant in the 3rd New Hampshire Regiment, had not only fought bravely at Bunker Hill but given "good advice to the men, to place themselves in right order and stand their ground well." No fewer than forty-one members of Lee's company, including his captain, Levi Spaulding, had testified to his "conduct and undaunted courage" and recommended him for a vacant ensign's commission. He was duly promoted.[20]

Washington was also keen to exploit the talents of proven fighters from the previous war. When a vacancy for a brigadier arose in August, he felt obliged to mention two veterans to Congress. Both Joseph Frye of Massachusetts and John Armstrong of Pennsylvania had served as colonels of their colonies' provincials during the French and Indian War. While quick to emphasize that he would accept either man "with the utmost deference and respect," Washington left no doubt of his own preference: while Frye enjoyed "the character of a good officer," he was not "distinguished by any peculiar service"; Armstrong, by contrast, had not only exhibited a conduct and spirit that won the approval of "all who served with

him"—including Washington himself—but he had also led the 1756
attack against the Ohio Indians at Kittanning, an enterprise "which
he planned with great judgment, and executed with equal courage
and success." Frye was a solid, respectable officer, but Armstrong
had the warrior's dash and fire that were central to Washington's
concept of leadership.[21]

Washington knew from hard personal experience that disease—
particularly dysentery—posed a greater threat than enemy action.
General Orders issued at Cambridge on July 14 emphasized the
importance of "cleanliness," upon which "the health of an army
principally depends." To that end, the privies were to be filled in
weekly and new ones dug; the streets of the encampments were to
be swept daily; "offal and carrion" were to be buried and all "filth
and dirt" removed. Perseverance in such sanitation would, it was
hoped, "remove that odious reputation, which (with but too much
reason) has stigmatized the character of American troops." Further
orders warned against drinking "new cider": as nothing was "more
pernicious to the health of soldiers, nor more certainly produc-
tive of the bloody-flux," locals hoping to peddle the beverage were
warned that their casks would be stove in.[22]

The first weeks of Washington's command also saw efforts to
instill traditional military protocol. As guards were tardy in turning out to salute Washington and his generals, orders were issued
for the correct honors to be observed: for example, the commander
in chief himself, who was now referred to as "His Excellency," was
to be received by the guard with their muskets "rested" while the
officer in charge saluted and the drummers beat a march. And as
neither sentries, nor even their officers, yet recognized their commanders, they were "to make themselves acquainted with the persons of all the officers in the general command." To avoid confusion,
high-ranking officers would wear different-colored ribbons across
their breast, between the coat and waistcoat: Washington's was light
blue, while the major generals and brigadier generals wore pink
and aides green. As the Continental Army lacked uniforms, further
"badges of distinction" were ordered to indicate rank: field officers

were permitted to wear red or pink cockades in their hats, captains yellow or buff, and junior officers green. Sergeants could wear an epaulette, or stripe of red cloth, on the right shoulder, with corporals designated by green.[23]

As always, Washington took great pains with his personal appearance. Soon after he arrived at Boston, Dr. James Thacher, a local man who had volunteered his medical skills to the patriot cause, was "gratified with a view of General Washington" on horseback and accompanied by several other officers. Young Thacher was impressed by Washington's demeanor, presence, and immaculate uniform, noting: "It was not difficult to distinguish him from all others. His personal appearance is truly noble and majestic, being tall and well proportioned. His dress is a blue coat with buff-colored facings, a rich epaulette on each shoulder, buff under-dress, and an elegant small sword; a black cockade in his hat."[24]

The dearth of uniforms for the rank and file prompted Washington to suggest that Congress issue them with simple, cheap, and utilitarian "hunting shirts" rather than traditional woolen regimental coats. Made of cloth or linen, either left "natural" or dyed, these loose, smock-like garments were popular on the Appalachian frontier, and Washington's proposal recalled his 1758 initiative to clothe part of his own Virginia Regiment in "Indian dress." In July 1775, however, Washington was not merely interested in practicality; indeed, he argued, this seemingly "trivial" step, by establishing a universal costume, "would have a happier tendency to unite the men, and abolish those provincial distinctions which lead to jealousy and dissatisfaction."[25] While Congress approved of the plan, it was shelved because not enough of the necessary "tow-cloth" could be found locally. In coming years, the "hunting shirt," or "rifle shirt," nonetheless became a popular "field" uniform for many members of the Continental Army—but not before it sparked the very provincial rivalries that Washington had hoped to surmount.

The original army gathered to besiege Boston in 1775 had been drawn exclusively from New England. During late summer, its homogeneous character slowly began to change as reinforcements trickled in from elsewhere. The riflemen sent by Pennsylvania, Maryland, and Virginia, now reinforced from ten to twelve companies, made a strong impression upon Yankees like James Thacher, who regarded them with wonder: "They are remarkably stout and hardy men," he wrote, "many of them exceeding six feet in height. They are dressed in white frocks, or rifle-shirts, and round hats. These men are remarkable for the accuracy of their aim, striking a mark with great certainty at two hundred yards distance." According to Thacher, these marksmen soon proved their worth, picking off redcoats rash enough to expose themselves, "even at more than double the distance of common musket-shot."[26]

The tough backwoods rifleman, clad in his fringed "hunting shirt" and dealing death from afar, was destined to provide one of the most enduring and popular images of the Revolutionary War and to become a cornerstone of its military mythology. Washington, who was already thoroughly familiar with rifles from his service on the Virginian frontier and had carried one himself during the 1754 Fort Necessity campaign, was less easily impressed than Dr. Thacher. Writing to Samuel Washington in late September, he grumbled that the riflemen had so far enjoyed little opportunity to demonstrate their skill, or indeed their ignorance, "for some of them, especially from Pennsylvania, know no more of a rifle than my horse, being new imported Irish, many of whom have deserted to the enemy."[27]

Washington's jaundiced perspective no doubt reflected an incident, just weeks earlier, when he was obliged to quell mutinous Pennsylvanians of Colonel Thompson's rifle battalion who had objected after comrades were confined in the guardhouse for minor crimes. About thirty of them, with loaded rifles, had marched for the main guard at Cambridge, vowing to free their friends or die trying. Already warned by Brigadier General Greene that "the rifflers" were "very sulky" and threatened to "rescue their mates," Washington reacted swiftly by turning out 500 men with fixed bayonets and loaded muskets. When he confronted the irate riflemen and ordered them to ground their arms, they meekly obeyed.

Thoroughly cowed, all were marched off under guard. According to one eyewitness, Washington was "extremely displeased" and vented his anger in an impassioned speech, declaring "that the rifle men were the men he depended on." Indeed, "to be so much disappointed seemed very much to affect him."[28]

This worrying episode underlined the ineffectiveness of the "Rules and Articles" governing discipline in the Continental Army that had been approved by Congress in June. Mutiny was a serious crime that struck at the very heart of military efficiency. It was accordingly punishable by death under the British *Articles of War* that American provincials had encountered during the previous conflict when serving alongside the redcoats. Yet in 1775, the Continental Army had no such sanction, with the capital sentence restricted to cowardice in the face of the enemy. Officers were not subject to corporal punishment, while the maximum sentence for other ranks was limited to the biblical thirty-nine lashes typical of provincial units in the last war. This was mild indeed compared with the five hundred or more lashes routinely inflicted in the British Army and which Washington had authorized during his drive to discipline the Virginia Regiment.

As it turned out, Thompson's riflemen suffered nothing more painful than their tongue-lashing from Washington: court-martialed for "disobedient and mutinous behavior," thirty-three were fined twenty shillings, while a ringleader also received six days in jail; previously excused fatigue and guard details, they had also forfeited their privileged status, sharing such irksome duties with the musket-toting soldiers in the rest of their brigade. The same episode was apparently responsible for a ruling by Congress, part of a general tightening of the *Articles of War* following a conference with Washington at his headquarters in October, which extended the death penalty to cover mutiny and sedition.[29]

The troubling unrest among Thompson's Pennsylvanians is not mentioned in Washington's own correspondence, but neither is another affray involving riflemen, in which his intervention allegedly took a far more physical turn. The evidence for this rests entirely on the testimony of Israel Trask, aged just ten years old in 1775, who recalled it seventy years later, when applying for a Revolutionary War pension. During the siege of Boston, young Israel acted as a cook and messenger to the Massachusetts regiment in which his father served. Sometime that winter, a party of Virginian riflemen attracted the attention of the Marblehead Regiment, which was recruited from local sailors and fishermen. As the mariners' curiosity at the riflemen's distinctive "ruffled and fringed" shirts turned to scorn and jeering, an opening exchange of snowballs escalated into a full-scale brawl. Inside five minutes, so Trask maintained, "more than a thousand combatants" were locked in a fierce struggle, biting, gouging, and knocking each other down. At that very moment Washington rode up, accompanied by only his black servant, the slave Billy Lee. The commander in chief's response to the crisis was swift and direct. "With the spring of a deer," Trask remembered, Washington "leaped from his saddle, threw the reins of his bridle into the hands of his servant," then plunged "into the thickest of the melee," where "with an iron grip, he seized two tall, brawny, athletic, savage-looking riflemen by the throat, keeping them at arms length, alternately shaking and talking to them." As the other brawlers became aware of Washington's presence, they scattered, leaving him alone with his two captives. And so, without recourse to courts-martial, and by sheer dint of physical and mental power, Washington extinguished "hostile feelings between the different corps of the army." It is tempting to dismiss this incredible story as the product of an old man's jumbled memory, heavily influenced by Washington's towering posthumous reputation. Yet, while perhaps conflating distinct episodes, including the earlier mutiny of Thompson's men, it likely preserves at least some semblance of truth.[30]

By early August, the fledgling American army faced a critical shortfall in munitions—both lead for casting bullets and the gunpowder to propel them—with just nine rounds per man. Reporting to Congress, Washington was desperate enough to contemplate any scheme to bolster supplies, however far-fetched. Hearing of a sizable powder magazine in a remote part of the far-off island of Bermuda, Washington hoped to send a privateer vessel to impound it. His justification for the venture reveals his attitude toward risk taking in general:

Enterprises which appear chimerical often prove successful from that very circumstance. Common sense and prudence will suggest vigilance and care where the danger is plain and obvious, but where little danger is apprehended the more the enemy is found unprepared and consequently there is the fairer prospect of success.[31]

It was a creed that Washington would put to the test soon enough.

Given the gunpowder crisis, it was fortunate for Washington that his opponent Thomas Gage stayed on the defensive, with military operations amounting to no more than bickering between outposts. This skirmishing had nonetheless yielded prisoners on both sides, raising the sensitive issue of their treatment. Washington and Gage had remained on friendly terms until the very eve of the rupture between Crown and colonies. Indeed, when Gage returned to England on leave in spring 1773, Washington had attended the farewell dinner given for him by the citizens of New York. Now things were different. Hearing that "officers engaged in the cause of Liberty" had been unceremoniously thrown into a "common gaol" in Boston, Washington warned his old friend that if such harsh treatment persisted, he would be reluctantly obliged to serve British prisoners the same way. He added: "But if kindness and humanity are shown to ours, I shall with pleasure consider those in our hands, only as unfortunate, and they shall receive the treatment to which the unfortunate are ever entitled."[32]

Replying to Washington's letter, Gage strongly denied allegations that prisoners had been mistreated. Indeed, he declared, "Britons, ever preeminent in mercy, have out-gone common examples, and overlooked the criminal in the captive." Although Gage did not use the word, such men were rebels "whose lives by the laws of the land are destined to the cord." Yet far from being hanged as traitors, as they could have been, prisoners had "hitherto been treated with care and kindness," he added. It was true that officers had fared no differently than others, but that was because Gage acknowledged "no rank that is not derived from the King."[33]

Gage's moderate stance would be followed by succeeding British commanders in America. Although a Royal Proclamation of Rebellion was issued in London on August 23, 1775, entreating all Crown officers to suppress the insurrection and "to bring the traitors to justice," the full awful force of the law was never unleashed against the American rebels;[34] there would be no executions like those that followed the Jacobite rebellion of 1745–46, which Gage himself had helped to suppress, or the draconian, drum-head justice administered to Irish rebels in 1798.

As the standoff at Boston continued, Washington became reacquainted with the frustrations of command, although these now dwarfed those he had encountered as colonel of the Virginia Regiment. At headquarters, he was immediately swamped by paper. The experienced Horatio Gates oversaw staff work, but the commander in chief was still obliged to handle a copious correspondence. Simply reading through this today is daunting enough: composing outgoing letters, digesting incoming reports, and acting upon them all amounted to a colossal and mind-numbing task.

Some of this paperwork was exasperatingly trivial. For example, Washington became snared in an ongoing correspondence with a captive British officer on a touchy issue of protocol. Major Christopher French of the 22nd Foot—the same officer who had served on James Grant's expedition against the Cherokees in 1761—had been captured after he disembarked in New Jersey, unaware that war had already erupted. While accepting French's word of honor not to escape from Hartford, Connecticut, where he was being held, the local committee of safety had ruled that the major must not strut around town wearing his sword, "as the lower class of townspeople took umbrage" at such provocative behavior. Major French appealed to Washington as one officer to another, trusting that the Virginian's "long service and intimate acquaintance with military rules and customs" would prompt him to intervene in his favor. It was soon clear, however, that Major French had talked himself into trouble, announcing that if he were able to join his regiment, he "should act vigorously against the country, and do every thing in his power to reduce it," sentiments that had caused the patriots of Hartford to regard him "as a most determined foe." Replying from headquarters, Washington was surprised at French's insistence upon "points of mere punctilo," particularly given the rough treatment endured by "those brave American officers who were taken fighting gallantly in defense of the liberties of their country." As French enjoyed "all the essential comforts of life," Washington hoped he would have the "prudence and good sense" to abide by the wishes of the Hartford folk. After all, he added wryly, the major's stay among them might be longer than anticipated.[35]

Major French's keen sense of honor was just one among many distractions as Washington grappled with an overriding problem destined to dog him to despair: an army composed of amateur part-timers must inevitably melt away as the men's stipulated periods of enlistment expired. Writing to John Hancock on September 21, he warned that, as the Connecticut troops were only engaged until December 1, and none of the others for longer than January 1, the "dissolution" of the army was therefore unavoidable, "unless some early provision is made against such an event." Washington's generals believed that, if the men were appeased with a spell of leave, it should be possible to reenlist them to serve the coming winter, but there was no guarantee.[36]

Using tactful and restrained language, which contrasted with his often intemperate rants to Governor Dinwiddie twenty years before, Washington warned Hancock and his colleagues of an impending crisis. "It gives me great pain," he wrote, "to be obliged to solicit the attention of the honorable Congress, to the state of this army, in terms which imply the slightest apprehension of being neglected." But he had no choice. With winter fast approaching upon poorly clad "naked" men whose time of service would expire within a few weeks and with military funds "totally exhausted," his situation was "inexpressibly distressing." *Someone* was to blame, although Washington diplomatically hesitated to point the finger against Congress: "I know not to whom I am to impute this failure," he continued, "but I am of the opinion, if the evil is not immediately remedied and more punctuality observed in future, the army must absolutely break up."

This firm but respectful stance, in which Washington acknowledged the primacy of the Revolution's civilian leadership while simultaneously emphasizing the genuine needs of the men fighting to uphold American liberty, would characterize his relations with Congress while commander of the Continental Army. By instinct Washington was a soldier rather than a politician, yet he had gradually learned to combine the roles of both to achieve his ends. His long and nuanced letter to Hancock is evidence of maturing political skills, acquired in Virginia's House of Burgesses since his first military retirement in 1759 and polished during the Continental Conventions of 1774–75. It had the desired effect: a committee of Congress was soon on its way to Cambridge to address the key issues.

Meanwhile, Washington was keen to attack Boston while he still had troops to command. In the same letter in which he informed Hancock of the Continental Army's dire situation, Washington emphasized his own wish "by some decisive stroke to relieve my country from the heavy expense, its subsistence must create." Indeed, no man in America hoped more earnestly for "such a termination of the campaign, as to make the army no longer necessary."

To that end, in early September Washington had sent a circular to his generals, priming them for a council of war to discuss his proposal for a surprise assault upon Boston. This would involve coordinated strikes: across the harbor using whaleboats and by land against the British fortifications at Roxbury, which defended the port's narrow "neck." Washington argued that dwindling powder supplies and rumors of British reinforcements both justified such a bold attempt. But, above all, with winter approaching, men already homesick would be still quicker to decamp; and even if an army could be kept together, it would be difficult and costly to maintain. These factors, among many others, inclined Washington to "wish a speedy finish of the dispute": with one knockout blow the war could be decided, and they could all go home. Despite his strong personal preference for decisive and aggressive action Washington was not blind to the hazards involved or "the probable consequences of a failure." After weighing the pros and cons, the council of war considered Washington's plan too risky, unanimously agreeing "that it was not expedient to make the attempt at present at least." The commander in chief abided by their judgment.[37]

Washington's hopes for an all-out offensive against Boston were soon revived, however, and this time with the blessing of the politicians in Philadelphia. On October 18, he summoned another council of war, "in consequence of an intimation from the Congress, that an attack upon Boston if practicable was much desired." Provided Washington considered the attempt "likely to defeat the enemy and gain possession of the town," he was to strike "upon the first favorable occasion"—and before the arrival of expected British reinforcements. If manpower was lacking, Washington was authorized to make up his numbers by mobilizing local minutemen. This was not the last occasion upon which Congress would encourage Washington to seek a swift, decisive victory—despite the risks. Given his temperament, such prompting was scarcely necessary. Once again, his generals reined him in: maintaining their previous position, they swiftly rejected the latest plan as unrealistic under the circumstances.[38]

In both instances, Washington had followed his original congressional instructions and sought the guidance of his senior officers. Faced with the uncompromising rejection of his own initiatives, he had accepted their overwhelming verdicts without caviling or seeking to overrule them. Despite his own hunger for action, Washington was undoubtedly right to do so: sending raw troops against regulars ensconced behind entrenchments would have played directly into his enemy's hands, likely destroying the young Continental Army.

But there remained another outlet for Washington's urge to do more than simply sit watching the British in Boston. In early summer, Congress had resolved to invade Canada, assembling a distinct "northern" army at Albany under General Schuyler and ordering it up the Champlain Valley. To support that advance and distract Britain's commander in Canada, Sir Guy Carleton, Washington authorized a bold strike against Quebec, using men from his own army. The city was believed to be virtually undefended and therefore "an easy prey." A detachment of more than 1,000 was to penetrate to the St. Lawrence Valley via the rugged course of Maine's Kennebec River. The force consisted of some 800 volunteers from the Continental regiments at Cambridge; given the wilderness terrain to be surmounted, all were to be "active woodsmen, and well acquainted with bateaus"—sturdy, flat-bottomed boats capable of carrying about twenty men and their provisions. There were also three companies of the feisty riflemen, one of them commanded by Captain Daniel Morgan. As a teamster during the French and Indian War, Morgan had received a severe flogging after striking a British officer and had never forgotten the pain and humiliation. Command of the expedition was entrusted to a zealous Connecticut colonel, the thirty-four-year-old Benedict Arnold.[39]

To Lord North's ministry back in London, which had received the shocking news of Bunker Hill on July 25, it was clear that Britain's commander in chief in North America lacked the stomach for suppressing an escalating rebellion. Orders were dispatched for Gage's recall, and on October 10 he was superseded by General Howe. Confronted with the reality of full-scale rebellion, the ministry agreed to give Howe a reinforced army of at least 20,000 men and to make New York, not Boston, its operational base for a campaign of reconquest.

Initially, there had been widespread political and military support for curbing the rebellion through a naval blockade, targeting American trade. But compared with what was expected to be a short, sharp land war, a blockade might prove a protracted business. With the Royal Navy run down in the years of peace since 1763, there was also the question of safeguarding home waters, particularly as it was notorious that the French were itching for a chance to exact vengeance for their crushing defeat in the previous war. On the other hand, mobilizing the fleet to a war footing could provoke the French to intervene from fear for their vulnerable Caribbean possessions. In addition, a purely naval response to the revolt would ignore those Americans—perhaps one-fifth of the white population—who were loyal to the Crown, failing either to protect them or to exploit their potential as auxiliaries for the British Army.* In August 1775, the ousted royal governors of North and South Carolina were both adamant that with minimal support from British regulars, large concentrations of Loyalists in the interior "Back Country" would willingly take arms and rise up to throw off the rebels. Such reports chimed with a common view that the American rebellion was a "conspiracy" involving a minority of agitators, rather than a more widespread movement. The notion that the majority of colonists were fundamentally loyal held particular appeal for Lord George Germain, who became American Secretary in late 1775, and would oversee Britain's strategy in coming years.[40]

Although Congress's "Olive Branch Petition" was ignored in London, to the delight of American radicals who favored outright independence rather than reconciliation, Lord North and his cabinet hadn't abandoned all hopes of a negotiated settlement. While gearing up for war, they gradually warmed to the notion of a Peace Commission; its basis for negotiation would be the so-called Conciliatory Proposition that North had announced back in February 1775. Regarded by even some of his own supporters as conceding far too much, this dangled a deal that the prime minister hoped would solve the crisis: where any colony agreed to pay for its civil government and its share of defense costs, Parliament would not attempt to impose revenue-yielding taxes. Since then, however,

---

* While a significant minority of North America's population opposed the revolutionary cause, for simplicity's sake the term "American" is henceforth used here to denote its supporters. Pro-British Americans are referred to as "Loyalist."

attitudes had hardened. By seeking to open negotiations with individual colonies, the proposed Peace Commission would ignore the very existence of Congress. Colonies that refused to talk would be obliged to do so—by force, if necessary.

A shortage of shipping prevented Howe from shifting his troops to New York by sea that autumn. And despite his well-earned reputation as an aggressive officer, he proved no keener than Gage to break the deadlock by storming the rebel siege lines. Although Washington chafed at the continuing inactivity, the lull provided a vital breathing space in which to reorganize the Continental Army—as Captain James Wilkinson of Maryland explained, "to make a selection of officers, to levy a new army, to organize his corps, to assimilate, partially, their modes of duty and exercise, to cherish the confidence of his troops, and to infuse among them some sense of the esprit de corps."[41]

On October 8, in forwarding their recommendations to Congress, Washington's generals had agreed unanimously that the new army, "sufficient for both offensive and defensive measures" over the coming winter, should consist of not fewer than 20,372 men. There would be twenty-six regiments of "battalion men," each mustering 728 of all ranks organized into eight companies, plus 1,444 riflemen and artillerymen. The proposed regiments were almost twice the strength of British battalions, which were lucky to field 400 men, officers included. On paper these were powerful formations, but there remained the question of filling them with flesh-and-blood recruits. It was initially agreed to seek enlistments to December 1, 1776, but in the following month, when the officers of the new regiments actually set about finding their men, that period was extended by thirty days. Recruiting officers were urged to observe ideological, physical, and racial criteria, being "careful not to enlist any person, suspected of being unfriendly to the liberties of America, or any abandoned vagabond to whom all causes and countries are equal and alike indifferent." Neither should they enlist "negroes, boys unable to bear arms, nor old men unfit to endure the fatigues of the campaign."[42] Before long, recruiters would learn to be less discriminating.

While there were no clashes between the rival armies at Boston, British warships based at the port began prowling the neighboring New England coastline, prompting cries for help from vulnerable communities. On October 18, two warships bombarded Falmouth, in what would become Maine, starting fires that consumed most of the town.[43] While deploring the "desolation, and misery" resulting from this calculated act of "ministerial vengeance," Washington was powerless to send either men or munitions to assist the townsfolk. However, he had fitted out several armed vessels as privateers, and they were soon preying upon British merchantmen bound for Boston. On November 28, Captain John Manley of the schooner *Lee* pounced upon the British ordnance ship *Nancy*. As Washington enthused to his secretary and friend Joseph Reed, this valuable haul of munitions was an "instance of divine favor; for nothing, surely, ever came more apropos." The *Nancy*'s cargo included a fine brass thirteen-inch mortar, assorted shot, and 2,000 muskets and bayonets; disappointingly, there was no gunpowder, a commodity that remained in desperately short supply.[44] In early December, Washington pleaded for Congress to do all in its power to remedy "the great want of powder." Stocks were so low that, far from mounting an offensive, Washington's army would scarcely have enough to defend its own lines against a sortie.[45]

On November 16, 1775, Washington had issued orders that would soon make the British occupation of Boston untenable. Keen to augment his artillery, he entrusted an important mission to twenty-five-year-old Henry Knox, a former Boston bookseller who had spent much time perusing his own stock, especially volumes devoted to gunnery and fortifications. Knox's knowledge and drive would soon gain him the job of Washington's chief of artillery, but in the meantime he was ordered to gather up the guns and ammunition currently in the province of New York. These included such cannon and mortars as could be fetched from the once-formidable but now run-down Champlain Valley fortresses of Ticonderoga and Crown Point, which had been captured in May by New Englanders under Arnold and Ethan Allen. Washington wrote: "The want of them is so great, that no trouble or expense must be spared to obtain them."[46] Knox, whose substantial girth belied his energy, took him at his word.

Knox's determination and zeal stood in marked contrast to the stance of many others who'd formed the first patriot army outside Boston. Their enthusiasm for the cause had proved short lived. By late November, Washington was fighting a losing battle to persuade the Connecticut men to extend their enlistments. Writing to Joseph Reed, who had now replaced Gates as adjutant general, he warned that "such a dirty, mercenary spirit pervades the whole that I should not be at all surprised at any disaster that may happen." To plug the yawning gap in the ranks it would be necessary to summon 5,000 minutemen and militia from Massachusetts and New Hampshire— undisciplined men who Washington feared would contaminate his army, destroying the "little subordination" that he had worked so hard to instill. Just five months after accepting Congress's offer to command the Continental Army, Washington was already ruing his decision: "Could I have foreseen what I have, and am like to experience, no consideration upon earth should have induced me to accept this command," he wrote.[47]

Ironically, what Washington condemned as the New Englanders' despicable desertion of the cause could also be interpreted as an expression of the very freedom they had been fighting for; such liberty was personal, and not just some high-flown ideological concept. While deploring the early return of men from his state and promising to punish the ringleaders, Connecticut's governor, Jonathan Trumbull, highlighted the difficulty of maintaining such a revolutionary struggle without simultaneously unleashing "licentious and leveling principles, which many very easily imbibe." He added: "The pulse of a New England man beats high for liberty." It followed that his enlistment was "purely voluntary": when his time was up, he considered himself free to go—unless a fresh engagement was made. As Trumbull correctly noted, this contract principle had prevailed with the New England provincial troops during the French and Indian War. For the present, he greatly feared "its operation among the soldiers of the other colonies, as I am sensible this is the genius and spirit of our people."[48] This was a paradox that Washington, the Virginian gentleman planter for whom strict hierarchy was the natural way of things, would never fully accept.

Since he had arrived at Cambridge, long, rambling letters from his Washington cousin Lund, describing the sometimes comical rhythms of rural life at Mount Vernon, had provided Washington with news of his home and family, offering welcome, if momentary, distractions from the strains of command. For example, Lund was happy to report that "after doing and undoing twenty times" Mount Vernon's chimney had finally been cured of its inveterate smoking. Regrettably, an attempt to saw short the horns of Washington's notoriously vicious bull, undertaken in Lund's absence, had proved less successful. That tricky operation had been supervised by the hapless Thomas Bishop, a soldier servant whom Washington had inherited from General Braddock in 1755; although "every man, woman and child" on the plantation had turned out to lend a hand, as Lund reported, "the bull proved too many for them."[49]

On December 11, Washington was cheered by far more tangible links with his old domestic life with the arrival in camp of Martha, her son, Jack, and his young wife, Nelly. The militiamen had also marched in on schedule and were far better troops than Washington had expected. As he informed John Hancock, they were not only "very fine looking men" but "go through their duty with great alacrity"—praise indeed from a soldier of Washington's antimilitia prejudices and further testimony to the intensive training of the Yankee minutemen in the months before Lexington and Concord.[50]

And as 1775 drew to an end, there was encouraging news from Canada. There the revolutionaries' offensive seemed a spectacular success. General Schuyler's force, spearheaded by his dashing second in command, Brigadier General Montgomery, had forged north up the Champlain Valley, taking the British posts at St. John and Chambly and then pushing on to capture Montreal. The indefatigable Colonel Arnold, meanwhile, had been advancing with incredible hardship through the frozen Maine wilderness to reach Point Lévis, opposite Quebec. Here was a man after Washington's own heart:

brave, tough, dauntless. Offering his heartfelt thanks for Arnold's "enterprising and persevering spirit," Washington bestowed the ultimate accolade upon him. Paraphrasing a passage from his favorite play, Addison's *Cato*, he added: "It is not in the power of any man to command success, but you have done more—you have deserved it."[51] To General Schuyler, Washington wrote of his satisfaction in learning that Arnold had overcome "almost insuperable difficulties," despite the fact that nearly a third of his force had forsaken him and turned back. In words that must have returned to haunt him, Washington added: "The merit of this gentleman is certainly great and I heartily wish that Fortune may distinguish him as one of her favorites."[52]

At Boston, Washington remained understandably fixated upon the problem of rebuilding and remodeling his army, all the while within cannon-shot of the enemy. Regrettably, as their enlistments terminated, the "same desire of retiring into a chimney-corner seized the troops of New Hampshire, Rhode Island, and Massachusetts . . . as had worked upon those of Connecticut." While Washington's old army trickled away, as inexorably as sand in an hourglass, frantic efforts were made to recruit a new one. Already, harsh reality was leading to change: General Orders on December 30 now permitted the recruitment of "free negroes" who had already served in the army before Boston and were keen to reenlist.[53]

On New Year's Day 1776, Washington issued orders announcing the "commencement" of the new army. To mark this fresh start, he pardoned all offenses committed in the old one and freed all prisoners. In truth, the army needed every man it could get in what remained a crisis situation. Offsetting his continuing anxiety with a touch of pride, Washington reported to his confidant Joseph Reed: "Search the vast volumes of history through, and I much question whether a case similar to ours is to be found," he wrote, and not without justification. They had held their position against the "flower of the British troops for six months together," disbanding one army and raising another in the teeth of "a reinforced enemy."[54]

As Washington's General Orders of January 1 underlined, the new army's bedrock must be "subordination and discipline." These were "the life and soul of an army"; without them, they would be "no better than a commissioned mob"; with them, the Continental Army would become "formidable to our enemies, honorable in ourselves and respected in the world." The men were "brave and good" and "addicted to fewer vices than are commonly found in armies," but forging them into an effective fighting machine would depend, above all, upon the exertions of the officers, from brigadiers down to ensigns.

Washington's own conception of the officer's role had not changed since the 1750s. It was outlined in a letter to William Woodford, the newly appointed colonel of the 2nd Virginia Regiment, who had sought guidance on how to proceed.[55] "The best general advice I can give," Washington replied, "is to be strict in your discipline; that is, to require nothing unreasonable of your officers and men, but see that whatever is required be punctually complied with." Woodford must reward and punish all by merit, "without partiality or prejudice." Vice must be discouraged "in every shape," while every man in the regiment, from the highest to lowest, should be impressed with "the importance of the cause, and what it is they are contending for." When dealing with his officers he should be "easy and condescending . . . but not too familiar, lest you subject yourself to a want of that respect, which is necessary to support a proper command."

Drawing upon his own combat experience during the French and Indian War, Washington urged Woodford to always be on his guard against surprises, marching with "front, rear, and flank guards" and securing all his encampments. When it came to the business of drill—both the basic "manual exercise" by which the individual soldier learned how to handle his musket and the far trickier "evolutions and maneuvers" for shifting a regiment across a battlefield, the most useful guide, in Washington's opinion, remained Humphrey Bland's *Treatise of Military Discipline*. This was the same text that Washington had recommended to his Virginia Regiment officers back in 1756. "Old Humphrey" was a veteran of Marlborough's legendary campaigns and had served under the Duke of Cumberland in Flanders and Scotland forty years later. By 1775, Bland's book was showing its age: the Connecticut militia, which had adopted it in 1743, abandoned it in 1769 as "prolix and encumbered with useless motions."[56] Washington's penchant for Bland underlines the conservatism of his own approach to warfare and a reliance upon the habits learned during his first military career. Yet, while failing to reflect the latest drill, Bland's work nonetheless emphasized basic tactical truths that remained as relevant in 1775 as they had done when he was learning his trade under "Corporal John." For example, Bland stressed the importance of receiving the enemy's fire first, reserving your own volley until close quarters and briskly following it up with a bayonet charge. That particular lesson had been taken to heart by General James Wolfe and put to good use on the Plains of Abraham in 1759.[57]

Other books recommended to Colonel Woodford by Washington, which likewise reflected his personal library, included translations of Turpin de Crissé's *Essay on the Art of War*—the work used by General Forbes in his 1758 campaign against Fort Duquesne— and Captain Louis Michel de Jeney's *The Partisan*, which concerned itself with the business of "Making War in Detachment." Another of Washington's suggestions, Major William Young's *Maneuvers, or Practical Observations on the Art of War*, incorporated another influential and useful text, *General Wolfe's Instructions to Young Officers*: this reprinted the regimental and general orders issued by Wolfe in the decade before his death at Quebec, presenting the thoughts of an unusually diligent and professional officer on everything from tackling drunkenness among the rank and file to rebuffing an attacking column of infantry.

As his recommended reading shows, Washington was well aware of both "regular" and "irregular" warfare. Interestingly, despite his extensive firsthand experience of backwoods campaigning in the 1750s, the American army Washington envisaged in the autumn of 1775 was geared toward waging a "conventional" conflict, not a guerrilla war and still less an "Indian" one. Given the frustrations he had experienced on the frontier, both in fighting Indians and enlisting their aid as allies, it is unsurprising that Washington should endorse Congress's policy of encouraging the "Indian Nations" to stay out of the fight, seeking nothing more from them than "a strict neutrality."[58]

Both the organization and the discipline of the Continental Army sought to emulate the old Virginia Regiment, which had itself imitated the British model; many general orders issued from 1775 onward used phrases identical to those employed by Washington between 1755 and 1758. Rather than embodying some free-spirited force of patriotic but amateur citizen militia, as advocated by the political and military radical Major General Charles Lee, Washington's military vision was fundamentally conventional, anchored upon a regular army of long-service professionals—the "standing army" that was anathema to so many of his fellow Americans, not least to members of Congress.

In early 1776, whether the Continental Army would survive in any shape at all remained a moot point. The first detailed rolls for the newly reorganized force, compiled on January 9, revealed that instead of the 20,000 considered to be the minimum required for the job, Washington had only 8,200 men: of those, just 5,600 were actually present and fit for duty.[59]

The gloom was soon compounded by news of a shattering defeat before Quebec. During the last hours of 1775, the combined forces of Montgomery and Arnold launched a desperate assault upon the fortified city under cover of a snowstorm. It was a gallant, but futile, effort. Cut down by a blast of canister, Montgomery provided the revolutionary cause with a high-ranking military martyr, one who would be commemorated in a spirited canvas by the painter John Trumbull. Recklessly brave as ever, Arnold was shot through the left leg; oozing blood and defiance, he limped back with the survivors to maintain a wary siege.

Washington's spirits received a badly needed boost when Henry Knox returned from Ticonderoga on January 18, followed soon after by his spectacular haul of some sixty guns. Through determination, ingenuity, and sheer backbreaking toil, these priceless field-pieces and mortars had been ferried down Lake George, then dragged on ox-drawn sledges across the frozen New England countryside. Knox's ordnance constituted the most formidable "train" of artillery that Washington had ever seen, stronger than those assembled by Braddock and Forbes and capable of raining shot and shell on Boston.

Gunpowder was still too scarce for such an intensive bombardment, but Washington resurrected his hopes for a direct offensive, seeking to exploit the solid ice that now stretched between his lines and Howe's defenses to launch "a bold and resolute assault." Not surprisingly, on February 16, the customary council of war vetoed the scheme, its members virtually unanimous in their opposition. Reporting this outcome to Hancock, Washington couldn't conceal his disappointment. Sensitive for his reputation and burning to be seen to be "attempting something against the ministerial troops," this time he had only bowed to the council's verdict with the greatest reluctance. Washington assured Hancock: "I was not only ready, but willing and desirous of making the assault; under a firm hope, if the men would have stood by me, of a favorable issue, notwithstanding the enemy's advantage of ground, artillery, etc." His frustrations were clear, reflecting an abiding obsession with honor and public reputation: with the "eyes of the whole continent fixed" upon him, with "anxious expectations of hearing of some great event," it was irksome "to be restrained in every military operation for want of the necessary means of carrying it on."[60]

Washington was once again wise to heed his generals' advice: sending ill-trained troops skittering across the ice against regulars itching to settle the score for Bunker Hill must have ended in a massacre. Even Providence would have been hard pressed to preserve her favored son under such circumstances: eager to prove his personal courage by leading from the front, Washington would likely have shared the fate of Montgomery at Quebec, depriving the Continental Army of its commander and dealing a potentially lethal blow to the Revolution.

There were soon less risky alternatives to an all-out assault. By March, Washington had finally stockpiled enough gunpowder to begin bombarding Boston with Knox's artillery. As early as February 11, Lieutenant Colonel Rufus Putnam—cousin to Israel "Old Put"—had proposed a plan for securing Dorchester Heights, which dominated Boston from the south and still remained unfortified by either side. Three weeks later, Putnam's plan was activated, with Knox's gunners providing a diversionary barrage. They had much to learn: as Washington reported to Joseph Reed, in a matter of days no fewer than five mortars burst, presumably through the "ignorance" of the bombardiers. Those wrecked so regrettably included the formidable mortar taken from the prize *Nancy* and nicknamed "Congress": it was one thing to read about artillery in technical treatises, quite another to operate it in action.[61]

Despite such teething troubles, the bombardment proved effective enough to thoroughly alarm and distract the British. Under its cover, more than 2,000 Americans worked feverishly to fortify Dorchester Heights through the moonlit night of March 4–5. The frozen ground defied pick and shovel, so it was impossible to construct the usual entrenchments, but viable gun batteries were made instead from timber frames known as "chandeliers" stuffed with fascines (long bundles of sticks); Elisha Bostwick of the 7th Connecticut Regiment remembered that they "labored incessantly all the night," raising breastworks and filling hundreds of barrels with gravel. These were placed at the edge of the defenses, "ready to be set rolling down the steep hill on the approach of the enemy."[62]

Waking to the sight of extensive and substantial siegeworks, the redcoats were no less astounded than they had been by the swift fortification of Breed's Hill the previous June. Howe now contemplated a similarly blunt response. Orders were issued for an attack on the heavily manned Dorchester Heights on March 5: this was the sixth anniversary of the "Boston Massacre"—an emotive date in every American patriot's calendar—and Washington reported his officers and men to be impatient for the onset, ready to face their enemies with "the most animated sentiments and determined resolution." According to intelligence provided by escaped prisoners from Boston, that afternoon some 3,000 redcoats were embarked aboard transport ships, glumly anticipating "another Bunker Hill affair"; if their anticipated attack on Dorchester Heights went ahead, Washington intended to launch a counterstrike of his own, sending 4,000 "chosen men" under Generals Putnam, Sullivan, and Greene to attack Boston itself.[63]

The redcoats were first ferried over to Castle William Island, close to their objective, ready for the final approach by landing craft. Howe's men were instructed to attack in a more "open order" than the elbow-to-elbow formation they had employed at Bunker Hill, and with unloaded muskets, trusting to cold steel alone: the attack on June 17, 1775 had become bogged down when the redcoats paused to return the rebel fire, losing impetus at a crucial moment.[64] This reliance upon looser lines and the bayonet would characterize British tactics throughout the American war but was not tested that day. Mercifully, a falling tide, followed by a "violent storm," provided Howe with an excuse for canceling the assault.

Secure on Dorchester Heights, Washington's men swiftly fortified Nooks Hill, even closer to Boston and its harbor. They were checked by British gunfire, but Howe's position was now clearly untenable and evacuation only a matter of time. In return for being allowed to leave without interference, Howe agreed to spare the town from burning. On March 19, Washington reported the outcome of the long and troublesome siege to Congress. Two days earlier, "the ministerial army" had evacuated Boston, which was now in the possession of the "forces of the United Colonies." Happily, President Hancock's own handsome townhouse had survived British occupation and American bombardment virtually unscathed, with his furniture in "tolerable order" and the cherished "family pictures" all "entire and untouched." Elsewhere, everything indicated that the redcoats had retired "with the greatest precipitation." They had left their barracks and fortifications standing, along with several cannon—"spiked" with nails in their touch holes, but capable of being drilled out and reused—and a large iron mortar, along with quantities of stores.[65]

The British flotilla hovered in Boston's outer harbor until March 27, raising fears that Howe would counter attack after all. Then the fleet made sail, where to, nobody knew for sure. Rumor suggested the British naval base at Halifax, Nova Scotia, but New York was the obvious destination, and Washington had already sent a brigade marching there. On April 4, once the British ships had hove out of sight, Washington, too, headed south with the bulk of his army. Command of the Boston sector returned to its original guardian, Major General Ward.

For all his misgivings and the myriad difficulties he'd faced, Washington had won the first round of the contest, and in fine style. The recapture of Boston, so long the hub of resistance against British tyranny, was both a symbolic and a concrete triumph, and a cause for widespread patriot jubilation. Washington, whose own education had been so perfunctory, now received an honorary degree from Harvard College, while Congress voted him a gold commemorative medal. Here was a taste of the public recognition that fueled him. It was Washington's first major victory and a moment to savor. Yet he was under no illusion that one success, however remarkable, would end the war. The redcoats were gone from Boston, never to return. But they had not left America. William Howe would be back, his likeliest target New York.

In the nine months since he had assumed command of the Continental Army, Washington had tried repeatedly to bring on a decisive engagement with the British, only to be disappointed. He left Boston still spoiling for a stand-up fight. At New York he'd get one.

7

THE TIMES THAT
TRY MEN'S SOULS

When Washington arrived at New York City on April 13, 1776, he expected to find a British fleet already riding at anchor in the harbor. But Howe had instead gone north to Britain's naval base at Halifax, Nova Scotia, to replace stores lost during the hurried evacuation of Boston, to await promised reinforcements from Britain, and to reorganize his forces for the coming campaign. In the previous summer it had already been agreed that Howe's army should make New York its base for an offensive aimed at crushing the American revolt. That port's fine, spacious harbor and Loyalist sympathies were strong arguments in its favor. In strategic terms, an advance up the Hudson River from New York, in conjunction with a drive south by strengthened British forces in Canada, would split the rebellion like a wedge hammered into a log, dividing New England from the Middle and Southern Colonies.

Knowing New York's value to their enemy, the American revolutionaries were no less determined to keep it. In February and March, before being ordered away to counter British designs upon the south, Major General Charles Lee had begun fortifying the city and its surroundings. This, as he confessed to Washington, was a futile task. New York was "so encircled with deep navigable water, that whoever commands the sea must command the town," Lee warned.[1] While overwhelming British sea power meant that the city was ultimately indefensible, Lee started works intended to ensure that any attack would at least incur heavy casualties. The East River, between Manhattan and Long Island, was protected by sunken vessels and the crossfire of batteries on Lower Manhattan and on Long Island's Brooklyn Heights. To the west side of Manhattan, the Hudson—or North River—was too wide to block or dominate by flanking batteries. Luckily, that shore, unlike the eastern, was mostly rocky enough to discourage landings. In the city itself, which still filled just the southernmost portion of Manhattan Island, waterside streets were barricaded, while the landward outskirts were screened by earthworks. A crucial component of Lee's defensive scheme was a powerful fortification on Brooklyn Heights. As its guns were capable of bombarding New York City, the British would have no choice but to subdue it, he reasoned. Washington was "much pleased" with Lee's efforts;[2] yet all this activity only disguised the unpalatable truth that New York lay open to amphibious attack: divided by the East River, defenders on Manhattan and Long Island alike were in danger of being outflanked, isolated, and eliminated. On strategic grounds, Washington would have been well advised to abandon New York City to the British. But both the wishes of Congress and his own inclinations persuaded him to make a stand there.

As Washington prepared to counter Howe at New York, it was becoming increasingly clear that continuing talk of a negotiated settlement was unrealistic, and that Great Britain aimed to bring her rebellious colonies to heel by force. This was no easy task, particularly given her shortage of military manpower and resources. Indeed, while it is common to read in modern works that Britain was the "superpower" of the age, such language is misleading. Faced with a full-scale rebellion rather than a localized insurgency, the British Army struggled to expand from its pared-down peacetime establishment of 29,000 men. Of these redcoats, some 10,000 were already in, or en route to, North America; a further 7,700 were based in other overseas garrisons. In England and Scotland together, there were only about 9,500 soldiers available—both for home defense and to reinforce the American army. Ireland had its own force, but that was already down to about half its theoretical strength, with just 7,000 men. Given the chronic scarcity of soldiers, efforts were made to plug the gaps with mercenaries: a first bid to hire 20,000 Russians from Empress Catherine the Great foundered, but the petty princelings of the miniature German states of Hesse-Cassel, Brunswick, and Hanau were keen to rent their well-trained troops for American service. Treaties signed in January 1776 secured the services of no fewer than 18,000 German professionals.[3]

Britain's resort to "Hessian" hirelings, the very antithesis of the amateur citizen-soldiers who had faced the redcoats at Boston, only hardened colonial opinion toward the Mother Country. Washington's own views of the conflict were already fixed. Writing on May 31 from Philadelphia, where he had been summoned by Congress to settle details of the coming campaign, he was overjoyed to learn that the Virginia Convention had voted to instruct its own delegates to propose that Congress declare the colonies to be free and independent states. Praising "so noble a vote" to his brother Jack, he observed that "things have come to that pass now, as to convince us, that we have nothing more to expect from the justice of Great Britain." Those who still believed in reconciliation and that the "dispute" would be "speedily, and equitably adjusted by commissioners" were dangerously deluded compared with men who realized that the only choice was to "conquer, or submit to unconditional terms . . . such as confiscation, hanging, etc."[4]

As the tense wait in New York continued, the situation in Canada went from bad to worse. Washington had diverted more regiments from his own army to reinforce that buckling front, but the tidings were dismal. Bolstered by fresh troops in the spring, the British made a vigorous counterattack. The ambitious Major General Burgoyne routed the invaders at Trois-Rivières, forcing the ardent Arnold to abandon Montreal. Weakened by combat and desertion, and scourged by smallpox, the beaten and despondent Americans withdrew in disorder to upstate New York.

Some 250 miles to the south, in New York City the presence of Washington and his expanding army buoyed patriot spirits. On

June 18, the New York Provincial Congress gave Washington and his generals and regimental commanders an "elegant entertainment." There were thirty-one patriotic toasts, including one to "the late noble Lord Howe"—the British officer killed at Ticonderoga in 1758, whose two surviving brothers, Admiral Richard and General William Howe, were at that very moment sailing for New York at the head of the forces intended to restore royal authority. While George Augustus Lord Howe is today virtually forgotten, his memory in 1776 remained strong. In the previous December, in a letter to William Howe deploring the disrespectful treatment of the captured Ethan Allen, Washington had observed "that the Americans in general esteem it not as the least of their misfortunes, that the name of Howe—a name so dear to them—should appear at the head of the catalogue of the instruments, employed by a wicked ministry for their destruction."[5]

On June 29, the leading ships of William Howe's task force anchored off New York. There were soon 110 vessels, carrying about 9,000 troops. An attack looked imminent, but Howe's first move was to put his men ashore on Staten Island, where they could recover from their cramped voyage from Halifax. Howe was waiting for two more fleets: one of them, commanded by his elder brother, Vice Admiral Lord Howe, carried long-awaited reinforcements from Europe, including a detachment from the famed Brigade of Guards and the first contingent of "Hessians"; the other, under Major General Henry Clinton, consisted of troops recently sent against Charleston, South Carolina.

The Charleston expedition had evolved from a far more ambitious British plan aimed at harnessing Loyalist sentiment in the south. Based upon wildly optimistic predictions of Crown support, and crippled by delays in assembling the troops and shipping, the southern strategy was a fiasco. By the time that British forces from Boston under Clinton and a larger contingent from Ireland commanded by Major General Charles Cornwallis, arrived at the appointed Cape Fear rendezvous, premature Loyalist attempts to throw off the rebels in Virginia and North

Carolina had been crushed. Seeking to salvage something from the botched campaign, the move against Charleston only compounded the loss of British prestige when it was decisively rebuffed on June 28.

The port's stalwart defense had been galvanized by Charles Lee. Writing to his friend the physician and congressman Benjamin Rush on the day after the battle, Lee reported how "the tyrant's mercenaries" had sent eight warships to subdue Charleston's key bastion, "a very imperfect and ill planned Fort on Sullivan's Island." The British men-of-war unleashed a furious cannonade, but the defenders, ensconced behind ramparts constructed of logs cut from spongy and resilient palmetto trees, were resolute. The vaunted wooden walls of the Royal Navy were beaten off with heavy losses, while Clinton and his redcoats, who had landed on the wrong side of an impassable inlet, remained mere bystanders. Drawing upon the classical era that inspired so many of his contemporaries, Lee enthused: "Our people, though quite raw recruits behaved like the Decima Legio"—Julius Caesar's famed Tenth Legion. Their sterling performance seemingly vindicated Lee's much-publicized belief that well-motivated citizen-soldiers would always beat paid professionals.[6]

Not surprisingly, this timely success gave a massive boost to Lee's military reputation. Rush wrote to him from Philadelphia: "It would take a volume to tell you how many clever things were said of you and the brave troops under your command after hearing of your late victory. It has given a wonderful turn to our affairs." He added that Lee's performance had done much to dispel the people's gloom at the failure of the Canadian expedition, reviving hopes that "we shall yet triumph over our enemies."[7] The total defeat of Britain's attempt against Charleston was no less significant for her unfolding strategy in North America. Disappointed in his hopes of pacifying the south, the American Secretary, Lord George Germain, now shelved that idea for the next two and a half years, when operations would focus on the Northern and Middle Colonies. The respite for the Southern Department also meant that Continental Army regiments raised there could be diverted for service in the northern theater.*

Meanwhile, the patriots' will to win was strengthened by Congress's formal declaration of American independence on July 4. Washington received official confirmation five days later, as the steady buildup of British forces off New York continued. General Orders for July 9, required each brigade to parade to hear the declaration read "with an audible voice." To Thomas Jefferson's ringing promise of "Life, Liberty and the Pursuit of Happiness," Washington added his own hopes that "this important event will serve as a fresh incentive to every officer, and soldier, to act with fidelity and courage, as knowing that now the peace and safety of his country depends (under God) solely on the success of our arms."[8]

That evening, Washington's soldiers joined the jubilant crowds of civilians who toppled and dismembered the impressive equestrian statue of George III on New York's Bowling Green. While conceding the zealous motives behind this action, Washington deplored the riotous manner in which his men had participated: such things were better "left to be executed by proper authority," he admonished. Washington's reaction to the disorder exemplified the stance of those wealthy property holders who had no wish to see events run out of their control: this was to be an orderly revolution.[9]

The real question was how long that movement would last in the face of the forces now assembling to crush it. At New York, Washington's defensive plans hinged upon an assumption that Howe would obligingly assault his entrenchments, taking losses

---

* In 1776 Congress created four administrative "Departments" for the Continental Army, designated "Southern," "Northern," "Eastern" (New England), and "Middle." A "Western Department," covering the frontiers of Virginia and Pennsylvania, was added in 1777. From spring 1776, the main field army under Washington's personal command was associated with the "Middle Department," embracing New York up to the Hudson Highlands, New Jersey, Pennsylvania, Maryland, and Delaware. Although commander-in-chief, Washington allowed the leaders of regional armies considerable autonomy.

he couldn't afford. "If our troops will behave well," he told Hancock on July 10, the redcoats would "have to wade through much blood and slaughter before they can carry any part of our works, if they carry 'em at all, and at best be in possession of a melancholy and mournful victory."[10]

Washington was anticipating another Bunker Hill. But New York City was not Boston, and the British were no longer the besieged; and with his brother's fleet at his disposal, Howe had other options than an unsubtle frontal attack. The flexibility gifted by unchallenged sea power was demonstrated on July 12, when two British frigates and three other vessels probed the Hudson. Washington's Manhattan batteries proved incapable of stopping them, with many of his awestruck gunners gawping at the spectacle rather than opening fire. One gun crew that did attempt to hit the ships was commanded by young Captain Alexander Hamilton, whose "zeal and diligence" had made his New York artillery company "conspicuous for their appearance and the regularity of their movements." Now, they fired so briskly that Hamilton's cannon burst, killing two of his men; they were buried on the Bowling Green, where King George had lately ridden.[11] The flotilla penetrated as far as the broad Tappan Zee, some twenty-five miles upriver, so severing Washington's water-borne communications with Albany.

That same day, July 12, Lord Howe's flagship, HMS *Eagle*, anchored off New York. Besides his military task as commander of the Royal Navy in American waters, Richard Howe had a contrasting and contradictory role to perform: Prime Minister Lord North had decided that the Howe brothers should simultaneously act as his peace commissioners, seeking a negotiated settlement between the Mother Country and its rebellious American offspring. Both Howes held well-known sympathies toward America, largely because of the "family connection" resulting from the colonists' reverence for the memory of their slain elder brother. As already seen, when the monument to George Augustus Howe funded by Massachusetts was unveiled in 1762, the gesture had a marked and enduring impact upon his surviving siblings. In 1766, while treasurer of the navy, Richard Howe was among just a handful of key office holders willing to receive the petition of the Stamp Act Congress; at Christmas 1774, when war looked ever more likely, he met Benjamin Franklin in London, spending weeks in a futile effort to persuade the Pennsylvanian polymath to work for an accommodation.[12]

But, like Washington, the Howes were born fighters who prized personal honor and martial distinction above all else; as faithful servants of the Crown, their pro-American sympathies didn't prevent them from accepting high command across the Atlantic. Indeed, such authority at least allowed them to act upon their inclination to temper force with negotiation. By early July 1776, Congress's declaration of independence made such a peaceful settlement increasingly unlikely, yet the admiral was determined to at least try.

Besides promoting reconciliation through circulars and a published declaration of his own, Lord Howe sought to open negotiations directly with Washington, sending a letter to New York on July 14 under a flag of truce. Howe's initiative stalled immediately on an issue of protocol: his letter failed to give Washington's military rank—which would have recognized and legitimized his position—and was instead addressed to "George Washington Esqr." Washington conferred with the general officers on hand, who agreed that he shouldn't receive any letter directed to him as a mere "private gentleman." Washington's trusted friend Colonel Reed was sent to "manage the affair," pointing out to Howe's messenger, Lieutenant Philip Brown, that "there was no such person [as 'Mr. Washington'] in the army, and that a letter intended for the General could not be received under such a direction." Brown was greatly concerned at this impasse, particularly as the letter was "rather of a civil than military nature" and because Lord Howe came with "great powers" to talk. But, as Reed made clear, unless Washington was addressed according to his correct "station," which was well known to the British, no letter could be accepted. As Washington explained to John Hancock, this was not simply a question of "punctilio," as "the opinion of others concurring with my own, I deemed it a duty to my country and my appointment to insist upon that respect which in any other than a public view I would willingly have waived."[13]

Nothing if not persistent, Howe made another attempt to open talks with Washington on July 16. This, as the admiral's personal secretary, Ambrose Serle, tartly noted, "was refused for the same idle and insolent reasons as were given before." While Howe was striving "to avert all bloodshed and to promote an accommodation," Serle continued sarcastically, it seemed "to be beneath a little paltry colonel of militia at the head of a banditti or rebels to treat with the representative of his lawful sovereign, because 'tis impossible to give him all the titles which the poor creature requires."[14]

While unwilling to concede Washington's rank in writing, the Howe brothers continued their efforts to open a dialogue with him. On July 19, an officer was sent to *ask* whether "General Washington" would consent to meet Lieutenant Colonel James Patterson, the British adjutant general. After an opening discussion about forms of address, which resolved nothing other than Washington's refusal to accept any letter that didn't officially acknowledge his rank, talk turned to the treatment of American prisoners of war in Canada. Patterson read a letter from General Howe promising to address that issue; then, as he was about to leave, he suddenly raised the all-important matter of reconciliation. Washington refused to be drawn. While agreeing that King George had chosen men of high reputation to act for him, he had no authority to negotiate with them. In addition, he understood that the Howe brothers were only empowered to issue pardons, and those who had committed no crime could surely have no need of *them*. At that, the interview ended.[15]

The following day, Washington wrote a revealing letter to his old comrade Adam Stephen, lieutenant colonel of the original Virginia Regiment, and now colonel of the Continental Army's 4th Virginia Regiment. After outlining his current tribulations at New York, Washington harked back more than two decades to recall the dangers that they had shared as young men during the French and Indian War. These remained etched indelibly on his memory.

Indeed, for all that now crowded his thoughts, he would not let July 3 and 9 pass by "without a grateful remembrance of the escape we had at the Meadows and on the Banks of Monongahela." For Washington, the knowledge that they had survived those bloody days offered comfort for the future. Indeed, he hoped that the "same Providence" that protected them both at Fort Necessity in 1754 and at Braddock's defeat in 1755 would "continue his mercies, and make us happy instruments in restoring peace and liberty to this once favored, but now distressed country."[16]

By early August, most of the expected British reinforcements had converged on Staten Island, swelling General Howe's strength to some 25,000 professional soldiers fit for duty. Washington's army also grew as new units marched in from the southern and middle states; he had about 20,000 men, although many of them were militia rather than regulars, and the sick list was longer than ever. Washington's command was at last becoming truly continental, but this diversity brought problems of its own: frustratingly, it seemed that the rivalries that had traditionally divided the American colonists would now hamstring their struggle for independence from Britain. Washington, who had shown himself such a vigorous champion of selfish Virginian interests in 1758, now urged a united front against the common enemy. Not everyone shared his breadth of vision. Orders from headquarters on August 1 announced Washington's "great concern" at the jealousies that had "arisen among the troops from the different provinces." The "reflections" being bandied about by officers and men alike could only "injure the noble cause," creating opportunities for the enemy to exploit. It was time, Washington appealed, for "all distinctions" to be "sunk in the name of an American."[17]

Now that Howe's entire force had concentrated, his attack was only a matter of time. During the tense wait, Washington sought to steel his men to face the battle ahead, using his customary combination of patriotic appeals and sage advice, backed by a blunt warning to those who shirked or ran. General Orders on August 13 urged the troops to remember "that liberty, property, life and honor, are all at stake." While the enemy would try to intimidate them by martial display, Washington's soldiers should remember how such redcoats had already been repulsed "on various occasions, by a few brave Americans." They were to be attentive to their orders, with each "good soldier" holding his fire "'till he is sure of doing execution." On a rather different note, the orders added that "it may not be amiss for the troops to know, that if any infamous rascal, in time of action, shall attempt to skulk, hide himself or retreat from the enemy without orders . . . he will instantly be shot down as an example of cowardice."[18]

Bickering, sickly, and outnumbered, Washington's army was obliged to defend a fifteen-mile front, stretching from the western end of Long Island to Upper Manhattan. This was a daunting task, made more so by the threat of amphibious attack: with the priceless asset of naval mobility, the Howe brothers could strike when and where they liked. On August 22—a calm, sunny morning that had succeeded a terrible night of awesome thunder and lightning— they did precisely that, landing 15,000 men and their supporting equipment on Long Island in a matter of hours and without the loss of a single soldier. Spreading over the island's meadows, fields, and orchards like a bloodstain, Howe's men were unopposed. Another 5,000 soon followed.

While it was obvious that Howe had now placed "a pretty considerable part" of his manpower on Long Island, Washington's intelligence reports badly underestimated the strength of the landing force, reckoning it at just "eight or nine thousand" men. In consequence, he remained unsure whether it would begin operations there or was intended as a feint to distract attention from an assault on New York City itself.[19] Washington responded to Howe's move by doubling his own forces on Long Island to about 9,000 men. The majority manned the strong fortifications at Brooklyn Heights, bordering the East River, but more than 3,000 of the best troops were ordered to hold an outlying position extending for several miles along the low, but steep and densely wooded line of the Heights of Guana. At first sight, these hills posed a formidable barrier, but their length obliged the defenders to spread themselves dangerously thin. In addition, the Heights were pierced by four "passes"; defensive forces covered three of them, but the most easterly, Jamaica Pass, was left unguarded.

In truth, the American dispositions on Long Island were badly flawed, with the advanced troops too far forward to enjoy support from their comrades at Brooklyn and vulnerable to annihilation piecemeal. Washington, as overall commander, must take the blame. Despite his four months at New York, he had failed to familiarize himself with its geography. The problem had only been compounded by a rapid succession of local commanders. When Charles Lee departed for the south in March, the responsibility for New York's defenses was turned over to Brigadier General William Alexander, a hard-drinking New Jersey man who called himself "Lord Stirling" because of his claim to an extinct Scottish earldom. The taxing assignment was soon after inherited by Nathanael Greene, who tackled it with his customary thoroughness. But on August 15, a week before the British landed on Long Island, Greene fell sick with a raging fever and was recalled to recuperate in Manhattan. His post was passed to Major General John Sullivan, who held it only briefly before an indignant Israel Putnam demanded that the command was rightfully his by seniority. "Old Put" got his way, which was unfortunate, as he knew even less about Long Island's topography than his predecessors.

Unlike his American opponents, General Henry Clinton was thoroughly familiar with New York City and its surroundings. The son of a former royal governor of the colony, he had spent his boyhood there before joining the British Army and seeing distinguished service against the French during the Seven Years' War's German campaigns as aide-de-camp to the celebrated Prince Charles of Brunswick. The straggling American position on the Heights of Guana tempted Clinton to devise an ambitious plan. Exploiting his local knowledge and also what he'd learned of the sophisticated war of maneuver waged in "High Germany," it aimed to turn both of the enemy's flanks. When William Howe proved skeptical of its complexity, Clinton persuaded him to adopt a modified version: while the rebels were preoccupied by fake attacks, or "demonstrations," to the right and center of their position, a powerful force would make a stealthy approach to the undefended Jamaica Pass under cover of darkness and then swing around the Americans' left.[20]

Late on the evening of August 26, the assault troops were ready. Major General James Grant, the bluff and portly Highlander who had been captured by the French and Indians outside Fort Duquesne in 1758 during Forbes's campaign, was deployed on the extreme left of the British line, facing the American right. The outspoken Grant had made himself a hate figure for the revolutionaries by mocking their fighting spirit and boasting in Parliament that he would march from one end of the colonies to the other with 5,000 men;[21] the same number were under his command that night. Lieutenant General Philip von Heister and 4,000 of his blue-coated Hessians held the British center at Flatbush. Meanwhile, Howe, Clinton, Cornwallis, and another 9,000 men were preparing for their long night march. At dawn on August 27, this flanking force had reached Jamaica Pass without incident. By then both Grant and Heister were already engaging the Americans strung along the Heights to their fronts. These units—New Englanders, Pennsylvanians, Marylanders, and men from Delaware—were commanded by Sullivan and Lord Stirling. In a series of fierce, isolated actions, the Continental troops fought coolly enough against what appeared to be genuine and determined assaults, offering "battle in the true English taste," as one of the Marylanders described it, and standing firm despite the incoming shot and shell that was "now and then taking off a head."[22] They were congratulating themselves on holding back the redcoats and Hessians from sunrise until noon when the unsuspected British flanking column struck suddenly from behind.

Surprise was total. Faced with the prospect of being cut off from the refuge of Brooklyn's fortifications and now attacked from the front in earnest, the weary and bloodied men of Sullivan's command quickly crumpled, scattering in flight across the intervening marshes. Lord Stirling's southern regiments fought harder, staging several stubborn stands "with more than Roman virtue," but the redcoats pushed on briskly with the bayonet, and they too were broken. Many ran fast enough to find safety within the Brooklyn lines, but about 1,500 were not so fortunate; perhaps 200 died—drowned in tidal Gowanus Creek or shot, clubbed, or bayoneted by their pursuers—the rest were rounded up as prisoners. At a cost of 370 casualties, Howe had inflicted a crushing defeat, eliminating some 40 percent of the Heights' defenders. Major General Grant crowed: "If a good bleeding can bring those Bible-faced Yankees to their senses, the fever of independency should soon abate."[23]

Washington had played no direct role in the grim fight for the Heights. Instead, he was among the general officers who looked on helplessly from a "high hill" within the Brooklyn defenses, viewing the rout through their telescopes. The same Maryland soldier who had fought all morning before escaping across Gowanus Creek later heard that "general Washington wrung his hands, and cried out, *good God, what brave fellows I must this day lose!*" Washington was seemingly bewildered by the swift and devastating British attack, which had made him and his generals look like bungling amateurs.

Reinforced by fresh regiments ferried across from Manhattan during the morning, 7,000 or so Americans were now hemmed within the fortifications of Brooklyn, their backs to the East River. To the chagrin of many of his officers, Howe refused to administer a coup de grâce to the shocked and demoralized rebels by ordering an immediate assault upon their redoubts and trenches. Howe didn't doubt that his men could have stormed them. But, as he informed Lord George Germain, it was pointless to incur unnecessary casualties when the same results could be achieved by more methodical and far less costly siege operations. Yet Henry Clinton, the chief architect of the stunning victory on Long Island, was not alone in maintaining that the enemy was too shaken to resist a bold attack and that a prime opportunity to destroy much of the Continental Army and perhaps snuff out the rebellion itself had been squandered.[24]

William Howe's stance was clearly influenced by personal experience of the bloodbath at Bunker Hill and the overriding need to conserve his precious manpower, but others factors also came into play. According to Charles Stedman, a Loyalist and British Army commissary who wrote a perceptive history of the American Revolutionary War, Howe considered he had already done enough to destroy his enemies' resolve to fight and had "no desire to shed the blood of a people so nearly allied to that source from whence he derived all his authority and power."[25] In addition, like his brother Richard, General Howe was also a peace commissioner: as events soon demonstrated, their conciliatory stance—which so woefully misjudged the determined mood of the revolutionaries—hinged upon more than just a broad sense of Anglo-American kinship.

Howe's failure to push on and storm the Brooklyn lines on August 27 gave Washington the chance to save his army and, with it, American independence. Over the next two days, heavy rain fell, further dampening the morale of Washington's dispirited men but also hampering the work of the redcoat sappers digging snaking trenches to within easy striking distance of Brooklyn's earthworks. It seemed as if Washington and the troops still with him must fight to the death or ignominiously surrender. Then, on the night of August 29–30, the blustery weather subsided and dense fog descended. Under its cover, in a stealthy and skillfully managed operation conducted by Colonel John Glover's versatile Continental regiment of Marblehead mariners, Brooklyn's defenders were ferried back to Manhattan. The British never realized what was happening until they were gone.

Reporting next day to John Hancock, Washington told how the retreat had been made without loss of men or ammunition and in better order than he would have expected; all the stores and cannon were evacuated, save for some heavy guns that got bogged down in the soggy ground. Washington also reported that the Howe brothers were still seeking a negotiated settlement: Major General Sullivan, who had been captured along with Lord Stirling during the desperate fighting on Long Island and released on parole, maintained that Lord Howe remained "extremely desirous of seeing some of the members of Congress." Washington had allowed Sullivan to travel to Philadelphia so that he could brief the delegates in person.[26]

Two days later, Washington wrote again to Hancock in an understandably pessimistic mood. "Our situation is truly distressing," he confessed. Since the setback on August 27, many of the troops had become dispirited, apprehensive, and despairing. Rather than steeling themselves to meet the emergency, the militiamen were deserting in droves. Their example was contagious, likewise their insubordination, to the extent that Washington was now obliged to admit his "want of confidence in the generality of the troops." Militia and short-service soldiers were inadequate to the gravity of the situation. There was but one remedy, a cure that any liberty-loving American patriot would find hard to swallow—"a permanent standing army." Washington was "fully convinced" that without such a force, "competent almost to every exigency . . . our liberties must of necessity be greatly hazarded, if not entirely lost. . . ." It was the old argument that he had voiced so often as colonel of the Virginia Regiment twenty years before, but now given added urgency. Whatever aid the militia might contribute was "nearly counterbalanced by the disorder, irregularity and confusion they occasion."[27]

If his troops could be relied upon, Washington assured Hancock, he would be confident of defending New York City. Regrettably, he could give no such guarantee. This was a harsh judgment, particularly as the recent crushing defeat stemmed from Washington's poor generalship rather than any obvious lack of spirit among his men; he had been totally outclassed, while they'd fought as well as anyone could have expected, with hundreds paying the supreme price. At that very time, as Lord Howe's secretary, Ambrose Serle, discovered, the woods near Brooklyn were strictly off-limits, being "noisome with the stench of the dead bodies of the rebels, whom the Hessians and the Highlanders followed thither and destroyed."[28]

Lacking confidence in his men, Washington now raised the possibility of abandoning New York City. In that case, he asked Hancock, should it be destroyed, or instead left intact to provide snug winter

Charles Willson Peale, *George Washington*, 1772. The earliest known portrait of Washington shows him wearing his uniform as colonel of the Virginia Regiment from 1755 to 1758.

Anonymous, *Lawrence Washington*, ca. 1740–50. Washington's much-loved half brother wears the red coat and green waistcoat of the American Regiment in which he served as a captain in the Caribbean from 1740 to 1742.

Duncan Smith, *Sarah "Sally" Cary Fairfax*. This 1916 copy of a naïve, and now lost, portrait by an anonymous artist suggests the qualities that captivated the young Washington.

Sir Joshua Reynolds, *Captain Robert Orme*, 1756. This dashing young British officer befriended Washington during the 1755 campaign against Fort Duquesne.

Allan Ramsay, *John Campbell, Fourth Earl of Loudoun*, 1754. Britain's commander in chief in North America from mid-1756 to early 1758 failed to afford Washington the patronage he expected.

William Mercer, after James Peale, *The Battle of Princeton*, c. 1786. Washington rallies his troops at the crisis of the fighting on January 3, 1777.

Xavier della Gatta, *The Battle of Germantown*, 1782. Early on October 4, 1777, redcoats prepare to defend the Chew House against the Americans, seen advancing in the distance.

Charles Willson Peale, *George Washington at Princeton,* 1779. This celebrated portrait commemorates Washington's pivotal victory on January 3, 1777. Hessian standards captured days earlier at Trenton lie at his feet.

Charles Willson Peale, *General Nathanael Greene,* 1783. Widely regarded as Washington's most able subordinate, Greene shared his instinctive aggression.

Charles Willson Peale, *General Henry Knox,* 1783. Washington's loyal artillery commander, shown wearing the insignia of the newly inaugurated Society of the Cincinnati.

General Sir William Howe, mezzotint published by John Morris, c. 1777. Washington's brave but sometimes lackadaisical British opponent during the campaigns of 1776 to 1777.

John Smart, *Sir Henry Clinton*, 1777. Howe's erratic successor, and Washington's principal enemy from 1778.

Thomas Gainsborough, *Charles Earl Cornwallis*, 1783. A deceptively tranquil portrait of the energetic general trapped at Yorktown in 1781.

James Peale, *General Horatio Gates at Saratoga*, c. 1799. Washington's colleague and rival at his greatest triumph, the surrender of General Burgoyne's army on October 17, 1777.

George Romney, *Joseph Brant*, c. 1776. Society artist Romney painted the charismatic Mohawk leader when Brant visited London.

H. Charles McBarron Junior, *Washington at Monmouth Courthouse*. A modern reconstruction of the battle on June 28, 1778, with Washington berating Charles Lee for retreating. The artist captures the day's intense heat, and the motley uniforms of the Continental Army.

Major John André, *Self-portrait*, 1780. Made on the eve of his execution on October 2, 1780, André's sketch reveals the debonair and carefree demeanor that so impressed his captors.

John Trumbull, *Surrender of Lord Cornwallis*, 1787–1828. Deputizing for Lord Cornwallis at Yorktown on October 19, 1781, Brigadier General O'Hara capitulates to Major General Lincoln, while Washington looks on.

Louis–Nicolas van Blarenberghe, *The British Surrender at Yorktown*, 1785. The garrison marches out to lay down its arms, watched by smartly uniformed French troops (left) and ragged Americans.

Gilbert Stuart, *George Washington,* "Athenaeum type", 1796. Perhaps the most familiar likeness of Washington, Stuart's portrait depicts features rendered puffy and distorted by badly–fitting false teeth.

Attributed to Frederick Kemmelmeyer, *Washington Reviewing the Western Army at Fort Cumberland, Maryland,* after 1794. Against the backdrop of the Allegheny Mountains militia assemble on October 16, 1794 to counter the Whiskey Rebels. Wearing an updated version of his old Revolutionary War uniform, Washington rides a horse of his favorite color.

John Trumbull, *George Washington,* 1780. The lean and vigorous forty-eight-year-old Washington shadowed by Billy Lee, his slave and constant companion during the Revolutionary War.

quarters for the British? By simply posing the question, Washington left no doubt of his readiness to torch the city. To Nathanael Greene, the continuing focus on New York City obscured a far graver danger, as the enemy had it in their power to land higher up on Manhattan, trapping all the Americans below. Greene not only favored burning the city and its suburbs, but also evacuating Manhattan Island without delay. Writing to Washington on September 5, he urged that "a general and speedy" retreat was "the only eligible plan to oppose the enemy successfully and secure ourselves from disgrace." Greene believed they now had "no object on this side" of King's Bridge—the only viable land exit from Manhattan.[29]

On September 7, as Greene had recommended, Washington summoned a council of war to respond to a threat that both intelligence reports and direct observation suggested was now looming ever closer: that the British intended to corner his army on "the island of New York . . . by taking post in our rear, while the shipping effectually secure the front." So positioned, the enemy could sever Washington's communications, obliging him to fight on their terms or "surrender at discretion." Facing "a choice of difficulties," only exacerbated by the unreliability of the troops, everything—"history—our own experience—the advice of our ablest friends in Europe—the fears of the enemy, and even the declarations of Congress"—pointed to the wisdom of a cautious, defensive stance. Explaining his conundrum to Hancock on September 8, Washington gave a classic statement of what would come to be characterized as his "Fabian" strategy: "that we should on all occasions avoid a general action or put anything to the risk unless compelled by a necessity into which we ought never to be drawn." Conforming to such a cautiously defensive "war of posts," and always shying away from a potentially decisive battle, ran directly counter to Washington's own far more aggressive instincts; it was soon clear that he was prepared to interpret this creed as flexibly as possible and even to ignore it completely.

For the moment, however, the key question remained whether to defend New York. As Washington reported to Hancock, while some general officers at the council had favored "a total and immediate

removal from the city," thus keeping the enemy at bay and preserving the kernel of troops around which a new army could be
built, they were overruled by others who were swayed by a belief
that Congress expected the city "to be maintained at every hazard."
A compromise was reached, although it only delayed the inevitable: "that for the present a part of our force might be kept here
and attempt to maintain the city a while longer." In consequence,
all save 5,000 men were shifted from Lower Manhattan: a strong
force of 9,000 was moved to the vicinity of King's Bridge, while the
balance—another 5,000 or so—were strung between them to fend
off a British strike against Manhattan's eastern shoreline.[30]

Given the obvious danger of being bottled up on Manhattan
Island, Washington's failure to not only quit New York City but
evacuate his entire army to the mainland without delay testifies
to the potentially baleful influence of the council of war and the
consequences of his misguided belief that it was vested with the
authority to dictate strategy. In addition, besides a desire to placate his civilian masters in Congress and an ingrained reluctance
to surrender territory without a fight, it is also likely that Washington's sense of urgency was blunted by his own exhaustion and the
enemy's inactivity.

For nearly a fortnight following his easy victory on Long
Island, William Howe had done little more than monitor the
Americans' positions. It took an ominous development on September 9, when the British occupied Montresor Island—a fine
base for staging an amphibious landing midway up Manhattan
Island—to convince Washington that he must withdraw the rest
of his troops from New York City before it was too late. Urged
on by six generals headed by Greene, he called another council of war on September 12 to reconsider the army's "critical and
dangerous" situation. This time, by a majority of ten votes to
three, it was decided that the city at least should be abandoned
forthwith. Significantly, the army was not yet quitting Manhattan: a substantial body of 8,000 men would be left at the northern end of the island, "for the defense of Mount Washington and

its dependencies." This description embraced the strongpoint known as Fort Washington, high on the east bank of the Hudson, and the fortified lines stretching south toward the rocky Harlem Heights.[31] Given the stores to be transported, the evacuation of New York was easier said than done. So long delayed, the decision was now barely in time. This dithering warned against the danger of placing too much reliance upon the opinions of politicians in distant Philadelphia with little grasp of strategic realities. With time, Washington learned to assert himself decisively as the commander on the spot. Before he did, such deference to the wishes of Congress would cost the cause dear.

The prolonged lull in British operations, which gave Washington and his generals such a timely reprieve, was deliberate and intended to allow a fresh diplomatic initiative. On September 11, the day before Washington and his commanders finally decided to abandon New York City, the peace conference that Lord Howe had proposed via General Sullivan went ahead on Staten Island. It was attended by three congressmen—Lord Howe's old friend Benjamin Franklin; another leading radical, John Adams; and the more moderate Edward Rutledge. The trio returned unimpressed by Howe's statement that the colonists' grievances could only be addressed *after* they had surrendered but struck by his explanation that his family's ties with New England left him with a strong desire for peace. The precise nature and importance of this personal bond is underlined by the explicit testimony of Adams. In his autobiographical recollection of the Staten Island conference, Adams wrote:

> *Lord Howe was profuse in his expressions of gratitude to the state of Massachusetts for erecting a marble monument in Westminster Abbey to his elder brother Lord Howe, who was killed in America in the last French war, saying, "he esteemed that honor to his family above all things in this world. That such was his gratitude and affection to this country, on that account, that he felt for America as for a brother, and, if America should fall, he should feel and lament it, like the loss of a brother."*

At this, as Adams recalled, the worldly-wise and witty Franklin had quipped that they would do their utmost to save Howe "that mortification."[32]

The conference collapsed because the Howes lacked any authority to negotiate with independent states. As Benjamin Rush informed his wife, the three commissioners had reported that Lord Howe's "powers extended no further than to confer with people of influence in America" upon their grievances: even that step depended upon the rebels first returning to their allegiance. Such backsliding was now unthinkable. Rush added: "When his Lordship asked in what capacity he was to receive them, Mr. Adams said, 'In any capacity your Lordship pleases except in that of British subjects.'"[33]

Despite his political naïvety, there is no reason to doubt the sincerity of Lord Howe's sentiments. During that crucial summer, therefore, the Howe brothers confronted their opponents with decidedly mixed feelings. If they'd been fighting the old enemy, France, as both of them demonstrated during the previous war and as "Black Dick" would prove many years later in combat with the French Revolutionary regime, they would have shown no such restraint. In 1776, however, the Howes' conflicting roles as military commanders and peacemakers compromised Britain's war effort at a critical moment: their clear reluctance to land a knock-out blow at New York, when Washington was willing to risk his unseasoned army in a stand-up fight, proved costly for the Mother Country; looking back, New Englanders may have considered the £250 voted for George Augustus Howe's monument to be money very well spent.[34]

The total failure of Lord Howe's latest peace initiative was swiftly followed by a fresh British offensive. As anticipated, this fell on Manhattan's eastern shore. On the evening of September 14, five frigates pushed up the East River and anchored off Kip's Bay. The shoreline had been entrenched and lined with a breastwork defended by Connecticut militiamen. The next morning, September 15, they watched in trepidation as some 4,000 British and Hessian troops—crack grenadiers and light infantry commanded by Clinton—were embarked in rows of flat-bottomed boats for an amphibious assault. As one young British officer, Captain Francis Lord Rawdon, noted, the Germans, who were new to such water-borne operations, steadied their nerves by singing hymns. By contrast, the redcoats countered the tension in their own way, "by damning themselves and the enemy indiscriminately with wonderful fervency."[35]

Then, with a continuous, deafening roar that left even seasoned British observers awestruck, the frigates unleashed their broadsides against the shore defenses. Not surprisingly, this intensive bombardment was too much for the Yankee levies. They promptly abandoned their trenches, scattering in a blind panic that swiftly infected two brigades of Continentals sent to stiffen them. Alerted by the gunfire, Washington rode toward the scene from his new headquarters at Harlem Heights, only to meet the defenders already "retreating with the utmost precipitation" and "flying in every direction and in the greatest confusion." Despite the best efforts of Washington and his staff, the fugitives could not be rallied until they were miles off. According to General George Weedon, Washington was "so exasperated that he struck several officers in their flight, three times dashed his hat on the ground, and at last exclaimed, 'Good God, have I got such troops as those!'" Another senior officer, Nathanael Greene, reported that Washington was abandoned by his men "within eighty yards of the enemy, so vexed at the infamous conduct of the troops that he sought death rather than life." It was only with difficulty that he could be persuaded to retreat.[36]

By pushing just a mile or more westward across Manhattan to the Hudson River, Clinton could have trapped about 3,500 Continentals still remaining in and around New York City under General Putnam. Unsure of the opposition and lacking orders to advance, Clinton instead consolidated his bridgehead until reinforcements arrived. By 5 p.m. Howe had come ashore with a further 9,000 men, but by then the city's defenders had already escaped. Jettisoning their cumbersome cannon, they had headed up the Hudson shore to rendezvous with Washington's main army at Harlem Heights that evening. Meanwhile, the British marched into New York, marveling at the strength of its fortifications and relieved that they had fallen without a fight. Washington's new position at Harlem was naturally strong, and he had no doubt of rebuffing an enemy attack—provided his troops showed "tolerable bravery." To his "extreme affliction," however, recent experience had only reinforced his growing conviction that such conduct was "rather to be wished for than expected."[37]

Here, at least, Washington was soon to be pleasantly surprised. On September 16, the day after the Kip's Bay stampede, his men went far to redeem themselves. During a sprawling engagement, several companies of impetuous British light infantry pushed forward against Washington's Harlem lines, leaving their supports far behind. These elite troops used bugle horns rather than drums to transmit orders; according to Colonel Joseph Reed, when they emerged from the woods into the open, they sounded the hunting call "in the most insulting manner," as if celebrating a kill. To Reed, this braying seemed to "crown" their "recent disgrace." For a passionate fox hunter like Washington, it must have been the final straw. Here at last was a chance to vent pent-up frustrations and hit back at the enemy. Rather than adopt a defensive stance in accordance with his recent assurances to Congress, he authorized several units to advance, engage, and surround the rash and impertinent redcoats. The plan failed to unfold precisely as envisaged, but it was effective enough all the same: outnumbered by determined Marylanders and Virginians, the light infantrymen were pushed back. Their retreat was covered by more redcoats, including Highlanders from the 42nd Foot, a famed regiment destined to become better known by its unofficial title, the "Black Watch." Dismissed by the British as no more than a scrimmage, in which the cocksure "Light Bobs" had gallantly fought their way out of a scrape, the so-called Battle of Harlem Heights was undeniably significant for Washington and his army. The Americans had not only faced some of Howe's best soldiers but had seen their backs. Morale soared accordingly; as the exultant Reed reported, they had "recovered their spirits and feel a confidence which before they had quite lost."[38]

Nathanael Greene, who had commanded the front line at Harlem Heights, downplayed his first battlefield engagement as a "skirmish" rather than an "action." But, like Reed, he knew that its results far outweighed its scale: the Americans "had advanced upon the plain ground without cover," driving the British before them. General Putnam, Colonel Reed, and the other officers present had acted with noble spirit. If all the colonies could field such fine leaders, Greene believed, there would be no need to doubt the rank and file: indeed, there "never was troops that would stand in the field longer than the American soldiery. If the officers were as good as the men, and had only a few months to form the troops by discipline, America might bid defiance to the whole world."[39]

Aptly enough, on the very day Washington's soldiers demonstrated their fighting spirit at Harlem, Congress authorized a major expansion and reorganization of the Continental Army along lines that he had been lobbying for since the previous summer. Shocked by the debacle on Long Island and further swayed by Washington's urgent pleas in its wake, delegates voted for what many patriots still considered unthinkable—a standing army of long-service troops. Congress resolved that eighty-eight battalions, each of 738 officers and men—a total force of 65,000—should be recruited forthwith, with state quotas based upon population: hence Massachusetts and Virginia were each required to raise fifteen battalions, Delaware and Georgia just one apiece. Crucially, given Washington's diatribes against the bane of short-term enlistments, recruits for this new army would serve "during the present war." As Washington knew from hard experience, it was one thing to authorize an army on paper, quite another to raise it. Above all, it was necessary to recognize that, for all the fine talk of liberty and freedom, men required to risk their lives for the cause of American independence had the right to expect realistic, concrete rewards. In line with another appeal from Washington, which had deplored the existing $10 bounty as derisory—especially when a man could get twice as much for a month or two in the militia—any Continental soldier who signed up for the duration would receive a bounty of $20. As Washington the land-hungry former surveyor appreciated only too well, a chunk of the country that they were fighting to defend would offer recruits an even stronger reason to shoulder a musket for American liberty. Congress agreed with his reasoning, adding 100 acres of land to each man's bounty. After debate, Congress decided to extend the land deal to men prepared to enlist for three years. Once he had heard the new recruitment terms Washington pushed for further incentives, including the annual issue of a suit of good clothes to each noncom and soldier.[40]

No less crucial was the question of the army's leadership, another long-standing Washington gripe and one underlined by Greene's pointed comments following the unexpected success at Harlem Heights. Before Washington received news of Congress's resolutions to form the new army, he had written to Hancock pleading for changes that would permit a reformation of the officer corps. Employing what he casually dismissed as "a few moments" borrowed from "the hours allotted to sleep," but which must have been a lengthy stint of brow-furrowing toil, he composed a long and closely argued letter.[41]

Washington believed that the "general run of the officers which compose the present army" fell far short of the ideal; great care must be taken in choosing those for the new army, even if it took twice as long to complete the regiments. The type of officer Washington had in mind was described in a letter to his Virginian friend Patrick Henry: when selecting the officers for the fifteen battalions to be raised by Henry's state, pains should be taken to guard against "the soldier and officer being too nearly on a level." In Washington's opinion, a clear distinction was necessary: when previous military experience was not an issue, he advised, "the true criterion to judge by . . . is to consider whether the candidate for office has a just pretension to the character of a gentleman, a proper sense of honor, and some reputation to lose."[42] In other words, men like Washington himself.

Just as the rank and file deserved decent bounties, so their officers should receive enough pay to allow them to live like "gentlemen." They, too, needed something more to fight for than a patriotic belief in the worthiness of their cause. As Washington emphasized to John Hancock, only this financial independence would encourage "men of character to engage; and till the bulk of your officers are composed of such persons as are actuated by principles of honor, and a spirit of enterprise, you have little to expect from them." After all, he added, surely something was "due to the man who puts his life in his hand, hazards his health and forsakes the sweets of domestic enjoyments." Recalling his frustrations at the unequal status of redcoats and provincials during the last war, he wondered why a Continental captain should receive half the pay of his British counterpart for performing the same duties. As soon as Washington received Congress's decision to place its faith in the new standing army he repeated his plea for higher officers' pay, enclosing an estimate covering all ranks from colonels to surgeons' mates.[43]

Alongside his calls for a well-led and reliable force of long-service regulars, Washington had consistently appealed for his army to be placed under tougher discipline. As he had informed Hancock on September 25, the sanctions available under the original *Articles of War* agreed by Congress in June 1775 were laughably weak. With one or two exceptions, for "the most atrocious offences" the maximum punishment was a mere thirty-nine lashes. Even when properly inflicted, this failed to intimidate offenders, with "many hardened fellows" boasting that they would endure it again for a bottle of rum. In consequence, desertion was rife, with thirty or forty men slipping off together; likewise "the infamous practice of plundering," which was pursued so indiscriminately that it threatened to alienate the civilian population—with consequences "fatal both to the country and army."

Here again Washington's persistent lobbying had already hit home. On September 20, Congress approved new and far stricter *Articles of War*. John Adams was a key player, egged on by his friend William Tudor. As judge advocate, Tudor shared Washington's view that the existing *Articles* were toothless: far from "making soldiers," they were "breeding highwaymen and robbers." Indeed, men who'd joined the fight from a sense of virtue had now lost their enthusiasm and were "sinking into an army of mercenaries" who must be restrained "by a fear of punishment." Adams, who recalled that he and Thomas Jefferson had formed a committee to thrash out the revisions, readily acknowledged that they had used the British Army's regulations as a template. Anticipating opposition within Congress regardless of what was proposed, Adams therefore resolved to forward "a complete system at once" and let it "meet its fate." As there was already a set of articles in existence "which had carried two empires to the head of mankind" (the British rules were no more than a literal translation of the Roman Army's, he claimed), they had been copied "totidem verbis." In fact, there had been some changes, not least the substitution of "the Congress" for "the King," but, as Adams proudly recalled, the *Articles* of September 1776 were essential for the new modeling of the Continental Army: "They laid the foundation of a discipline, which in time brought our troops to a capacity of contending with British veterans, and a rivalry with the best troops of France."[44]

The revised *Articles* came close to what Washington wanted to impose his notions of discipline. Now deserters and plunderers, as well as mutineers and cowards, could face the death penalty, while the maximum number of lashes for less heinous offenses was upped to 100. This was less than Washington had often inflicted upon the men of his Virginia Regiment, while the redcoats regularly faced far heavier floggings: that January, for example, a British court-martial in Boston had sentenced private Thomas MacMahan to a thousand lashes for receiving stolen goods; his *wife*, Isabella, received a hundred lashes at the "cart's tail" for the same crime.[45] The stiffening of the Continental Army's discipline nonetheless signaled a commitment to increased order and professionalism; it also acknowledged that many recruits for the new, long-service army would be a different breed from those who had flocked to the siege of Boston, driven primarily by patriotic zeal: as the new Continentals increasingly resembled the soldiers of traditional European armies, not least the British, they would need to be kept in line by tough discipline akin to that customary within those organizations.[46]

Coming after all of that summer's humiliations and frustrations, Washington's success in persuading Congress to recognize that the real advantages of a disciplined "standing army" far outweighed the remote "evils to be apprehended from one" was a significant victory, as important for the future of American independence as any scored on a battlefield. In the autumn of 1776, however, Congress's new model Continental Army existed only in theory. Until it materialized, Washington was left with soldiers whose enlistments mostly expired at the end of the year or earlier. As he complained to his cousin Lund on September 30, the army's strength was "fluctuating, uncertain, and forever far short of report—at no time, I believe, equal to twenty thousand men fit for duty." That day, the hale men numbered 14,759, with another 3,427 detached "on command," and that with the "enemy within stone's throw of us." It was driving Washington to distraction: "In short, such is my situation that if I were to wish the bitterest curse to an enemy on this side of the grave, I should put him in my stead with my feelings; and yet I do not know what plan of conduct to pursue."[47]

It was the old story that Washington had faced in 1756–57 on the raid-lashed frontiers of Virginia, but now writ large: "I see the impossibility of serving with reputation," he told Lund, "or doing any essential service to the cause by continuing in command, and yet I am told that if I quit the command, inevitable ruin will follow, from the distraction that will ensue." Washington had accepted the trust that Congress had placed upon him; he was honor-bound to uphold it while he could. Despite being "wearied to death all day with a variety of perplexing circumstances," he was now resolved to stand his ground at Harlem while he'd breath to do so. As the enemy could not afford "to waste the season that is now fast advancing," a few more days should bring matters to a head.

The three weeks following the clash at Harlem Heights had seen another halt in Howe's operations as he took stock before making his next move. Howe was clearly wary of Washington's latest position and unwilling to risk his precious men in an all-out assault that was likely to incur heavy casualties. According to Lord Howe's well-informed secretary, Ambrose Serle, on September 17, when the general came on board the *Eagle*, he told how the rebels had been "driven back to some immensely strong works . . . on very advantageous ground."[48]

It is also possible that Howe was hoping to coordinate his next offensive move with a British advance against Albany from Canada. Intelligence from Quebec certainly suggested the likelihood of a link-up. In the days after the action at Harlem Heights, Serle noted optimistic reports that the "Northern Army" was rolling south down the Hudson Valley. Indeed, a rebel deserter from that front maintained that General Burgoyne had taken several of their armed vessels, was passing over lakes Champlain and George, and expected to reach New York "very shortly."[49]

In fact, there would be no junction between Britain's New York and Canadian armies that year, or in any other. Despite Burgoyne's promising beginning in shunting the demoralized rebels out of Canada, by late summer his offensive had lost momentum, owing largely to the courage, drive, and initiative of the ever-resourceful Benedict Arnold. As Arnold had hastily assembled a ramshackle fleet on Lake Champlain, Britain's commander in chief in Canada, Governor Guy Carleton, was obliged to construct a flotilla capable of facing it. The miniature navies clashed on October 21, and, although the British blasted Arnold's fleet into splinters, its dogged resistance bought enough time to discourage Carleton from pushing on from Crown Point to Ticonderoga and to halt his campaign by pulling back to the northern end of Lake Champlain. Because of Arnold, another fine opportunity to snuff out the rebellion was lost.[50]

Following William Howe's capture of New York City, his brother had built on that success to play another conciliatory card. Rebuffed by Congress, he now tried a direct appeal to the colonists at large. On September 19, the Howes issued a joint declaration. In vague terms, it invited Americans to discuss ways by which peace and unity could be restored to the empire, indicating that King George III was inclined to revise the legislation that had sparked the rebellion in the first place. Not surprisingly, this latest initiative was greeted with derision, not only by the rebels, but also by Loyalists and, not least, by British Army officers. Everyone—save, it seemed, for the Howe brothers themselves—could see that the time for talk was over. Hostilities would cease only if Washington and his generals were pounded into submission by hard fighting. Yet General Howe continued to favor a war of maneuver, methodically reclaiming territory rather than seeking a decisive battle that might inflict unhealable wounds, while Lord Howe maintained his hopes for a negotiated settlement. In doggedly pursuing reconciliation, the brothers seemed untroubled that this approach was utterly at odds with the objectives of the strategists in London, who sought decisive victories that would crush the rebellion.[51]

Washington knew that the enemy's command of the waterways around New York gave them the mobility to land wherever they chose, and high enough up Manhattan Island to sever his own retreat route to the north, via King's Bridge. Yet he still stayed put at Harlem Heights, now seemingly fixated on the idea of fighting a defensive action that would oblige Howe to risk a bloody frontal assault; instead of preempting him by abandoning the Harlem lines and moving north, he awaited his attack. Given his amphibious capacity, Howe had other, less costly options. On October 12, Richard Howe's ships disembarked 4,000 troops at Throg's Neck, on the East River and above Washington's position.

The peninsula selected for the landing was a poor choice, too constricted and marshy for a rapid breakout in the teeth of determined defenders ensconced behind stone walls. Howe would have to strike elsewhere. Abortive or not, the Throg's Neck landing left Howe's intentions beyond doubt. Washington must withdraw his troops from Manhattan Island while he still could. On October 16, he urged retreat to another council of war and was forcefully seconded by Major General Charles Lee, who had now returned from

South Carolina. The next day, most of the army began falling back from Harlem Heights. However, it was also agreed that Fort Washington in northern Manhattan should be "retained as long as possible." This dubious decision was justified on the grounds that the fort would maintain communications with New Jersey and block further British efforts to push ships up the Hudson.[52]

Baffled at Throg's Neck, on October 18, Howe tried again at Pell's Point, four miles farther north, this time concentrating the bulk of his army. An American brigade of about 750 men under the reliable Colonel John Glover took advantage of the district's woods and walls to mount a stubborn delaying action, skirmishing with the grenadiers and light infantry of Howe's advance guard before falling back. In his last orders from Harlem Heights, issued on October 21, Washington paid tribute to their "merit and good behavior."[53] Rather than pushing forward vigorously, hounding Washington's heels, Howe advanced warily, with obvious deliberation. Unmolested, Washington left Manhattan Island by King's Bridge that same day; on October 22, he established another strong position ten miles upcountry at the village of White Plains.

As Lord Rawdon wryly noted, "plains" was a misnomer for what was in fact "as hilly and difficult a country" as he had ever clapped eyes on.[54] Washington's latest position covered a three-mile frontage, its right anchored on the steep, rocky, and partially wooded Chatterton Hill. Washington was still learning the rudiments of battlefield command. Repeating his error on Long Island, he failed to reconnoiter the ground carefully: despite its obvious importance, he neglected to fortify Chatterton Hill, instead entrusting it to the care of a few hundred of the jittery militia who so exasperated him.

Skirmishers from Howe's army reached White Plains on the morning of October 28. Only now did Washington begin to take his bearings, assessing developments from the summit of Chatterton Hill. He was accompanied by Major General Lee, who scanned the horizon and pointed out what he reckoned to be a much stronger defensive position, still farther back, at North Castle. They were about to ride off and inspect it when it became clear that a determined British attack was developing, targeted at Chatterton Hill. About 1,000 Continental troops, along with a few cannon, were sent to bolster the militia there.

Like Washington's command, Howe's army at White Plains con-sisted of about 13,000 men; almost as many remained behind on Manhattan Island. Preceded by an intensive and effective cannon-ade, his assault columns of Hessians and redcoats waded across the shallow Bronx River at the foot of Chatterton Hill, deployed as best as they could on the constricted ground, then ascended the slope with fixed bayonets. True to Washington's predictions, the mere sight of cold steel was enough to panic the militia into flight, but the Continentals mounted a more respectable resistance before falling back. Once again, Howe failed to capitalize upon this vic-tory with a determined pursuit of Washington, who had estab-lished reserve positions to the east. One frustrated officer wished that the army had instead been led by Howe's old commander, the bold Wolfe. Of course, such critics failed to appreciate that the gen-eral's aim was not the annihilation of the Continental Army, but rather its continued withdrawal at the minimum cost in British and German blood.[55]

Howe was poised to resume his methodical offensive on the morning of October 31, but a rainstorm on the evening before the intended assault drenched his ammunition and made the going heavy for his artillery, giving Washington an opportunity to slip away once more. Now conforming to the "Fabian" pattern, he fell back some five miles to North Castle, the formidable position recently identified by Lee. Howe made no effort to dislodge him from there; as he subsequently reported to Germain, he could not see the "least consequence" in merely "driving their rearguard fur-ther back."[56] Indeed, Washington's army had been driven quite far enough for Howe's purposes. On November 4, the British com-mander quit White Plains and returned to Manhattan, where a more tempting target awaited.

Baffled by Howe's sudden withdrawal, Washington couldn't credit that he was retiring into winter quarters so soon. He would surely strike again, but where? If Howe shifted into New Jersey, he might venture a lunge at Philadelphia, the Revolution's capital. Intelligence also suggested that Fort Washington would attract the enemy's "earliest attention." Washington summoned another council of war to mull things over. If the enemy continued toward New York, would it not be wise to "throw a body of troops" into New Jersey? The reply was a unanimous yes. It was agreed that the regiments raised west of the Hudson should be detached for that duty, with the proviso that the units "belonging to the eastern side of Hudson's River"—the New Englanders—should remain there if circumstances permitted. Finally, as it was necessary to safeguard the rugged Hudson "Highlands," which not only barred the route to Canada but also secured the Americans' communications between New England and the middle and southern states, a hefty contingent of 3,000 men would be sent there.[57] Washington's army, which was already shedding manpower as the militia levies' enlistments expired, would now be fragmented and dispersed in the face of a powerful enemy.

Although Howe's precise intentions remained unclear, the threat to Fort Washington was obvious enough. Despite that strongpoint's vulnerability, Washington faced considerable pressure to maintain it. In conjunction with Fort Lee, which lay opposite on the New Jersey shore, its cannon were supposed to prevent British shipping from penetrating the Hudson. Congress had cautioned Washington to spare no effort or expense to block the river, an injunction underlined by the council of war of October 16. Such a stance made sense only if Fort Washington was defensible; men whom Washington trusted believed that it was. The complex was commanded by the bullish Pennsylvanian rifleman Colonel Robert Magaw, but overall responsibility for the sector rested with Major General Greene, a conscientious and capable officer whose judgment Washington had grown to value. Based at Fort Lee, Greene monitored the situation on Manhattan closely, making frequent trips back and forth across the Hudson. Like Magaw, Greene was adamant that the fort could be held. Washington initially accepted this verdict but had second thoughts after three British ships pushed up the Hudson on November 5, heedless of its guns. Washington asked Greene, "What valuable purpose can it answer to attempt to hold a post from which the expected benefit cannot be had?" He was now "inclined to think" it would be unwise to "hazard" the men and supplies at Fort Washington. However, while revoking previous orders that Greene must hold the fort at all costs, Washington failed to act upon his instincts and order its immediate evacuation. Greene meanwhile was sure that Washington's fears were unfounded: indeed, not only was the garrison "of advantage" but it was in no "great danger."[58]

On November 9, Washington began shifting part of his army to New Jersey by a roundabout route, crossing the Hudson River higher up at Peekskill. Once over, he aimed to bolster his command with enough local reinforcements to rebuff any advance by Howe. Meanwhile, William Heath was left with the contingent to secure the Hudson Highlands; the strongest force remained around White Plains under Charles Lee. As Howe's plans were still obscure, Washington's instructions for his second in command, in whom he placed "the most entire confidence," allowed him discretion to react to developments: as the enemy's "appearances of embarking troops for the Jerseys" might be no more than a feint, Washington took the liberty to "suggest" that Lee guard against an attack on his own command. On one point, however, Washington made his wishes crystal clear: "If the enemy should remove the whole, or the greatest part of their force to the west side of Hudson's River, I have no doubt of your following with all possible dispatch."[59]

By November 14, Washington and most of his men were over in New Jersey. Writing to Hancock from Greene's headquarters at Fort Lee, Washington confessed that "the movements and designs of the enemy" were no clearer: while there was a general agreement that they would besiege Fort Washington, that would only employ a small part of their force. As for the rest, only time could tell.[60]

That same night, a flotilla of flatboats carrying British troops rowed silently up the Hudson, passing unnoticed beneath Forts

Washington and Lee before peeling off into a creek leading to the Harlem River. Utterly oblivious to this ominous development, the next morning Washington rode out from Fort Lee and headed for Hackensack, six miles deeper into New Jersey. There he received alarming intelligence, forwarded by Greene. A British flag of truce had delivered a blunt ultimatum to Magaw: he had two hours to surrender or risk "every man being put to the sword." Magaw remained defiant, prepared to defend his post to the death.[61] Washington lost no time in heading back to help. Even now, his urgency was blunted by poor advice. Halfway across the Hudson, Washington met a boat with Greene and Putnam aboard, bound for New Jersey. When he called over for a situation report, they both maintained that the threatened garrison was in "high spirits" and capable of "a good defense." By now the fort had been reinforced: nearly 3,000 Continental troops were concentrated there, manning the cramped five-sided earthwork and its extensive outlying defenses. Reassured, Washington returned to Fort Lee, spending the night there.

The next morning, November 16, Howe ordered an all-out assault on Fort Washington. This bold action suggests that it was not simply fear of another Bunker Hill–style butcher's bill that had stopped him short of the Brooklyn lines on August 27, but rather his hopes for a negotiated settlement—hopes that had now withered. Howe's troops struck from three sides—the east, north, and south. At about 10 a.m., Hessians and redcoats began fighting their way up the surrounding slopes, encountering punishing terrain and determined resistance. Alerted by the firing, Washington once again crossed the river to assess the situation in person. By noon, despite heavy casualties, Howe's men had cleared the outworks and were closing in on the fort itself. For all of Magaw and Greene's assurances, its fall now seemed inevitable. Washington and his generals must get out while they still could. Greene recalled: "We all urged his Excellency to come off. I offered to stay. General Putnam did the same and so did General Mercer, but his Excellency thought it best for all of us to come off together, which we did about half an hour before the enemy surrounded the fort."[62]

Rather than face a final assault and risk the slaughter of his men, Magaw reluctantly capitulated. More than 50 of the fort's defenders had been killed; all the rest—about 2,800, of whom several hundred must have been wounded—were captured. These survivors were lucky to escape with their lives: excited troops who have just subdued a formidable defensive position, seeing comrades slain or maimed alongside them, are notoriously reluctant to spare opponents whose weapons are still warm. Howe's men were no exception. A massacre of the surrendered garrison by the incensed Hessians, who had "been pretty well pelted" as Major General Grant put it, was only averted by the prompt intervention of their officers.[63] Even then, many captives were roughed up, abused, and otherwise humiliated; owing to the combatants' failure to agree upon a workable system for the exchange of prisoners of war, most of them subsequently endured a harsh confinement within the fetid prison hulks moored in New York's harbor, an ordeal that eventually killed two-thirds of them through illness and neglect.

Mercifully, Washington had no inkling of the garrison's ultimate fate. He already felt bad enough, racked by self-reproach. As he reported to his brother Jack three days later, this "most unfortunate affair" had given him "great mortification." Not only had Howe bagged a significant percentage of Washington's scarce manpower, but also much artillery and some of the army's best muskets. Worst of all, the blow had fallen because Washington failed to follow his own convictions, instead accepting bad advice. He wrote: "And what adds to my mortification is that this post, after the last ships went past it, was held contrary to my wishes and opinion, as I conceived it to be a dangerous one." But urged on by a full council of general officers, and with Congress pressing for the Hudson to be blocked, Washington "did not care to give an absolute order for withdrawing the garrison till I could get round and see the situation of things." By then it was too late.[64] The council of war had proved a dangerously double-sided tool: at Boston it repeatedly checked Washington when he was bent upon sacrificing his army in suicidal frontal assaults; at New York it persuaded him, against his own better judgment, to throw away the defenders of Fort Washington.

As Lieutenant John Peebles of the Royal Highland Regiment noted, these men were some of Washington's "best troops," including many riflemen. Peebles recognized their commander, Magaw, as "an old acquaintance"; he didn't elaborate, but it is likely they had served alongside each other in western Pennsylvania during the last war.[65] Like many other Scots—the rebel officers Adam Stephen and Hugh Mercer, for instance—Peebles had come to America with a medical background, serving first as a surgeon's mate with the 2nd Virginia Regiment in 1758. Transferring to Montgomery's Highlanders, he fought as a volunteer during Henri Bouquet's celebrated 1763 clash with the Ohio Indians at Bushy Run, earning an ensign's commission in the 42nd for his bravery.[66]

Other British and Hessian observers were unimpressed by Magaw's garrison. According to Lieutenant Frederick Mackenzie of the Royal Welch Fusiliers, the prisoners were a dirty and shabby bunch. Mackenzie noted that "many of them were lads under 15, and old men" who cut odd, unsoldierly, and even comical figures.[67] Strikingly similar observations had been made by Ambrose Serle in August after the Long Island rout. He scornfully dismissed the rebel army as "the strangest that ever was collected"; it was a "motley crew," composed of "old men of 60, boys of 14, and blacks of all ages, and ragged for the most part." Serle also noted the "vast numbers of Irish" in the rebel ranks, convinced that many of them were convicts who had been transported into the colonies, and were consequently "glad of an idle vagabond life, and well-disposed to any bad purpose they may be set on."[68] Making due allowance for prejudice and exaggeration, such eyewitness testimony indicates that in 1776, Washington's army was already drawing on the very sources of manpower that its recruiting officers had been warned to shun; coming years would do little to change its profile.

The disaster at Fort Washington was swiftly compounded by another. On November 20, as Washington informed Hancock next day, a powerful enemy force landed on the seemingly inaccessible cliff-lined Jersey shore between Dobbs Ferry and Fort Lee. Like Wolfe's men at Quebec in 1759, the redcoats scaled the cliffs and, led by a vigorous veteran of the Seven Years' War's German campaigns, Major General Charles Cornwallis, rapidly pushed onward to Fort Lee. Warned by Washington, that strongpoint was abandoned in the nick of time, and the garrison escaped across the Hackensack River. But crucial stores and almost all of the artillery were lost.[69]

Reporting this blow to Lee, Washington appealed for him to bring his troops to his assistance. With no more than 3,000 "much broken and dispirited" men under his own command, he had no option but to retreat across a "dead flat" landscape that offered no potential for making a stand, even though it meant exposing "a very fine country" to the enemy's ravages. As Howe had shifted "the seat of war" to New Jersey, and its inhabitants would naturally expect the Continental Army to protect them, Washington and his generals now believed that "the public interest" required Lee to bring his troops across the Hudson. "Unless therefore some new event should occur, or some more cogent reason present itself, I would have you move over by the easiest and best passage," Washington wrote. Even now he fought shy of issuing an explicit order, so allowing his subordinate leeway for ignoring his appeal.[70]

Unknown to Washington, another letter had been inserted with his, written by his trusted adjutant general, Joseph Reed. This diminished Washington and fed Lee's already inflated ego: "I do not mean to flatter or praise you at the expense of any other," Reed had written, "but I confess I do think it is entirely owing to you that this army, and the liberties of America, so far as they are dependent on it, are not totally cut off." While lauding Lee, Reed blamed Washington for the loss of the fort named after him, lamenting that "an indecisive mind is one of the greatest misfortunes that can befall an army."[71]

Washington, meanwhile, had no option but to continue his headlong retreat, crossing the Passaic River at Aquackanock and then marching south to Newark. His troops now numbered about 5,400, but of those, more than 2,000 were at liberty to leave for home on

December 1, when their enlistments expired; the time of another 950 would be up on New Year's Day.[72] With his own army disintegrating, Washington needed Lee's help more badly than ever. But, far from responding to his commander's call, Lee was following his own inclinations. Instead of coming west himself, he had ordered Major General Heath to send 2,000 of *his* men from the Hudson Highlands. Aware that such a move would be "extremely hazardous," and determined to obey Washington's specific instructions to hold his ground, Heath wrote to warn him that Lee was interpreting his own commands as "a recommendation not a positive order."[73] As events would show, this was an astute analysis.

Luckily for Washington, the British pursuit of his demoralized force had initially been slowed by wet weather, but on November 25, Cornwallis set out after him in earnest at the head of an elite force: British grenadiers and light infantry and Hessian grenadiers and jägers—green-clad marksmen armed with rifles that were shorter, but no less accurate, than those used by the Americans. As Washington's rear guard left Newark on November 28, these advance troops were already entering the town. Fearful that Howe would sever their line of withdrawal by landing a detachment on the New Jersey shore at Perth Amboy, Washington and his generals resolved to keep falling back as fast as they could. By hard marching, they covered another twenty-five miles to reach Brunswick, on the south bank of the Raritan River, by the next day. Reporting to Hancock on November 30, Washington believed that two enemy divisions were now converging on them, intending "to push every advantage resulting from the small number and state of our troops."[74]

Meanwhile, Charles Lee still refused to shift his men across the Hudson. His motives remain unclear, but it seems likely that he distrusted Washington's abilities and genuinely felt his own would serve the cause better. Replying to Reed's letter of November 21, Lee had likewise regretted that "fatal indecision of mind which in war is a much greater disqualification than stupidity, or even want of personal courage." This response was opened by Washington, who had assumed that it related only to public business. In a brief, formally polite note, he informed his adjutant general of his unwitting discovery.[75]

A shame-faced Reed promptly sent his resignation to Congress, but Washington persuaded him to stay on; given such an ill-timed display of disloyalty, it was long before the old rapport between them was reestablished. For Washington, Reed's underhandedness was just one among many dispiriting circumstances. While his poorly clothed, ill-supplied, and shrinking army was continuing its forced march across the depressing and featureless New Jersey landscape to Brunswick, the weather had turned suddenly wintry and grim. Far from rallying to Washington's army as militiamen, the state's inhabitants were flocking to safeguard themselves and their property from the triumphant British by pledging allegiance to King George: true to their tradition of alternating the velvet glove with the mailed fist, the Howes had capitalized upon the captures of Forts Washington and Lee to declare an amnesty for all who took an oath of loyalty within sixty days. Thousands seized the opportunity.[76]

By early evening of December 1, the redcoats and Hessians were once again snapping at Washington's heels. As artillery batteries dueled across the Raritan, his dejected troops abandoned Brunswick and pushed on for Trenton, where boats would be held ready to ferry them across the Delaware River.[77] Before quitting Brunswick, Washington fired off yet another appeal to Lee: "I must entreat you to hasten your march as much as possible or your arrival may be too late to answer any valuable purpose," he pleaded. Even now Lee remained on the New York side of the Hudson. Writing from Peekskill the day before, he expected to enter New Jersey with 4,000 "firm and willing troops" on December 2. Lee would then be pleased to receive Washington's instructions, although he hoped they would not prove too binding, "not from any opinion, I do assure you, of my own parts—but from a persuasion that detached generals cannot have too great latitude—unless they are very incompetent indeed."[78]

Falling back via Princeton, Washington reached Trenton on December 2; Lord Stirling and Adam Stephen were left behind at the little college town with two brigades to keep watch for the enemy, still believed to be at Brunswick. This intelligence was correct: to the consternation of many British and Hessian officers, who'd been confident of catching and destroying the rebels before they reached the Delaware, the army had halted there on December 1. As William Howe explained to Lord George Germain, his "first design extending no further than to get and keep possession of East Jersey," Lord Cornwallis had orders to stop at the Raritan River. Captain Johann Ewald of the Hessian jägers, who had already been puzzled by the sluggishness of the march from Fort Lee, concluded that General Howe hoped to end "the war amicably, without shedding the blood of the King's subjects in a needless way." But Howe's advance had gone better than expected, and he was now alive to "the advantages that might be gained by pushing on to the Delaware and the possibility of getting to Philadelphia." After a leisurely journey from New York City, he arrived at Brunswick on December 6 with General Grant and the British 4th Brigade, and the next day Cornwallis's crack corps resumed its stalled pursuit. The earl's troops reached Princeton that evening, only to find the rebels already gone.[79]

Tired of running and itching to shed his Fabian mantle, Washington had hoped to take a stand at Princeton. As he informed Hancock on December 5, duty and inclination alike impelled him to fight back "as soon as there shall be the least probability of doing it with propriety." With most of his baggage and stores now safely across the Delaware, he had intended to double his rear guard at Princeton and await developments. Washington was on his way there to take command when an express messenger had brought warning of Cornwallis's advance, and that one of his columns aimed to encircle the town. Faced with these heavy odds, the rear guard retreated to Trenton. By the morning of December 8, all of Washington's men had been ferried across the Delaware River into Pennsylvania, the last of them embarking just as the enemy's advance troops arrived. To prevent pursuit, Washington had issued urgent orders for all craft on the river to be either secured or destroyed. But as intelligence suggested that the enemy were bringing up boats of their own, and his army was too small to cover a wide enough front to foil a crossing, Washington now feared for "the security of Philadelphia."[80]

By the time Washington quit New Jersey, Lee had at last entered the state. He now headed about 2,700 men, exclusive of militia. Assured that Washington was "very strong," instead of marching to join him, Lee imagined that he could "make a better impression" by keeping behind the enemy. Even when he learned the true situation and that Washington's "inadequate" force had been hustled back across the Delaware, Lee kept his distance. Given the difficulty of linking up, he wrote on December 8, might it not be better for him to attack the enemy's rear?[81] If Lee had been acting independently, this would have been a permissible strategy; it is also significant that he wrote from Morristown, a secure highland region that would become a preferred base for Washington's own army. But Lee was expected to join Washington, not fight his own campaign, and his stubborn disregard of his commander in chief's repeated appeals for help amounted to blind disobedience.

Increasingly anxious for Philadelphia, Washington continued to urge Lee to join him "with all possible expedition." Some 2,000 local reinforcements now came into camp: they consisted of a Continental regiment recruited from Germans settled in Pennsylvania and Maryland and a brigade of well-equipped and disciplined Pennsylvania militiamen, the Philadelphia Associators, under the feisty Colonel John Cadwalader; among them was Charles Willson Peale, who'd painted Washington's portrait at Mount Vernon in 1772 and who would make many more likenesses of "His Excellency" in coming years. These reinforcements increased Washington's force to more than 5,500. It would be stronger still if Lee's command joined, too. Yet still he did not come. Within the week Washington learned why. The American cause "had received a severe blow in the captivity of General Lee," he reported to his cousin Lund. Lee's misfortune was blamed on his own "imprudence" in venturing several miles from camp when the enemy was just twenty miles off. When a "rascally Tory" informed the British, Lee was quickly snapped up by a patrol of the 16th Light Dragoons—the same cavalry regiment in which he had served with distinction in Portugal in 1762—and unceremoniously bundled off, still wearing his slippers, and without his hat or overcoat.[82]

To many British officers, Lee—their fellow countryman and professional, and the victor at Charleston—was the rebels' most impressive general, not Washington, the amateur who had been soundly drubbed at New York and since driven before them across New Jersey. Led by Lieutenant Colonel William Harcourt and a fiery red-haired young cornet named Banastre Tarleton, the troopers who captured Lee were so delighted with their exploit that they celebrated by making his horse drunk before following suit themselves.[83]

Disaster though it seemed to many Americans, Major General Lee's ignominious capture was, on balance and with hindsight, a blessing to the patriot cause, removing a fickle and unstable character. Just minutes before being taken prisoner, Lee had finished a letter to his old friend General Horatio Gates, blaming his own "choice of difficulties" in New Jersey upon Washington's glaring incompetence. "There never was so damned a stroke" as the loss of Fort Washington, Lee opined. "*Entre nous*, a certain great man is most damnably deficient."[84]

Washington could only watch helplessly as enthusiasm for the revolution reached a low ebb. On December 12, Congress abandoned Philadelphia, withdrawing far southward to the security of Baltimore in Maryland; before doing so, it passed hasty legislation giving Washington "full power to order and direct all things relative to the department, and to the operations of war," until further notice.[85] This was an act of desperation, but Washington immediately seized upon it to enhance his army's fighting strength. At the urging of Colonel Henry Knox, he issued orders for the corps of artillery to be strengthened by three more battalions. Explaining this action to Hancock, Washington emphasized that the "present exigency of our affairs will not admit of delay either in council or the field." Referring "self evident" matters to Congress, "at a distance of 130 or 40 miles," would only cost crucial time, he argued. Besides the gunners he had already authorized, Washington also wanted to recruit more Continental regiments—110 instead of the eighty-eight approved by Congress. Given the long-standing patriot suspicion of standing armies, all this had an ominous resonance, suggesting that Washington aspired to a military dictatorship like Cromwell's, founded upon his own New Model Army of devoted shock troops. Washington had anticipated that suspicion and sought to allay it. He pledged: "I can only add, that desperate diseases, require desperate remedies, and with truth declare, that I have no lust after power but wish with as much fervency as any man upon this wide extended continent for an opportunity of turning the sword into a ploughshare." In a supporting letter, Nathanael Greene assured Hancock that there was "no evil nor danger to the states in delegating such powers to the General." Indeed, Greene added: "There never was a man who might be more safely trusted nor a time when there was louder call."[86]

Writing to his brother Jack on December 18, Washington confided that the struggle now seemed all but over. The disaffection of New York, Pennsylvania, and most especially New Jersey, which had prevented Washington's army from turning at bay at Hackensack or Brunswick, was worrying enough, but the greatest bane was the old one: "the accursed policy of short enlistments, and placing too great a dependence on the militia the evil consequences of which were foretold 15 months ago with a spirit almost prophetic." Many Continentals would be entitled to go home within a fortnight, and unless every nerve was strained to "recruit the new army with all possible expedition," the game would be "pretty near up."[87]

But the recruiting prognosis was bleak indeed. Benjamin Rush believed that "the four eastern states" of New England would struggle to raise their quotas, "owing to that excessive rage for privateering that now prevails among them." Serving Continental troops were impatient "for the extirpation of their enlistments" so that they, too, could "partake of the spoils of the West Indies." Rush believed that at least 10,000 New Englanders were manning privateers, men who by rights should be enlisting in the army destined to decide the fate of America. That force "must consist of seventy or eighty thousand men, and they must all be fit for the field before the first day of May next," he warned. The gossipy Rush, who accompanied the

Pennsylvanian militia, also voiced grave doubts about the army's leadership. He was not alone. "Since the captivity of General Lee," he observed, "a distrust has crept in among the troops of the abilities of some of our general officers high in command. They expect nothing now from heaven-taught and book-taught generals." Although Rush didn't mention names, Washington and his henchmen Nathanael Greene and Henry Knox were the obvious targets.[88]

Congress had fled, the British and Hessians were scouring the east bank of the Delaware for a way across, and by New Year's Day Washington expected to have little more to stop them than the raw Philadelphia militia and a handful of Virginian and Maryland Continentals. Even now he did not despair. After reporting these dire developments to Lund, his thoughts suddenly turned to a topic of no less interest and importance: the stables at Mount Vernon. He had sent Lund "a very pretty mare" and also "a very likely, as well as a very good horse to match the bay you have for Mrs. Washington." Having suffered a cut, he was "troublesome" and "vicious," but also amorous—"as much so I think after mares, as any stallion I ever met with," Washington believed.[89]

Happy thoughts of horseflesh offered Washington a brief respite from the daily grind of the grueling war to preserve the Revolution. The stark reality of the situation was laid bare on December 19, 1776, with the publication of the first part of Thomas Paine's *The American Crisis*. Paine, who had earlier rallied public opinion behind American independence with his phenomenally popular pamphlet *Common Sense*, and who'd shared the army's dispiriting withdrawal across New Jersey as an aide to Nathanael Greene, opened with a blunt and uncompromising statement: "These are the times that try men's souls." Many in Washington's army, not least its commander, would have agreed, watching helplessly as those Paine stigmatized as the "summer soldier and the sunshine patriot" slunk off. Yet, reading on, they might have found consolation and hope in Paine's prediction that those who now stood firm would merit "the love and thanks of man and woman." After all, "the harder the conflict, the more glorious the triumph." Within a week, those words would reverberate in one of the most remarkable turnarounds in military history.

8

VICTORY OR DEATH

Lacking the boats he needed to ferry his troops across the Delaware River and continue hounding Washington's army, on December 14, 1776, William Howe called a halt to the victorious campaign that had begun on Long Island four months earlier, quartering his redcoats and Hessians in a great swathe across New Jersey. The general himself retired to New York, keen to enjoy its pleasures. He no doubt felt that he'd earned them: with Charles Lee captured, Congress fled to Baltimore, and Washington chivvied into Pennsylvania, the revolutionaries' cause appeared to be teetering on the very brink of collapse. To cap his triumph, Howe had just received the coveted red ribbon of the Order of the Bath from King George III as a reward for trouncing the rebels.

The temptation to push future operations into Pennsylvania and capture Philadelphia now prompted Sir William to drastically revise his projected strategy for 1777. At the end of November, he had envisaged that no fewer than 10,000 of his men would strike north up the Hudson when the new campaign opened, cooperating with a fresh expedition down the river by British forces in Canada. An equal number would attack Boston; that force would advance from a new base at Newport, Rhode Island—which a detachment under Clinton captured on December 8. Allowing 7,000 men to garrison that port and New York, Howe's plan allocated 8,000 troops to cover New Jersey and pin down Washington by menacing Philadelphia. This scheme involved 35,000 men in all, and Howe had requested a hefty reinforcement of 15,000 to implement it. However, the unexpectedly rapid recovery of New Jersey convinced him to reshuffle his priorities: under a fresh plan, sent to Lord George Germain on December 20, the main offensive was now to be directed against Washington in Pennsylvania. In consequence, the projected drive against New England from Rhode Island was postponed until the reinforcements arrived, while a mere 3,000 men would hover on the Lower Hudson, to screen New Jersey and "facilitate in some degree the approach" of the northern army from Canada.[1]

To ensure that his army could push swiftly forward across the Delaware River as soon as it froze thick enough to support his men and guns and give the maximum protection to New Jersey's Loyalists, Howe's army was spread along a very extensive line of cantonments, stretching from Paulus Hook on the Hudson to the banks of the Delaware River. The chain's southern end, on the Delaware itself, was tethered to outposts at Bordentown, Burlington, and Trenton. Each settlement was held by brigade-strength detachments of three battalions; save for the Highlanders of the 42nd, all were Hessians. Some twelve miles farther back at Princeton was a strong supporting force of redcoats: five battalions of infantry plus three troops of light dragoons. Farther back still, on the Raritan River, sizable detachments held Hillsborough and Brunswick. Smaller bodies of troops were distributed between another twelve posts running north. Overall command of the occupying forces in New Jersey rested with Howe's crony, Major General James Grant, who made his headquarters at Brunswick, more than thirty miles from the Delaware.

By any usual rule of military procedure, Grant's three advanced posts would have been deemed dangerously isolated and exposed. But as intelligence suggested that patriot morale was in a tailspin and Washington's performance during the summer and autumn had scarcely suggested audacity, there seemed little reason to fear for them. This was certainly the view of Grant, whose recent experiences on Long Island and Manhattan had done nothing to alter the opinions of the rebels he'd notoriously voiced in the House of Commons. Grant's perspective was shared by the commander at

Trenton—the most vulnerable post of all—Colonel Johann Rall. Although advised to construct a redoubt for his artillery, Rall neglected to do so. Trusting to their bayonets alone, his men had already routed the American rebels at White Plains and Fort Washington; should they have the temerity to attack him at Trenton, they would meet the same response.[2]

Far from dissolving, as Howe and his commanders believed, Washington's army on the Pennsylvanian side of the Delaware was slowly regaining strength. The indefatigable Major General Sullivan had joined on December 20 with 2,000 of the troops recently commanded by the unfortunate Charles Lee. Another 500 Continentals under Horatio Gates arrived from Ticonderoga, salvaged from Philip Schuyler's shattered northern army; Gates soon left for Philadelphia, but his men stayed. Among them was a sixteen-year-old fifer, John Greenwood of Boston, later to become Washington's dentist. As Christmas approached, Washington commanded a respectable force of about 6,000 men fit for duty. With many Continental enlistments due to expire at midnight on December 31, Washington was determined to preempt Howe's advance on Philadelphia and land a blow of his own while he still had an army to command. Indeed, Washington had been contemplating an "important stroke" against the enemy as early as December 14; a week later, on December 21, Pennsylvania congressman Robert Morris wrote to him hoping that the rumors he had heard of his plans to "cross into the Jerseys" were true.[3]

Washington's precise objective was influenced by a series of independent spontaneous risings against the royal forces. Goaded by the rampant and indiscriminate plundering of Howe's foraging parties, in late December, New Jersey's inhabitants finally began turning upon their occupiers; rebel militiamen, who had been conspicuous by their absence during Howe's advance, now mobilized and fought back on the Delaware front. Rall's exposed brigade at Trenton came under mounting pressure, with constant, niggling harassment leaving his men exhausted and edgy. The strain on the Germans only intensified when bands of Pennsylvanian militia pitched in, mounting raids across the Delaware. Although spurning advice to fortify Trenton, Colonel Rall repeatedly appealed for reinforcements. After he wrote to General Grant *three* times in one day the Scot replied that there was no cause for alarm. After all, he reasoned, the rebel army in Pennsylvania numbered no more than 8,000 men, and they were shoeless, "almost naked . . . and very ill-supplied with provisions." Beyond sending this blithe reassurance, Grant did nothing.[4]

Six miles south of Trenton, at Bordentown, Rall's sector commander, Colonel Carl von Donop, was also becoming increasingly troubled by another force of New Jersey militia, under Colonel Samuel Griffin. The significance of their activities was emphasized in a message that arrived on December 22, sent by Washington's adjutant general, Joseph Reed. Just weeks earlier Reed had wounded Washington deeply by criticizing his leadership to Charles Lee, but he now made ample amends. Raised in Trenton and educated at New Jersey College—the future Princeton University—Reed knew the locality intimately. Colonel Griffin's progress at the head of a spirited militia had created a fine opportunity for action, Reed argued. He suggested that they should either reinforce the aggressive Griffin or mount a separate attack. In his opinion, "the latter bids fairest for producing the greatest and best effects." Above all, Reed urged, it was necessary to do *something*, and soon. With the credit of the cause expiring, "even a failure" was preferable to inaction. Surely, the "scattered divided state of the enemy" afforded "a fair opportunity" for an offensive. He added: "Will it not be possible my dear General for your troops or such part of them as can act with advantage to make a diversion or something more at or about Trenton—the greater the alarm, the more likely success will attend the attacks." There was no time to lose: "Our affairs are hasting fast to ruin if we do not retrieve them by some happy event."[5]

As emphasized, in urging an offensive, Reed was recommending a response that Washington was already pondering. If, as seems likely, the customary council of war was summoned to debate the best course of action, no official record survives.

Beyond doubt, it was swiftly decided to follow Reed's advice. On December 23, Washington replied that the "attempt on Trenton" was scheduled for "Christmas day at night," with the attack to go in "one hour before day" on December 26. The need for secrecy was paramount. "For heaven's sake keep this to yourself, as the discovery of it may prove fatal to us, our numbers, sorry I am to say, being less than I had any conception of—but necessity, dire necessity will—nay must justify any attempt." Indeed, Washington told Reed, he now had "ample testimony" of Howe's intention to push on to Philadelphia immediately the ice in the Delaware River was strong enough. His plan was to strike first while the enemy was distracted by the militia: in conjunction with Colonel Griffin, Reed was ordered to attack as many of their posts as possible, thereby causing maximum confusion.[6]

By then, Griffin's militia had already played a crucial role in Washington's unfolding plan. News of a sizable concentration of rebels at the village of Mount Holly, some twelve miles south of Bordentown, had prompted Donop to march there with his entire command and confront them on December 23. After a brisk skirmish the militia was swiftly dispersed, but events then took an unexpected, and momentous, turn. That arch-professional, Captain Ewald of the jägers, could scarce credit what he witnessed with his own eyes: Donop, "who was extremely devoted to the fair sex, had found in his quarters the exceedingly beautiful young widow of a doctor." The smitten colonel stayed put for the next three nights, only shifting on the morning of December 26. Instead of being poised with his men at Bordentown— within supporting distance of Trenton—"to the misfortune of Colonel Rall," Donop was more than a day's march away at Mount Holly, "detained there by love."[7]

On Christmas Eve, as preparations for the attack on Trenton were under way, Washington's intelligence-gathering operation continued. In New Jersey, Reed liaised with Griffin and his militia, seeking to pinpoint the whereabouts of Donop's roving command. That same day, Captain Ewald recalled, "a trumpeter arrived in Mount Holly from General Washington," inviting Donop to exchange prisoners. This, as Ewald soon divined, was no more than "a ruse" to confirm the colonel's absence from Bordentown.[8]

Washington meanwhile finalized the details of the Boxing Day assault on Trenton, although once again there is no formal record of any council of war. The senior officers who were on hand for consultation that Christmas Eve provide a cross-section of the army's unusually diverse leadership. Like Washington himself, Brigadier Generals Adam Stephen and Hugh Mercer had cut their teeth fighting the French and Indians in the Ohio Valley in the 1750s; during that same war, another of his brigadiers, Arthur St. Clair, had been an officer in the Royal American Regiment, soldiering alongside General Wolfe at the famous sieges of Louisbourg and Quebec; before winning acclaim for his courage and leadership at Bunker Hill, John Stark of New Hampshire had already survived many scrapes on New York's frontier as an officer in the celebrated Rogers's Rangers, serving with the late Lord Howe and still venerating his memory. Others present with Washington's army—Major Generals Nathanael Greene and John Sullivan and Colonels John Glover and Henry Knox—had learned their new trade since 1775. Despite their differences in age, experience, and background, all were now veterans and, like their commander, eager to avenge the humiliations of the past summer.

Washington and his officers agreed upon an ambitious, three-pronged attack. The strongest column, consisting of 2,400 Continentals under Washington's personal command, would cross the Delaware at McConkey's Ferry about nine miles above Trenton, then surprise the town from the north. That force would split into two divisions, headed by Greene and Sullivan, with each taking different roads. Washington's old comrade Adam Stephen and his brigade of Virginian Continentals formed the advanced guard; they were to be accompanied by a detachment of artillerymen without cannon, but carrying drag ropes to haul away the enemy's guns should opportunity offer and tools to spike them if they couldn't be moved. The succeeding brigades were allocated no fewer than eighteen field-pieces, an exceptionally high ratio of guns to men;[9] for a small force, it packed a potentially powerful punch. Washington's artillery commander, Colonel Knox, was entrusted with directing the embarkation of the men and guns at McConkey's Ferry, to proceed "as soon as it begins to grow dark." Once across the Delaware, the detachment would advance in "profound silence" with "no man to quit his ranks on the pain of death." If all went smoothly, the leading brigades would hit Trenton at 5 a.m. on December 26.[10]

Meanwhile, a force of about 800 Pennsylvania militia under Brigadier General James Ewing was to cross the Delaware close to Trenton, secure the bridge over Assunpink Creek, which marked the southern limit of the settlement, and occupy its far bank, so blocking any breakout by the garrison in that direction. The third column, consisting of 1,800 Philadelphia Associators and Rhode Island Continentals under Colonel John Cadwalader, who had been appointed brigadier general of militia, was to cross the Delaware farther downstream, at Bristol and attack any Hessians and Highlanders still in the vicinity of Bordentown and Black Horse. If Cadwalader could "do nothing real," he should "at least create as great a diversion as possible," Washington implored.[11]

Despite Washington's efforts to impose secrecy, Major General Grant received advance intelligence that the rebels were contemplating attacks on both Trenton and Princeton; the spy has never been identified, but whether leaked by accident or design, his or her information must have originated with someone privy to the deliberations of December 22. Still inclined to underestimate the Americans, Grant doubted whether such a bold attempt would actually be made, yet he didn't question the veracity of the report and therefore urged Rall to be on his guard. Grant's warning reached Rall on the evening of Christmas Day, by which time two American deserters and a pair of local loyalists had already informed him that Washington's army was preparing to move: a crossing of the Delaware, targeted at Trenton, looked imminent. But Rall remained unperturbed. Like Grant, he couldn't credit that the rebels would dare to attack him in strength. And if they did, so much the better: the colonel was confident that his grenadiers and fusiliers, wearied though they were by incessant alarms, would deal with Washington's rabble as they had done before—with professional discipline and cold steel.[12]

Washington's daring plan to strike at Rall hinged upon precise timing. The troops must be ready to cross the Delaware by nightfall, giving them long enough to reach Trenton before dawn. Yet the operation was soon lagging badly behind schedule. Many of the Continentals were weary, poorly clothed, and ill shod, and their advance to the three assembly points adjoining the west bank of the Delaware was painfully slow. The weather, which had been sunny, now worsened with a vengeance. With darkness, drizzle began to fall; it soon thickened into rain, and by late evening, as the men neared the river, they were shuffling into the teeth of a storm loaded with snow, sleet, and hail. That evening, the increasingly severe conditions stymied both of the downriver operations intended to support the main attack under Washington. At their designated crossing point below Trenton, Ewing's militia met an impassable combination of jumbled ice and swiftly flowing channels that defied attempts to cross either by boat or on foot. Brigadier Cadwalader's command, which now hoped to target Donop at Mount Holly, encountered equally discouraging obstacles; after moving downriver to Dunks's Ferry, several hundred men managed to reach the Jersey shore, but the bulk of the brigade and its artillery were unable to follow. Benjamin Rush, who was with Cadwalader, recalled how "great bodies of floating ice rendered the passage of the river impracticable," forcing them to turn back "in a heavy snow storm in the middle of the night."[13]

At McConkey's Ferry, Washington still had no inkling that everything now depended upon his own column. By midnight on Christmas Day 1776, the crossing finally got under way as the troops embarked aboard a motley assemblage of craft: these included swart, sturdy, and stable flat-bottomed Durham boats, usually used for carrying freight on the Delaware but now packed with shivering soldiers, and ferries capable of transporting and unloading the guns, their ammunition carts, and teams of draught horses. Here, too, the river was a daunting obstacle. Besides the challenges posed

by the unrelenting storm, the biting cold, and the intense darkness of the night, the boatmen had to counter a swift current that
brought great cakes of ice swirling down the main channel, then
find a way through the crusts that buttressed the river's banks. Ply-
ing their oars and setting poles and urged on by the booming commands of the colossal Knox, they succeeded in getting the column
across without losing a single man or gun.

It was a remarkable achievement, but, as Washington reported
to John Hancock, "the quantity of ice, made that night, impeded the
passage of boats so much, that it was three o'clock before the artillery could all be got over, and near four, before the troops took up
their line of march."[14] There was now no chance of surprising Trenton under cover of night. But a withdrawal, with the enemy likely to
interrupt any reembarkation, was unthinkable. The day before, Dr.
Rush had called upon Washington at his headquarters to give assurances of Congress's continuing support in such trying times and
noticed him "play with his pen and ink upon several small pieces of
paper." Rush remembered: "One of them by accident fell upon the
floor near my feet. I was struck with the inscription upon it. It was
'Victory or Death'": Washington had been writing the "countersign,"
or password, to be used by his commanders during the impending
attack.[15] True to his uncompromising motto, he now "determined to
push on at all events."

Screened by an outlying cordon of sentries, Washington's detachment prepared to march onward. Two forty-strong advance parties
under Captains William Washington—a distant cousin—and John
Flahaven moved out first: their task was to establish roadblocks
three miles outside Trenton, detaining anyone coming in or out of
the town. They were followed by Stephen's advance guard of Virginians, then the main body. This marched off in one long column,
sodden, numbed, and lashed all the while by the continuing storm.
In the grim conditions, several dog-tired men fell out. At least two
froze to death. The icy weather nearly proved fatal to Washington,
who rode along the column, encouraging his troops. As Lieutenant Elisha Bostwick of the Connecticut troops testified, in "passing

a slanting, slippery bank," the hind feet of Washington's horse slid from under him. He was only preserved by his strength and horsemanship, gripping his mount's mane and yanking back its head until it recovered balance. Bostwick was equally impressed by the calm advice he heard Washington give to his weary men—"Soldiers keep by your officers. For God's sake, keep by your officers"—delivered "in a deep and solemn voice."[16]

After about five miles, when the column reached the halfway mark at the Birmingham crossroads, it split into its two divisions for the final approach. Greene's took the upper or Pennington Road to Trenton, Sullivan's the lower River Road. Each had roughly the same distance to march and were to attack as soon as they had pushed in the enemy's pickets. Now, as his still-undetected troops neared their objective, Washington was astounded by the unexpected appearance of a band of Virginians heading toward him from the direction of Trenton. On Stephen's orders, but without Washington's authorization, these men had crossed the Delaware on Christmas Day on a mission to exact vengeance for a comrade killed in recent skirmishing with the Hessians. That very night, while Washington's command was converging on McConkey's Ferry, they had attacked a Hessian picket at Trenton and alarmed the whole garrison. This allegedly caused Washington to round on his old comrade and angrily accuse him of jeopardizing the entire operation. In fact, Stephen's raid worked to Washington's advantage, convincing Rall that *this* was the attack that Major General Grant had warned against and that the immediate danger was over; as Joseph Reed put it, this "truly casual or rather providential" event "baffled his vigilance."[17]

At 8 a.m. on December 26, when the men of Greene's division emerged from sheltering woods and began trotting across a field on the outskirts of Trenton, surprise was still on their side. The Hessian guard post on the Pennington Road spotted them but, with the storm in their faces, had trouble establishing their identity and numbers. After the Americans opened fire, the Hessians waited for them to come closer, gave a volley of their own and then made a disciplined and orderly withdrawal. Washington, who longed to have such professional troops under his own command, noted with admiration: "They behaved very well, keeping up a constant retreating fire from behind houses."

Remarkably, Sullivan's division on the lower road launched its attack just three minutes after Greene's. Both advanced with determination, pushing on at "a quick step."[18] As Washington testified in his report to Hancock, all the hardships of the night did nothing to "abate their ardor" as they closed in on the enemy. Indeed, "each seemed to vie with the other in pressing forward." Confronted by this sudden onslaught, the Hessians tumbled out of their billets and barracks and began forming up across the town's two main thoroughfares, King Street and Queen Street. To Washington, who was observing developments from high ground to the north, they seemed bewildered, "undetermined how to act"; despite the enduring legend, they weren't drunk, just worn out by sleepless nights— and understandably shocked to find hundreds of ragged rebels advancing upon them from out of a swirling snowstorm. When the Hessians wheeled out two guns, the advance party under William Washington rushed forward and captured them. Captain Washington and his young second in command, Lieutenant James Monroe, were severely wounded during the fight; Washington survived to win a reputation as a brave and effective cavalry commander, Monroe to become the fifth president of the United States of America.[19]

By now, Knox had placed six guns under Captain Thomas Forrest and Alexander Hamilton at the northern heads of both streets, which acted like funnels for round shot and canister, and immediately opened fire on the cramped enemy; crucially, although most of the muskets on both sides were immediately made useless by the wet, the artillery was still able to function.[20] When the Hessians sought refuge in side streets they became embroiled in a close-quarters fight with Washington's Continentals. All the while, snow fell and the storm howled. As Nathanael Greene wrote to his wife, Catherine, the combined violence of man and nature evoked "passions easier conceived than described."[21] On horseback in the midst of his confused, milling men, Colonel Rall tried to regain the initiative by ordering a bayonet charge to punch through the encircling Americans. But Knox's massed artillery took its toll, forcing Rall to retreat to an apple orchard on the eastern outskirts of the town.

Early in the engagement, several hundred Hessians had withdrawn across the Assunpink Bridge and the creek's upstream fords—the very openings that Ewing's aborted column had been sent to seal. Rall's prospects of saving the rest of his command by following suit were dashed after Sullivan's men swung round the southern end of Trenton. When Rall fell from his horse, mortally wounded, his men swiftly lost heart. Outgunned and hemmed in on three sides, they lowered their regimental colors and laid down their muskets. In just forty-five minutes, Rall's three crack regiments had been smashed. Some 500—about a third of the garrison—escaped before Washington's net drew tight, but of the rest, more than 100 had been killed or wounded and 900 captured. Remarkably, given the confused and congested nature of the fighting, Washington's troops sustained just a handful of killed and wounded.

Elated by this swift victory, Washington pondered his next move. After all their hardships, capped by the adrenalin rush of combat, his men were mentally and physically exhausted. In addition, many of them were toasting their success in captured rum, an understandable reaction to their ordeal, but one that rendered them unfit for further duty. Above all, Washington's force was perilously small. As he explained to Hancock, if the supporting columns under Brigadiers Ewing and Cadwalader had been able to cross the Delaware, his combined army could have driven the enemy from all their posts below Trenton. But without them he was outnumbered, while the presence of British troops at nearby Princeton only increased the dangers of dawdling in New Jersey. Momentarily satisfied, Washington therefore "thought it most prudent to return" to Pennsylvania, recrossing the Delaware at McConkey's Ferry with his haul of prisoners and captured cannon that same evening.

Small in scale, Washington's raid on Trenton had momentous results. Indeed, it would be difficult to exaggerate its significance, in both the short and long term. As Lord Howe's personal secretary, Ambrose Serle, predicted in his diary on December 27, "the very unpleasant news" of Trenton would "tend to revive the drooping spirits of the rebels and increase their force." Days later, Captain Ewald of the jägers noted reports that the rebel army had since swollen to 16,000 men. Ewald didn't credit them, but they were nonetheless symptomatic of the psychological change wrought, almost overnight, by Washington's "coup." He observed: "Since we had thus far underestimated our enemy, from this unhappy day onward we saw everything through a magnifying glass."[22]

By following his warrior instincts and attacking the enemy when the first opportunity presented itself, Washington had not only given a timely boost to American morale but gone far to restore his own self-esteem following the defeats and humiliations of the past year. Victory was all the sweeter because it had been won over the fearsome Hessians, who'd played such a prominent role in his darkest hour, the loss of Fort Washington. For all their unbending Prussian-style discipline, bristling mustaches, and tall, brass-fronted caps, even they were not invincible.

Washington's euphoria was clear in the ungrudging tributes he paid to his men, which provide a striking contrast to the biting criticisms that had peppered his correspondence following the routs at Long Island and Kip's Bay. Reporting his victory to Hancock on December 27, he wrote that the behavior of officers and men alike reflected the "highest honor upon them." But it was Washington's General Orders, issued that same day, which gave the clearest sign of his intense, personal satisfaction:

The General, with the utmost sincerity and affection, thanks the officers and soldiers for their spirited and gallant behavior at Trenton yesterday. It is with inexpressible pleasure that he can declare, that he did not see a single instance of bad behavior in either officers or privates; and that if any fault could be found, it proceeded from a too great eagerness to push forward upon the enemy.[23]

Having lauded his men, Washington seized the moment to appeal to those whose terms of enlistment were due to expire at the year's end, urging them to stay on for long enough to maintain the momentum of the counterattack. As they had "begun the glorious work of driving the enemy," he hoped that they would "not now turn their backs upon them, and leave the business half finished at this important crisis, a crisis, which may, more than probably determine the fate of America."

Learning that Cadwalader and his Philadelphians had managed to cross the Delaware on December 27, and that other militia units were coalescing in lower New Jersey, Washington decided to capitalize upon the shock waves that news of Trenton had sent through the enemy's garrisons. On December 30, despite appalling conditions, he crossed the Delaware once more and began concentrating his troops at their old battleground of Trenton. There he followed up his recent General Orders with a far more direct appeal to the men whose enlistments would soon be up.

Although Washington disliked making speeches, he addressed each regiment in person, spiking his patriotic rhetoric with an offer of hard cash: on his own initiative and trusting that Congress would give retrospective approval, he offered a substantial bounty of $10 to any man willing to extend his service for a further six weeks. Washington's weary, homesick Continentals were not easily swayed. Sergeant Nathaniel Root of the Connecticut troops recalled how the commander in chief opened by highlighting the victory at Trenton and emphasized that "we could now do more for our country than we ever could at any future period; and in the most affectionate manner entreated us to stay." But when the drums beat for volunteers, the sergeant continued, not a man stepped forward. Undeterred, Washington tried again, dramatically wheeling his horse about and delivering a forceful and heartfelt speech from the saddle: "My brave fellows, you have done all I asked you to do, and more than can be reasonably expected; but your country is at stake, your wives, your houses, and all that you hold dear. You have worn yourselves out with fatigues and hardships, but we know not how to spare you." By consenting to stay on for the short spell requested, they would render an unequaled service to their country and to the "cause of liberty." At this, a few in Sergeant Root's 20th Continental Regiment stepped forward, followed immediately by almost all who were still fit for duty.[24]

Including the New Englanders with Cadwalader's column at Crosswicks who agreed to soldier on and the Virginians whose enlistments continued until February 1778, about 3,000 Continentals remained. Many others had already endured enough, and no amount of fine words from Washington or his officers could keep them from going off. They included young John Greenwood: promised promotion to ensign, he bluntly retorted that he "would not stay to be a colonel." In his memoirs, Greenwood explained his decision: "I had the itch then so badly that my breeches stuck to my thighs, all the skin being off, and there were hundreds of vermin upon me." Clutching a tasseled, brass-hilted sword taken from the Hessians at Trenton, Greenwood journeyed home to Boston, ultimately joining a privateer under the celebrated Commodore Manley. As Benjamin Rush had predicted, many other New Englanders succumbed to the lure of the sea and the prospect of rich hauls of prize money, including most of Colonel Glover's Marblehead Regiment.[25]

Washington was realistic enough to recognize that for all his appeals to patriotic duty, the cash bounty had been the decisive factor in preserving the kernel of a viable army: reporting to Hancock on New Year's Day, 1777, he conceded that such an unorthodox advance was inconvenient, but unavoidable. "The troops felt their importance," he wrote, "and would have their price." He added: "Indeed, as their aid is so essential and not to be dispensed with, it is to be wondered, they had not estimated it at a higher rate." No sooner had Washington authorized the emergency payment than he received confirmation that Congress, on December 27, had already approved of his action by granting the extraordinary powers that he'd requested a week earlier. Although Congress avoided the emotive title, several commentators styled him "dictator." The devoted Nathanael Greene enthused that Washington had been granted "full powers to do and act as he thinks proper, to make such establishments and take such measures as the safety and interest of the states may require." Although these powers fell short of dictatorial, they were extensive enough: Washington had the right to raise sixteen new regiments of Continental infantry, along with 3,000 cavalrymen and fresh artillery units; significantly, the commander in chief, rather than the individual states, would personally appoint or demote all officers below the rank of brigadier general. He could also requisition supplies and deal with "disaffected" civilians—those loyal to King George—requiring them to swear allegiance to Congress or leave their home states. These powers were to last for a maximum of six months. Acknowledging this "honorable mark of distinction," Washington assured Hancock that he had no intention of exceeding his military authority and shrugging off "all civil obligations." On the contrary, as he informed the Executive Committee of Congress, "as the sword was the last resort for the preservation of our liberties, so it ought to be the first thing laid aside, when those liberties are firmly established."[26]

In his dispatch to Hancock, Washington revealed that he and his generals were "concerting a plan of operations" to be executed as soon as possible and which would hopefully be "attended with some success." This phrasing suggested another attack to second that already made upon Trenton. Such boldness was all the more remarkable given that Washington's most reliable intelligence revealed that General Howe in New York had reacted to news of Trenton by authorizing a formidable counterattack, with 5,000–6,000 men already concentrated at Princeton.

In fact, that same day, January 1, 1777, one of Howe's best officers, Lord Cornwallis, had arrived at the little college town to assume command. Including the reinforcement he had brought with him, his force actually totaled about 8,000 redcoats and Hessians, with twenty-eight guns. Cornwallis had been about to go home on leave to visit his gravely sick wife, Jemima, when Howe suddenly recalled him to stabilize the situation in western New Jersey; he therefore had strong personal as well as professional reasons for eliminating Washington's army without delay.

For his fresh "plan of operations" Washington could draw upon a strong force of more than 6,500 men, with a very powerful artillery train of forty guns: besides his remaining Continentals, there were another 3,600 militia downriver at Crosswicks and Bordentown under Brigadier Generals Cadwalader and Thomas Mifflin. Late on New Year's Day, following a council of war, urgent orders were dispatched for them to march their brigades to Trenton without delay, and they came in the following morning.[27] Washington's decision to gather his troops in "an exposed place," dangerously close to a strong enemy force, was influenced by knowledge that retreat into Pennsylvania would undo much of what had already been achieved, "destroying every dawn of hope which had begun to revive in the breasts of the Jersey militia."[28] In addition, the plan exploited a prime piece of intelligence that Cadwalader had communicated on New Year's Eve and which Washington and his commanders must have considered during their deliberations next day.

Drawing upon information supplied by a "very intelligent young gentleman" familiar with Princeton, Cadwalader made a detailed map of the vicinity; crucially, this revealed the presence of a little-used farmer's track, the Saw Mill Road; connecting with the Quaker Bridge Road, it approached Princeton from an undefended direction rather than by the main Post Road to Trenton, a front that the British had fortified with redoubts. The chance to exploit this nugget would depend upon Washington's ability to fend off the impending blow from Cornwallis. On the morning of January 2, he arrayed most of his troops and guns along the east side of Assunpink Creek, stretching for some three miles from its junction with the Delaware River to cover the fords upstream. It was a formidable position—the very one that Colonel Rall's many critics believed he should have adopted on the fateful December 26. In addition, an elite detachment of about 1,000 men, including Colonel Hand's regiment of riflemen, Captain Forrest's gun battery, and other Continental units, had been pushed far up the Princeton Road to slow the British advance; these troops had already clashed with Hessian jägers and redcoat light infantry on January 1, where the Eight Mile Run stream crossed the highway, defending the "pass" stubbornly until a reinforcement of grenadiers obliged them to fall back.[29]

As anticipated, Cornwallis began his march to Trenton early next day. He left a 1,500-strong brigade of three infantry regiments and a detachment of dragoons at Princeton to guard his rear, with instructions for two of the battalions to follow on the next day. En route, another 1,500 men were left at Maidenhead, with similar orders to move up later. Cornwallis meanwhile pushed on with his main column of about 5,500 troops. From the start, its progress was hindered by heavy mud that clogged the high road and the fields to either side and, beyond Maidenhead, by the same defending force that had proved so troublesome the previous morning. Backed by musket-armed Continentals and Forrest's well-served guns, at Sha-bakunk Run, within three miles of Trenton, Hand's riflemen forced Cornwallis to deploy his men from column of march into line of battle: a time-consuming business. Although his casualties were light, it took Cornwallis ten long hours to cover as many miles. Another determined stand, supervised by Washington and Greene, was mounted on the outskirts of Trenton before the delaying force finally fell back through the town and across the bridge over Assun-pink Creek, covered by artillery on the east bank. By the time Corn-wallis arrived with his main body, the light was dwindling fast. As the earl "displayed his column," arraying his battalions in line, it seemed to Major James Wilkinson that "a crisis in the affairs of the Revolution" had been reached. Rival gun crews now traded fire in a prolonged and "pretty smart cannonade," and skirmishes flickered in the twilight.[30]

British and Hessian units probed the creek at the lower ford and bridge but were thwarted by Washington's massed guns and infan-try. Cornwallis summoned a council of war to consider whether to continue operations or postpone them until daylight. Given the risks of a frontal assault upon such a strongly defended position and the difficulties of maneuvering in the darkness to turn Washington's right flank, Cornwallis opted to give his exhausted men a much-needed rest, then "bag the fox" in the morning.[31]

While the British settled in for the night, Washington called another council of war, at the headquarters of the Scottish veteran Major General Arthur St. Clair. Although well posted to rebuff a direct attack, the army was vulnerable to a flanking move that would pin it against the Delaware River. A retreat to Philadelphia via Bordentown was likewise risky. Major Wilkinson, who was serving as an aide to St. Clair but did not attend the meeting, was told that Washington, "yielding to his natural propensities," had been ready to hazard everything on a "general engagement." St. Clair later claimed that it was he who "had the good fortune to suggest" the bold alternative "of turning the left of the enemy in the night," and he was "forcibly" supported by his countryman Hugh Mercer. Washington, who may have been contemplating such a move himself, "highly approved it," and not a single council member dissented.[32] Under cover of darkness, the army would give Cornwallis the slip, take the back road to Princeton, and attack the isolated British brigade still waiting there. If all went well, it might be possible to push on and capture the crucial British supply depot at Brunswick. As Washington reported to Hancock, this would avoid the "appearance of a retreat . . . or run the hazard of the whole army being cut off" while also offering a chance to "give some reputation to our arms."[33]

Leaving several hundred men as decoys to keep the camp fires burning, shout challenges, wield pickaxes, and generally create the illusion that his lines remained occupied, Washington's force moved out in silence, the wheels of its cannon muffled in cloth. Like Howe at Long Island, Cornwallis was oblivious to this stealthy withdrawal. Captain Ewald wryly described the dénouement: "We intended to renew the battle at daybreak, but Washington spared us the trouble." When dawn came they were surprised to discover that "this clever man" was gone. At that very same moment, Ewald continued, "we heard a heavy cannonade in our rear." Cornwallis's command turned out and marched off at the "quick step" toward the sound of the guns. But by then Washington had already landed his blow.[34]

In one long column led by local guides, Washington's men and guns started moving out from their defensive positions facing Trenton at midnight. Owing to a sharp drop in temperature, the mud that had hampered Cornwallis's advancing troops was now frozen solid and capable of supporting the weight of artillery. The intense dark of the night helped screen the withdrawal but also contributed to a potentially disastrous episode when a regiment of Pennsylvania militia in the rear panicked and fled after mistaking another American formation for Hessians.[35] Their fear infected several other bodies of nervous militia, but the rest of the column pushed on grimly through the early hours of January 3, 1777, the troops often halting to drag cannon over tree stumps.

The going was easier after the column struck the Quaker Bridge Road, and shortly before 7 a.m. they reached Stony Brook, some three miles from Princeton, having already covered about twelve miles. Here, while getting his guns across the stream, Washington reorganized his force for the final assault: as at Trenton, there would be converging divisions, intended to swing wide and encircle the enemy. Such dispersal was risky, and it assumed that the redcoats would obligingly stay put at Princeton. According to Captain Thomas Rodney of Delaware's Dover Light Infantry Company, Major General Sullivan was "ordered to wheel to the right and flank the town on that side"; another force, of two brigades, played a similar role to the left; on its march it was to demolish the bridge that carried the Post Road over Stony Brook, thereby stopping the British garrison from leaving Princeton by that route or being reinforced from Trenton. A third column, formed of Mercer's weak brigade of Continentals backed by Cadwalader's much larger brigade of Philadelphia militia "was to march straight on to Princeton without turning to the right or left."[36] During the halt, Sergeant Joseph White of the Massachusetts Artillery recalled, each man in his company was ordered to drink half a gill from a bucket full of rum mixed with gunpowder. White "took a little" of the potent concoction, reputedly the favored tipple of the pirate Edward Teach, alias "Blackbeard."[37]

When the army moved onward the sun was rising, dashing Washington's hopes of attacking under cover of darkness: that hadn't stopped him at Trenton, and neither did it now. But Washington's plan soon unraveled when a column of British infantry was spotted marching south on the main road toward Trenton, in keeping with Cornwallis's orders for two of the brigade's three regiments to rejoin him that day. Sighting the main body of Washington's army, these redcoats swiftly turned "to the right about."[38] The column commander was Lieutenant Colonel Charles Mawhood of the 17th Foot. Sending his wagons back to Princeton, where the 40th Foot remained to guard the stores, and posting the 55th Foot and most of his artillery in a defensive position outside the town, Mawhood boldly advanced the rest of his little force against the rebels that he had seen in the distance across the frosted landscape. He was unaware that Mercer's column, masked by the undulating terrain, was between him and his objective. Mercer was likewise innocent of Mawhood's move forward.

Although the British brigade at Princeton numbered about 1,500 men, just a quarter of the size of Washington's army, the force under Mawhood's immediate command was far smaller. Besides about 250 of own 17th Foot, he led a motley contingent of mounted and dismounted men of the 16th Light Dragoons, gunners of the Royal Artillery, and drafts and convalescents for other units, including grenadiers, light infantry, and Highlanders: in all, perhaps 650 men with two brass six-pounder cannon. While some 1,100 of Cadwalader's militia were advancing behind him, Mercer had no more than 350 men and a pair of iron three-pounder cannon in his own denuded spearhead brigade of Pennsylvanians, Virginians, and Marylanders. Despite the heavy overall odds against Mawhood's redcoats, Washington's decision to split his own force meant that the British would initially have numbers on their side.[39]

Passing a farmhouse and barn, Mercer's men emerged from an orchard to find Mawhood's regulars arrayed behind a rail fence, just fifty yards off. Sergeant Root recalled kneeling and loading his musket with ball and buckshot—"Yankee peas" in the redcoats' slang. He and his comrades unleashed a devastating opening volley. Ensign George Inman of the 17th Foot believed that it accounted for most of the 101 rank and file of his battalion killed or wounded during the battle; he was the sole officer on the right wing to escape serious injury, "receiving only a buckshot through my cross belt which just entered the pit of my stomach and made me sick for the moment."[40]

Despite their heavy casualties the British gave a volley of their own, clambered over the fence, and immediately charged with the bayonet. Mercer's men recoiled through the orchard, leaving him unhorsed and surrounded by baying redcoats. When the stubborn Scot refused to surrender, lashing out with his sword, he was clubbed to the ground with a musket butt, bayoneted repeatedly, and left for dead. As the victorious British surged forward, capturing the enemy's abandoned cannon, the survivors of Mercer's broken brigade collided with the Philadelphia Associators coming up behind them. Deploying from column into line, the militiamen were thrown into confusion and fell back, too. Crucially, two more American field pieces, under Captain Joseph Moulder, were now unlimbered and brought into action. Manned bravely and efficiently, they stemmed the British advance with blasts of canister.

At this crisis, when the battle's outcome hung in the balance, Washington spurred up. Sergeant Root remembered that he "appeared in front of the American army, riding toward those of us who were retreating, and exclaimed, 'Parade with us, my brave fellows! There is but a handful of the enemy, and we will have them directly!'" The sergeant and his comrades rallied, but the militia had been badly shaken and were still disinclined to face the British bayonets. In his attempts to halt their flight Washington "exposed himself very much, but expostulated to no purpose." It was only after the Philadelphians had retreated another 100 yards that Brigadier Cadwalader managed to steady them. Now, as New England Continentals from the rear of Sullivan's column turned back to help, the emboldened militia rejoined the firefight, and the lengthening odds against Mawhood's men began to tell. After making what Washington acknowledged to be "a gallant resistance," they finally broke and ran for it. The exultant Virginian galloped after them, urging on his own men by shouting: "It's a fine fox chase, my boys!" Major Wilkinson reported these words at second hand, but, given Washington's love of the hunt, they sound characteristic enough to be credible. Wilkinson observed: "Such was the impetuosity of the man's character, when he gave rein to his sensibilities."[41]

While some of his scattered soldiers fought their way through to the west, Colonel Mawhood headed north, toward Princeton, accompanied by about twenty men. The very epitome of gentlemanly nonchalance, he trotted across the front of the astonished Americans, with two spaniels frisking about his pony's hooves.[42] During the savage fighting at the orchard, the 55th Foot outside Princeton had been confronted by units from Sullivan's strong division; heavily outnumbered, it fell back in a series of delaying actions. A group of redcoats prepared to defend the college buildings but soon surrendered after artillery opened up on them with round shot. Having played little part in the action—despite Mawhood's pointed orders to support him—most of the 55th and 40th retreated to Brunswick; the bloodied survivors of the 17th eventually rallied at Maidenhead.[43]

Some two-thirds of Mawhood's brigade, along with its supplies and most of its guns, escaped. Yet without doubt Washington had notched up another stunning victory, albeit one that had come perilously close to defeat. This time, as Washington conceded, the militia had played their part alongside the Continentals; indeed, the Philadelphia Associators had "undergone more fatigue and hardship" than he would have expected at such an "inclement season." Nathanael Greene, who like Washington, was typically critical of militia, proved far more unstinting in his praise of the Philadelphians: their conduct at Princeton was "brave, firm and manly," he reported. Although broken, they had rallied and reformed "in the face of grapeshot, and pushed on with a spirit that would do honor to veterans."[44]

Reporting the outcome to John Hancock, Washington tallied the enemy's losses in killed, wounded, and prisoners at 500, with "upwards of one hundred of them left dead" on the ground: only a slight exaggeration. His own casualties were far less numerous—about twenty-five to thirty privates killed, with the wounded yet to be reckoned up—although some "brave and worthy" officers had been lost: besides Mercer (who died of his wounds a week later), they included Colonel John Haslet, the stalwart commander of the old Delaware Continentals, shot through the head.

Thrusting himself into the thick of the fighting, Washington had been lucky to escape a similar fate. Several of his officers and men expressed relief at his survival, mingled with disapproval at his rashness. James Read, a sailor who volunteered for service with the Philadelphia Associators, told his wife that he would never forget the concern he felt for Washington, seeing "him brave all the dangers of the field, and his important life hanging as it were by a single hair with a thousand deaths flying all around him." Major Samuel Shaw of the artillery observed that, while the army loved Washington "very much," they had one thing against him: "the little care he takes of himself in any action." The major added: "His personal bravery, and the desire he has of animating his troops by example, make him fearless of any danger. This, while it makes him appear great, occasions us much uneasiness." Shaw attributed Washington's deliverance to the "shield" of "Heaven."[45] Judged by his reaction to the Monongahela and other fights, he may have thanked Providence instead.

Under his original plan, Washington had hoped to push on to Brunswick, on the Raritan River, and deal another devastating blow by destroying Howe's stores there. But his troops were now exhausted, "many of them having had no rest for two nights and a day." After once again canvassing his officers, and mindful of the danger of squandering what had been gained by "aiming at too much," Washington wisely decided to fall back to the north. With a British brigade just five miles off at Maidenhead, more redcoats were soon converging upon Princeton. But Washington's precaution of demolishing the bridge over Stony Brook delayed their pursuit until he had got clear. By the time Cornwallis's own force arrived from Trenton that afternoon, the "fox" was long gone, although the evidence of his handiwork was all too apparent. Captain Ewald noted: "We found the entire field of action from Maidenhead on to Princeton and vicinity covered with corpses." Unaware that Washington and his exhausted men had camped overnight at Rocky Hill, just two hours from Princeton, the anxious Cornwallis immediately marched to Brunswick to safeguard his supply depot. Washington meanwhile retired to the wooded hills of Morristown in northern New Jersey, where Greene had already identified a promising site for the Continental Army to finally march into winter quarters.

The ten day Trenton-Princeton campaign of December 1776 to January 1777 was the highpoint of Washington's military career. War with Britain would drag on for another six years, during which time Washington faced, and overcame, many other crises. But he never again displayed such control over men and events, and with such momentous consequences. Although Washington's official and personal correspondence was characteristically restrained, the spectacular success of his whirlwind winter campaign must surely have given immense personal satisfaction. Some hint of this, and also the extent to which the twin victories were complementary, is revealed in Charles Willson Peale's famous painting *George Washington at Princeton*, in which the Hessian standards captured at Trenton lie spread at his feet and his subject betrays the hint of a smile. Here, at long last, was a true taste of the military glory that Washington had craved since his youth.

Taken together, the victories at Trenton and Princeton swept away the lingering stigma of the defeats at Long Island and Fort Washington just months before. The decisive and aggressive leadership that underpinned them couldn't have been more different from the dithering that had led to disaster at New York. In a matter of days, and by following his warrior's instinct to fight back, George Washington had redeemed his battered reputation, silencing, for the moment at least, those critics who were starting to question his capacity to lead the military struggle against Britain. For congress-men who had just granted Washington his enhanced powers, reach-ing their decision *before* news of the first victory at Trenton arrived, here was swift confirmation that they'd acted for the best. Above all, given the nadir of the revolutionary cause at Christmas 1776, Wash-ington's offensive could not have been better timed. As Nathanael Greene expressed it to Tom Paine from the new camp at Morris-town, "The two late actions at Trenton and Princeton have put a very different face upon affairs." Greene, for whom the campaign had likewise delivered badly needed redemption, told his cousin Christopher that adversity had brought out the best in his revered commander: "His Excellency General Washington never appeared to so much advantage as in the hour of distress," he wrote.[46]

Washington's resilience had indeed been remarkable. During those crucial days, his leadership and generalship were also exem-plary, a fact recognized by contemporaries and later commentators alike. In his history of the American war—published in 1780 while it was still being fought—one serving British officer praised Washing-ton as a general "capable of great and daring enterprise." His night march to Princeton was "conducted in a masterly manner," deserv-ing a place among "distinguished military achievements"—worthy indeed "of a better cause." Writing at the height of the Edwardian empire in the early twentieth century, the British Army's historian, Sir John Fortescue, gave ungrudging praise, acknowledging that "the whole cause of the rebellion in America was saved by Washing-ton's very bold and skillful action." More recently, the Howe broth-ers' biographer, Ira D. Gruber, agreed that the campaign "had an immediate and decisive influence on the war," restoring "the spirits of thousands of languishing patriots and damping the rising hopes of loyalists." Not only had Washington guaranteed the rebellion's sur-vival, but, after Princeton, "the British government had very little chance of winning the war and retaining its colonies."[47]

For the British Army in America, the impact of Princeton was both immediate and long-term. While the high command had sought to minimize the destruction of Rall's brigade at Trenton,

Washington's subsequent strike could not be dismissed so lightly. It convinced Howe to pull back his outposts from the Delaware River to the Raritan and on a drastically constricted line from Brunswick to Perth Amboy. This not only meant that his army relinquished a rich foraging region, but ensured that any future campaign against Philadelphia via New Jersey must first regain the ground that had been lost. In broader strategic terms, however, Washington's spectacular double blow did nothing to deflect Howe from his intention to focus on Pennsylvania in 1777. Sir William's growing obsession with capturing Philadelphia and destroying the main rebel army under Washington reversed the cautious strategy that he had followed in 1776. Crucially for the outcome of the war, Howe's "fixation" would ensure that cooperation with the scheduled British advance from Canada that spring would become even less of a priority than it already was.[48]

Having given full rein to his aggressive instincts, and with devastating results, Washington now reverted to defensive mode as he sought time to build his new army. In February he took a farsighted step that was to prove vital to his unending search for manpower. Smallpox had erupted among the troops. According to Sergeant Root, who fell sick himself at Morristown camp, "many of our little army died there of that disease." Faced with a repetition of the epidemic that had culled the regiments ejected from Canada in 1776, Washington introduced systematic inoculation of all soldiers who'd not yet had smallpox. Not only were the doctors busy at Morristown and Philadelphia, but, to keep his army "as clean as possible of this terrible disorder," Washington had recommended that every state contributing men to the army should ensure that their recruits were inoculated immediately. The mass operation was kept as secret as possible, with patients inoculated in "divisions" at intervals of five or six days to ensure their phased return to active duty.[49]

Meanwhile, in their cramped and cheerless billets Howe's redcoats and Hessians endured a grim and sickly winter. They were soon embroiled in a frustrating and costly guerrilla war as expeditions to gather forage in the surrounding countryside encountered the region's reinvigorated militia and Continentals from Morristown. Resistance was so stiff that British wagon trains required substantial escorts. For example, on February 23, 1777, a column sent out from Perth Amboy under Colonel Mawhood was accompanied by a battalion of light infantry, another of grenadiers, the entire 3rd Brigade of three regiments, and several artillery pieces. Even this substantial force was roughly handled when it skirmished with Continentals near Woodbridge. In his diary, Lieutenant Peebles of the 42nd reported that the column returned "much fatigued" with the loss of sixty-nine men killed and wounded and another six missing. Peebles's own grenadier company had been heavily engaged, suffering twenty-six casualties. Visiting his wounded, Peebles considered it a pity to throw away such fine men on "shabby ill managed occasions." With the Scottish Highlands already scoured of military manpower by intensive recruitment in 1775 and steady emigration to North America during the previous decade, the loss of a veteran grenadier like William McIntosh, who died of his wounds on March 11, was a high price to pay for a few cartloads of hay.[50]

From Morristown, Washington was well placed to monitor Howe's movements, whether into Pennsylvania or up the Hudson River. In spring 1777, the direction in which Sir William would strike was hard to predict. In April, a British raid on Danbury, Connecticut, which burned munitions that might have been used to contest the expected advance from Canada, suggested that Howe intended to cooperate with Burgoyne's northern army. That same episode had given Benedict Arnold another chance to enhance his reputation as one of the bravest officers in the Continental Army. When Arnold's horse was shot dead, he extricated himself from beneath its carcass and in the face of the enemy coolly retrieved his pistols from their holsters. John Adams was so impressed by an exploit sufficient to make Arnold's "fortune for life" that he wanted to commemorate it with a medal.[51] Washington held an equally high opinion of the famed Connecticut fighting man. Supporting Arnold's claim for the date of his promotion to major general to be adjusted to give him greater seniority, Washington wrote: "It is universally known, that he has always distinguished himself, as a judicious, brave officer of great activity, enterprise and perseverance."[52]

Despite the boldness of his Christmas and New Year offensive, Washington was now coming under criticism for failing to quit his Morristown fastness and make another assault on Howe's army. Writing to Nathanael Greene, John Adams's cousin and fellow congressman Samuel Adams suggested that, while "Europe and America seem to be applauding our introduction of the Fabian method," such classical comparisons were misleading. After all, he continued, Fabius's foe—the great Carthaginian general Hannibal—was hamstrung by a lack of supplies from his own state; under those circumstances, Fabius was wise to grind his opponent down by "frequent skirmishes." In contrast to Hannibal, General Howe was kept well provisioned by the Royal Navy and had "the fullest assurances of early reinforcements from Britain." If Fabius had been in Washington's place, Adams asked, would he not have sought a decisive result, by destroying Howe's army at Brunswick? The loyal Greene was quick to set the Bostonian straight. True, there was a difference between the situations of Hannibal and Howe, but it was not so great as to justify Washington "taking a resolution to attack the troops at Brunswick," particularly as they were fortified, and his own army was inferior in both numbers and discipline.[53]

Greene's words echoed the response of a council of war called by Washington on May 2 to consider the advisability of a "general attack upon the enemy in Brunswick and at the neighboring posts": its unanimous opinion was that the available troops were still too few and inexperienced for such an undertaking. There had been some tentative support for a more limited attack on the enemy post at Bergen, although Major General Adam Stephen's suggestion that Bonhamtown or Piscataway, east of Brunswick, could be targeted at little risk was summarily dismissed as unviable.[54] The stubborn Scot went ahead with his pet plan anyway, using Continentals from his own division. On May 10, they were badly mauled by the 42nd Regiment and a battalion of light infantry and were lucky to get clear. Stephen reported the clash to Washington in very different terms as a "considerable advantage gained over the enemy's best troops." It was a "bold enterprise," he continued, and the British must have lost at least 200 killed and wounded. In a dispatch to John Hancock, the president of Congress, Washington duly reported this "smart skirmish" in which the American troops had "behaved well and obliged the enemy to give way twice." He was therefore incensed to learn, just hours later, that Stephen had been economical with the truth and promptly fired off a withering reprimand. "Your account of the attempt upon the enemy at Piscataway is favorable, but I am sorry to add, widely different from those I have had from others (officers of distinction), who were of the party," Washington wrote icily. Indeed, he added, "the disadvantage was on our side, not the enemy's, who had notice of your coming and was prepared for it, as I expected."[55]

For all their shared history of hardships and danger, to Washington his old comrade's unwarranted bragging was unforgivable. Not only did it flout his own code of restrained, gentlemanly honor, but it turned the Continental Army into a laughing stock, a force that had to invent victories. Its reputation clearly mattered to Washington, and on a very personal level: back in February he'd rebuked Major General William Heath after he staged a half-hearted attempt to capture the British post of Fort Independence, which guarded the route to Manhattan via King's Bridge. Despite his obvious incapacity to carry out an assault, Heath had warned the garrison to surrender or risk the consequences. Washington could only wish the summons had never been sent, "as I am fearful it will expose us to the ridicule of our enemies."[56]

In mid-June, Howe took the offensive himself, leading a powerful force from Brunswick up the Raritan, seeking to lure Washington down from his strong defensive position behind the hills of Middlebrook and into the kind of potentially decisive engagement that he had been ready to risk at New York. But Washington had learned from his mistakes in 1776. With fewer than 8,000 Continentals, he refused to be drawn, instead sending detachments to observe and harass the enemy. After several days of skirmishing,

Howe retired, his frustrated troops burning and plundering as they went. Nothing daunted, Sir William soon tried again. When Howe's redcoats and Hessians began embarking aboard transport ships at Perth Amboy, Washington moved forward to hinder him, deploying Lord Stirling's brigade to Metuchen and leading the bulk of the army to Quibbletown, farther to the northwest. Howe's embarkation was merely a ruse, calculated to tempt Washington into the open, and his coat-trailing tactics had apparently worked. On the night of June 26, he quickly disembarked his troops, sending columns against Stirling and Washington. While the wary Washington reacted swiftly enough to evade Howe and retired to Middlebrook unscathed, Stirling's division was more sluggish, losing about eighty men before disengaging. For Howe, this petty victory was small consolation for the priceless weeks lost in a futile attempt to bring his enemy to battle. Stymied by Washington's careful defensive strategy—the closest he ever conformed to the classic "Fabian" template—Howe once more embarked his army at Perth Amboy, and this time in earnest. He sailed for Staten Island, relinquishing all of New Jersey to the rebels.

On July 9, Howe's formidable force of more than 14,000 men began boarding transport ships in New York Harbor; another 7,300 under Henry Clinton remained to garrison New York City. When the flotilla finally sailed two weeks later, its destination remained a mystery to friend and foe alike. In fact, Sir William was heading for Philadelphia; with Washington's army still intact in New Jersey, and now supported by a vigorous and effective militia, he had decided to reach his objective by sea rather than land.

When Howe's troops were still embarking, Washington had conjectured that they would strike at Philadelphia by way of the Delaware River. In consequence, he called for accurate and detailed maps of the region, "which is or may be the seat of war," to be compiled as soon as possible, particularly "as regards the shores of the Delaware where the enemy may probably land and march."[57] However, logic dictated that Howe must surely cooperate with the northern army on the Hudson, a view reinforced when Washington learned that Burgoyne had taken Ticonderoga on July 5. That assumption initially led Washington to preempt such a move by shifting his army north from Middlebrook and Morristown, pushing two divisions across the Hudson at Peekskill and securing a pass, known as the Clove, through the strategically vital Hudson Highlands. They stayed there until July 24, when news that Howe's fleet had sailed out to sea from Sandy Hook, rather than up the Hudson, required a rethink. Although Washington still had his doubts, as all his commanders agreed that Philadelphia was now Howe's objective, he changed front once more, marching south to reach Coryell's Ferry on the Delaware, about thirty miles above Philadelphia, on July 27. Warned by Congress that Howe's force was hovering off the Capes of Delaware, indicating that an attack on the city was imminent, Washington's footsore soldiers pushed on to defend it. Within a day of reaching Germantown, on the outskirts of Philadelphia, they received fresh reports that Howe's fleet had disappeared on July 31. Describing these puzzling and worrying developments to his brother Jack some days later, Washington was clearly perplexed: "We remain here in a very irksome state of suspense," he confessed. While some now believed that the British had continued south, the majority—including Washington—were "satisfied" that they had "gone to the eastward," back toward the Hudson. The prospect of further punishing marches in the strength-sapping heat of summer left Washington reluctant to move again until firmer intelligence arrived. Wrapping up his letter to Jack with a P.S. on August 9, by which time there'd been no further news of Howe's whereabouts, Washington now concluded that he had indeed gone east and was slowly shifting his own forces in that direction.[58]

Washington's original hunch that Howe aimed to attack Philadelphia via the Delaware was in fact correct. But after receiving intelligence that Washington was waiting for him upriver at Wilmington, Sir William instead kept sailing south and then turned into Chesapeake Bay to make a landing in Maryland. His army finally disembarked at Head of Elk on August 25, after nearly seven weeks aboard ship. Already delayed by his fruitless maneuvering in New

Jersey, this protracted voyage put Howe's Philadelphia campaign even further behind schedule. Incredibly, Howe remained as far from his objective as he had been when still occupying his New Jersey bridgehead. Crammed into transport ships for weeks, his troops landed in poor shape; the dragoons' horses suffered so badly that Howe now had precious few cavalry. More worryingly, the summer campaign season was swiftly running out: focused on his own objectives, Howe would have precious little time to cooperate with Burgoyne, even if he wanted to.

By August 22, when Howe's fleet was reported to be well within Chesapeake Bay, the dire implications for Burgoyne were already clear to Washington. He ordered Major General Israel Putnam, who was watching Clinton above New York, to send the latest information on Howe's whereabouts to Governor Trumbull of Connecticut, who was to forward it farther to the east. As there was now no danger of Howe heading for New England, Washington hoped that "the whole force of that country" would turn out to "entirely crush" Burgoyne, emulating the example of New Hampshire militia under Brigadier General John Stark, who had already overwhelmed a foraging column of Brunswickers, Loyalists, and Iroquois Indians near Bennington, Vermont, on August 16. As Howe's objective was now clearly Philadelphia, albeit by "a very strange" route, Washington summoned Major General John Sullivan's division to bolster his own army for the impending clash.[59]

With confirmation of Howe's landing place, Washington pivoted south once more at the head of 11,000 men. Arriving in Philadelphia, he paraded his new army through the city to contest Howe's advance. Congress was adamant that Washington should defend the Revolution's capital, and he clearly relished the prospect of a rematch with Sir William. In his General Orders, Washington emphasized that the coming engagement would offer a prime opportunity to both end the war and win renown. By seeking battle, he announced, the enemy put everything at stake: "If they are overthrown, they are utterly undone—the war is at an end." Just one "bold stroke" would "free the land from rapine, devastations and burnings, and female innocence from brutal lust and violence." They must take their cue from Stark's New Hampshire militia, who had fought with the resolution of veterans. Washington's men should also remember that *they* constituted their country's "main army." In consequence, he added: "The eyes of all America, and of Europe are turned upon us . . . glory waits to crown the brave."[60]

Reinforced by local militia to about 14,000 men, Washington decided to confront Howe from behind Brandywine Creek. This offered a strong defensive barrier, snaking amid wooded hills, with the only crossings at readily defensible fords. Washington's troops were arrayed in detachments over a six-mile front to cover them but were mostly concentrated about Chadds Ford, where the high road to Philadelphia crossed the creek. Despite his recent appeal for decent maps, Washington's knowledge of the terrain was badly flawed; he was unaware of other fords beyond the far right of his line, and they were left unguarded. Armed with excellent intelligence from local Loyalists, Howe knew about this weakness in Washington's position and resolved to exploit it with a long flanking march. This recalled the maneuver that had delivered a stunning victory on Long Island; once again, the Americans would be distracted by a "demonstration" to their front, allowing time for the flanking force to get into place. The diversionary attack against Chadds Ford was entrusted to the Hessian Lieutenant General Wilhelm von Knyphausen with 6,000 men. By about 10 a.m. on September 11, he had pushed Washington's light troops across the creek and opened fire with his artillery. Some six hours earlier, the 8,000-strong column under Cornwallis, accompanied by Howe, had begun its march upstream to turn Washington's right.

While artillery batteries exchanged fire across Chadds Ford, Washington received warning of Howe's march. Yet he failed to react swiftly and decisively to this threat or to exploit the opportunity to overwhelm Knyphausen in Howe's absence, later explaining to John Hancock that his reports were "uncertain and contradictory." This was true enough: initial intelligence that "a large body of the enemy" with a formidable train of artillery was marching along the Great Valley Road toward the fords on the right was followed by another dispatch, from Major General Sullivan, maintaining that Major Joseph Spear of the Pennsylvania militia had heard nothing of the enemy "in that quarter" and was "confident" that any reports to the contrary "must be wrong." Washington allowed himself to be swayed by Spear's wildly inaccurate information, concluding that the reported flanking move was just a feint, and that Knyphausen was less vulnerable than he seemed.[61]

With some eighteen miles to cover in the summer heat, it was early afternoon before Howe's men crossed the Brandywine at Jeffries Ford and began advancing against Washington's right. By now, the danger was all too clear, and Washington hastily redeployed the divisions of Sullivan, Stirling, and Stephen in a belated attempt to counter it. At about 4 p.m., Howe's troops engaged them.

The fighting was fierce and confused. One British light infantry officer struggled to describe it in a letter for a friend back home. Indeed, the Battle of Brandywine was nothing like the theatrical performances at London's Covent Garden or Drury Lane, or the celebrated tapestries of Marlborough's great victories hanging at Blenheim Palace. Instead, there was "a most infernal fire of cannon and musketry" mingled with the incessant bellowing of orders: "'Incline to the right! Incline to the left! Halt! Charge!' etc." All the while, cannonballs were "plowing up the ground" and the branches of trees cracking overhead, their "leaves falling as in autumn by the grapeshot."[62]

For two hours, the three American divisions fought to stem the British onslaught; as the same officer acknowledged, "The misters on both sides showed conduct." But, as Washington conceded, his dispositions were not "adequate to the force with which the enemy attacked us on our right."[63] Before that flank collapsed, the intensity of the firefight had drawn Washington to the scene from Chadds Ford, with Nathanael Greene and a brigade of his division close behind. As Greene recalled, he arrived to find "the whole of the troops routed and retreating precipitately, and in the most broken and confused manner." He was ordered to cover the retreat and held off Howe's weary troops for long enough to prevent "hundreds of our people from falling into the enemy's hands."[64]

Likewise alerted by the sustained, distant gunfire, Knyphausen's command had meanwhile attacked across Chadds Ford, encountering fierce opposition from Anthony Wayne's division, but after "a severe conflict" gradually pushed it back. In contrast to the rout at Long Island, these units withdrew steadily, in reasonable order. By preoccupying Howe, Greene's stand bought time for them, too, giving credence to his later claim that he had saved the army from "ruin."

Washington had been soundly beaten, suffering more than 1,000 killed, wounded, or captured—double the casualties sustained by Howe's attacking troops. While Sir William had notched up another notable victory and once again shown himself no contemptible commander when he chose to be, the action had begun too late in the day to permit a chivvying pursuit that might have delivered a more decisive result. In any event, Howe's army lacked enough cavalry to hound the enemy through the night, and his men were exhausted from their long trek and the hard fight that followed. That evening, as Ensign Inman of the 17th Foot recalled, they were finally able to "sit down and refresh ourselves with some cold pork and grog"—watered rum—"on the ground the enemy had first posted themselves, which we enjoyed much as our march before the battle was better than 18 miles."[65]

Washington was not discouraged by the outcome of the Battle of Brandywine. Neither were his men. "Notwithstanding the misfortune of the day," he informed Hancock, "I am happy to find the troops in good spirits; and I hope another time we shall compensate for the losses now sustained." During the ensuing fortnight, as he shifted his forces to shield Philadelphia, Washington remained keen to fight Howe. Another major action looked imminent at Warren Tavern, west of the city, but a prolonged rainstorm, which soaked through his men's shoddy cartridge boxes, obliged Washington to withdraw to a strong defensive position until fresh ammunition could be issued;[66] wags dubbed this nonevent "the Battle of the

Clouds." No less eager for a fight, the British soon demonstrated their ability to strike whatever the weather. In the early hours of September 21, a force of redcoats under Major General Charles Grey made a surprise attack on Wayne's sleeping Pennsylvanian Continentals at Paoli. To avoid any accidental firing that might betray the enterprise, the flints were removed from their muskets. In what one British officer described as a "nocturnal bloody scene," they used their bayonets to kill or wound more than 300 of Wayne's men, taking another 100 prisoners. This coup was deplored as a "massacre" by the survivors, although it was a legitimate, if unusually ruthless, act of war; its commander won the acclaim of the British Army and the nickname "No Flint Grey."[67]

The following night, after "a variety of perplexing maneuvers," Howe crossed the Schuylkill River at Fatland and Gordon's Fords, so taking the lead in the race for Philadelphia. Washington had once again been hampered by lack of reliable intelligence, the heavily Loyalist population "being to a man disaffected" toward the patriots' cause. The army's ability to make forced marches was hindered by a dearth of shoes: at least 1,000 men were now barefoot;[68] in that respect the new army fared little better than the old one that had left bloody footprints in the snow at Trenton.

On September 26, Howe claimed his prize, marching his army into an undefended Philadelphia. Congress, which had returned from Baltimore after the Trenton-Princeton campaign, now decamped once again, this time to York, Pennsylvania. So long anticipated, Howe's conquest proved a hollow triumph. Indeed, the capture of the revolutionaries' capital, and North America's largest city, did not have the expected impact. Rather than signal the collapse of American morale, it scarcely dented it. Patriots were already buoyed by reports from the upper Hudson, where Burgoyne's army, which had begun its southward advance from St. John's in mid-June, while Howe was still seeking a clash with Washington in New Jersey, now faced serious problems. The expedition had begun promisingly enough, when Arthur St. Clair abandoned the pivotal fortress of Ticonderoga rather than risk the loss of his garrison, but the rugged wilderness terrain slowed Burgoyne's advance to the Hudson River to a snail's pace. Worse still was the bloody check administered to his foragers at Bennington by Stark's militia. Despite these ominous developments, Burgoyne pushed on regardless, determined to reach Albany. Near Saratoga, he found his path blocked by a substantial rebel force manning fieldworks on Bemis Heights. Consisting of more than 7,000 militia and Continental troops, including Daniel Morgan's riflemen loaned from Washington's own hard-pressed army, the force was commanded by Major General Horatio Gates, who had replaced the listless Philip Schuyler on August 19. When Burgoyne attempted to turn Gates's left on September 19, he was countered by troops led by Benedict Arnold. After stubborn fighting across the clearing at Freeman's Farm, the British held the field, gaining a technical victory but suffering heavy casualties and failing to spring Burgoyne's army from the jaws of the trap into which it had marched.

No less important for patriot morale than developments to the north was the fact that, for all Howe's best efforts, Washington and his main field army had not only endured but remained a force to be reckoned with. Although enlistments for the new army fell far below the numbers approved by Congress in September 1776, by the following summer the commander in chief and his Continentals, rather than Congress or its capital, had become both the symbol and defender of American liberty: as long as they remained in being, surviving the British Army's attempts to destroy them, so did their cause. And, as would soon be seen, for all their disappointments and hardships, Washington and his army were still capable of taking the offensive.

When Howe occupied Philadelphia, he encamped most of his army at the settlement of Germantown, about five miles to the north. The camp was not fortified with redoubts, as that would have suggested weakness; like Rall at Trenton, Howe had no doubt that his veteran regulars could handle any rebel assault. Yet Howe's deployment proved too tempting for Washington and his generals to resist. A council of war on September 28 voted ten to five against attacking before anticipated reinforcements arrived; but another, on October 3, which benefited from intelligence that Howe had weakened his army with detachments, was unanimous that "a favorable opportunity offered to make an attack upon the troops which were at and near Germantown."[69]

The resulting plan shared elements with the daring assault on Trenton, involving a nighttime approach march by four converging columns to deliver a surprise attack at dawn. In fact, the plan was even bolder than the Trenton operation, as the target was not simply a single Hessian brigade, but a full British army estimated at 9,000 men. Washington's attack force numbered about 11,000 men; 3,000 were militia, the rest Continentals. The two largest columns, each composed of two divisions plus a flanking brigade of Continentals, were once again commanded by Sullivan and Greene. The first would approach Germantown by the main road, Greene by a more looping route, respectively aimed at the center and right of the British camp. The other two columns, consisting of far weaker forces of militia, had a supporting role: operating out on the flanks, they were to swing round the British rear.

Marching out on the evening of October 3, all four columns were expected to be in place, and ready to attack, by 2 a.m. on October 4. After a breather to finalize their dispositions, they were to assault the British pickets at exactly 5 a.m., and, like Grey's men at Paoli, "with charged bayonets without firing."[70] Predictably enough, expectations of clockwork timing proved optimistic. Sullivan's column, which Washington accompanied, had the most direct route. But his footsore Continentals, who had spent weeks making arduous forced marches, were unable to meet the schedule; it was daybreak before they reached within a mile of Howe's outposts. Sent on a far longer route, Greene's column lost a valuable hour after its guide took the wrong road. Despite these problems, when Sullivan's advance units suddenly emerged from the thick fog that masked the countryside, surprise was achieved. The startled British pickets were forced back, and the heavily outnumbered light infantry behind them obliged to make a fighting withdrawal, contesting every fence and ditch. When Howe rode up to assess the situation, convinced that it was nothing more than a skirmish, he was swiftly disabused as a blast of canister rattled past him. In the confusion of the attack, Sir William's dog went missing, falling into the hands of the rebels; a dog lover himself, Washington duly returned the hound with his compliments.[71]

Despite initial success, crucial momentum was lost when Washington was persuaded to pause and tackle a small force of redcoats—Lieutenant Colonel Thomas Musgrave and about 120 of his 40th Foot—who had barricaded themselves inside the substantial stone-built Chew House. For the gunner Henry Knox, this "castle" was an irresistible target. Rather than isolate and bypass the strongpoint, Washington waited while Knox commenced an ineffective bombardment, and the infantry tried to break in. Musgrave's band defied all efforts to pry them out, and in the time they bought, Howe's main force formed itself to face the American attack.

There were other consequences to the misguided assault on Chew House. Hearing the sound of heavy gunfire to his rear and assuming that Sullivan was in trouble, Anthony Wayne turned his lead division back to help. At much the same time, Greene's delayed column came up on the left. Without consulting Greene, Major General Adam Stephen shifted his division toward the firing at Chew House. With the dense fog now thickened by clouds of gunsmoke, visibility was worse than ever, down to fifty yards. When Stephen's men encountered Wayne's, they opened fire on each other. To Washington it was this, "more than anything else," that "contributed to the misfortune which ensued." At that moment, Howe counterattacked, sending Major General James Grant's brigades against the bewildered Americans. Wayne's and Stephen's men soon broke in panicked flight, defying all efforts to rally them; their ammunition dwindling, Sullivan's also retreated, but steadily. Having entertained "the most flattering hopes of victory," Washington and his men now saw it snatched away.[72]

With each side suffering casualties similar to those sustained in the previous battle—Howe conceding 520 dead and wounded,

Washington 650, and 400 more taken prisoner—Germantown was another victory for Howe, yet, once again, one from which he derived little concrete advantage. Washington told Hancock that "the day was rather unfortunate, than injurious." The troops were "not in the least dispirited" and had gained invaluable combat experience. The British, too, were impressed with their enemy's audacity and aggression: Captain Peebles of the Black Watch ranked the attack on Germantown as the "most spirited" that the Americans had ever made.[73]

Congress agreed with Washington's own optimistic assessment, unanimously resolving to thank him for his "wise and well concerted attack" and his officers and men "for their brave exertions." It was even ordered that Washington should receive a commemorative medal.[74] Alongside the praise came criticism. Major General Stephen, whose unauthorized advance was credited with triggering the disastrous outburst of "friendly fire," was widely believed to have been drunk at the time. If the veteran Scot was inclined to tilt the rum jar or whiskey jug, he was not alone. In his journal, British Captain John André noted: "Several, not only of their soldiers, but officers, were intoxicated when they fell into our hands."[75] It was a hard-drinking age. Although Washington contented himself with a modest glass or two of Madeira in good company, such temperance was clearly unusual, particularly among military men: for example, the diary of John Peebles contains frequent references to becoming "fou"—drunk. Brigadier General Lord Stirling was equally fond of a drink, as Benjamin Rush observed, seeking relief in "toddy"—rum mixed with water and sugar; and just weeks after Germantown, Dr. Rush urged John Adams to convince his fellow congressmen to resolve "that if any major or brigadier general shall drink more than one quart of whiskey, or get drunk more than once in 24 hours, he shall be publicly reprimanded at the head of his division or brigade."[76] Whatever his drinking habits, it seems likely that Stephen, who had angered Washington with his rogue scout before Trenton and bogus reports since, was a marked man: a preliminary court of inquiry headed by Nathanael Greene was followed by a full court-martial. Presided over by John Sullivan, it found Stephen guilty of "unofficerlike behavior" and being "frequently intoxicated . . . to the prejudice of good order and military discipline." Washington approved the verdict, and Stephen was dismissed on November 20.[77]

While Stephen became the scapegoat for Washington's exasperating defeat, Colonel Musgrave was hailed as the hero of Howe's hard-won victory. Visiting the battered and blood-spattered Chew House on the day after the battle, when the bodies of seventy-five Americans were still sprawled beneath its splintered doors and windows, Captain Ewald of the jägers marveled at Musgrave's stand— and its ramifications: "This example of a single brave and intelligent man, through whom the entire English army was saved, shows what courage and decision in war can do." Had Howe's army been defeated, he added, "all honor truly would have been lost."[78] Ewald was scarcely exaggerating. The destruction of Howe's army, added to the elimination of Burgoyne's, would have crippled Britain's ability and resolve to continue waging the war: instead of denying the fact for a further six years, she must surely have acknowledged American independence far sooner. Long after the loss of America, the defense of Chew House was remembered by the 40th Foot, not least because it wiped away the stain left by its poor performance at Princeton. In 1790, Colonel Musgrave awarded a handsome silver medal to each survivor of the fight, stamped with a depiction of their regiment's finest hour.[79]

After his close shave at Germantown, Howe withdrew all his troops to Philadelphia. They were denied supplies from the surrounding countryside by Washington's patrols, while American strongpoints on the Delaware River south of the city prevented British provision ships from getting through. An attempt to subdue Fort Mifflin, on Mud Island, was a miserable failure, while Fort Mercer, on the Delaware's eastern shore at Red Bank, rebuffed a determined but misguided effort to take it by storm on October 22. Nearly 400 Hessians were killed and injured in the assault: their commander, the gallant Colonel Donop, was mortally wounded: he'd courted his last widow. The Americans finally evacuated their river defenses in mid-November, but by then the full cost of Howe's obsession with Washington and Philadelphia had become all too apparent with the confirmation of Burgoyne's capitulation at Saratoga.

Soon after his Pyrrhic victory at Freeman's Farm, Burgoyne had received a letter from Sir Henry Clinton, promising to support him by attacking the American forts on the Hudson River, guarding the vital Highlands some forty miles above New York City. True to his word, on October 3, Clinton advanced with 3,000 men and was soon making steady progress. The fort at Verplanck's Point surrendered without a fight two days later, and on October 6, Forts Montgomery and Clinton, north of Peekskill, were both stormed. The next day the British had advanced another five miles up the river to capture the evacuated Fort Constitution. Clinton now detached 2,000 men under Major General John Vaughan to push upriver with supplies for Burgoyne. On October 15, within forty-five miles of Albany, Vaughan's pilots refused to go farther; the general torched Esopus in his vexation. Worse still, Clinton was now ordered to send reinforcements to Howe's army, necessitating the recall of the upriver detachment and placing him "under the mortifying necessity of relinquishing the Highlands and all the other passes over the Hudson, to be reoccupied by the rebels whenever they saw proper."[80]

By then the fate of Burgoyne's army had already been sealed. Spurning the advice of a council of war which urged retreat, Burgoyne decided upon a fresh attempt to break through Gates's lines. On October 7, this blow was checked at Bemis Heights. Once again General Arnold demonstrated his consummate combat leadership, intervening without authority at a pivotal moment and helping to shatter the British assault. Taking more casualties than he could afford, late on the following evening Burgoyne reluctantly began to withdraw. But he was now too late. With his own ascendant army swollen by incoming militia to twice the size of Burgoyne's force, Gates blocked his retreat on October 12. Five days later Burgoyne surrendered on Gates's pledge that his 6,000 men would be sent back to Europe. He had secured such generous terms because Gates remained uncertain of Clinton's progress to the south and was unaware of his withdrawal. Realizing that Burgoyne's repatriated troops would free others for service in America, Congress promptly repudiated the terms of the surrender "Convention."

Regardless of such wrangling, the fact remained that the Americans had knocked an entire British field army out of the war. Howe was widely blamed for the catastrophe: many rued his lost opportunities to crush the rebellion in 1776; others lamented his failure to cooperate with Burgoyne, with dire consequences that some officers had predicted when the fleet sailed from New York. Others, too, had played their part in the disaster: the ambitious and overconfident Burgoyne, who had refused to turn back when he still could; and Lord George Germain, the mastermind behind British strategy in London, for neglecting to ensure that his American campaigns of 1777 were sufficiently coordinated to complement each other.

Besides its impact upon American morale, Saratoga had a fundamental effect on opinion in France. Although the government of the young Louis XVI had been negotiating with the American revolutionaries for some time and would surely have entered the war eventually, Burgoyne's defeat, along with Washington's strong showing at Germantown, expedited the process. Just months earlier, in August, Washington had doubted whether France would ever do more than "give us a kind of underhand assistance, that is supply us with arms etc. for our money and trade." France would only enter the conflict if Britain had "spirit and strength to resent" her interference in the quarrel and declared war on the old enemy, he believed.[81]

French-supplied munitions had been crucial in maintaining the revolutionary war effort: in 1777, they accounted for 90 percent of the Continental Army's powder and shot, while five brass cannon captured by Howe's army at Brandywine were French made. Volunteers from the French Army were also conspicuous among the foreigners who besieged Congress for commissions in the Continental Army, which only complicated Washington's already chaotic command. They included the nineteen-year-old Marquis de Lafayette, the son of a colonel killed fighting the British at Minden in 1759. Lafayette arrived at Philadelphia in July 1777, just months after a visit to London, where his obliging hosts remained unaware of his ambitions to join the American rebels: he had thoroughly enjoyed the city's delights, dancing at the house of Germain and meeting General Henry Clinton at the opera. While confessing himself young and inexperienced, to Washington's consternation Lafayette clearly assumed that the major general's rank he'd been given by Congress was not merely honorary and that a full Continental Army division would soon be at his disposal; as Washington explained to Congressman Benjamin Harrison, Lafayette had meanwhile agreed to accept a smaller command and had already applied, at the direction of John Hancock, for two aides-de-camp.[82]

Many of the foreigners with the revolutionary forces were little more than mercenaries—adventurers hungry for employment, experience, and fast-track promotion. Lafayette was well aware that, by the time of his arrival, Americans were already "disgusted by the conduct" and pretensions of several Frenchmen who had gone before him. But Washington, who took Lafayette into his military "family" as a volunteer aide, swiftly discovered that he was no braggart or charlatan but was motivated by an unswerving belief in the cause. Lafayette was no less impressed by Washington. When he first met "that great man," he recalled that "the majesty of his figure and his height were unmistakable," while his welcome was "affable and noble." The Virginian planter and the French aristocrat soon forged a strong and enduring friendship. For Lafayette, Washington may have helped to fill the void left by the soldier-father he had lost in infancy; yet while the marquis is often cast as a surrogate for the son Washington never had, despite the age difference between them their affectionate, bantering relationship was more fraternal; it recalls the bond between Washington and his half brother Lawrence, with the older man acting as mentor and role model for the younger. Like Washington, Lafayette was both a gentleman and a warrior; when the Frenchmen was shot in the leg at Brandywine, his commander made a point of reporting it to Congress. The marquis was still limping on November 25 when he distinguished himself at Gloucester, New Jersey, in a skirmish with a foraging party led across the Delaware River by Lord Cornwallis. With Washington's backing, this "little success," as Lafayette modestly called it, convinced Congress to give him a Continental division. On December 4 he inherited the Virginians of the disgraced Major General Stephen.[83]

For all Washington's skepticism about the intentions of Lafayette's countrymen across the Atlantic, when news of Burgoyne's capitulation reached Paris in December 1777, the French government swiftly committed itself to recognizing the United States and entering into an official alliance. The formal treaties were signed in February 1778, with a declaration of war with Britain following in July.

Unquestionably, the Franco-American alliance changed the nature—and course—of the American War of Independence. In the sense that Burgoyne's nemesis stemmed largely from Howe's fixation upon Washington and Philadelphia, the earlier victories at Trenton and Princeton certainly contributed to this development. Yet Washington's feelings about the momentous patriot victory at Saratoga were mixed. The contrast with his own defeats at Brandywine and Germantown was galling, his frustration and envy difficult to conceal. After news of Gates's success over Burgoyne's troops at Bemis Heights reached Washington's army on October 15, General Orders announced that thirteen cannon would be fired that afternoon to salute the "Northern Army." However, while congratulating his own men upon such a "signal victory," Washington pointedly hoped that it would stimulate the army under "his immediate command" to win laurels of its own. After all, he announced, "this is the Grand American Army; and that of course great things are expected from it. . . . What shame and dishonor will attend us, if we suffer ourselves in every instance to be outdone?"[84]

Washington's concern that his own performance in Pennsylvania might be judged harshly against Gates's at Saratoga emerged in a letter to his trusted friend Landon Carter, who had known him since he was a callow youngster defending Virginia's frontier. Seeking to explain their mixed fortunes, Washington contrasted the situation of the two armies. Gates's northern command had enjoyed support from a spirited force of "upwards of 12,000 militia." His own situation in Philadelphia couldn't have been more different: "the disaffection of [a] great part of the inhabitants of this state— the languor of others, and internal distraction of the whole, have been among the great and insuperable difficulties I have met with, and have contributed not a little to my embarrassments this campaign," he wrote. Washington assured Carter that he did "not mean to complain," although his anger and bitterness at the disadvantages he'd toiled under were all too evident.[85]

Washington's mood was scarcely improved by the seemingly disrespectful stance that Gates now adopted toward him. Instead of reporting his victory directly to Washington, the commander in chief, Gates left it to Congress to convey the news at second hand. As his Northern Department army was a separate force, technically independent of Washington, Gates could claim some justification in writing to Congress first. At the very least, however, this was a breach of etiquette guaranteed to goad a stickler for protocol like Washington; at worst, it suggested that Gates now considered himself Washington's equal, or even superior. After congratulating Gates on his victory, Washington regretted "that a matter of such magnitude and so interesting to our general operations, should have reached me by report only, or through the channel of letters not bearing that authenticity, which the importance of it required, and which it would have received by a line under your signature, stating the simple fact."[86]

This mild rebuke was the first rumble in a storm that would soon reverberate through the Continental Army's high command, presenting Washington with yet another crisis to surmount. Meanwhile, the continued presence of a powerful British force in

Philadelphia was a more pressing concern. As Gates had disposed of the immediate threat within his department, Washington had sent his trusted aide Captain Alexander Hamilton to explain the plight of the main army and to request reinforcements. By now, Washington was contemplating a blow of his own to rival that landed against Burgoyne. It was nothing less than a full-scale assault to "dislodge the enemy from Philadelphia." In advance of a scheduled council of war he briefed his general officers with a list of questions. When they met on October 29, Washington explained that, while Howe now commanded about 10,000 rank and file fit for duty, their own force numbered about 11,000 exclusive of garrisons; however, some 2,000 militia from Virginia and Maryland would be leaving camp soon when their enlistments expired. Asked whether their present strength and circumstances justified an attack, Washington's generals were adamant that they did not.[87]

But the notion of attacking the formidable and well-fortified British force in Philadelphia refused to die. It was revived in late November when Brigadier General Cadwalader, himself a Philadelphian, proposed a detailed plan for ejecting the invaders. Seeking to capitalize upon the absence of hefty British detachments in New Jersey, Cadwalader envisaged a coordinated assault involving divisions attacking both overland and by boat from the Delaware River. Ultimately, Cadwalader's plan fared no better than Washington's, yet a minority of generals—the Bavarian veteran Johann de Kalb, Lord Stirling, Anthony Wayne, and Charles Scott—supported his offensive. Their opinions, and those of other senior officers, were presented to Washington in writing and make for revealing reading. While some responses, from John Armstrong and John Paterson, for instance, were brief and forthright rejections of a "hazardous" plan likely to be attended with "fatal consequences," other officers articulated their opposition in detailed reports that not only grappled with the practicality of the proposal, but sought to demonstrate their extensive knowledge of military affairs. For example, both John Sullivan and Henry Knox cautioned wariness of the redoubts that screened Howe's army: in the course

of his reading—which by the way had not been "inconsiderable"—
Major General Sullivan had never come across a single instance
where "a chain of redoubts covering the whole front on an army"
was successfully assaulted; indeed, those thrown up by Peter the
Great of Russia in a single night at Poltava in 1709 had defeated
the "best army in the world," led by the Swedish warrior-king
Charles XII, one of the heroes whose busts Washington had hoped
to install at Mount Vernon. Drawing upon more recent history
to make the same point, Sullivan highlighted the fate of Donop's
Hessians at Red Bank. Knox also mentioned Poltava, reinforcing
his argument by referencing the renowned French Army general
and military theorist of the 1740s, Marshal Maurice de Saxe, who
rated redoubts as "the strongest and most excellent kind of field
fortification."[88] Saxe's *Reveries; or Memoirs upon the Art of War*,
first translated into English in 1757, would have been among the
volumes that Knox perused in his Boston bookshop before turning from the theory to the reality of war.

Such reasoned and informed feedback testified to the serious-
ness with which George Washington's officers were approaching
their task of defending American liberty. Ironically, this keen
interest contrasted with the typically casual approach adopted
by their professional British counterparts, who, when not fighting the enemy or one another, preferred to amuse themselves
with gambling, drinking, and whoring. That December, Captain
Ewald noted that the Americans had now "trained a great many
excellent officers who very often shame and excel our experienced officers, who consider it sinful to read a book or to think
of learning anything during the war." Rummaging through the
enemy's haversacks, he had often found translations of "the most
excellent military books"—for example, "the Instructions of the
great Frederick to his generals." Ewald's comment was characteristically perceptive: a redcoat ensign who'd read Bland's *Treatise* en route to Boston in 1774 and who had suggested that his
brother officers might benefit from doing likewise, was mocked
mercilessly for his pains: ribbing him as "Humphrey Bland" and

"the young general," they "soon laughed him out of his scheme for reforming the army."[89]

While Cadwalader's proposal was understandably rejected as too risky, Sir William Howe soon emerged from behind his defenses, looking for a fight. Late on the evening of December 4, a powerful British column moved out from Philadelphia to attack the rebels: according to General Grey's aide-de-camp, Captain André, their encampment extended along a ridge of hills for about three miles to the east of Whitemarsh. After testing both the right and left of Washington's position, on December 6 Howe sought to repeat the strategy that had yielded results on Long Island and at Brandywine. A "demonstration" by Grey would distract Washington from the "real attack," to be delivered by a larger force under Sir William's personal command. But this time the plan failed, with no more than lively skirmishing as American units fell back to their formidable main position, from which Washington wouldn't budge. By the next day, André noted, "most people thought an attack upon ground of such difficult access would be a very arduous undertaking" and also a fruitless one, as the enemy had secured a viable line of retreat. The army thereupon returned to Philadelphia, the rebels occasionally nipping at its heels.[90] As in New Jersey six months earlier, Washington's selection of a strong defensive position and careful "Fabian" tactics had kept Sir William at arm's length.

As 1777 drew to a close, and Howe's well-supplied troops stayed snugly ensconced in Philadelphia, the overriding issue for Washington was to find viable winter quarters for his own cold and tattered army. In his General Orders of December 17, he acknowledged that the site he'd chosen was unlikely to be popular. Withdrawal to the heart of Pennsylvania, already crowded with refugees from Philadelphia, would expose a vast tract of fertile land to the ravages of the enemy, he argued. It was therefore essential for the army to adopt a position where it could not only "prevent distress" and "protect the country" but also enjoy "the most extensive security" from a surprise attack. In such a place they must make the best of things, building huts to keep them warm and dry through the coming winter. Washington was confident that officers and soldiers alike would "resolve to surmount every difficulty" with the same "fortitude and patience" that had sustained them through their last campaign. He pledged to "share in the hardship, and partake of every inconvenience."[91]

The location Washington had decided upon was a tiny settlement about eighteen miles northwest of Philadelphia, protected by the Schuylkill River and screening hills: Valley Forge.

9

TREASON OF THE
BLACKEST DYE

Washington's army had scarcely occupied its new winter quarters at Valley Forge when it became clear that it faced a potentially disastrous supply crisis. On December 23, 1777, Washington reported to Henry Laurens, Hancock's successor as president of Congress, that a dearth of provisions left him utterly helpless to act against the enemy. That was bad enough, but with little to eat for days on end his long-suffering troops were growling and mutinous. Unless supplies reached camp immediately, Washington warned, the army faced a stark trinity of choices: "Starve—dissolve—or disperse."[1]

The troops were not only ravenous, but also lamentably clad: of the 11,000 who marched into camp, nearly 3,000 were "barefoot and otherwise naked." Private Joseph Plumb Martin, a hard-bitten veteran of Kip's Bay, White Plains, and Germantown who wasn't given to exaggeration, witnessed a recurrence of what had become the Continental Army's winter calling card, remembering how its path to Valley Forge could be tracked by yet more bloodstained footprints in the snow. Martin and his comrades now had little more than tatters of old clothing to defy the cutting wind and numbing cold of winter and were mostly without blankets. Lafayette recalled that the soldiers' "feet and legs turned black with frostbite and often had to be amputated."[2]

Even now, Washington opposed coercing civilians into supplying his men with the provisions and clothing they needed so badly.

Small seizures of food made in late December 1777, "in consequence of the most pressing and urgent necessity," had "excited the greatest alarm and uneasiness," even among those best disposed toward the Revolution. If repeated, Washington warned, such tough measures would have "the most pernicious consequences," destroying popular support for the Continental Army.[3]

The situation was all the more galling because the food, clothing, and equipment that the army needed so desperately lay stockpiled in storehouses and depots: the root cause of the problem was logistical, resulting from a total breakdown in the transportation network needed to shift supplies over rural Pennsylvania's muddy roads. Both the commissary and quartermaster departments were to blame, with Congress, which controlled them, ultimately responsible for the shambles; for example, although General Thomas Mifflin resigned his post of quartermaster general in November 1777, it was three months before that vital vacancy was filled. As the Americans' elected central government, Congress was already revealing the inherent weakness that would increasingly thwart Washington's ambitions to take the war to the enemy: unsurprisingly for a body spawned by a revolt against British taxation policies, it lacked power to tax the states to fund the revolutionaries' national war effort or even to enforce its requests for supplies and manpower.

If food and clothing were scarce at Valley Forge, wood at least was plentiful, and by New Year's Day 1778 the army was under cover, with the rank and file hunkering in the crude huts they had built for themselves. True to his word, and unlike many of his officers, Washington stayed with his men throughout their winter ordeal in Pennsylvania, just as he had kept close by them at Boston and Morristown. This contrasted with his attitude as commander of the Virginia Regiment between 1755 and 1758, when he'd often left his men in their spartan frontier posts to seek respite in more civilized quarters. At Valley Forge, Washington didn't share all of his army's hardships: given his rank and responsibilities, there was no expectation among contemporaries that he should. While the privates, sergeants, and junior officers roughed it in shanties, Washington and his staff were accommodated in cramped but relatively warm stone buildings or wooden farmhouses and ate regular, if rudimentary, meals. There was also a semblance of domesticity as Martha Washington, along with the wives of high-ranking officers such as Greene, Knox, and Lord Stirling, joined their menfolk in camp.

Washington's continued physical presence at Valley Forge was crucial for the army's survival. Even if *he* was not shoeless, cold, hungry, and lousy, as he went his daily rounds he saw many men who were all of these things and through his unending correspondence spared no pains to ensure that Congress knew of their sufferings and sacrifices in the cause of American liberty. Following the stance that he had adopted since first accepting command of the Continental Army in June 1775, Washington sought to achieve his objectives though careful, respectful lobbying of key players in Congress. This, too, was a marked change from his attitude during the 1750s, when his letters to Virginia's Lieutenant Governor Dinwiddie grew petulant and brusque, and ultimately self-defeating.

Prompted by Washington's frequent reports from headquarters, which chronicled his army's trials in telling detail, Congress took action. In January it appointed a "Committee at Camp," instructed to work with Washington to overhaul the army's organization, addressing such key issues as recruitment, clothing, supply, and discipline. The measures that Washington believed essential to address the "numerous defects" in the "present military establishment" were presented to the committee members in an extraordinarily detailed and comprehensive document. Besides urging pensions as a means of motivating his officers, Washington called for a formal annual draft from the militia to fill his depleted battalions. While certainly a "disagreeable alternative" to voluntary enlistments, drafting was now "an unavoidable one," he argued: with the Continental Army more than 35,000 men short of the paper establishment, something drastic needed to be done. Earlier that month, Virginia had already resorted to conscription to fill its quota of fifteen Continental regiments, targeting unmarried militiamen, who received a $15 bounty and were obliged to serve for a year. Like militiamen balloted for the old Virginia Regiment during the 1750s, those wealthy enough to provide an able-bodied replacement could dodge the draft. In fact, when the "new army" was first authorized in September 1776, with the states each required to provide their share of men, the hiring of substitutes had become common. Having already served a six-month stint in the Connecticut "levies," in early 1777, young Joseph Plumb Martin resolved to enlist in the Connecticut Continentals for "three years, or during the war." Badgered to take the place of one of a squad of militiamen and act as their "scapegoat," he recalled: "I thought, as I must go, I might as well get as much for my skin as I could." While deploring such auctions, Washington was nonetheless prepared "to provide a man" in place of his cousin Lund, should he "happen to draw a *prize* in the *militia*." To Washington, Lund was more valuable overseeing Mount Vernon than toting a musket against the British, but such responses merely exacerbated the extent to which the war for American liberty was fought by the most underprivileged and unfree members of American society, white and black alike.[4]

Once the initial wave of martial enthusiasm, or *rage militaire*, of 1775 subsided, and it became clear that the war with Britain would be both long and bitter, most of those who endured the greatest dangers and hardships to secure American independence by serving in the Continental Army were not the land-owning citizen-soldiers of hallowed tradition, but rather drifters and marginalized men with little real stake in the society they were defending. Such propertyless men resembled the "volunteers" of the ill-fated American Regiment sent off to Cartagena in 1740 and likewise those who had filled the ranks of Washington's Virginia Regiment during the French and Indian War. Many Continentals undoubtedly believed in their cause, but as Washington had acknowledged in the late summer of 1776, they soldiered on as much from necessity as from high-flown ideological reasons.[5]

Drawn increasingly from the "lower orders" of American society, as the war ground on, the profile of the Continental Army's manpower grew ever closer to the redcoats they faced across the battlefield. While the British Army's rank and file typically took the king's shilling because they needed a steady wage, they, too, were far from being the mindless scum lambasted by Charles Lee and other commentators. Many of them were unskilled "laborers," but a significant proportion had worked at trades before enlisting, often in their early twenties. For example, forty-three-year-old Private William Bragg of the 63rd Foot, who was examined for his Chelsea pension in May 1787, was a weaver from Darlington, County Durham. He'd spent twenty-one years with his regiment and not only was "worn out" but had been wounded in the left thigh at Germantown. His comrade, Corporal John Ingram, aged forty-two, had enlisted in the 63rd at the same time. Born in Taunton, Somerset, and formerly a barber, Corporal Ingram was described as "wounded in the head, right leg and left thigh on Long Island, North America." A veteran of the 23rd Foot (or "Royal Welch Fusiliers"), who appeared before the Chelsea Board in 1790, must have been among the very first British casualties of the conflict. A forty-four-year-old laborer from Burnley, Lancashire, Corporal Matthew Haymer was "wounded in his right thigh and in his left foot at Lexington, in New England, on the 19th April, 1775, also in the right shoulder at Bunker's Hill on the 17th June 1775." These injuries had not stopped him serving throughout the American war, accumulating a total of twenty-four years with his regiment. Unsurprisingly, he too was "worn out."[6]

As these cases show, British soldiers normally enlisted for "life," although during the American Revolutionary War, shorter terms, for "three years or the duration," were introduced, along with more generous bounties, paralleling practice in the Continental Army.[7] Even with such incentives, after 1776, Britain struggled to keep her battalions across the Atlantic up to strength. With precious few injections of manpower, regiments were loath to shed any trained soldier still capable of marching and fighting, which is why multiply wounded men like Bragg, Ingram, and Haymer were back on duty as soon as they could walk. For all his frustrations with the Continental Army's fluctuating strength, unlike his opponents, Washington could at least draw upon a reservoir of local replacements.

Although Congress shied away from enforcing conscription, other states besides Virginia authorized their own drafts, offering wildly different bounties, conditions, and terms of service. This meant that besides a kernel of long-term veterans like Private Martin, the Continental Army was topped up by relays of recruits drafted for shorter spells—twelve, nine, or even six months. The system was wasteful, as the short-timers had scarcely been trained before their enlistments expired, yet they sustained Washington's army after the initial pool of "volunteers"—the kind of rootless, hard-up and adventurous men most likely to succumb to the blandishments of the recruiting parties—had run dry.[8]

Washington's manpower headaches never were resolved, but at Valley Forge the supply situation slowly began to improve, helped by the appointment of competent administrators to two crucial jobs: Jeremiah Wadsworth, a rich Connecticut merchant, became head of the commissary department, while Washington's right-hand man, Major General Nathanael Greene, reluctantly swapped his field command for the onerous and distinctly inglorious staff appointment of quartermaster general. But by then, corruption and inefficiency had already exacted a far higher toll upon the Continentals than Howe's redcoats and Hessians: in the six months following the army's arrival at Valley Forge, about 2,500 men—almost a quarter of the army—died as exposure and malnutrition exacerbated the customary campground killers of dysentery and typhus.[9]

Washington's standing as a commander whom Congress could work with—indeed, whom it couldn't work without—was consolidated by another crisis during the trying winter of 1777–78. It arose from grumbling, both within and outside the army, about Washington's style of leadership. Such criticism was scarcely surprising given the disappointing results of his Pennsylvania campaign, which looked lamer still alongside Gates's decisive victory over Burgoyne. For example, while admiring Washington's bravery and devotion to the cause, Brigadier General Anthony Wayne and Major General Johann de Kalb both complained about his tendency to defer too readily to the opinions of councils of war, rather than following his own good sense. Such gripes were not without foundation; although Washington had known since March 1777 that "it never was the intention of Congress, that he should be bound by the majority of voices in a council of war, contrary to his own judgment," by then the habit of doing so was already ingrained.[10]

Inside Congress, John Adams, who had been instrumental in securing Washington's elevation to commander in chief in 1775, was now concerned at his near-deification. Indeed, for many Americans, Washington's emergence as the symbolic figurehead of their new republic had invested him with a quasi-royal status; the title "Father of his Country" first appeared in print in 1778. Such popular veneration, which threatened to replace one King George with another, rubbed against the republican grain of men like Adams. As he confided to his wife, Abigail, another reason to offer thanks for Saratoga was that the "glory of turning the tide of arms" did not belong to Washington. Had it done so, he cautioned, "idolatry and adulation would have been unbounded," even to the extent that American liberties might be endangered. Adams added: "We can allow a certain citizen to be wise, virtuous, and good, without thinking him a deity or a savior."[11]

Despite their criticisms, none of these men suggested that Washington should be supplanted as commander in chief. One prominent revolutionary who *did* urge such a drastic measure was the outspoken Dr. Benjamin Rush, now surgeon general of military hospitals in Washington's own Middle Department. An ardent admirer of Washington when the war began, before the end of 1776 Rush was already turning against him. By the following autumn, his attitude had hardened into outright opposition. On October 21, 1777, in a letter to John Adams, he extolled his good friend Horatio Gates at the expense of Washington: "Look at the characters of both!" Rush exclaimed. "The one on the pinnacle of military glory—exulting in the success of schemes planned with wisdom, and executed with vigor and bravery . . . the other outgeneraled and twice beated [*sic*]." Rush then proceeded to quote another soldier he greatly admired: Brigadier General Thomas Conway, an Irish-born French Army officer now in the American service. In "a letter to a friend," Rush reported, Conway had said that: "A great and good God has decreed that America shall be free, or _____ [Washington] and weak counselors would have ruined her long ago."[12]

Conway's "friend" was none other than Gates. This surprising intelligence reached Washington some weeks later in roundabout fashion. The officer charged with carrying the Saratoga victory dispatches to Congress was Gates's aide-de-camp, the Trenton and Princeton veteran Colonel James Wilkinson. Stopping at Reading en route to York, Wilkinson fell into company with other officers belonging to the "family" of Major General Lord Stirling. It was a convivial occasion, with his Lordship reminiscing, at some length, about his adventures during the Battle of Long Island.[13] As the drink and conversation flowed, Wilkinson divulged Conway's criticisms of the commander in chief. These reached Stirling via his aide Major William McWilliams. A staunch Washington devotee whom Conway had recently derided as a drunkard, his Lordship felt duty-bound to expose "such wicked duplicity." As forwarded to Washington, Conway's words read: "Heaven has been determined to save your country; or a weak general and bad counselors would have ruined it."[14]

Without verifying this unauthenticated gossip, Washington immediately took the offensive, writing Conway a terse note quoting what he was alleged to have declared. That same day, November 5, 1777, Conway replied, conceding that he *had* written a congratulatory letter to Gates, in which he had spoken his mind "freely" but denying using the words attributed to him and offering to have the original retrieved as proof. Conway's letter to Gates is now lost, but judging by a surviving paraphrased extract, it was scarcely complimentary to the commander in chief. Conway now took the opportunity to clear the air by offering his opinion of Washington, "without flattery or envy," writing "you are a brave man, an honest man, a patriot, and a man of great sense." He added a less flattering rider that nonetheless echoed the sentiments of some other senior officers: "Your modesty is such, that although your advice in council is commonly sound and proper, you have often been influenced by men who were not equal to you in point of experience, knowledge or judgment."[15] In a subsequent letter to Washington, written after his olive branch had been brushed aside, the indignant Irishman pointed out that in Europe it was common for officers to express frank criticisms of superiors in their personal correspondence: indeed, it would be ironic if such "an odious and tyrannical inquisition" should be introduced by the commander of an army "raised for the defense of Liberty."[16] Had Conway known of Washington's persistent attempts to undermine his own commander, John Forbes, in 1758, he might have added hypocrisy to his charge of despotism.

Despite his anger, Washington had no wish to escalate the quarrel and so highlight damaging rifts within the Continental Army at a critical time: that was achieved, albeit unwittingly, by Congress. On November 7, it appointed Thomas Mifflin, the former quartermaster general, to the reorganized Board of War. On Mifflin's recommendation, Congress soon after chose Gates as president of the board; and on December 13, it selected Conway to fill the new staff post of inspector general to the army, with promotion to major general. Although founded on Conway's reputation as an experienced professional soldier and effective drillmaster who came strongly recommended by Major General Sullivan, this posting and jump in rank immediately made him a focus for jealousy and resentment among the other brigadiers who had been passed over and raised suspicions that his new influence would be wielded against Washington and his henchmen.

While historians have discredited the existence of a conspiracy to replace Washington with Gates—alliteratively dubbed the "Conway Cabal"—given the timing of Congress's appointments, that is precisely how things appeared to him and his devoted followers.[17] For example, Washington's old friend the army physician Dr. James Craik wrote on January 6 to warn him that "a strong faction" was forming against him "in the new Board of War and in the Congress." Craik believed that General Mifflin was among the most "active" of those "secret enemies who would rob you of the great and truly deserved esteem your country has for you." At the same time, Lafayette was warning Henry Laurens against attempts to discredit Washington by "Gates's faction, or Mifflin's forces." Laurens was quick to reassure the marquis that criticism of Washington within Congress amounted to "little more than tittle-tattle." He added: "I think that the friends of our brave and virtuous general, may rest assured that he is out of the reach of his enemies, if he has an enemy, a fact which I am in doubt of."[18]

In fact, Washington certainly had detractors inside Congress, notably James Lovell of Massachusetts, whose private opinions reflected civilian distrust of professional soldiers in general and of the commander in chief's close-knit and prickly military entourage in particular. For example, after Congress allowed Washington extra staff officers, Lovell wrote to Sam Adams complaining that it seemed the "13 United States" together could not supply enough "honest men" as "aides de camp, secretaries and privy councilors to one great man, whom no citizen *shall* dare even to talk about say the Gentlemen of the Blade."[19]

Yet the only prominent revolutionary to actively call for Washington's replacement was former congressman Dr. Rush. On January 12, 1778, he rashly sent an anonymous letter to Virginian delegate Patrick Henry: "The northern army has shown us what Americans are capable of doing with a GENERAL at their head," he wrote. "The spirit of the southern army is no ways inferior to the spirit of the northern. A Gates, a Lee, or a Conway would in a few weeks render them an irresistible body of men." Rush then quoted the now infamous words attributed to Conway that he had first cited to John Adams three months earlier. Henry sent the letter to Washington, who swiftly suspected the identity of its author.[20]

In the face of the perceived threat, Washington's most loyal supporters, men like Greene, Lafayette, and Hamilton, closed ranks in what amounted to a "cabal" of their own. When General Conway appeared at Valley Forge to assume his duties as inspector general, he received a reception as frosty as the weather. After Washington explained that Conway must await instructions from the Board of War before starting work and hinted that his promotion was unjustified, the quarrelsome Hibernian countered with a letter sarcastically comparing "the great Washington" to Frederick the Great of Prussia.[21]

Whatever his personal feelings at such slights, as commander in chief Washington was unable to resent them privately by issuing a challenge to a duel, particularly as such conduct was banned under the Continental Army's *Articles of War*. But there was no lack of men willing to pick up a sword or a brace of pistols on his behalf. Conway discovered this soon enough. He had swiftly been cold-shouldered by his colleagues, including his former friend Lafayette, who now disowned him as "an ambitious and dangerous man";[22] when Congress appointed the marquis to lead another proposed "irruption" into Canada, he refused to accept Conway as his second in command. In April, the exasperated Conway offered Congress his resignation; to his chagrin it was promptly accepted. But the matter didn't rest there. In July, before Conway left for France, an angry exchange with another Washington loyalist, Brigadier General John Cadwalader, prompted a duel. In the ensuing encounter Conway was shot in the mouth; the ball emerged from the back of his neck, beneath his pigtailed hair. Apparently convinced he was dying, Conway took the opportunity to make Washington a fulsome apology, acknowledging him to be a genuinely "great and good man."[23]

Neither was Washington inclined to let Horatio Gates off the hook. Even though Gates had done no more than receive an unsolicited letter from Conway, he'd made no attempt to defend Washington against criticism. The two generals exchanged a series of letters that did neither of them credit. Gates's outraged appeal for help in tracking down the miscreant who had rifled his private correspondence did nothing to dispel Washington's impression that he was implicated in intrigue with "a dangerous incendiary." Beaten down by Washington's reproaches, Gates finally expressed his innocence of any conspiracy: "I solemnly declare that I am of no faction," he wrote, adding, "I cannot believe your Excellency will either suffer your suspicions or the prejudices of others to induce you to spend another moment upon this subject." Washington agreed to bury the hatchet, consigning the controversy "as far as future events will permit" to "oblivion."[24]

Without doubt, Washington emerged from the affair stronger than ever, with an enhanced standing inside Congress. In addition, the vociferous reaction of Washington's partisans against those suspected of plotting against "His Excellency," which has been compared by one respected historian to a "witch hunt," served notice that future critics would be swiftly silenced: there'd be no more talk of replacing Washington with Gates—or with anyone else.[25]

Both the Conway episode and the shared hardships of the Valley Forge winter fostered the emergence of an officer corps that increasingly conformed to Washington's vision of the type of men he had always wanted to lead the Continental Army. Unlike many of the amateur officers who had served against the British at Boston and New York in 1775–76, these long-term professionals came mostly from the propertied ranks of society; they saw themselves as "gentlemen" and expected to be treated as such. Just as the rank and file of the Continental Army had changed since 1776, with those men signed up for "three years or the duration" increasingly resembling the redcoats they viewed down the barrels of their muskets, as the war dragged on, so Washington's officers drew closer to the British model in background, outlook, and aspirations. Above all, they were concerned with two intertwined concepts that had driven Washington since his youth: status and honor.

By the time the army encamped at Valley Forge, many officers felt that they had been slighted by their civilian masters in Congress on both counts. Not only were they often denied the promotions they believed they'd earned by hard service, but their pay, which was increasingly devalued by rampant inflation, provided small compensation for lost civilian incomes; such cavalier treatment was bitterly resented, not least by Major General Benedict Arnold. In an attempt to address their financial problems, officers again looked to British precedent and demanded the right to half pay for life—essentially a pension for retired officers—to commence at the war's end. When first approached with the notion in November 1777, Washington was doubtful, aware that congressmen suspicious of standing armies would resist such a move on ideological grounds. But faced with a mounting wave of resignations from disenchanted officers, Washington swiftly changed his mind. Resurrecting the desperate arguments that he had used in the summer of 1776, when urging solid material incentives for recruits, in his detailed address to Congress's Camp Committee Washington underlined the need for realism: "Motives of public virtue" were no longer enough; if his officers' "languishing zeal" was to be revived, their "private interest" must also be considered: half pay was the only answer. Conscious that the Continental Army was now the torchbearer of American liberty, in May 1778, Congress approved the pensions, although limiting them to seven years. Even this partial consent was grudging, with accusations of antirepublicanism and extortion only salting the wounds of officers who already believed their precious honor had been impugned.[26]

As Thomas Conway could testify, one consequence of a heightened sense of personal reputation among officers who considered themselves "gentlemen" was a mania for duelling.[27] Unsurprisingly, the volatile mixture of touchy young men, lethal weapons, and an unbending code of conduct ensured that dueling was already endemic within European armies: for example, jäger Captain Ewald soldiered through the American War of Independence with just one good eye: he had lost the other in 1770, when, as a young lieutenant in the Leib Regiment, a night of revelry in Cassell's "Hof von England" inn led to a disastrous encounter with a drinking companion.[28] Although proscribed under the Continental Army's British-based *Articles of War*, "affairs of honor" were nonetheless common: just like his counterpart serving King George, the American officer who refused a challenge faced the social stigma of cowardice. Continental Army surgeon James Thacher was often required to attend such "meetings" and patch up the survivors: in

August 1780, after duels on successive days sacrificed "two valuable lives . . . to what is termed principles of honor," he railed against "this fashionable folly, this awful blindness and perversion of mind, this barbarous and infernal practice, this foul stain on the history of man!"[29] Yet such appeals to rationalism fell on deaf ears: in coming years, dueling would add a dangerous edge to politics in the young American Republic; in the southern states it would linger on into the middle decades of the nineteenth century, another "peculiar institution" to set alongside slavery.[30]

The growing distinctiveness of Washington's honor-conscious officer caste—Lovell's "Gentlemen of the Blade"—was exemplified by an extraordinary theatrical performance at Valley Forge. In an expression of group solidarity and as a mark of esteem for Washington, they presented an amateur production of his favorite play, Addison's *Cato*. It was *Cato* that Washington had quarried to express the true depth of his feelings for Sally Fairfax in 1758 and his admiration for Benedict Arnold in 1776. This was an exclusive event, for officers only. Underlining the social gap between leaders and led, it also indicated the growing gulf between American soldiers and civilians, incurring the derision of men like Sam Adams, who considered such performances as a decadent and un-Republican imitation of the plays often staged by British Army officers.[31]

That same month, in fact, the British officer corps in Philadelphia gave a very different but no less remarkable performance as a farewell for Sir William Howe, who was being replaced as commander in chief in North America by Henry Clinton. This elaborate "Mischianza" (from the Italian for "medley") reflected a growing interest in the medieval "Gothic" past, with rival teams of mounted officers in fancy dress—the "Knights of the Blended Rose" and the "Burning Mountain"—fighting mock combats to champion the honor of their chosen ladies. Given Washington's own love of horses and his youthful penchant for knight-errantry, this lavish and colorful echo of the age of chivalry would surely have appealed no less than the sterner fare of *Cato*. Captain Peebles of the Black Watch certainly enjoyed himself. The spirited tourney was followed by a spectacular firework display, after which the carefree company relished "a very elegant supper" and "danced and drank till day light." But with the rebels still ensconced nearby at Valley Forge, others considered the elaborate and costly celebration to be ill timed and tasteless. Lord Howe's secretary, Ambrose Serle, observed sourly: "Our enemies will dwell upon the folly and extravagance of it with pleasure."[32]

While Howe's officers clashed sabers under the admiring eyes of Philadelphia's Loyalist belles, Washington's men were honing their skills for the serious business of war. That spring the Continental Army underwent a training program that underpinned its emergence as a professional, European-style force. On February 23, 1778, a former officer in the Prussian army, Friedrich Wilhelm von Steuben, arrived in camp. Like other foreign officers, he had been recommended to Congress by Benjamin Franklin and his fellow American commissioners in Paris, Silas Deane and Arthur Lee. Aided by Franklin's celebrity among Europe's intellectuals for his pioneering work on electricity, they had been lobbying since 1776 to orchestrate French backing for the revolutionaries' struggle against Britain. Unlike many of the military adventurers who preceded him, Steuben was an asset rather than a liability. Following the lead of Lafayette, the "baron" aspired to the rank and pay of major general, but was willing to serve as a volunteer until he had proved his worth. Washington was impressed by Steuben from the outset. One of his own military heroes was Frederick the Great: in 1759, he'd tried in vain to order a bust of "Old Fritz" to ornament Mount Vernon; here was an officer who had actually fought under the great man in his epic clashes with the Austrians, French, and Russians, encounters dutifully chronicled in the *Virginia Gazette*.

To Washington, Steuben's graduation from "the first military school in Europe" along with "his former rank" made him "peculiarly qualified" to fill the post of inspector general left vacant by Conway's resignation. Steuben's daunting task was to impose a single, uniform method of drill—what Washington characterized as "a well combined general system"—upon an army within which each battalion followed its own inclinations. Just months after Steuben's arrival at Valley Forge, a delighted Washington was singing his praises to Henry Laurens. Indeed, Steuben's "knowledge of his profession added to the zeal which he has discovered since he began upon the functions of his office" led Washington to "consider him as an acquisition to the service" and to recommend that Congress forthwith ratify his rank and appointment.[33]

At Valley Forge, Steuben found an army already steeped in British military traditions, which he was reluctantly obliged to accommodate within his own system of drill. Writing to his patron Franklin, after his *Regulations for the Order and Discipline of the Troops of the United States*—the famous "Blue Book"—had been published, the baron apologized that "circumstances have obliged me to deviate from the principles" typically used in European armies. "Young as we are," he explained, "we have already our prejudices as [have] the most ancient nations; the prepossession in favor of the British service, has obliged me to comply with many things which are against my principles." Regrettably, these included the redcoats' characteristic "formation in two ranks," rather than the three used by other nations, including the Prussians. Another veteran of European warfare, Sir Henry Clinton, also disapproved of "the open, flimsy order of two deep in line" adopted by the British in America. Yet when he succeeded William Howe as commander in chief, he kept it all the same: not only had it proved effective enough on the battlefield, but the rebels used it too.[34]

While falling short of his own Germanic ideals, Steuben's training methods, which concentrated upon the essential skills required to maneuver and fight in a disciplined fashion, had a profound impact upon the confidence and effectiveness of the Continental Army; crucially, by exploiting his knowledge of a radically new French drill, Steuben trained his men in a simplified approach to the notoriously tricky business of deploying from column of march to line of battle: to achieve this, unflustered, in the face of the enemy, was the acid test of the true veteran.[35]

An opportunity for the troops to demonstrate their new proficiency on the drill field came in early May, when confirmation arrived that France had formally entered into alliance with the United States. A great parade was staged to celebrate an event that promised to establish American "liberty and Independence upon lasting foundations." On the morning of May 6, all the brigades assembled for a thanksgiving service and general inspection before marching off to form two long lines. After thirteen cannon fired a salute, the infantry began a continuous fire of musketry that rippled along the battalions. Twice repeated, this *feu de joie* was punctuated by "huzzas" to the "King of France, the friendly European powers," and "the American states." Each man was issued a gill of rum to celebrate the occasion. Daniel Morgan's veteran riflemen missed the party: they were ordered to patrol through the night to make sure the redcoats didn't arrive uninvited.[36]

For British strategists, the Franco-American alliance altered the focus of the war: already struggling to suppress a colonial insurrection, they now faced a far wider conflict against the old Bourbon enemy. Its impact upon Germain's priorities was immediate and profound. In late March 1778, Clinton was directed that the main war effort must now be against the French rather than the Americans and therefore switched from the mainland to the Caribbean. He was to send 5,000 redcoats to St. Lucia, and another 3,000 to Florida, which seemed a likely objective for France's traditional ally, Spain, who was soon expected to join the fight against Britain. Meanwhile, Clinton must evacuate Philadelphia and withdraw what was left of his army to New York. In another sure sign of the radical shift in London's objectives, a fresh set of peace commissioners, headed by the Earl of Carlisle, were sent across the Atlantic to open negotiations with the rebels. Empowered to concede anything short of total independence, it only compounded the soldiers' sense of humiliation and betrayal. Jotting in his journal on June 10, a disgusted John Peebles commented: "Alas Britain how art thou fallen."[37] Congress likewise saw the initiative for what it was—a sign of British weakness and desperation—and ignored it.

Although Philadelphia had proved of precious little strategic value to the British, its evacuation after so much hard fighting was a glum prospect for officers already depressed by the resignation of Howe. For all his faults and errors, brave, lazy, uncomplicated Sir William had remained popular with the army's rank and file and most of the officer corps. Clinton was a very different proposition: arrogantly intelligent yet fundamentally insecure. A man who could characterize himself as a "shy bitch" was unlikely to work well with colleagues and subordinates of different temperaments.[38]

Clinton viewed his inherited command as a poisoned chalice but resolved to make the best of things. While obliged to abandon Philadelphia, he decided to delay the dispatch of the detachments earmarked for other fronts until he had reached New York, keeping his seasoned army together for the risky march across New Jersey. Some 3,000 Loyalists who feared the reprisals of returning revolutionaries were put aboard ship, along with stores and German troops deemed too unfit, or unreliable, to complete the punishing cross-country trek. On the morning of June 18, Clinton's army crossed the Delaware River and headed east. Encumbered by a lengthy wagon train, its progress was sluggish. Six days found it no farther than Allentown, just thirty-five miles from Philadelphia. There, in order to avoid a hazardous passage of the Raritan River at Brunswick, Clinton veered northeast, heading for Sandy Hook.

Clinton's lumbering column was shadowed at a respectful distance by Washington's reformed and reinvigorated army. Most of its senior officers were so delighted to see their enemies quit Philadelphia that they felt inclined to let them go unmolested. This group included Charles Lee, who had recently rejoined the army following an exchange of prisoners and resumed his place as senior major general. While still a captive, Lee had sent Washington a detailed plan for reorganizing the "American Army" and simplifying its drill. The latter task had already been undertaken, during Lee's prolonged absence, by Baron Steuben. But Lee's paper also included a pessimistic assessment that was utterly at odds with Washington's vision of his revamped army and its capabilities. To claim that the Americans were now disciplined enough to risk a "decisive action in fair ground" was "talking nonsense," Lee maintained. Rather than subscribe to the "insanity" of seeking battle, they should put their faith in a defensive strategy of "harassing and impeding" the enemy and, if necessary, falling back behind the Susquehanna River. Lee continued to promote his plan when he reached Valley Forge; he was convinced that the British in Philadelphia would soon take the offensive, so obliging the Continental Army to fight on "very dis-advantageous" terms; he couldn't credit that the enemy would "pass through the Jerseys to New York."[39]

Not only did Lee totally misread Clinton's intentions, but his cau-tious, "Fabian," mentality was now badly out of step with the mood of Washington and his more hawkish acolytes—Greene, Wayne, Hamilton, and Lafayette—for whom the enemy's extended column offered a target too tempting to resist. With opinion within the high command divided, however, a vague and potentially danger-ous compromise was reached. At a council of war held at Hopewell Township on June 24, it was decided to avoid "a general action." Instead, a corps of 1,500 men would shadow the British, menacing their flanks and rear and reinforcing "the other Continental troops and militia" who were "already hanging about them." A disgusted Alexander Hamilton identified Lee as the prime mover behind that "sage plan," which "would have done honor to the most honorable society of midwives, and to them only." [40]

That same day, Greene, Lafayette and Wayne all wrote to Wash-ington, making it clear that the council's decision did not truly reflect their own opinions. While agreeing that an unnecessary bat-tle should be avoided, all felt that more should be done than simply harassing Clinton's army. Greene wrote: "I am clearly of opinion for making a serious impression with the light troops—and for hav-ing the army in supporting distance." Like Washington, Greene was aggressive by instinct, and keen to fight. If they allowed the enemy to pass through New Jersey without "attempting any thing upon them," he added, they would always regret it. Lafayette agreed, pushing for the advance detachment to be reinforced to 2,000 or 2,500 "selected men"—enough to engage part of the enemy's force and even beat their "tremendous grenadiers." Wayne also wanted to bolster the detachment, while keeping the main army close enough to the enemy's rear to act swiftly, although not to provoke a major engagement contrary to Washington's wishes. Lieutenant Colonel Hamilton underlined another, and equally pressing, justification for more decisive action: "We feel our personal honor as well as the honor of the army and the good of the service interested, and are heartily desirous to attempt whatever the disposition of our men will second and prudence authorize."[41]

Washington was receptive to these arguments: the vanguard was therefore tripled to more than 5,000 men and placed under Lafayette. Major General Lee, who had been happy to relinquish command of the original, far smaller force to the young Frenchman, now changed his mind: as second in command of the army, he must assume what was "undoubtedly the most honorable command" next to Washington's.[42] On June 27, when the baking sun forced both armies to rest, it was agreed that this swollen vanguard should chivvy Clinton as soon as his march resumed.

Early the next morning, June 28, 1778, the British moved out in two divisions: the first consisting of about 4,000 men and the baggage under General Knyphausen; the second, which followed an hour or so later, numbered another 6,000 troops led by Clinton. Alerted to this movement, Lee's detachment crossed a series of three ravines to attack the British rear guard near Monmouth Court House. The Americans were soon in trouble. The tail of the snaking British column, commanded by the omnipotent and ever-aggressive Cornwallis, delivered a lethal sting. It comprised the army's best units: Guards, grenadiers, light infantry, and light dragoons. These crack troops riposted effectively, and as Clinton swiftly reinforced them, Lee's outnumbered force was pushed back. Those who grudgingly retreated included Private Joseph Plumb Martin. As he and his comrades were taking a breather while the artillery negotiated a muddy defile, Washington suddenly rode up on his "old English charger," surrounded by his staff. Martin heard him ask "by whose orders the troops were retreating." When told that Lee was responsible, Washington said something else, but, as he was riding forward, Martin didn't catch his words. Men nearer to the general heard him say "damn him." Mild as this might seem, it was an unusual outburst from the typically restrained Washington: Private Martin remarked that such language was certainly "very unlike" him, although, as he "seemed at the instant to be in a great passion," his looks conveyed exactly the same sentiments.[43] Moving on toward the enemy, Washington soon encountered Lee in person. In a rare explosion of temper, he apparently subjected him to a verbal flaying, then, regaining his composure, calmly set about restoring order; for once, Lee was lost for words, cowed by the Virginian's uncharacteristic rage.[44]

Besides Lee's advance guard there were about 6,000 men in the main body of Washington's army, so the odds remained even—provided they would stand and fight. Now, as at Princeton, Washington's inspiring, personal leadership was crucial in ensuring that they did. His aide Alexander Hamilton wrote admiringly: "By his own good sense and fortitude he turned the fate of the day." In a dig at Horatio Gates, whose victory at Saratoga was attributed by many to the courageous battlefield leadership of Benedict Arnold, Hamilton added that Washington had not let another man win his laurels for him, "but by his own presence, he brought order out of confusion, animated his troops and led them to success." Another Washington devotee, Major General Greene was equally certain that his intervention was decisive: "The commander-in-chief was every where, his presence gave spirit and confidence and his command and authority soon brought everything into order and regularity."[45]

Arraying his Continentals in a strong defensive position on high ground behind the most westerly ravine, and with powerful support from well-sited artillery, Washington rebuffed a succession of determined but poorly coordinated British assaults. With casualties mounting and dozens of men dropping dead from heat exhaustion alone, Clinton broke off the fight. Washington's soldiers were exultant at facing "the flower of the British army" in open battle. Their discipline had prevented Lee's withdrawal from escalating into a general rout and vindicated Steuben's training regime at Valley

Forge. That fair-minded professional Captain Ewald conceded: "Today the Americans showed much boldness and resolution on all sides during their attacks."[46]

In his General Orders of June 29, Washington congratulated his army "on the victory obtained over the arms of his Britannic Majesty yesterday," while a brief dispatch to Henry Laurens reported how the enemy had been "forced . . . from the field."[47] Yet the Battle of Monmouth Court House was an indecisive affair, in which neither side could truly claim a clear-cut success: Washington had failed to destroy or even deflect Clinton's column, and on June 29, it continued on its way without further interruption, reaching Sandy Hook on July 1 to rendezvous with Lord Howe's fleet. By July 6, Clinton's troops were all safely inside the fortifications of Manhattan.

If Monmouth—the last major engagement to be fought in the war's northern theater—failed to deliver the unambiguous battle-field victory that Washington still wanted, it was decisive in another sense, by eliminating his sole remaining rival within the Continental Army. In the immediate aftermath of the battle, while still smarting from Washington's stinging public rebuke, General Lee penned three notes to him in quick succession, the last of them demanding a court-martial to clear his name. Washington acquiesced and, given Lee's intemperate choice of language, added a charge of disrespect to counts of failing to engage the enemy and "making an unnecessary, disorderly and shameful retreat."[48] Evidence was heard over several weeks as the army marched toward a new position on the Lower Hudson. The court's verdict, delivered on August 12, was unanimous: Lee was found guilty on all three charges. Although the first could have brought a death sentence, he was merely suspended from service for a year.[49]

While Lee was clearly guilty of disrespect toward Washington, the other two crimes laid to his charge were by no means proven. Yet, as historian John Shy has pointed out, an acquittal on *them* would have been tantamount to a vote of no-confidence in Washington;[50] the surprising leniency of Lee's sentence certainly supports this interpretation. Interestingly, vindication for Lee's withdrawal at

Monmouth came from his opponent. Henry Clinton did not doubt that, if Lee had stood his ground, "his whole corps would probably have fallen into the power of the King's army," long before Washington's force could have succored him.[51]

Incensed at what he considered to be unjust treatment, Lee refused to accept his fate and keep quiet, instead attacking Washington and his inner circle in the press. This so incensed Washington's aide John Laurens that he challenged Lee to a duel. The Englishman had already shrugged off similar invitations from Wayne and Steuben, who both felt that he had disparaged them while publicly defending his own conduct at Monmouth. But Laurens was more persistent, and Lee finally agreed to accept. When they fought with pistols in a field outside Philadelphia, Lee sustained a flesh wound; both combatants were ready to continue, but their seconds persuaded them that honor had been satisfied.[52] Lee never returned to the Continental Army. On balance, this was just as well: as his behavior after Monmouth confirmed, whatever his merits as a general officer—and these are by no means clear from his service record—Lee was disqualified from high command by his cantankerous character. Even Lee's most ardent admirers, men like Benjamin Rush, conceded that his "knowledge and experience" was offset by "his oddities or vices." Given his volatile personality, it is hard to imagine him ever working loyally under Washington, let alone providing an alternative figurehead for a concerted revolutionary war effort.[53]

For the British, meanwhile, Henry Clinton's return to New York City proved timely. Less than a week later, on July 11, the French alliance bore fruit when Vice Admiral Charles-Hector, Comte d'Estaing, appeared off Sandy Hook with a formidable fleet of sixteen "ships of the line"; these powerful vessels, typically with two gun decks in North American waters, were so designated because of their ability to join the formal lines of battle in which rival fleets customarily fought each other. Outgunned and undermanned, Lord Howe's ships stayed safe within New York Harbor, denying d'Estaing the chance to inflict a decisive defeat. While more than 2,000 privateering craft sailed under American colors

during the Revolutionary War, creating havoc among British merchantmen, the official Continental Navy never amounted to above
a score of single-deck frigates, often commanded by dashing
officers capable of fighting morale-boosting ship-to-ship actions
but insignificant in broader strategic terms. The appearance of
d'Estaing's formidable squadron therefore gave a hefty jolt to the
balance of sea power: while William Howe's land operations had
been conducted confident in the knowledge that his brother's warships dominated North American waters, Henry Clinton enjoyed
no such guarantee.[54]

Acutely aware of d'Estaing's significance, Washington took
pains to welcome him and to give assurances that he would spare
no effort to foster a "cordial and lasting amity" between the new
allies.[55] With the British still too strong at New York, d'Estaing and
Washington instead resolved to strike at Newport, Rhode Island.
Its garrison of 3,000 British, Germans, and Loyalist provincial troops offered a seemingly soft target. At the end of July the
French fleet entered Narragansett Bay; soon after, Major General
John Sullivan was menacing the British garrison with 10,000 men,
mostly militia but with a stiffening of Continental regiments. All
looked set for an overwhelming combined assault by land and sea
when the indefatigable "Black Dick" Howe unexpectedly arrived
off Newport on August 9 with a reinforced fleet. D'Estaing sailed
out to meet him, but a gale kept the rivals apart. Meanwhile, the
dogged Sullivan pushed on with his siegeworks. On August 14, an
attack was repulsed, and the dejected militia began to disband. By
now d'Estaing, too, was keen to depart and refit his damaged ships
in Boston before Howe sought another battle. Sullivan's appeals
could not dissuade him. Bitterly disappointed at this "betrayal,"
the New Englander couldn't contain his disappointment. When he
was forced to lift the siege, the garrison staged a sally to help him
on his way; on September 1, 1778, Howe's ships brought Clinton
with a relief force of 4,000 men from New York. It was a shambolic
start to the Franco-American alliance and a clear reminder that,
even with the entrance of the French, sea power remained in the

balance, dependent upon the resolution of local commanders, the commitment of resources, and the fickleness of the wind.

No less disappointed than Sullivan, but far more diplomatic in his reaction, Washington worked to minimize any long-term damage. Having fought the French as a young man, he knew as well as anyone that old enmities still lurked just beneath the surface: they must be smothered for the greater good of the cause. As he wrote to the crestfallen Nathanael Greene, who'd eagerly joined the expedition to reconquer his birthplace and who distinguished himself during the fighting withdrawal, while the campaign's failure was regrettable, "a still worse consequence" would be the sowing of "seeds of dissention and distrust between us and our new allies." Given the "universal clamor" against the French—which had triggered murderous brawls in Boston—the tactful Greene was to exert himself to pacify d'Estaing, "heal all private animosities," and stifle "all illiberal expressions and reflections" from American officers that threatened to scupper the alliance.[56]

Clinton sought to exploit his enemy's embarrassment and the local superiority of Howe's fleet by taking the offensive. Under the command of Major General "No Flint" Grey, the Newport relief force was sent to raid the New England coast, burning New Bedford and rounding up cattle on Martha's Vineyard. Some hard-line British officers, the "fire and sword men," approved of such devastation and believed more of the same would bring the rebels to heel; others saw the raids as futile, even counterproductive.[57] Eager to land a telling blow while he still commanded the men soon to be siphoned off to other battle fronts, Clinton now proposed attacking Boston and destroying the French fleet sheltering there. When Lord Howe vetoed the plan as too risky, Clinton sought to provoke a decisive engagement with Washington's army encamped amid the hills north of Manhattan. But when a powerful British force entered New Jersey, Washington resurrected the Fabian strategy that he had used against Howe for much of the previous year, refusing to be enticed from his strong ground. During the winter of 1778–79, Washington's army was quartered in an arc above Manhattan, with concentrations at Danbury in Connecticut, West Point in the Hudson Highlands, and Middlebrook, New Jersey.[58]

Meanwhile, direct French intervention had prompted Congress to revive its long-cherished plans to invade Canada. While he had backed such an offensive in 1775, Washington now opposed it, and on good grounds. In an official letter to Congress, sent on November 11, 1778, he emphasized the notorious logistical problem of pushing troops across the intervening wilderness. But in a private letter, sent three days later to his friend the president of Congress Henry Laurens, Washington revealed that his real misgivings concerned the motives of his French allies. Alarmed "for the true and permanent interests" of his country, Washington feared the consequences of sending a French army into what was until recently a Bourbon possession—"attached to them by all the ties of blood, habits, manners, religion." Displaying his firm grasp of political realities, he told Laurens: "I fear this would be too great a temptation to be resisted by any power actuated by the common maxims of national policy." For Americans, the ramifications of a rebuilt New France were frightening to contemplate: with her Spanish relatives in possession of New Orleans and controlling the Mississippi River and well-disposed tribes of Indians arching along the western frontier between the two Bourbon territories, France would "have it in her power to give law to these states." Although "heartily disposed" to think the best of America's new ally, he added that "it is a maxim founded on the universal experience of mankind, that no nation is to be trusted farther than it is bound by its interest, and no prudent statesman or politician will venture to depart from it."[59]

When the French and Americans next acted together, the objective could not have been more distant from Canada; their presence in Georgia, the most southerly rebel state, resulted from a significant shift in British operations. In early November 1778, Clinton had reluctantly embarked the hefty detachments that Germain demanded, a development, as he dolefully informed the American Secretary, which would preclude future offensives by his own main army. The increasingly despondent Clinton had already tendered his resignation, without success. Tied to a command he no longer wanted, Sir Henry still sought to use his limited resources on other fronts. When Germain had first recommended the abandonment of Philadelphia, he had also suggested a southern expedition to exploit the reportedly strong Loyalist sentiments in Georgia and the Carolinas. Clinton acted on that recommendation, sending a capable officer, Lieutenant Colonel Archibald Campbell, with 3,000 men, including his own 71st Regiment of Highlanders, to reconquer Georgia. When Campbell's force landed, shortly before Christmas 1778, resistance was insignificant. On December 29, Savannah fell to the British, and in January 1779, Augusta followed suit. Campbell's successor, Brigadier General Augustine Prevost, aimed a stroke at Charleston, South Carolina, but was obliged to turn back after Congress's new commander in the Southern Department, Major General Benjamin Lincoln, headed north from Georgia to relieve the port.

While the British were making headway in Georgia, d'Estaing had been preoccupied in the Caribbean. A soldier before turning sailor, on St. Lucia he returned to his old trade, encountering the veteran redcoats that Clinton had sent from New York under the ubiquitous Major General James Grant. These troops soon demonstrated the combat skills they had acquired in more than two years of tough campaigning against the American rebels. On December 18, 1778, a single brigade of 1,300 men under Brigadier General William Medows successfully defended the brushwood-covered peninsula of The Vigie against a determined attack by 5,000 French regulars. In "this Bunker Hill of the Caribbean," which gave a taste of things to come in Spain and Portugal thirty years later, the thin red line shredded the oncoming assault columns, with round shot and canister from four heavy eighteen-pounder cannon increasing the carnage: the British suffered 171 casualties, the French a staggering 1,600, including 400 killed.[60] When they finally arrived, tidings of this brilliant success over the old enemy heartened Clinton's troops now watching Washington's army from Manhattan. In his diary Captain Peebles noted approvingly: "Well done little Meadows. He licked them handsomely."[61]

That summer, Clinton still hoped to tempt Washington into a decisive engagement. He calculated that a drive against the American forts guarding the strategically vital Highlands on the Hudson River—the same objectives that he'd briefly, captured and then reluctantly relinquished in October 1777—would draw Washington's army from its current position in New Jersey. When Stony Point and Verplanck's Point were both seized on June 1, 1779, so threatening to rupture the Americans' communications with New England, Washington shifted troops to bolster the newly erected fortifications farther north, overlooking the Hudson at West Point, but once again avoided battle. Meanwhile, Sir Henry tried another ploy, sending Major General Tryon to raid the coast of Connecticut. Tryon fulfilled his task with a zeal that exceeded Clinton's orders: between July 5 and July 11, New Haven, Fairfield, and Norwalk were all torched. Although Washington ordered troops to Connecticut, he refused to fall into Clinton's trap by marching his main army into New England.

Instead, Washington struck back by authorizing a surprise attack on Stony Point. The mission was entrusted to the aggressive and flamboyant Brigadier General Anthony Wayne. Like the redcoats of "No Flint" Grey who had inflicted such a stinging defeat on his Pennsylvanians at Paoli, by Washington's specific order Wayne was to attack "with fixed bayonets and muskets unloaded." His command consisted of "chosen men" drawn from the light infantry companies that each Continental regiment had been ordered to form in May 1778; following British Army practice, these elite units were temporarily brigaded together. On July 15, 1779, they justified their privileged status, swiftly overpowering Stony Point's garrison: at a cost of fifteen killed and eighty-five wounded, including Wayne himself, the Americans slew sixty-three redcoats, wounded another seventy, and took 442 prisoners. An elated Wayne reported that his light infantry had "behaved like men who are determined to be free."[62]

Shaken by this coup, Clinton immediately recalled Tryon's command, while Washington ordered the destruction of the fortifications at Stony Point and fell back. Soon after, on August 19, the Americans deepened Clinton's depression with another daring hit-and-run raid that further demonstrated the Continental Army's growing élan. This time the blow fell against the post of Paulus Hook, on the New Jersey shore within cannon shot of New York City. In a well-planned and audacious operation conducted by the Virginian Major Henry Lee—father of the legendary Confederate commander Robert E. Lee—another 150 prisoners were taken. As Washington appreciated, while "small on the great scale" such exploits increased his army's confidence, while disgracing the enemy.[63] In their wake the disheartened Clinton once again tendered his resignation: as before, Germain refused to accept it.

During the summer of 1779, while Washington's main army fenced warily with Clinton on the Lower Hudson, a substantial detachment was sent to the northwest to punish Britain's allies among the Six Nations of the Iroquois, who had unleashed destructive raids on the frontiers of New York and Pennsylvania during the previous year. While the Iroquois contribution to Burgoyne's 1777 campaign had proved short lived and ultimately insignificant, their attacks in 1778 had a far greater impact on the revolutionary cause, not simply terrorizing settlers, but destroying rich farmlands crucial for feeding the Continental Army. They had also highlighted the stark difference between the European-style war being fought on the eastern seaboard and the less-restrained conflict characteristic of the western frontiers. That dichotomy was brought home to Captain Ewald of the Hessian jägers one evening in June 1779 after "a captain of the Indians," who had served with the Loyalist rangers led by Colonel John Butler and the Mohawk chief Joseph Brant, reached the British lines in the Hudson Highlands. This mixed-race warrior, whose father was an English-born gunsmith among the Iroquois, had participated in the notorious raid on the Wyoming Valley in July 1778. It had been a gory business: "I had worked so hard with my tomahawk and scalping knife that my arms were bloody above the elbows," he told his listeners. Asked why Colonel Butler hadn't prevented such cruelties, the warrior patiently explained another reality of frontier warfare that had been clear to French officers operating alongside the Shawnees and Delawares in the 1750s: had Butler dared to "meddle" with the Indians' "customs and laws," they would have taken umbrage and deserted him instantly. According to the Indians' ways, he added, enemy officers never received quarter. If taken alive, such war leaders faced death by torture. Indeed, one rebel major was subjected to a three-day ordeal, "during which the Indians danced continually around this poor fellow among their prisoners of war. Since he was a brave and distinguished soldier, they shouted to him that he should now act like a man at the end of his life." Appalled, yet clearly fascinated at this insight into a parallel world of war at its most savage, Ewald noted that the narrator's "heart seemed to rejoice with this tale."[64]

In fact, Ewald had already experienced something of the ferocity of frontier-style warfare at first hand. During the previous summer, he and his jägers had cooperated with Loyalist cavalry in mounting a devastating ambush near Philips's Manor, New York. The victims were Massachusetts Continentals and a band of Mahican Indians from Stockbridge in the same state. As Ewald acknowledged, it had been a "hot fight" in heavily wooded terrain, with the cornered Americans—white and Indian alike—defending themselves "like brave men." After about three hours, many of them were dead, either dropped by the jägers' rifles, or cut down by the dragoons. It was an unusually ruthless engagement. Ewald noted: "No Indians, especially, received quarter . . . save for a few." When he later walked over the ground, the curious Ewald examined the dead Mahicans and was impressed by "their sinewy and muscular bodies" and their expressions, which testified "that they had perished with resolution"; they put him in mind of his own Germanic ancestors under Arminius, who had massacred the legions of Varus in AD 9. A dedicated soldier, but clearly a humane man, Ewald wrote nothing of why the Stockbridge warriors should be virtually annihilated, while about fifty of their white comrades were spared and taken prisoner. The mere fact that they were Indians was apparently sufficient explanation: the bloody episode suggests that even when tribal fighters operated far from the frontiers and alongside "conventional" forces, they were deemed to fall outside the customary "Rules of War" and treated without mercy.[65]

Washington's punitive expedition to exact retribution upon the Iroquois was commanded by the conscientious, if conspicuously unlucky, Major General Sullivan. As Washington knew from his own hard experience, Indian fighting was a chancy and unpredictable business, and he gave Sullivan detailed advice intended to minimize the risk of another Braddock-style fiasco. Above all, he was to maintain the aggressive initiative. Sullivan should "make rather than receive attacks, attended with as much impetuosity, shouting and noise as possible, and to make the troops act in as loose and dispersed a way as is consistent with a proper degree of government, concert and mutual support." Mimicking the celebrated tactics of his old colleague Henri Bouquet, developed during the Forbes campaign of 1758 and tested at Bushy Run in 1763, Washington urged that "wherever they have an opportunity," Sullivan's men should "rush on with the war whoop and fixed bayonet: nothing will disconcert and terrify the Indians more than this." While Washington had shunned a plundering, destructive war in the east and deplored Tryon's recent coastal raids on New England, the western frontier was a different matter. Against "savage" Indians, there was no need for civility or restraint. Sullivan's object must be the utter devastation of the Indian settlements: indeed, Washington emphasized, these should "not be merely *overrun* but *destroyed*"; there could be no negotiation "until the total ruin of their settlements is effected." If the Indians then showed some "disposition for peace," they should be required to prove their sincerity by delivering up such "principal instigators of their past hostility" as Butler and Brant.[66]

Although marked down for vengeance, Joseph Brant, or Thayendanegea, had sought to minimize the sufferings of the frontier settlers; despite his "savage" background, he, too, exemplified the qualities of gentleman and warrior that Washington prized. Among the most remarkable of all Native American leaders, Brant was a protégé of Britain's influential Indian superintendent, Sir William

Johnson, and in 1758, while aged about fifteen, had accompanied him to fight the French at Ticonderoga. After schooling in New Hampshire, in late 1775, Brant had traveled to England as part of a delegation intended to secure British backing to guarantee the integrity of tribal lands against the incursions of the American revolutionaries. In London the dignified and articulate Mohawk became the toast of the town. He was interviewed by James Boswell for an article in the *London Magazine*, and his portrait was painted by the leading society artist George Romney; it would be painted again in 1786 by none other than Gilbert Stuart, later to achieve acclaim for his iconic likenesses of President Washington. By August 1776, Brant was with the British forces poised off New York and struck up an enduring friendship with a kindred spirit, the aristocratic and chivalrous General Hugh, Lord Percy.[67]

As a guest aboard the *Eagle*, Brant also won the admiration of Lord Howe's personal secretary, Ambrose Serle, who noted that he "was remarkably easy and sensible in his discourse," expressing "an air of gravity, which rendered it to me the more engaging. His remarks were pertinent, and bespoke a strong natural understanding." Serle was especially impressed that Brant had "translated [a] great part of the English New Testament into the Mohawk language." Indeed, in Serle's opinion, Brant and a fellow chief were "abundantly less savages" and "more refined and more sensible than half at least of our ship's company."[68]

To tackle Brant's people, Sullivan was given an army of 2,500 veteran Continentals, supplemented by artillery and militia: about 4,000 in all. He proceeded with caution, and on August 29, defeated a force of outgunned Iroquois warriors and Loyalist rangers at Newtown. When they fell back to the British fort at Niagara on the Canadian border, the Iroquois heartlands—the Mohawk Valley and Genesee Country—lay undefended. Following Washington's instructions, which reflected the strategy used against the Cherokees by James Grant in 1761, Sullivan implemented a systematic scorched-earth policy that destroyed the Iroquois cornfields and villages. Reporting the results of Sullivan's "plan of chastisement" to Lafayette in September, Washington believed it would convince the Iroquois that their "cruelties are not to pass with impunity" and that they had been incited to "acts of barbarism by a nation which is unable to protect them." Sullivan had "burnt between 15 and 20 towns," along with "their crops and every thing that was to be found," sending the inhabitants "fleeing in the utmost confusion, consternation and distress towards Niagara, distant 100 miles through an uninhabited wilderness."[69]

As the Seneca chief Cornplanter reminded Washington a decade later, by authorizing this comprehensive devastation, he had given new resonance to his old Indian name: "When your army entered the country of the Six Nations," Cornplanter told him, "we called you Town Destroyer; and to this day, when that name is heard, our women look behind them and turn pale and our children cling close to the neck of their mothers."[70] Although Sullivan's expedition avenged Iroquois depredations, it did not cow the Six Nations' warriors: incensed by their losses and increasingly reliant upon British support, in both 1780 and 1781, they fell upon the New York frontier with renewed fury.

For all its ferocity, this ongoing Indian war remained distinct from operations on the eastern seaboard. There, the strategic situation had undergone a dramatic and, for Washington, perplexing shift. Requested to help Congress's commander in the Southern Department—Major General Benjamin Lincoln—d'Estaing returned from the Caribbean and by September 1, 1779, was anchored off the Georgian coast. He'd no intention of lingering, but as long as the West Indian hurricane season ruled out further operations there, he was willing to join a Franco-American offensive against Savannah. On September 12, he landed 4,500 troops; combined with Lincoln's army of about 3,000, they surrounded Prevost's outnumbered garrison. But the siege moved slowly—far too slowly for d'Estaing, whose crews rapidly succumbed to sickness. When a bombardment failed to intimidate Prevost and his men, d'Estaing boldly resolved to storm the city's defenses; always a risky undertaking, this decision went against the advice of a majority of officers. Like Washington's cautious counselors during the siege of Boston, they were right to be wary. When the assault was launched on October 9, it was beaten back with more than 800 casualties; d'Estaing himself was seriously wounded. Although Lincoln wished to continue operations, d'Estaing had no desire to stay in Georgia. The siege was lifted on October 18, 1779. For a second time, direct French intervention had failed utterly to deliver the expected results.

That September, after first intelligence arrived of d'Estaing's appearance off Savannah, Clinton had gathered all of his available forces in New York City, evacuating Newport, Rhode Island, and his remaining posts in the Hudson Highlands. While these withdrawals indicated that a fresh British offensive in the north was unlikely, this massing of manpower nonetheless made it possible for Clinton to contemplate a strike elsewhere. Building upon the tidings of d'Estaing's total defeat, on Boxing Day 1779, Clinton set sail from New York with 7,600 men: his objective was Charleston, South Carolina, where he had been thwarted so ignominiously by Charles Lee in 1776. If South Carolina was restored to Crown control, Lord George Germain now believed, it could become the base for a British thrust northward, harnessing resurgent Loyalists to methodically overrun and pacify the remaining rebel states.

Although he longed to attack New York—the hub of British strength in America since the summer of 1776, and the scene of his own most humiliating defeats as commander of the Continental Army—Washington was powerless to exploit the absence of Clinton and thousands of his men far to the south. He was reduced to inactivity by a formidable combination of circumstances that were all beyond his control. The winter of 1779–80 was the coldest on record, and his army's sojourn at Jockey Hollow, near Morristown, New Jersey (the same ground where it had quartered in January 1777, after Princeton), proved unremittingly grim, worse even than Valley Forge. On December 16, 1779, just days after occupying his new winter quarters, Washington sent a blunt circular letter to the states. The army's supply situation was "beyond description alarming," with all its magazines bare and the commissaries lacking the cash or credit to replenish them, he wrote. His troops had already been on half rations for five or six weeks; there was scarcely enough bread for three more days, and once that was gone they must glean the surrounding countryside. In the past there had been temporary glitches caused by "accidental delays in forwarding supplies," Washington added, but this latest crisis was different in magnitude: "We have never experienced a like extremity at any period of the war," he warned. Without "extraordinary exertions" by the states from which the army drew its supplies, it must "infallibly disband in a fortnight."[71]

The crisis was exacerbated by the unrelenting weather. Snowstorms were bad enough for poorly clad, shivering soldiers obliged to shelter under canvas until they had built ramshackle huts, but the deep drifts that soon accumulated also made the region's roads impassable for supply wagons. Once local depots were emptied, there would be no prospect of relief from farther afield for weeks to come. Yet with the economy undergoing financial meltdown, local farmers refused to sell their surplus produce for the drastically depreciated Continental dollars. By the onset of 1780, Washington's ravenous Continentals were plundering surrounding farmsteads of whatever they could find. Washington was well aware of the dire consequences of such pilfering for his army's discipline and also for its precarious base of civilian support but, given the genuine distress of his men, hesitated to punish them. To prevent an escalation of marauding, Washington appealed to the county magistrates of New Jersey to impose requisitions of cattle and grain. Given the urgency of the situation, he had no doubt that the specified quotas would be delivered voluntarily: if not, they would be taken by force. According to Dr. James Thacher, Washington's uncompromising invitation was "attended with the happiest success," yielding sufficient supplies to save "the army from destruction."[72]

But this respite was temporary. With their bellies soon empty again, Washington's desperate veterans continued to scour the vicinity for any morsel. General Orders of January 28, 1780 announced that Washington would no longer excuse "the plundering and

licentious spirit of the soldiery"; according to the outraged magistrates, scarcely a night passed "without gangs of soldiers going
out of camp and committing every species of robbery, depredation
and the grossest personal insults." For the future, any man found
straggling beyond the sentries after retreat beating risked a hundred lashes on the spot; those detected in robbery or violence might
receive up to *five hundred* lashes, at the discretion of the officer of
the guard.[73] The situation was so desperate that Washington was
now prepared to exceed the penalties laid down in the army's *Articles of War*. As Dr. Thacher testified, during the crackdown, heavy
floggings were inflicted, although many of the recipients made a
point of receiving "the severest stripes without uttering a groan, or
once shrinking from the lash." Thacher attributed this to "stubbornness or pride"—along with the men's habit of chewing a lead bullet
"while under the lash, till it is made quite flat and jagged."[74]

Like the harsh weather, the supply crisis continued well into the
spring of 1780. When Joseph Plumb Martin of the Connecticut Continentals arrived in camp in late May, he once again encountered
his familiar companion, "the monster hunger." For several days
after rejoining the main army, Martin and his comrades "got a little
musty bread," with "a little beef about every other day": but before
long, he recalled bitterly, "we got nothing at all." Now "exasperated
beyond endurance," such veterans faced a stark choice: starve to
death or quit the army and go home. It was a cruel dilemma for men
who, Martin maintained, were "truly patriotic," who "loved their
country" and had already suffered "every thing short of death in its
cause." Their discontent finally erupted on May 25. According to
Private Martin, after a day spent "growling like sore headed dogs,"
by evening roll call the soldiers were showing their teeth, defiantly
back-talking their officers and ignoring orders. When the adjutant
of Martin's regiment called one of the men "a mutinous rascal," his
comrades spontaneously turned out and formed up on the parade
ground beside him in a menacing show of solidarity. In an ensuing
brawl, several officers were roughed up, and Colonel Return Jonathan Meigs of the 6th Connecticut Regiment was wounded with a

bayonet. The outbreak was contained before it could escalate by a timely issue of provisions and the arrival of steady Pennsylvanian troops but nonetheless served warning that many seasoned Continentals were nearing the end of their patience with Congress.[75]

This latest crisis had barely subsided when Washington received news of a shattering patriot defeat in the south. There Clinton's switch of front had yielded spectacular dividends. On February 11, 1780 his storm-lashed force was within striking distance of its objective, Charleston. General Lincoln awaited Clinton's advance within the port's fortifications. On the night of April 1–2, the British began digging their siege lines. Enduring heavy bombardment, and with his escape route cut, Lincoln was ready to surrender the city on condition that he and his army went free. Disinclined to haggle, Clinton offered the alternatives of unconditional surrender or a bloody storm. Pressurized by Charleston's skittish citizens, on May 12, Lincoln capitulated. Some 2,500 Continentals—virtually the entire regular army of the Southern Department—became prisoners of war, while hundreds of captured militiamen were released on parole. Captain Peebles of the 42nd described the Continentals as a "ragged dirty looking set of people as usual, but [with] more appearance of discipline than what we have seen formerly." Some of their officers were "decent looking men"; they included another "old acquaintance" of Peebles from happier days, Colonel Nathaniel Gist of the 3rd Virginian Continentals, the son of Washington's wilderness guide, Christopher.[76] The fall of Charleston was an American defeat to rival Fort Washington, and it kindled British hopes that the revived southern strategy might yet hold the key to victory. Warned of the approach of a fresh French expeditionary force and fearing for his New York garrison, Clinton returned north on June 8, 1780 with 4,000 men, leaving Lord Cornwallis to continue the reconquest of the south.

In the north, by contrast, the strategic situation remained stagnated. Even the arrival of the long-anticipated French fleet, which decanted 5,500 regular troops onto Rhode Island in mid-July, failed to break the deadlock. Although the French general, Jean-Baptiste

Donatien de Vimeur, Comte de Rochambeau, would fall under Washington's orders, his naval colleague Commodore the Chevalier de Ternay held an independent command; this meant that he could veto any joint operations that the French disliked.[77] As Ternay's fleet had been promptly blockaded in Newport by the Royal Navy, obliging Rochambeau to summon help from the New England militia to reinforce the defenses, there was clearly no immediate prospect for a new Franco-American offensive, whether against New York, or anywhere else.

The fifty-five-year-old Rochambeau was an experienced officer with a distinguished record of service in both the War of the Austrian Succession and the Seven Years' War. From the outset, Washington set about building a professional relationship with him and his countrymen. As he spoke no French himself, he used his trusted confidant Lafayette as a go-between: "All the information he gives and all the propositions he makes," he told the French commander, "I entreat you will consider as coming from me." Mindful of the tensions and resentments that had followed the collapse of the Franco-American attempt upon Rhode Island two years before, in announcing the arrival of Rochambeau's force, Washington's General Orders expressed a hope that "the only contention" between the Americans and the troops of His Most Christian Majesty would be to "excel each other in good offices and in the display of every military virtue."[78]

That summer brought more bleak tidings from the south. Against Washington's advice, Congress sent Horatio Gates to assume command in that troubled sector. On August 16, 1780, the victor of Saratoga suffered a crushing defeat at Camden, South Carolina. Faced with Cornwallis's veterans, Gates blundered by forming his entire left wing of militia, without the customary backbone of Continentals. The militia fled immediately, many without even firing their weapons, although the Continentals on the right staged a stubborn stand before being outflanked and broken; their bravery cost them dear, and the slain included the tough Bavarian veteran Baron de Kalb. One survivor, Colonel Otho Williams of the 6th Maryland

Regiment, blamed the utter rout upon the "infamous cowardice of the militia of Virginia and North Carolina [which] gave the enemy every advantage over our few regular troops." To Alexander Hamilton, Camden demonstrated "the necessity of changing our system" and eschewing amateur soldiers: Gates's "passion for militia, I fancy will be a little cured, and he will cease to think them the best bulwark of American liberty," he wrote.[79]

For Washington, too, "the late disaster in Carolina" bolstered his consistent argument that it was fatal to depend upon militia. Writing to the latest president of Congress, Samuel Huntington, he rammed home the old message yet again: "Regular troops alone are equal to the exigencies of modern war, as well for defense as offence." While useful as "light troops to be scattered in the woods and plague rather than do serious injury to the enemy," militia could never acquire the "firmness requisite for the real business of fighting": *that* prized quality "could only be attained by a constant course of discipline and service."[80] In fact, as Washington's trusty subordinates in the south would soon demonstrate, provided their limitations were recognized, militiamen had the potential to complement the Continentals, not simply as hovering skirmishers, but in set-piece engagements.

Building upon his success, Cornwallis marched into North Carolina, once again chasing the chimera of active Loyalist support. On September 26, he reached Charlotte, pausing to give his weary troops a breather. Meanwhile, to the west, Major Patrick Ferguson—the same officer who'd had Washington in his sights at Brandywine three years earlier—was advancing toward Charlotte at the head of a force of Loyalist provincials and militia. But the wild backcountry of the Carolinas was a hostile environment for Crown sympathizers: on October 7, Ferguson's little army, which had taken up a defensive position on King's Mountain, was overwhelmed by Tennessee backwoodsmen in a pitiless encounter. The gallant Ferguson died in a hail of rifle balls, along with many of his men; the major's body was treated with unmerited disrespect, with the victors taking turns to urinate upon it.[81] Some survivors were singled out for summary execution. Small in scale, King's Mountain epitomized the brutality and vindictiveness of what had become a virtual civil war in the south—exactly the kind of unrestrained irregular conflict that Washington had been so keen to avoid elsewhere.

Back in New York after his Charleston triumph, Clinton faced his own share of frustrations in 1780. Still in aggressive mode, he had wanted to attack Rochambeau's infantry on Rhode Island, but his curmudgeonly naval colleague, Lord Howe's successor, Vice Admiral Marriot Arbuthnot, was lukewarm, and the strike was canceled. In addition, an advance by Washington toward King's Bridge—the route from Manhattan Island to the mainland—gave cause for caution. On September 14, a far more dynamic sailor than Arbuthnot, Admiral Sir George Brydges Rodney, reached New York bringing ten more ships of the line. Unlike Arbuthnot, Rodney was game to join Clinton's redcoats in a crack at the French. But by now the mercurial Clinton had changed *his* mind: with all the delays, the enemy had fortified themselves too strongly to justify an attack.

Still adjusting to their new surroundings, Rochambeau and his naval partner Ternay were determined to maintain a defensive stance. At a strategic summit held at Hartford, Connecticut, on September 20–22, 1780, Washington secured their agreement to his contention that "of all the enterprises which may be undertaken, the most important and decisive is the reduction of New York, which is the center and focus of all the British forces." However, his suggestion that the French land and sea forces should separate, with the fleet heading for Boston and the troops reinforcing the American army above Manhattan, was rejected, Rochambeau and Ternay "observing that they had pointed instructions from their court for the fleet and army to support each other." In an admission that boded ill for future allied operations, Versailles had ordered that the French troops should be confined "as much as possible on islands," so minimizing friction with "American citizens." Even the incentive of a joint "winter expedition to Canada"—a prospect that Washington had only recently regarded with horror—failed to excite Rochambeau: before "concerting" any such plan he must consult the ministry in France, "as he imagined there might be some political objections to the measure." In short, there would be no offensive that year.[82]

Meanwhile, Clinton's gaze had been drawn inexorably back to his perennial objective, the rugged Hudson Highlands. Sir Henry's latest plan to seize them hatched one of the most notorious and remarkable episodes in the American Revolutionary War, which affected both him and Washington more profoundly than any other. It hinged upon the treason of the revolutionary hero Major General Benedict Arnold, now commandant of the crucial fortifications at West Point. In an act of breathtaking duplicity, the discontented Arnold agreed to sell his post to the British for £20,000 and the rank of general in the royal service.

Since early 1779, as he informed Germain, Clinton had been given reason to believe that Arnold was "desirous of quitting the rebel service and joining the cause of Great Britain" owing to his "displeasure at the alliance between France and America." Under a false identity, Arnold embarked upon a secret correspondence that yielded "most material intelligence," dangling the tantalizing information that he expected to be "employed in the American service" in an important role and was willing to surrender himself "under every possible advantage to His Majesty's arms." In July 1780, when Arnold gained command of 4,000 men and all the rebel forts in the Hudson Highlands, Clinton put two and two together: not only was Arnold the mysterious correspondent, he concluded, but he promised an "object of the highest importance"—control of the Hudson River as far as Albany. Admiral Rodney was keen to offer all naval assistance to Clinton's projected "movement up the North River": it only remained to confirm Arnold's identity beyond all doubt, settle the details of the plan, and ensure that there was no risk of the king's troops falling victim to a counterplot. A meeting was fixed, with Arnold adamant that the person sent to confer with him should be Clinton's adjutant general, twenty-nine-year-old Major John André, who had handled the secret correspondence from the outset.[83]

André was ferried upriver by the sloop HMS *Vulture*, and the clandestine meeting with Arnold went ahead early on September 22. So far, all had gone to plan, and the plot looked set to fulfill Clinton's hopes. But the next day, André's luck ran out. Carrying a pass from Arnold and using the alias "John Anderson," the major set out overland to reach safety at New York. This journey took him through the no-man's-land that stretched between the British and American armies, a violent and lawless zone contested by rival bands of irregulars hardened by years of guerrilla warfare and mutually addicted to plunder. In Westchester County, André encountered three American militiamen whom he mistook for Loyalists, not least because one of them, John Paulding, was wearing the "green, red-trimmed coat" of a Hessian jäger.[84] Spurning a bribe, the trio searched the major and found incriminating documents in his boot. Out of uniform and beyond his own lines, André was arrested as a spy. Arnold was alerted to this development by a letter from one of his unsuspecting subordinates; he opened it on the morning of September 25, shortly before his treachery became clear to Washington, who arrived at Arnold's headquarters later that same day on the way back from his discouraging conference with Rochambeau at Hartford. There he read the documents seized from André: in Arnold's handwriting, these disclosed details of West Point's defenses. Immediate steps were taken to detain Arnold, but by then he had embarked on a barge, coolly bluffed his way past the American outpost at Verplanck's Point, and reached safety aboard the *Vulture* moored downriver.

The ensuing shock and horror at Arnold's crime was mingled with relief at the precariously narrow margin by which disaster had been averted. Washington's General Orders issued the following day, September 26, expressed all three emotions:

Treason of the blackest dye was yesterday discovered! General Arnold who commanded at West Point, lost to every sentiment of honor, of public and private obligation, was about to deliver up that important post into the hands of the enemy. Such an event must have given the American cause a deadly wound if not fatal stab. Happily the treason has been timely discovered to prevent the fatal misfortune. The providential train of circumstances which led to it affords the most convincing proof that the liberties of America are the object of divine protection.[85]

Coming so close to success, Arnold's plan left Washington badly shaken. Among the most stalwart fighters in the revolutionary cause and severely wounded for his pains, Arnold had been one of Washington's favorites; in symbolic recognition of his courage on the battlefield he had given him a handsome set of epaulettes. Yet while undoubtedly a warrior, Arnold was plainly no gentleman. André, by contrast, was both. A professional soldier, he'd fought at Brandywine, Paoli, Germantown, and Monmouth. No stranger to the sight of blood and smell of gunsmoke, André was also courteous, debonair, and cultivated, fluent in four languages and a gifted artist to boot; a keen amateur actor, he had not only ridden in the "Mischianza" tournament at Philadelphia in May 1778 but also designed the risqué "Turkish" costumes worn by those ladies daring enough to participate.

Arnold was beyond retribution, but there remained the question of what to do with André, who had been captured under circumstances that left no doubt of his involvement in espionage. As Washington reported to Sir Henry Clinton, a board of general officers appointed to examine the major swiftly concluded that he "ought to be considered as a spy from the enemy, and that agreeable to the law and usage of nations it is their opinion he ought to suffer death."[86]

Clinton, who ordinarily struggled to form friendships, was devoted to his young adjutant general and deeply concerned at his plight. Believing that Washington's officers had reached their verdict without all the relevant facts, Clinton sent a three-man delegation upriver in a desperate bid to save André. Only

Lieutenant General James Robertson was permitted to land, meeting Major General Nathanael Greene in the private capacity of "gentleman" rather than "officer." Greene had warned Robertson that the distinction was irrelevant, as "the case of an acknowledged spy admitted no official discussion." With a "blush," Greene added that "the army must be satisfied by seeing spies executed." However, it appeared just one thing would placate them: for André to be set free, Arnold must be given up. Of course, such a solution was unthinkable to Clinton, and Robertson had answered this offer "with a look only, which threw Greene into confusion." He left the meeting "persuaded" that André would not be harmed.[87]

Robertson had misread the determined mood of Washington and his generals. André was under no such illusion. On September 29, he had written Clinton a letter absolving him of any responsibility for his predicament. Now "perfectly tranquil in mind and prepared for any fate to which an honest zeal for my king's service may have devoted me," the major asked only that any proceeds from the sale of his officer's commission would go to his mother and three sisters.[88] André's impeccable conduct in the face of impending death deeply impressed his captors, winning admirers like young Alexander Hamilton. Indeed, he personified the very qualities that they aspired to as officers and gentlemen. Knowing he must die, André hoped at least to be shot like a soldier, not hanged as a spy: he wrote to Washington requesting that indulgence but received no reply. According to Hamilton, as a firing squad would have been "incompatible with the customs of war," it was decided to withhold an answer to spare André "the sensations, which a certain knowledge of the intended mode would inflict."[89]

André's execution on October 2 was a solemn, awe-inspiring occasion. One of the many bystanders, Dr. James Thacher, reported that almost all the American army's senior officers attended—with the notable exception of Washington and his immediate staff. Calm and dignified as he walked through the crowd dressed in his scarlet regimentals and polished boots, André had smiled and exchanged polite bows with several acquaintances. When the gallows suddenly came in sight, he momentarily recoiled. Asked what was amiss, he replied: "I am reconciled to my death, but I detest the mode." André's courage was all the more impressive because, as Dr. Thacher noted with rather too much clinical detachment, he was fighting to master his physical fear: while standing near the gallows, the major revealed "some degree of trepidation; placing his foot on a stone and rolling it over, and choking in his throat, as if attempting to swallow." But in his last minutes André gave the performance of his life, coolly blindfolding himself with a handkerchief and adjusting the hangman's noose. In contrast to André's composure, by now many of the onlookers were openly weeping. Another witness, Major Caleb Gibbs of Washington's elite Life Guard, reported that, when André was asked for any last words, he simply "called on all the gentlemen present to bear witness that he died like a brave man." Gibbs added: "and did."[90]

When news of André's hanging reached Clinton's army, his officers wore black crepe armbands for eight days as a mark of mourning. Captain Ewald especially regretted André's fate, as he'd met him before the war while he was visiting Cassell. The captain recalled that he had "shown much friendship for me and the Jäger Corps."[91] Unsurprisingly, the execution of the popular young major provoked an unprecedented storm of opprobrium against Washington from both British officers and civilian commentators. When André's mock-heroic poem "The Cow Chase," written in 1780 to lampoon a foraging expedition by Lord Stirling, was republished in London in the following year, its "Advertisement" condemned the "inhuman Washington."[92] The opening stanza of Ann Seward's "A Monody on the Death of André" exemplified the tragic episode's impact upon perceptions of a man that many Britons had previously admired:

Oh Washington! I thought thee great and good,
Nor knew thy Nero thirst for guiltless blood;

Severe to use the power that fortune gave;
Thou cool determined murderer of the brave.[93]

Years later, Sir Henry Clinton remained bitter at André's execution, which he blamed upon Washington's vindictive rage "at the near accomplishment of a plan which might have effectually restored the King's authority and tumbled him from his present exalted situation" and which had left him burning "with a desire of wreaking his vengeance on the principal actors in it." Heedless of "the acknowledged worth and abilities of the amiable young man who had thus fallen into his hands, and in opposition to every principle of policy and call of humanity, he without remorse put him to a most ignominious death." [94]

There is no evidence that Washington bore André any such malice. Reporting the execution to his aide and close friend Lieutenant Colonel John Laurens, he wrote: "Andre has met his fate, and with that fortitude which was to be expected from an accomplished man and gallant officer." All of Washington's animosity was channeled at Arnold. While Laurens believed that the turncoat was destined to endure the "torments of a mental Hell," Washington was convinced that Arnold was immune to self-reproach. "From such traits of his character which have lately come to my knowledge," he wrote to Laurens, "he seems to have been so hackneyed in villainy, and so lost to all sense of honor and shame that while his faculties will enable him to continue his sordid pursuits there will be no time for remorse."[95]

Indeed, while André attracted almost universal sympathy and admiration, Arnold became the most hated man in America. As Dr. Thacher observed, "Could Arnold have been suspended on the gibbet erected for André, not a tear or sigh would have been produced." It has been plausibly suggested that the unprecedented invective directed against Arnold screened the guilt of many of his countrymen who had themselves betrayed the revolutionary cause in less spectacular fashion, by failing to join the fight against

Britain, or by not even expressing solidarity with the hard-pressed Continental Army.[96]

Yet, for all the vilification he incurred, Arnold was scarcely unique in his disillusionment with Congress and its broken promises or, as he expressed it in a letter to Washington, "the ingratitude of my country."[97] Other soldiers who'd risked life and limb for American liberty, only to find their efforts ignored by apathetic civilians, were no less embittered: Arnold's treason was merely the most dramatic and infamous manifestation of a discontent that would soon surface far more widely.

10

THE WORLD TURNED
UPSIDE DOWN

For George Washington and the dwindling band of officers and men who remained under his command, 1781 would prove to be the decisive year in the struggle for American independence. Yet at its outset there was precious little cause for optimism; indeed, the year opened with an episode that suggested that the patriot cause had reached its nadir and was crumbling from within.

While not as cruel as its predecessor, the winter of 1780–81 was harsh enough for the Continentals still billeted in their old huts at Morristown, New Jersey. The bitter weather did nothing to improve the mood of men who were increasingly irate at their treatment by a Congress and states that seemed indifferent to either their services or sufferings. Besides the usual shortages of food, pay, and clothing that had caused unrest among the Connecticut Continentals in May 1780, veterans of the "Pennsylvanian Line" now nursed more specific grievances. Back in 1777, when the "new army" was recruited, they had been enlisted for "three years or during the war": a dangerously ambiguous wording. In 1779, as the end of the three years approached, the Pennsylvanian Continentals maintained that their enlistments would expire then, not continue as long as the war lasted. Given the army's chronic shortage of manpower, Washington and the Pennsylvania state authorities not surprisingly upheld the "duration" argument instead. As a *douceur* to reconcile the men to the fact that they were indeed signed up for the war, each received

$100; yet the way in which the dispute was settled, with some men bullied into accepting the payoff, left a bad taste behind it.[1]

Deep-seated resentment finally erupted on New Year's Day 1781, when about 1,500 Pennsylvanian Continentals mutinied at Morristown. As their state was now paying cash bounties for new recruits and for men enlisted on short terms who were willing to sign up for another hitch, these veterans felt betrayed by the settlement they had accepted in 1779. While now insisting that their own enlistments were up, most were ready to reenlist—provided they reaped the same generous benefits as the latecomers and short-timers. The mutineers' mood was angry. Officers who attempted to restore order were roughly handled, with several of the most unpopular killed or badly hurt by bayonets, musket butts, or stones. For all their violence, the Pennsylvanians were well organized. Electing a "Board of Sergeants" to present their grievances, they resolved to march on Philadelphia—where Congress had presided since the British evacuation of the city in 1778—and confront the revolution's civilian leadership. The Pennsylvanians' commander, the fire-eating Brigadier General Anthony Wayne, was unable to quell the discontent, although his men were at pains to assure him of their loyalty to the patriot cause, arresting two agents that Sir Henry Clinton sent from New York in hopes of exploiting the unrest. As Wayne's determined and defiant men marched through New Jersey to Princeton, he was swept along with them, like a cork on a stream.[2]

Such signs that the American revolutionary cause was imploding shocked Rochambeau; if the unrest spread and the Continental Army dissolved, the French court directed, he was to sit tight on Rhode Island until his men could be evacuated to the West Indies.[3] At his headquarters at New Windsor, above West Point, George Washington was no less concerned at the "unhappy and alarming defection of the Pennsylvania line," but, with no guarantee that the men under his immediate command wouldn't follow suit, he was reluctant to leave them and deal with the mutiny in person. Instead, he urged Wayne to contain the situation, staying with his men and negotiating with them. Mass resistance by armed and livid veterans required delicate handling, and Washington desperately needed their manpower: Wayne should "draw from them what they conceive to be their principal grievances and promise to represent faithfully to Congress and to the state the substance of them and to endeavor to obtain a redress," he advised. Above all, the notoriously hot-headed "Mad Anthony" Wayne should avoid a heavy-handed use of force. Such a tactic might fail to intimidate determined soldiers or backfire by driving them into the open arms of the British.[4]

Washington's advice was sound: talk, not intimidation, defused the crisis. When the mutineers reached Trenton, they were met by Pennsylvania's state president, the former Continental Army adjutant general and Washington aide Joseph Reed, accompanied by representatives from Congress. Negotiating directly with the sergeants, Reed agreed to discharge every man who claimed to have enlisted for three years only, without awaiting confirmation from the regimental muster rolls. The mutineers were also offered new clothing and back pay, along with immunity from prosecution. Many of them promptly reenlisted for the new bounty. Temporarily paralyzed, within weeks the Pennsylvanian Line had resumed its place within the Continental Army.

Washington's fears of further unrest were well founded. The Pennsylvanians' success encouraged several hundred of the New Jersey Continentals, based at Pompton, New Jersey, to mutiny on January 20. Although they had recently received $5 in cash in a gesture toward their arrears of pay, these veterans were also angry at the better terms being offered to recruits. The New Jersey troops, who had been urged to march on Congress by their leaders, were swiftly appeased by concessions, and the upheaval at Pompton subsided. Unlike the Pennsylvanians, they didn't escape punishment. Braced for fresh unrest, Washington was determined that the "dangerous spirit" running through the ranks must now be "suppressed by force." Unless it was, he warned the president of Congress, "there is an end to all subordination in the Army and indeed to the Army itself."[5]

To hammer home his message, Washington sent a 500-strong detachment under Major General Robert Howe to chastise the New Jersey units. By dawn of January 27, after a punishing march through the snow, they were in view of the soldiers' huts. Howe harangued his own New Englanders to remind them of their duty, then closed in on the unsuspecting erstwhile mutineers. Surrounded and faced with loaded cannon, they quietly submitted. According to Dr. James Thacher, who accompanied Howe's command, three ringleaders were tried on the spot, "standing on the snow," and sentenced to be shot immediately. A dozen of their comrades were forced to form the firing squad, shedding tears as they primed their muskets and rammed down cartridges. But they obeyed orders. After two men had been shot to death, the third was pardoned. Thacher believed that the "tragical scene produced a dreadful shock, and a salutary effect on the minds of the guilty soldiers." He regretted the severity of the punishment inflicted upon men with "more than a shadow of [a] plea to extenuate their crime," who had "suffered many serious grievances . . . with commendable patience" before finally losing "confidence in public justice." Echoing Washington's own mantra, Thacher added: "But the very existence of an army depends on proper punishment and subordination."[6]

The latest storm had dissipated, but another was already brewing. In the last days of 1780, the renegade Benedict Arnold, now a brigadier general in the British Army, had arrived off the coast of Virginia with 1,200 men. He had been sent south by Clinton to establish a British naval base in the Old Dominion and mount raids that would divert attention from Lord Cornwallis in North Carolina. Arnold relished his new assignment. Virtually unopposed, his troops sailed up the James River and on January 5 marched into Richmond, now the state capital. The next day, Arnold's raiders made a pungent bonfire of public buildings and tobacco warehouses. Despite the best efforts of Baron Steuben, who was in Virginia to help rebuild the shattered army of the Southern Department, the militia failed dismally to check the destruction. Reembarking aboard their transports, the British sailed back down the James and began fortifying Portsmouth, near Norfolk.

So far Arnold had rampaged with impunity. The first challenge to his position came in mid-February, when a small French flotilla—one sixty-four-gun ship and a pair of frigates commanded by Captain Arnaud le Gardeur de Tilly—slipped through the British blockade of Newport to reach the Chesapeake. This move was totally unexpected, and Tilly exploited the surprise to capture several British craft, including the forty-four-gun *Romulus*. His presence suggested that a joint Franco-American attack on Portsmouth was looming, and Arnold was sufficiently concerned to concentrate his forces within its new defenses. But when one of Tilly's frigates grounded while attempting to get upriver, the Frenchman opted to withdraw before the precarious balance of naval superiority tilted against him. By February 24, he was back at Newport.[7]

While disappointing in its results, the miniature expedition demonstrated the potential for another, heavier blow at the same target. This held strong appeal for Washington. Before Tilly's command had sailed, he'd suggested that the entire French squadron at Rhode Island should go south, along with 1,000 of Rochambeau's soldiers. Washington would contribute a supporting force of American troops under Lafayette, who would make for the Chesapeake overland. By the time Washington sent out his orders to Lafayette, Tilly's ships were already at sea. After their return, however, no time was lost in forging ahead with plans for a far more ambitious expedition along the lines Washington had envisaged, to be led by the new squadron commander, the Chevalier Destouches.

For his mission, Lafayette was given command of a 1,200-strong detachment of Continental Light Infantry. Working in conjunction with the hard-pressed Steuben, the Virginian militia, and the anticipated French ships, the marquis was to curb Arnold's depredations and ensure that he did not evade the just desserts for "his treason and desertion." Indeed, should the traitor fall into Lafayette's hands, Washington directed, he must receive his punishment "in the most summary way." Even the fearless Arnold was momentarily unnerved by the prospect of the noose that Washington clearly longed to tie around his neck: Captain Ewald, who served alongside him in Virginia, noticed that when the appearance of Tilly's ships caused anxiety for the security of Portsmouth, Arnold's "former resolution" was "mixed with cautious concern due to his fear of the gallows if he fell into the hands of his countrymen." To escape such a fate, Ewald noticed, Arnold "always carried a pair of small pistols in his pocket as a last resort."[8]

Meanwhile, Washington held high hopes for Destouches's expedition and, to speed it on its way, traveled to Newport himself. This visit gave the French officer corps a first sight of their illustrious ally. Thanks to his well-publicized exploits, Washington already enjoyed a tremendous reputation in Europe, especially among Britain's inveterate enemies. Far from being disappointed by the reality, his allies found him even more impressive in the flesh. As one young officer, Napoleon Bonaparte's future chief of staff Louis-Alexandre Berthier, observed: "The nobility of his bearing and his countenance, which bore the stamp of all his virtues, inspired everyone with the devotion and respect due his character, increasing, if possible, the high opinion we already held of his exceptional merit."[9]

Berthier was not alone. Rochambeau's Bavarian aide-de-camp, Baron Ludwig von Closen, was no less impressed when he met Washington at Newport that March and never altered his opinion of him:

Throughout my career under General Washington, I had ample opportunity to note his gentle and affable nature; his very simple manners, his very easy accessibility; his even temper; his great presence of mind, in sum, it is evident that he is a great man and a brave one. He can never be praised sufficiently. In military matters, he does not have the brilliance of the French in expression, but he is penetrating in his calculations and a true soldier in his bearing. This is the opinion of the entire army, which no one can applaud more sincerely than I.[10]

Washington's combination of gentleman and warrior had once again served him well, swiftly forging bonds with the aristocratic Old World professionals. His prolonged exposure to the assured gentility of the *English*-born members of the Fairfax dynasty at Belvoir during his formative years had bequeathed a lasting and vitally important legacy: as another of Rochambeau's aristocratic aides, Baron Cromot du Bourg, observed that summer, Washington's "manners are those of one perfectly accustomed to society, quite a rare thing certainly in America."[11] Whatever else worried the French about their allies—their folksy lack of sophistication, their threadbare and undermanned regiments, and their chaotic finances, for example—Washington's character and conduct did much to redress the balance, leaving an overwhelmingly positive impression; here was a man they could relate to and work with. Indeed, Washington's reception at Newport resembled a triumph: French soldiers in full parade dress lined the streets, while warships in the harbor fired thirteen-gun salutes in his honor, just as they would have done for a full marshal of France: the "assassin of Jumonville" had come a long way since 1754.[12]

Destouches's squadron sailed from Newport on March 8, 1781. It carried fourteen field pieces and more than 1,100 men, many of them grenadiers and "chasseurs," as the French called their light infantry. Yet it never reached its destination. In another demonstration of the vagaries of sea power, Destouches arrived off Virginia's Cape Henry on March 16 to find the entrance to Chesapeake Bay blocked by Arbuthnot's roving squadron. The fleets were evenly matched, and although the British admiral enjoyed the advantage of a following wind—the prized "weather gage"—the ensuing encounter was indecisive. Unable to penetrate the Bay, Destouches called a council of war, then took its advice to return to Newport.[13] Clinton meanwhile reinforced Arnold with another 2,000 men under a new commander, Major General William Phillips, a highly experienced officer who had distinguished himself by his skillful handling of the British artillery in Germany during the Seven Years' War; it was his guns that had killed Lafayette's father at Minden in 1759.

Despite Destouches's failure—the latest in a lengthening list of disappointments—that spring, Washington apparently sensed that the seemingly stalemated war was entering a new and potentially decisive phase. On May 1, he recommenced his diary, or more precisely "a concise journal of military transactions etc": apart from a terse record of the brutal weather at Morristown in early 1780, he had written nothing since his last entry on June 19, 1775, just days after his appointment as commander in chief.[14]

Events in the Carolinas, hitherto the source of little save gloom for Washington, now gave him some badly needed encouragement. Finally freed from his punishing, thankless, and distinctly inglorious stint as the Continental Army's quartermaster general in October 1780, Nathanael Greene had succeeded the tarnished Horatio Gates as commander of the Southern Department. Greene quickly made his mark. Boldly splitting his army at Charlotte in December, he sent about 700 Continentals and militia under Daniel Morgan westward to gather provisions and test British strength in the South Carolina backcountry. Cornwallis ordered his vigorous light cavalry leader Lieutenant Colonel Banastre Tarleton in hot pursuit with a sizable detachment, including his own crack formation of Loyalists, the British Legion. "Bloody Ban" caught up with the reinforced Morgan at Hannah's Cowpens on January 17, 1781. There, the wily "Old Waggoner" drubbed the impetuous dragoon in a devastating encounter that demonstrated the potential of well-handled militia when working in conjunction with dependable Continentals. Faced by oncoming British bayonets, the militia fell back as usual, but only after inflicting significant casualties with their muskets and rifles. Breathless and disordered from their pursuit of the retreating militiamen, Tarleton's infantry were then caught off guard when Morgan's well-drilled Continentals, who had staged a disciplined withdrawal, launched a decisive counterattack: of Tarleton's 1,100 men—mostly British regulars—more than 800 were killed or captured, a grievous loss to Cornwallis's command.[15]

Goaded by news of Cowpens, Cornwallis gave chase to Greene, pursuing him north all the way to the Dan River. Greene won the frantic "race to the Dan" and crossed into Virginia, while Cornwallis pulled back to Hillsborough in hopes of rallying the North Carolina Loyalists. They failed to materialize in worthwhile numbers. When Greene recrossed the Dan, Cornwallis advanced to meet him. Carefully shunning battle until he had been reinforced, Greene finally stood his ground on March 15, 1781, near Guilford Court House. Although his 4,400 men outnumbered Cornwallis's troops by more than two to one, the wary Greene adopted a defensive position, intended, like Morgan's at Cowpens, to extract the maximum value from his shaky militia: they formed his first two lines, with Continentals in the third. Although the militia crumpled under the British assault, before taking to their heels they inflicted enough damage to ensure that the redcoat line was thinner than ever when it reached the veteran Continentals. Even then, by dint of sheer hard fighting, Greene was forced to retreat after a savage seesawing engagement. Cornwallis held the field, but it was another costly victory, with the British suffering twice as many casualties as their enemies. Washington noted the outcome with approval, informing Greene that he was "truly sensible of the merit and fortitude of the veteran bands" under his command and that war was a chancy business, with the "most flattering" prospects deceptive, especially when militia were involved.[16]

Despite Washington's own abiding distrust of militia, both Morgan and Greene had demonstrated that the contribution of such part-timers was not confined to the kind of harassing, irregular warfare that had flared in New Jersey in 1777 or to the intimidation of Loyalist civilians. Indeed, by 1781, many American militiamen had already completed a tour of duty in either the Continental Army or the regular regiments raised by the individual states for their own defense and were more seasoned than their amateur status suggests. In addition, at a time when every redcoat or Hessian casualty was increasingly difficult to replace, the Americans' ability to boost their own itinerant Continental forces with short-term transfusions of local manpower was starting to tell. Also, while the Continental Army was always far below its theoretical strength, often at barely a half or even a third of the figures voted by Congress, the militia drew many more Americans into the revolutionaries' armed struggle, albeit for shorter periods and at less risk of death or disability; indeed, the relative attractiveness of militia service strongly discouraged enlistment in the Continentals.[17] Some indication of the extraordinary level of involvement is provided by the response to 1832 legislation that belatedly offered pensions for all Revolutionary War veterans who could prove at least six months' service in any formation—Continental, state regular, or militia: half a century after the end of the conflict, some 65,000 eligible claimants were still alive; taking into account wartime fatalities of perhaps 25,000 and those who had died since 1783, it has been estimated that between 175,000 and 200,000 Americans saw *some* kind of military service in the revolutionary cause. Based upon the total population of whites and blacks—and allowing both for Loyalists and a widespread reluctance to permit mass enlistment of slaves—almost one in two of all males of "fighting age" served. This was a truly revolutionary scale of mobilization—but one that makes the efforts of Washington's hard core of long-service Continentals even more remarkable.[18]

While Cornwallis recuperated from his blooding at Guilford Court House, Greene seized the initiative, marching against vulnerable British outposts in South Carolina. Greene, like Washington, was naturally aggressive; although forced by circumstances to adopt an essentially defensive strategy, he hankered for the crowning glory of battle that he'd read about as a youth. But the decisive victory that Greene craved continued to elude him: on April 25, 1781, as he advanced against the British base at Camden, the young Francis Lord Rawdon marched out to confront him at Hobkirk's Hill. Rather than await the attack, Greene boldly attempted to envelop Rawdon's flanks, sending in his veteran Virginian and Maryland Continentals with fixed bayonets. By lengthening his own line, Rawdon baffled Greene's plan and after another fierce fight obliged him to retreat. Cornwallis rated Rawdon's victory as "by far the most splendid of this war" although he knew from hard experience that in the Carolinas such tactical successes, however glorious, meant all too little in broader strategic terms.[19]

Within weeks there were the first hints of a development that would decide the conflict in a far more dramatic fashion than Cornwallis, or Washington, could have imagined. On May 8, the French frigate *Concorde*, which had left Brest on March 26, arrived in Boston. It brought General Rochambeau's son, the Vicomte de Rochambeau, with dispatches for his father from the French minister of war, Philippe-Henri-Marie, Comte de Ségur, and a new commander for the naval squadron at Rhode Island, the Comte de Barras; crucially, they bore news that another fleet, under Rear Admiral François Joseph Paul, Comte de Grasse and consisting of no fewer than twenty-six ships of the line, eight frigates, and numerous transport vessels, had left France for the West Indies. Ségur had added the tantalizing intelligence that this powerful armament would be available for operations on the North American coast in "July or August."[20]

The implications for the balance of naval power on the eastern seaboard were momentous: here at long last was a chance to achieve the overwhelming maritime superiority upon which a decisive land campaign could be based. Rochambeau and his new naval colleague both wanted to discuss the strategic situation with Washington without delay, and a meeting was fixed at Wethersfield, Connecticut. Ominously, Admiral Barras was unable to attend the conference on May 22; in yet another indication of the existing limitations upon sea power, he had been obliged to remain at Newport by the sudden appearance off Rhode Island of a British fleet under Arbuthnot. Rochambeau was instead accompanied by Major General François Jean le Beauvoir, Chevalier de Chastellux, a distinguished officer and enlightened *philosophe* who had already struck up what would become an enduring friendship with Washington. Like his colleagues in the French high command, Chastellux was a nobleman: he, too, was deeply impressed by Washington's character and wrote a famous sketch that appeared in his popular *Travels in North America*. To Chastellux, Washington was "the greatest and the best of men" in whom there was a "perfect harmony . . . between the physical and moral qualities." Such balance extended to Washington's physiognomy, which was "mild and agreeable" with "neither a grave nor a familiar air." But there was a striking exception to this calm, carefully moderated character: on horseback Washington was a different man. He was a bold and skillful equestrian, breaking in his own mounts, galloping even when there was no need for haste, and jumping the highest fences with reckless abandon.[21] All those long days chasing foxes across Virginia's Northern Neck like some Rutlandshire squire had not been wasted; the Neck's proprietor and young Washington's patron, that fanatical huntsman Lord Fairfax, would most certainly have approved.

Washington's rapport with Chastellux, which was lubricated by a shared appreciation for fine wine, now yielded useful dividends: for security reasons, war minister Ségur was adamant that Washington should know nothing more than that de Grasse was bound for the West Indies; in the days before the conference, however, Chastellux not only let his hard-riding American friend in on the details but took the liberty of enclosing a memorandum: this urged Washington to set Rochambeau marching for New York; then, once de Grasse had rendezvoused with Barras, the fleet and allied troops should move together against Virginia.[22]

With hindsight this was prophetic advice; but at Wethersfield Washington was fixated upon his old objective, New York. Indeed, the recent reduction of Clinton's garrison through the "several detachments" sent to the south now made it a more attractive target than ever. In consequence, it was agreed that the French and American armies should join forces on the Hudson River as soon as possible before moving down toward New York, ready to exploit any chink in Clinton's Manhattan defenses. *If* the West Indian fleet arrived off the coast, the combined force could either besiege New York or act "against the enemy in some other quarter, as circumstances shall dictate." Washington's diary reveals that such alternative zones of operation included "the southward," which suggests that Chastellux's recent hint had at least struck a chord. Yet

Washington left Rochambeau in no doubt of his own priorities, piling up the reasons *against* a southern campaign: the likely wastage of men from long and punishing marches, the lateness of the season for such a far-flung venture, and the difficulties and expense of land transportation all underlined "the preference which an operation against New York seems to have, in present circumstances." Writing to Major General Sullivan, Washington noted another point in favor of attacking New York: as the garrison was weak, there were fine prospects for success unless Clinton recalled substantial forces from the south. In that case, he added, "the same measure which might produce disappointment in one quarter would certainly, in the event, afford the greatest relief in another."[23]

Rochambeau dutifully prepared to shift his troops from Rhode Island to the Hudson. Shortly before they were due to depart, the French general received a dispatch from de Grasse, confirming that he expected to arrive off the North American coast in mid-July and requesting directions on what course to steer. Now determined to keep Washington fully briefed, on June 10, Rochambeau sent him a copy of the admiral's letter, along with another of his own revealing that he had urged de Grasse to head first for the Chesapeake instead of New York. At first sight, this seemed to overturn the consensus reached at Wethersfield. However, Rochambeau didn't yet envisage a full-fledged campaign in Virginia; his letter to de Grasse proposed another raid on the British base at Portsmouth, after which the admiral could exploit the prevailing winds to reach New York in just two days. In a postscript to de Grasse, Rochambeau added that, if Washington still wanted the fleet to make directly for New York, then he would fall in line with his wishes. Even though he had recently pressed for the French squadron at Newport to make another effort in the Chesapeake, Washington was taken aback by Rochambeau's letter. He swiftly replied, reminding him of what they had agreed—"that New York was looked upon by us as the only practicable object under present circumstances." But he now added a significant qualifier: if naval superiority was secured, other objectives *might* become "more practicable and equally advisable."

Washington knew that the final decision on the fleet's destination must rest with de Grasse. He did *not* know that France's ambassador to America, Anne-César, Chevalier de la Luzerne, had also written to the admiral, drawing his attention to the worsening position of the patriots in Virginia; in conjunction with Rochambeau's advice, this influenced de Grasse's ultimate decision to choose the Chesapeake, not the Hudson.[24]

By early July, Rochambeau's command had marched south from Rhode Island and rendezvoused with Washington's army near his old 1776 battleground at White Plains. To one French officer, Jean-François-Louis, Comte de Clermont-Crèvecoeur, the American troops looked much the same in 1781 as they had to their British opponents five years earlier—poorly clad and with youngsters and men of African descent both conspicuous in the ranks. "In beholding this army," he wrote, "I was struck, not by its smart appearance, but by its destitution: the men were without uniforms and covered with rags; most of them were barefoot. They were of all sizes, down to children who could not have been over fourteen. There were many negroes, mulattoes, etc." Aside from the officers, only the artillerymen—"very good troops, well schooled in their profession"—wore uniforms. Rochambeau's aide, Baron von Closen, corroborated this snapshot of Washington's tough, tattered and multiracial army: "It was really painful to see these brave men, almost naked, with only some trousers and little linen jackets, most of them without stockings," he wrote. But for all that they appeared "very cheerful and healthy." Closen added: "A quarter of them were negroes, merry, confident, and sturdy." By this stage in the war, besides being scattered throughout Washington's army, black soldiers were also clustered within individual units: "Three-quarters of the Rhode Island regiment consists of negroes," Closen noted, "and that regiment is the most neatly dressed, the best under arms, and the most precise in its maneuvers."[25]

Making due allowance for exaggeration, the black presence among the rank and file of the Continental Army was clearly significant enough to attract comment from outsiders: the only surviving returns to specify the number of black soldiers, for February 1778, indicate that they already comprised 10 percent of the rank and file, a proportion that is highly unlikely to have declined after a further three years of war. Washington, the slave-owing southern planter, was obliged to overcome the ingrained cultural prejudices that had barred the enlistment of African Americans into the old Virginia Regiment during the 1750s and had attempted to limit their contribution to the army besieging Boston in 1775–76. From Long Island onward, he needed every fighting man he could find—whatever the color of his skin.[26]

That summer, Washington's customary lack of manpower steadily undermined his long-held hopes of ejecting the British from Manhattan. By July 20, when Admiral Barras requested a "definitive plan of campaign" that could be forwarded to de Grasse, a despondent Washington was obliged to acknowledge that the ambitious New York plan was becoming increasingly unrealistic: his own army was woefully weak for such a daunting task, with few recruits forthcoming for either the Continentals or the militia; in addition, the states were ignoring his repeated pleas for help. Under these discouraging circumstances, the most he could now do was "to prepare, first, for the enterprise against New York as agreed to at Wethersfield and secondly for the relief of the Southern States"—if, despite his best endeavors, the arrival of de Grasse found him with "neither men, nor means adequate to the first object." Prospects for the projected New York operation were now so bleak that Washington had requested Henry Knox to suspend the transportation of heavy artillery and stores from Philadelphia in case they had to be conveyed back again.[27]

For all that, on July 21, a 5,000-strong allied force was sent marching in four columns to test Clinton's defenses. By 5 a.m. on July 22, they were arrayed in line of battle on the heights above King's Bridge. A few British dragoons rode out from the Manhattan lines to investigate, and the forts' cannon commenced a bombardment, but the defenders wisely stayed behind their formidable earthworks. For much of that day and the next, Washington and

Rochambeau conducted an extremely thorough reconnaissance of New York's defenses. To the consternation of the French general, on Throg's Neck, where the engineers lingered to calculate the precise distance to Long Island, they were cut off by the incoming tide and obliged to swim their horses to dry land.[28]

As such dedication shows, in late July, Manhattan still remained a potential allied objective. If the states had raised their requested troop quotas, by August 1, all would have been "in perfect readiness" to start the campaign against New York, Washington noted in his diary. Regrettably, "not more than half the number asked of them have joined the army." With "little more than general assurances of getting the succors called for," Washington could "scarce see a ground" for continuing his preparations against New York, especially as there was good reason to believe that Clinton would be reinforced from Virginia. Therefore, he added, "I turned my views more seriously (than I had before done) to an operation to the southward."[29]

Events in the southern theater now exerted an irresistible pull of their own. While Nathanael Greene was preoccupied with tackling British outposts in South Carolina, his archrival Cornwallis made a move that would ultimately present Washington with the opportunity he had awaited for so long. In late May, and in defiance of Clinton's orders, the earl had pushed north into Virginia. His junction with the British forces already operating there under Phillips and Arnold and the arrival of further reinforcements from New York gave him a powerful army of more than 7,000 men: it was this very threat that had prompted ambassador Luzerne to urge de Grasse to sail directly for Virginia.

The earl's first objective was the elimination of Lafayette's command, which had been operating in Virginia since April. Badly outnumbered even before the arrival of Cornwallis, the marquis was obliged to give ground before his forces, which included strong formations of cavalry spurred on by the aggressive Tarleton and the equally vigorous if more cerebral Lieutenant Colonel John Graves Simcoe, who headed another Loyalist "legion" comprising both mounted dragoons and infantry, the Queen's Rangers. By June, Washington had reinforced Lafayette with 1,000 more veteran Continentals. These Pennsylvanians were marched south by "Mad Anthony" Wayne, although only after continuing defiance in the ranks obliged him to execute eleven of them; as a further safeguard against insurrection, the rest proceeded with their ammunition and bayonets kept under guard.[30] Despite fears for their reliability, the Pennsylvanians were desperately needed by Lafayette, and he was overjoyed when they joined him in early June. Including local militia and newly raised Virginian state "levies," he now had about 5,000 men with which to counter Cornwallis.

After obliging Lafayette to abandon Richmond, Cornwallis headed for Williamsburg, where he hoped to receive orders clarifying Sir Henry Clinton's intentions for Virginia. On 26 June, near a tavern known as Spencer's Ordinary, Cornwallis's rear guard—a crack force consisting of Simcoe's Queen's Rangers and Captain Ewald's company of Hessian jägers—clashed with a larger detachment from Lafayette's army. It was a hard-fought but indecisive skirmish, with both sides claiming victory. That same day letters arrived from Clinton: dated June 11 and June 15, they caused what Ewald characterized as a "swift change from the offensive to the defensive." This turnabout was dictated by the threat posed to New York by the united armies of Washington and Rochambeau. Now discounting Lafayette's burgeoning force as insignificant, Clinton instructed Cornwallis to "take a defensive station in any healthy situation" such as Williamsburg or Yorktown, then, after retaining such troops as he needed to hold that strongpoint, detach the rest to reinforce the endangered New York garrison.[31] Cornwallis, who was keen to wage an active campaign in Virginia, reluctantly acquiesced. After reconnoitering possible defensive posts, he returned to Williamsburg with the intention of crossing the James River and then moving on to Portsmouth, where transports would be waiting to embark the men Clinton wanted.

To Lafayette, this planned withdrawal looked more like a retreat—and a fine opportunity to strike a glorious stroke. After celebrating the 4th of July with a review of his army, he set out after Cornwallis, hoping to disrupt his march and fall upon his rear guard. Some 500 Pennsylvanian Continentals under Wayne were pushed ahead. If the bulk of Cornwallis's army was already across the wide James River, as seemed likely, then those units that remained behind would be easy pickings. On the morning of July 6, Wayne was fed false intelligence suggesting precisely that scenario: but when he hurried onward from Green Spring, following a causeway across a swamp, he discovered that Cornwallis had set a trap and was lying in ambush with virtually his entire army. Faced with field pieces spraying canister and by advancing bayonets, Wayne lived up to his fire-eating reputation: deploying his Continentals in line and placing three guns of his own, he gamely counterattacked. Heavily outnumbered, Wayne's men were soon floundering back through the marshes in confusion. Lafayette was unable to rally them. Only darkness and the softness of the ground stopped Cornwallis from sending in his dragoons to complete the rout with their slashing sabers.[32]

Unmolested by the chastened Lafayette, Cornwallis completed his crossing of the James and continued on his way to Portsmouth. Two days after the engagement at Green Spring, he received another dispatch from Clinton. Dated June 28, it called for the troops earmarked for New York to be instead diverted to join a raid on Philadelphia, where Clinton hoped "by a rapid move to seize the stores" assembled there; only after that enterprise would they reinforce New York. The exasperated Cornwallis was about to embark the troops for Pennsylvania as ordered when yet more instructions arrived from Clinton. Written at New York on July 11, these now told the earl to halt the embarkation until further orders: indeed, as both Clinton and Admiral Graves, who had succeeded Arbuthnot in command of the North American squadron, were "clearly of opinion that it is absolutely necessary we should hold a station in Chesapeake for ships of the line as well as frigates," steps must be taken to fortify Old Point Comfort, which secured the best anchorage, at Hampton Roads. If Cornwallis felt that Old Point Comfort could not be held without possessing Yorktown, and that the whole scheme couldn't be undertaken with fewer than 7,000 men, the earl was at liberty "to detain all the troops now in Chesapeake" for that purpose.[33]

Nothing was now said of the threat to New York: Captain Ewald concluded that the enemy's advance toward the city "had been nothing more than a demonstration" intended to prompt a recall of troops from their real objective, Virginia.[34] Reeling under the barrage of Clinton's contradictory orders, after investigating the alternatives Cornwallis resolved to shift his entire army to Yorktown. In early August, his troops began work on extensive fortifications around the little town, with more earthworks protecting Gloucester, across the York River. From a prowling, aggressive command, Cornwallis's veteran army had become a static and vulnerable target.

By the time Cornwallis was digging in at Yorktown, Washington's other old enemies, the feebleness of Congress, and the apathy of the states had already dashed any realistic hope of besieging New York. That cherished plan was finally abandoned on August 14, when Washington received dispatches from Barras. These announced the intended departure of Admiral de Grasse from Cape François, Saint-Domingue (Haiti), on August 3. In command of "between 25 and 29 sail of the line and 3200 land troops" he was making for Chesapeake Bay. As de Grasse must return to the West Indies by mid-October and was anxious "to have every thing in the most perfect readiness to commence our operations in the moment of his arrival," there was no time to lose. Presented with this narrow but enticing window of opportunity, Washington didn't hesitate to jettison his original strategy and "give up all idea of attacking New York." Instead, the French troops and a detachment of the Americans would march to Head of Elk in Maryland, "to be transported to Virginia for the purpose of cooperating with the force from the West Indies against the troops in that state."[35]

Two days latter, on August 16, Washington received a letter from Lafayette informing him that Cornwallis was "throwing up works" at Yorktown and Gloucester.[36] But for the moment, at least, the

full significance of this intelligence didn't register. In a joint letter
to de Grasse next day, announcing their decision to "give up for
the present the enterprise against New York and to turn our attention toward the South," Washington and Rochambeau outlined far
broader strategic objectives than cornering Cornwallis: instead,
emphasis was placed upon the recovery of Charleston, the bastion
of British power in the south; if that city could not be attacked, then
they should aim to "recover and secure the states of Virginia, North
Carolina and the [back]country of South Carolina and Georgia."[37]
So, while the rendezvous with de Grasse was fixed at Chesapeake
Bay, the geographical scope for the campaign was initially more
ambitious and flexible.

On August 19, the united allied force began moving south. A few
days later, Admiral de Barras sailed from Newport with the army's
heavy siege guns to meet de Grasse's fleet. Still anxious for the security of New York, like Washington in the early summer of 1777,
Clinton struggled to fathom his enemies' intentions. Washington
and Rochambeau kept him guessing for as long as they possibly
could; at first their troops followed a route suggesting that they were
bound for Staten Island or Sandy Hook—both potential jumping-
off points for an assault on New York. For crucial days, Clinton was
baffled and distracted. It was only after Vice Admiral Sir Samuel
Hood arrived from the Caribbean bringing thirteen more ships of
the line and confirmation of de Grasse's departure that Clinton and
Admiral Graves realized where the real danger lay and resolved to
help Cornwallis. Even then, the true scale of the threat was badly
underestimated.

As Washington and his allies headed down through New Jersey on the scent of future victory there was a chance to revisit past
triumphs. On August 29, Rochambeau and his staff dined with
Washington at Princeton, then accompanied him to Trenton on
what amounted to a "staff ride" across battlefields that were already
celebrated among the French officers. Plainly fascinated, Closen
recalled that Washington explained "the dispositions, movements
and other circumstances" of the "famous" twin engagements.[38]

Sadly for future historians, Closen failed to record Washington's words. Another of Rochambeau's aides, Baron Cromot du Bourg, who covered the same ground two days later, gave his own detailed account of the famous battles in his diary. He rightly characterized Washington's night march to Princeton in the early hours of January 3, 1777 as "an extremely bold and well combined movement," yet his report of the standoff at Trenton on the previous evening indicates that the distortions of legend were already creeping in: according to Bourg, Washington's army had numbered less than 4,000, while Cornwallis had a mighty host of 10,000; in fact, as already seen, Washington had led about 6,500 men, his opponent 5,500.[39]

Making steady progress, Washington's men paraded through Philadelphia on September 2 in hot, dry weather. Knowing that the ladies were watching from their windows as they passed through the "splendid city," Dr. Thacher regretted the thick dust that obscured the tramping columns.[40] Given their ragged condition, some Continentals may have welcomed the dense pall kicked up by their bare feet. The French, who marched in over the next two days, had no such reason to hide their blushes. As Closen proudly reported, they "were much acclaimed by the inhabitants, who could never have imagined that French troops could be so handsome." Compared with Washington's threadbare Continentals, they must have seemed like soldiers from some fanciful oil painting: Closen's own unit, the German-speaking Royal Deux-Ponts Regiment, wore sky-blue coats set off with citrus-yellow facings, although he conceded that it was the Soissonnais Regiment, "with its rose-colored lapels and facings, in addition to its grenadiers' caps with great rose and white plumes," that especially "impressed the fair sex."[41]

During the march to Philadelphia through New Jersey, Washington had remained unsure whether Cornwallis would maintain his positions straddling the York River. By the time he reached the city on September 2, it seemed clear that the earl intended to stand his ground, but Washington was now racked with anxiety over the whereabouts of de Grasse. He confided to Lafayette that he was "distressed beyond expression," particularly as a British fleet was also reported to be steering for the Chesapeake. This worrying intelligence was correct: Admirals Graves and Hood, with nineteen ships of the line, had sailed from New York on August 31, while Clinton had embarked 4,000 troops ready to follow in their wake once the seas had been cleared of the enemy. If the British ships reached the Chesapeake first, Washington fretted, it would "frustrate all our flattering prospects in that quarter." By now those hopes rested upon the elimination of Cornwallis: should the earl's retreat by sea be cut off by French naval superiority, then Washington didn't doubt that Lafayette would do everything he could to baffle his escape by land. Two days later, when he reported developments to Nathanael Greene, Washington remained in an agony of uncertainty. There was still no news of de Grasse or of Barras, who had left Rhode Island with his squadron carrying the French siege artillery on August 24. Washington added: "From the circumstances related, you will readily conceive, that the present time is as interesting and anxious a moment, as I have ever experienced." He nonetheless hoped for "the most propitious issue of our united exertions," which would trap Cornwallis and force him to surrender.[42]

On September 5, Washington finally learned that de Grasse had arrived safely in Chesapeake Bay. Normally so restrained, he could no longer contain his excitement. Sailing with Rochambeau on the Delaware River toward Chester, Pennsylvania, Closen spotted "General Washington, standing on the shore and waving his hat and white handkerchief joyfully." When they disembarked, Washington reported that de Grasse had brought twenty-eight ships of the line and 3,000 troops: the infantry had already landed to strengthen Lafayette's force and prevent Cornwallis from breaking out overland, while the admiral would block his escape by sea. Baron du Bourg noted in his diary: "From this moment it was openly announced that we were marching upon Yorktown." With so much at stake it was an emotional moment. Washington and Rochambeau "embraced warmly," and the whole army shared their "joy in having their calculations work out so well." For once, events had run like clockwork. Closen mused that Rochambeau "must indeed have felt deep satisfaction in having the time draw near when his long-considered plans would be executed and in winning the approval of General Washington, who originally had been bent upon a campaign against New York."[43]

In 1788, when quizzed about his own role in the genesis of the Yorktown campaign, Washington remembered things rather differently. He maintained that for almost a year he'd had no intention of attacking New York. Every attempt had been made to convince the enemy otherwise, but that was just an elaborate smoke screen. Even before the intervention of de Grasse, Washington remembered, it was "the fixed determination *to strike the enemy on the most vulnerable quarter*." As New York was too strong, "the only hesitation that remained was between an attack upon the British army in Virginia or that in Charleston." Following "several communications" and "incidents," he recalled, the enemy's "post in Virginia" was upgraded from a *"provisional and strongly expected"* target to "the *definitive and certain object* of the campaign." [44] Either Washington's memory was playing tricks upon him, or he was guilty of wishful thinking; as already seen, from the time of the Hartford conference in September 1780 until the following August, his gaze remained fixed upon the garrison of New York: if the men and supplies he wanted had materialized, he would have assaulted Manhattan. Yet neither could Rochambeau claim the lion's share of the credit that the loyal Closen considered his due. When the French general proposed the Chesapeake as an objective in May 1781, he had envisaged a hit-and-run raid, not a full-blown commitment of sea and land power: and, as Washington's subordinate, he was ready to abide by his wishes should he insist that New York must remain the priority. More than anything, it was de Grasse's unilateral decision to sail for Virginia that paved the way for the operation, although only Cornwallis's sudden vulnerability, which no one could have predicted when the admiral left the West Indies, provided the opportunity for the combined allied forces to land a devastating and potentially decisive blow. Given these exceptionally fortuitous circumstances, the real father of the Yorktown campaign was surely Washington's faithful friend "Providence."

Yet as the allies moved south in September 1781, there was no guarantee of victory. In Maryland, Washington was once again served notice that, while his tattered and shoeless Continentals might not look like proper soldiers, they regarded themselves as such and expected to be treated accordingly. When Major General Benjamin Lincoln marched the New York, New Jersey, and Pennsylvania Continentals to Head of Elk, they refused to continue without part of the back pay owed to them. These were not men to be trifled with: despite the firing squads of January, they were still demanding their "rights." Given their timing Washington had little choice but to appease them. When desperate appeals to the newly appointed superintendent of finance, Robert Morris, yielded just $20,000, Washington was obliged to approach Rochambeau, who selflessly donated 50,000 of the 150,000 livres that he still had with him; this made it possible to issue the men a month's pay in coin. Like the extraordinary bounty tendered after the Battle of Trenton, money talked. As Closen noted, this hard cash "raised spirits to the required level." The next day, September 8, the pacified Continentals happily embarked for the voyage down Chesapeake Bay.[45]

Having surmounted the latest hurdle in his path, Washington rode on ahead of his army, keen to start laying the groundwork for the impending siege of Yorktown. On September 9, Washington reached his "own seat at Mount Vernon." It was more than six years since he had last seen his beloved home on the bluff above the Potomac River, and his long letters to cousin Lund leave no doubt that it was never far from his thoughts. Frustratingly, if predictably, Washington's diary reveals nothing of the emotions he must have felt at that moment, simply noting that he stayed for three nights before pushing on again for Williamsburg. During that time, Rochambeau and the Chevalier de Chastellux were Washington's guests. According to Washington's secretary, Colonel Jonathan Trumbull, Mount Vernon had accommodated a "numerous family" of staff officers who enjoyed "great appearance of opulence and real exhibitions of hospitality and princely entertainment." This sociable interlude was all too brief, as Washington was eager to meet Admiral de Grasse and agree "upon a proper plan of cooperation." On September 13, while on the road to Williamsburg, the allied generals and their staffs heard reports that de Grasse had left Chesapeake Bay on September 5 to engage a British fleet; agonizingly, the outcome of the encounter was not yet known. Closen captured the tense mood, reporting that all were "very anxious to learn the result of the battle and if M. de Grasse [had] re-entered the bay, since we were aware of the *absolute* necessity for us to have his fleet in the Chesapeake to protect our operations."[46]

The wait for news was mercifully short. The following day, on the final leg to Williamsburg, the generals received intelligence that de Grasse was back on station after fending off the combined fleets of Graves and Hood. They had left New York on August 31, unaware that de Grasse had already reached the Chesapeake the day before. His pronounced superiority in ships was another unpleasant surprise: on the assurance of Admiral Rodney, they'd expected him to leave the West Indies with part of his fleet, not all of it. After an inconclusive cannonade, the fleets shadowed each other for two more days as they drifted south, allowing Barras's squadron from Newport to slip into the bay with the vital siege artillery. No less crucially, after assessing the damage to his ships, Graves reluctantly returned to New York to refit.

Increasingly concerned for Cornwallis, Clinton authorized a belated diversion intended to draw Washington's attention back to the north. Benedict Arnold led a ferocious attack on the coast of his native Connecticut, torching New London and unleashing an assault on Fort Griswold, near Groton, in which the garrison was massacred after rejecting a summons to surrender.[47] But Washington now refused to be deflected from his purpose, even by the hated Arnold. His arrival at Williamsburg on September 14, attended by just a handful of hard-riding aides and servants, quickly turned into another triumphal entry, with the French and Continental regiments parading and townsfolk flocking to catch a glimpse of him.

According to Major St. George Tucker of the Virginian militia, the presence of the commander in chief had an immediate effect upon morale, giving "new hopes and spirits to the Army."[48]

On September 17, Washington and Rochambeau left for the meeting with de Grasse aboard his flagship, the *Ville de Paris*, off Cape Henry. The admiral agreed to extend his stay for a further fortnight, until the end of October. However, it was unlikely that he would be able to lend his strength to any other combined operations, which ruled out the attack on Charleston that the allied generals had mooted. Washington and Rochambeau returned to Williamsburg on September 22, knowing that they now had little more than a month in which to subdue Yorktown before the screening fleet departed, taking 3,000 French troops with it. Facing a fixed deadline, the allies couldn't simply sit back and blockade the town in hopes of starving out the defenders. They would have to prosecute a formal siege, digging trenches and bombarding the garrison into submission or, if Cornwallis stubbornly refused to yield, taking his fortifications by storm.[49]

Writing to de Grasse on September 25, Washington was confident that with "their superiority of strength and means" they had enough time, particularly for an operation that was "reducible to calculation."[50] This was quite literally true: of all the branches of eighteenth-century warfare, siegecraft was the most scientific, following a recognized sequence of moves that methodically yet inexorably increased pressure on the besieged: given enough men, guns, and munitions, the result should not be in doubt. By the time Washington wrote to de Grasse, the entire allied army had concentrated at Williamsburg: some 16,000 strong, of which just 3,000 were local militia; it outnumbered Cornwallis's forces by two to one. In addition, in its swampy fastness, the earl's army was rapidly succumbing to fevers, with barely 5,000 men fit for duty.

After entering the James River, most of the transports carrying the American and French troops had disembarked near Jamestown. As the erudite Dr. Thacher observed, this "was the place where the English first established themselves in Virginia, in 1607." Despite its historical significance, with just two houses still standing, the settlement no longer deserved to be called a town; its decline symbolized the degree to which the Old Dominion, like the rest of Britain's former colonies, was outgrowing its roots and slaking off the past. By a remarkable coincidence, the birthplace of British America lay within an easy march of Yorktown, where the old regime would soon receive its deathblow.

For a Yankee like Thacher, Virginia's Tidewater presented an unfamiliar and sometimes disturbing scene. The region was famed for its excellent tobacco, while cotton, Indian corn, hemp, and flax were also cultivated. Yet, as Thacher reported with disgust, these crops all depended upon the labor of slaves, "a species of the human race, who have been cruelly wrested from their native country and doomed to perpetual bondage, while their masters are manfully contending for freedom, and the natural rights of man."[51]

For the many black soldiers in Washington's army—both freedmen and slaves hoping to win their liberty as substitutes for whites unwilling to fight—the Virginian campaign must have stirred still stronger emotions. Such men included a veteran of the 2nd New Jersey Regiment with the suitably Republican name of Oliver Cromwell. "Brought up a farmer" and enlisting in the Continental Army in 1776 while in his early twenties, Cromwell had already fought under Washington's command at Trenton, Princeton, Brandywine, and Monmouth. Cromwell's story was highlighted in the spring of 1852, when his local newspaper interviewed him on his one hundredth birthday. As New Jersey's *Burlington Gazette* informed its readers, while many of them were familiar with this "old colored man," few knew that he was "among the survivors of the gallant army who fought for the liberties of our country 'in the days which tried men's souls.'" It is a remarkable story, but Cromwell's discharge certificate, signed by Washington himself, survives to affirm it.[52] Cromwell died in January 1853: old as he was, even he hadn't lived long enough to see the slave-owning Thomas Jefferson's trinity of "Life, Liberty, and the Pursuit of Happiness" become the inalienable rights of all his countrymen. It would take another, far bloodier civil war to redress the glaring irony behind America's fratricidal struggle for independence from Great Britain.

At Williamsburg, the allies braced themselves for their final push to Yorktown, some twelve miles off. As he prepared to close in for the kill, Washington reverted to aggressive mode. General Orders issued to the American troops now recommended them to "place their principal reliance on the bayonet, that they may prove the vanity of the boast which the British make of their particular prowess in deciding battles with that weapon." Joseph Plumb Martin remembered that they were directed to "exchange but one round" with the enemy before deciding matters with the bayonet.[53]

General Wolfe, who had zealously championed such "volley and bayonet" tactics in the British Army during the 1750s and had famously demonstrated their effectiveness on Quebec's Plains of Abraham, would certainly have approved of Washington's methods, if not his cause. Such pointed directives offer further evidence of the striking extent to which Washington's army now resembled its British enemy. Despite enduring popular perceptions of an organization that prided itself upon marksmanship, by the climax of the long war with Britain the Continental Army was increasingly putting its faith in cold steel, the trademark of the professionals. This gave immense satisfaction to Washington's drillmaster, Baron Steuben. Reporting on the progress of his reforms to Franklin in September 1779, Steuben wrote proudly: "Though we are so young that we scarce begin to walk, we can already take Stony Points and Paulus Hooks with the point of the bayonet, without firing a single shot."[54]

The same trend was taken even further in orders governing the arming of Washington's officers. Rather than shouldering the "fusils," or light muskets, carried by their British counterparts, American officers were required to equip themselves with spear-like "espontoons." At first sight, this was a curiously conservative move: while traditionally seen as the European officer's badge of rank, the espontoon had long since been abandoned by the British Army in America; General Braddock, so often taken to epitomize outmoded Old World methods, had ordered his officers to leave theirs behind before marching for Fort Duquesne in 1755. Yet it is clear that Washington regarded the espontoon as especially suited to his conception of the ideal officer. At Valley Forge in December 1777, he ordered every officer "to provide himself with a half-pike or spear as soon as possible—fire-arms, when made use of, withdrawing their attention too much from their men." Washington had a point: at White Plains, as Clinton noted with annoyance, the British attack on Chatterton Hill almost stalled after an officer paused to fire and reload his fusil. In American hands, the espontoon was not simply a symbol of authority, but a lethal weapon: Anthony Wayne requested fifty for his officers in 1779 and wielded one himself at the storming of Stony Point. Orders issued at Morristown in April 1780 warned that no officer, including captains, was "to mount guard or go on detachment" or "appear with his regiment under arms" without an espontoon. Two years later, Washington was still extolling the virtues of "that useful and ornamental weapon." In another intriguing throwback to the clashes of antiquity that so fascinated Washington and his contemporaries, the Continental Army's officers went into battle at Cowpens, Guilford Court House, and Yorktown armed much like the Spartans at Thermopylae.[55]

While at Williamsburg Washington's army received tidings of a bloody engagement in South Carolina in which Major General Nathanael Greene and his veterans had gathered fresh laurels. In his diary, Major St. George Tucker of the militia excitedly noted news of "a complete victory obtained over the British." In fact, although Greene had written those very words to Lafayette, on September 8, he'd once again seen victory slide from his grasp. His attempt to surprise a British force at Eutaw Springs under Lord Rawdon's successor, Lieutenant Colonel Alexander Stewart, came frustratingly close to success. In what would be remembered as one of the most stubbornly contested fights of the war, Greene's North and South Carolina militiamen performed well, standing firm and trading close-range volleys with Stewart's redcoats. When Greene advanced his veteran Continentals, much of the British line caved in. But the right wing, under Major John

Marjoribanks, held firm, repelling a cavalry charge and wounding and capturing its leader, Colonel William Washington. By now, Greene's men had overrun Stewart's camp. When their looting and drinking caused a breakdown of discipline, the redcoats' staying power slowly turned the scales, just as it had at Germantown four years earlier. In another echo of that battle, the British rallied behind the walls of a substantial house before launching a decisive counterattack that drove the mortified Greene from the field.[56]

Eutaw Springs was the last major battlefield confrontation of the American Revolutionary War. But for all its ferocity it was a minor affair compared with the impending siege in Virginia. The allied army marched to Yorktown on September 28, in one long column, then split and encamped before the little town that night. The Americans assumed the traditional post of honor and seniority on the right, the French, as their auxiliaries, took the left. Despite the forces massing against him, Cornwallis remained optimistic of holding out until help arrived. His confidence was bolstered the next day, September 29, when he received a dispatch from Clinton. Sent five days earlier, this assured him that relief would soon be on its way. Sir Henry had met with Graves and his replacement, Vice Admiral Robert Digby, who'd arrived at New York on September 21 with another three ships of the line. Finally alert to the full danger facing Cornwallis, they had agreed that 5,000 troops should be embarked, and the "joint exertions of the navy and army" made to rescue him. The force should be ready to sail by October 5. Cornwallis immediately replied that Sir Henry's letter had given him the "greatest satisfaction." He added: "I shall retire this night within the works, and have no doubt, if relief arrives in any reasonable time, York and Gloucester will be both in possession of His Majesty's troops."[57]

Acting on Clinton's pledge, Cornwallis promptly abandoned three outlying redoubts that buttressed the center of his position, so enabling him to deploy his diminishing manpower along a shorter defensive perimeter. Yet by giving up his first line without a fight, Cornwallis allowed his enemies to shave vital days off their schedule and to burrow forward to within effective artillery range far more swiftly than they had anticipated. Rather than approaching Yorktown's fortifications by the customary triple line of trenches or "parallels," as the methodical Clinton had done at Charleston, they would be able to get by with just two. In addition, as Washington reported in his diary, the evacuated British defenses proved "very serviceable" to the allies in coming days as they began their own works, reconnoitered the enemy's lines, stockpiled stores, and brought up artillery.[58]

The Connecticut veteran Joseph Plumb Martin, who was now a sergeant in the army's corps of sappers and miners, remembered that work on the first parallel commenced on October 6 —but only after Washington himself had "struck a few blows with a pickaxe." This was, as Martin sardonically observed, "a mere ceremony, that it might be said 'Gen. Washington, with his own hands first broke ground at the siege of Yorktown.'"[59]

Despite the defenders' gunfire, the diggers made good progress in the light sandy soil. Three days later, on October 9, the first parallel had been established at a range of 600 yards from Yorktown's ramparts, and the allied artillery batteries were ready for action. Washington's role as supreme commander of the land forces was now acknowledged in another symbolic act: Dr. Thacher reported that he formally initiated the bombardment, putting a glowing portfire to the touch hole of the first gun to be fired, at which "a furious discharge of cannon and mortars immediately followed."[60]

The French and American gunners subjected Yorktown's defenders to a remorseless pounding. Rochambeau was an old hand at sieges—according to Closen, this was his fifteenth; but it was only Washington's second, and in scale and intensity it bore little resemblance to Boston in 1775–76, which had been more like a blockade until Henry Knox's guns arrived from Ticonderoga. Washington was clearly fascinated by what he now witnessed, especially the expertise of the gunners. In his diary he noted how accurate cannon fire subdued the enemy's batteries, allowing the mortars to lob in their shells with devastating effect. Baron von Closen maintained that the French gun crews were "so skilled and sure in their aim that they used to wager that they could hit the same embrasure"—the narrow opening from which guns were fired—"six times in succession. General Washington often admired their ability."[61]

James Thacher was awestruck by the sheer spectacle of the "tremendous and incessant" bombardment. On October 10, the French surpassed themselves when they used forge-heated cannonballs—"red hot shot"—to burn a British forty-four-gun ship, HMS *Charon*, and three transports anchored in the York River. "I had a fine view of this splendid conflagration," Dr. Thacher wrote.

The ships were enwrapped in a torrent of fire, which spreading with vivid brightness among the combustible rigging, and running with amazing rapidity to the tops of the several masts, while all around was thunder and lightning from our numerous cannon and mortars, and in the darkness of the night, presented one of the most sublime and magnificent spectacles which can be imagined.

During daylight, the shells from the mortars were clearly visible as black balls, but at night they became "like fiery meteors with blazing tails," appearing "most beautifully brilliant" before descending "to execute their work of destruction." Thacher shared Washington's admiration for the technical proficiency of the gunners, who could calculate that a shell would "fall within a few feet of a given point, and burst at the precise time, though at a great distance." Such blasts caused "dreadful havoc" among the defenders, sending body parts spinning far up into the air. The deadly traffic was not all one way: on duty in the trenches, the doctor was kept busy ministering to his comrades: more than a dozen were killed or wounded on one day alone.

As the specialist engineers and artillerists went about their business Washington and many of his officers became little more than bystanders. Yet even a static siege could provide a stage for the displays of cool courage in which they delighted. By visiting the trenches, Washington showed his men that he was sharing their dangers; in his journal Dr. Thacher recorded how, during a considerable "cannonading from the enemy, one shot killed three men, and mortally wounded another." The chaplain of Thacher's regiment, the Reverend Evans, was standing close to Washington when another shot hit the ground nearby, showering his hat with sand. Evans, who was "much agitated" by this near miss, doffed his hat and showed it to Washington, exclaiming, "See here, General!" With his "usual composure," Washington had replied: "Mr. Evans, you had better carry that home and show it to your wife and children."[62]

Washington's presence in the front lines was also recalled by Sarah Osborn, a cook and washerwoman whose husband was a commissary sergeant in the 3rd New York Regiment. At Yorktown, Sarah regularly braved the British batteries to bring up the rations she had cooked for her husband and his comrades as they toiled in the trenches. On one occasion "she met General Washington, who asked her if she 'was not afraid of the cannonballs.'" As a veteran of the Continental Army, and clearly at ease in the presence of "His Excellency," Sarah had chaffed back that she couldn't let the bullets "cheat the gallows"; besides, "It would not do for the men to fight and starve too."[63] As both she and Washington knew only too well, many of the Continentals now besieging Yorktown had done precisely that many times before.

By October 12, work had begun on the allies' second "parallel," within only 300 yards of the British lines. For the work to progress it was necessary to eliminate two redoubts that outflanked it on the right. It was agreed that both should be stormed on the night of October 14. French grenadiers and chasseurs were given the task of assaulting the larger of the strongpoints, "Redoubt No 9," while the Continental Light Infantry were allocated "No 10." Lafayette was in overall command of the American operation and gave responsibility for leading the attack to his aide-de-camp and fellow countryman the Chevalier de Gimat. Washington's former aide Lieutenant Colonel Alexander Hamilton objected to this: on grounds of seniority, the honor belonged to him, not Gimat, he argued. After examining the dates of the rival claimants' commissions, Washington—who had long believed in strict military protocol—ruled in Hamilton's favor.[64]

As Washington reported to Congress, both the French and Americans secured their objectives with "firmness and bravery"; carrying unloaded muskets, the troops "effected the business with the bayonet only."[65] In fact, the French had been obliged to load and open fire: they'd taken heavy casualties as they waited for ax-wielding pioneers to hack a path through the stout wooden palisade that surrounded their objective; the Americans, who simply tore down the obstructions with their bare hands, suffered just nine killed and thirty-two wounded—about a third of the French losses.[66]

Alexander Hamilton was unscathed, although having just recently married he clearly felt a pang of guilt at the dangers he'd needlessly courted. Two days later, he wrote to his wife, Elizabeth, seeking to justify the behavior that could easily have left her prematurely widowed: "My honor obliged me to take a step in which your happiness was too much risked," he explained. Hamilton reassured his bride: "There will be, certainly, nothing more of this kind." Honor had now been satisfied and, with the exploit duly reported "in the Philadelphia papers," properly recognized.[67]

Washington's own rank and responsibilities barred him from participating in such overtly aggressive displays, but he continued to find other ways to demonstrate his sangfroid in the face of the enemy. Soon after the storming of the redoubts, a young Virginian soldier laboring on the siege lines witnessed "a deed of personal daring and coolness in General Washington which he never saw equaled." John Suddarth, who was sixteen at the time, recalled that this occurred when the British unleashed "a tremendous cannonade" in a desperate effort to demolish the besiegers' steadily encroaching works. Noticing activity in the British lines, and determined to establish exactly what was happening, Washington took his telescope and climbed up onto the "highest, most prominent, and most exposed point of our fortifications." There, as Suddarth remembered, he "stood exposed to the enemy's fire, where shot seemed flying almost as thick as hail and were instantly demolishing portions of the embankment around him." Washington stayed put for ten or fifteen minutes, despite the repeated efforts of his aides to coax him back under cover: they "were remonstrating with him with all their earnestness against this exposure of his person and once or twice drew him down." They were "severely reprimanded" for their trouble, and Washington resumed his place until he was completely satisfied.[68]

Cornwallis's own position under the allies' bombardment was now growing increasingly hopeless: on the night of October 15, a spirited sortie to spike enemy guns in the advanced batteries brought only temporary respite, and a last-ditch attempt to break out by ferrying his garrison across the river to Gloucester was stymied by a storm. On October 17, Cornwallis bowed to the inevitable and proposed a negotiation of terms; two days later it was agreed that the garrison must surrender themselves as prisoners of war.

All shipping, weapons, stores, and money were to be handed over to the victors; officers could keep their swords, while all ranks were allowed their "baggage and effects"—with the exception of "property taken in the country."[69]

Such "property" embraced former slaves who had thrown in their lot with the British. They included eighteen-year-old Barnard E. Griffiths, a "negro man" and "laborer" born at Charleston who'd joined the British forces besieging the city in 1780 and enlisted in the Queen's Rangers. According to his colonel, John Graves Simcoe, not only was he "very useful as a guide" but he served as a dragoon. Indeed, Griffiths was "frequently distinguished for his bravery and activity," particularly at the skirmish near Spencer's Ordinary, where he had fought hand to hand with a French officer and in a subsequent charge against the rebel infantry "by his gallantry preserved the life of his captain and was severely wounded." When Yorktown surrendered, Simcoe successfully interceded with Baron Steuben to ensure that Griffiths "might not risk the hazard of being sent prisoner into the country." The extraordinary efforts taken by an officer and gentleman like Simcoe on behalf of a former slave testify not only to his own enlightened humanity, but to the powerful bonds of comradeship; like the friendship between the Mohawk Joseph Brant and English aristocrat General Lord Percy, they also demonstrate the potential of a shared warrior's code to surmount barriers of class and race.[70]

Sir Henry Clinton's promised help for Cornwallis had never arrived, although here at least he was not to blame: Graves's naval repairs had progressed with agonizing slowness. Waiting to embark at New York to make a "spirited exertion for the relief of Lord Cornwallis," on October 6, Captain Peebles of the 42nd already knew that "the fate of America" was probably hanging in the balance; despite that, ten days later, when a desperate plea for help arrived from Cornwallis, the "Navy people" were still dragging their feet: it was October 19 before the fleet left port.[71]

That same day, Yorktown's defenders marched out to lay down their arms. Pleading an indisposition, Cornwallis delegated the duty of surrendering to his subordinate, Brigadier General Charles O'Hara, who had led the Brigade of Guards throughout the bloody southern campaign. Firsthand accounts of what happened next disagree over details, especially the mood of the key players, but the following sequence is as plausible as any: O'Hara at first rode up to Rochambeau to formally surrender his sword, apparently because he was confused rather than seeking to deliberately snub Washington; at this, a French officer, Comte Mathieu Dumas, indicated the rightful recipient; taking off his hat, O'Hara apologized to Washington for Cornwallis's absence; as etiquette required that Washington refuse to accept the surrender of an officer of inferior rank, he in turn politely directed O'Hara to his own second in command, Major General Lincoln, the same officer who'd been obliged to capitulate at Charleston; Dumas recalled that Washington had softened his rejection of the proffered weapon with the words "Never from so gallant a hand."[72] Such magnanimity in the moment of victory, particularly toward a respected fellow soldier like O'Hara, would certainly have been more characteristic of Washington than the studied disdain with which he has sometimes been credited by later writers, and more in keeping with the courtesy enshrined in the *Rules of Civility* that he had transcribed as a teenager.

With O'Hara and Lincoln now riding at their head, the long column of vanquished British and German veterans marched out down a corridor formed by the victors: ragtag Americans to their left, pristine French on the right. Sarah Osborn left her cooking and washing to watch the procession. Although she didn't know his name, Sarah never forgot Brigadier O'Hara's "full face" or the tears that rolled down his cheeks. Perhaps the tough Irishman wept from sheer shame at the British Army's humiliation; more likely he was remembering his son Augustus, a lieutenant in the Royal Artillery killed six months earlier at Guilford Court House; O'Hara himself had been severely wounded in that same terrible fight. Now, as the survivors of Cornwallis's army marched out to surrender, such sacrifices must have seemed all too pointless.[73]

The precise terms of the capitulation reflected those imposed upon Lincoln's men at Charleston, deliberately withholding some of the traditional honors of war: Yorktown's defenders were required to keep their regimental colors cased rather than flying bravely on the breeze, while the drummers and fifers, whose instruments were decked in black cloth as if for a funeral, were denied the privilege of playing one of the victors' tunes and restricted to a British or German march. According to a hallowed story, which has never been satisfactorily verified or debunked, they chose the melody of a popular, and singularly apt, English song: "The World Turned Upside Down." If, as has been suggested by music historians, the tune was identical to that of an older song, "When the King Enjoys His Own Again," the choice was both wistful and defiant.[74]

Arriving at the field appointed for their formal surrender, the British and Hessians relinquished their weapons. It was now, "the last act of the drama," as Dr. Thacher styled it, "that the spirit and pride of the British soldier was put to the severest test, here their mortification could not be concealed." Indeed, the redcoats' platoon officers seemed chagrined when giving the command to "ground arms," and their men only did so in a "sullen temper," throwing down their muskets with violence. Such truculence is scarcely surprising: for many of Cornwallis's men, it was their first defeat at rebel hands. Malcolm McKenzie and Neill Thomson of the 71st Highlanders were typical. As their pension applications testified, before "at last being taken prisoner with Lord Cornwallis," both had already helped to win an impressive string of victories at Long Island, Fort Washington, Brandywine, Briers Creek, Camden, Guilford Court House, Jamestown Point, the capture and defense of Savannah, and the taking of Charleston, along with "numberless petty skirmishes too tedious to mention."[75]

Thacher, who had joined the American army besieging Thomas Gage's redcoats at Boston in 1775 and tended the war's casualties ever since, clearly found the surrender of McKenzie, Thomson, and their surly comrades a moment to savor. For George Washington, commander of the Continental Army throughout those six long years of danger, hardship, and frustration, the thronged field outside the battered Virginian town must likewise have offered a supremely satisfying sight: nothing less than the humbling of the proud military organization that had rejected his youthful advances during the 1750s and inflicted humiliating defeats upon him twenty years later.

Ironically, that same British Army had provided not only a focus for Washington's enduring resentment but a blueprint for the American regular force that he had built and ultimately led to partake of a stunning victory. The Continental Army that maintained the long war for independence, the force that Nathanael Greene believed to embody the "stamina of liberty," mirrored the British prototype, and at Washington's insistence.[76] Just like the Virginia Regiment that he had sought to shape into a unit proficient enough to join the British Army, the Continentals were drawn from much the same strata of society as the redcoat rankers, served under harsh regular-style discipline, and took orders from a distinct caste of gentlemen officers. Given the English roots of Washington and many of his countrymen, as Baron Steuben had acknowledged, *some* imitation was only to be expected. But it is also clear that, despite his distinctly ambivalent relationship with the British Army, Washington never ceased to admire it as a military organization. As late as November 1780, when settling a point of administration, he referred the president of Congress to the "British Army, from whence most of our rules and customs are derived, and in which long experience and improvement has brought their system as near perfection as in any other service." [77]

The indelible British brand on Washington's army was clear enough to one of the thousands of royal soldiers snared at Yorktown. Now able to scrutinize the rebels at closer quarters and with greater leisure than he had been accustomed to since 1776, jäger Captain Ewald cautioned against equating them with some "motley crowd of farmers." On the contrary, he observed, their "so-called Continental, or standing, regiments are under good discipline and drill in the English style as well as the English themselves." At Yorktown, the Continentals were still showing the British habits that Steuben had been unable to curb at Valley Forge. Ewald, another German weaned on Prussian principles, "was greatly surprised that the Americans were not in close formation, arm to arm, but"—like the redcoats—"had consistently left a place for a man between every two men." The captain believed that if the war against the French, who used the traditional close-order formation, should continue, the British might "come out dirty in the first affair." Then again, Ewald hadn't been with Brigadier Medows at The Vigie in '78.

Besides noting striking similarities between the rival armies at Yorktown, Captain Ewald also detected important differences. For all their crisp drill, the Americans, who were "handsome . . . well-built men," remained lamentably clad and shod. Ewald reported: "I have seen many soldiers of this army without shoes, with tattered breeches and uniforms patched with all sorts of colored cloth, without neckband and only the lid of a hat, who marched and stood their guard as proudly as the best uniformed soldier in the world, despite the raw weather and hard rain in October." To Ewald, here was the key distinction between the American revolutionaries and their enemies. He marveled:

> *With what soldiers in the world could one do what was done by these men, who go about nearly naked and in the greatest privation? Deny the best-disciplined soldiers in Europe what is due them and they will run away in droves . . . But from this one can perceive what an enthusiasm—which these poor fellows call "Liberty"—can do!*[78]

When considering the motivation of the average Continental soldier, Ewald's objective testimony is surely worth considering. As the memoirs of even that jaundiced veteran Joseph Plumb Martin make clear, material gain and patriotism were not mutually exclusive incentives for Washington's regulars; the underlying loyalty of the exasperated mutineers of 1780 and 1781 suggests that many other men must have been motivated by a combination of both—bolstered of course by a strong measure of allegiance to their comrades. It was not the least of Washington's strengths that he recognized, almost from the outset of the Revolutionary War, that high-flown ideology alone was not enough to sustain men—whether officers or rank-and-file soldiers—who risked their lives and livelihoods for long years while so many of their countrymen sat idly on the sidelines.

While it was by no means clear to Washington in October 1781 or for many months to come, the swift and unexpected elimination of an entire British army at Yorktown marked the real end of Britain's attempt to deny the fact of American independence. When the news reached London on November 25, it caused widespread gloom, compounding dissatisfaction with Germain's strategy and reinforcing opposition to an unpopular and costly struggle. On February 27, 1782, the Commons voted to suspend hostilities in America; Lord North resigned soon after. The new ministry, headed by Charles Watson Wentworth, Lord Rockingham, was committed to settling a comprehensive peace with the Americans.[79]

If, in the short term, the decisive outcome of the Yorktown campaign hinged upon the help of Rochambeau and especially de Grasse, the foundations for the victory had been laid by Washington long before. Without his resilience and leadership of the Continental Army, particularly during those pivotal weeks in New Jersey in December 1776 and January 1777, the revolutionary cause would have foundered long before French intervention made such a stroke even a possibility. According to another anecdote that is impossible to verify but nonetheless rings true enough, the essence of this was acknowledged by none other than Cornwallis himself. At a dinner held after his surrender, so the story goes, the earl rose to respond to a toast and addressed Washington with these words: "When the illustrious part your Excellency has borne in this long and arduous contest becomes a matter of history, fame will gather your brightest laurels rather from the banks of the Delaware than from those of the Chesapeake."[80] Without Trenton and Princeton there could have been no Yorktown.

Unconvinced that Britain would relinquish the struggle, and braced for a counterstroke, Washington kept his troops in fighting trim, drilling them to a peak of efficiency. Back in its old positions above Manhattan, by the summer of 1782 the Continental Army looked very different from the force that had besieged Yorktown. That September, when he attended a review at Washington's headquarters in the Hudson Highlands, Rochambeau's aide-de-camp, Baron von Closen, was "struck by the sight of these troops, armed, in new uniforms, and with excellent military bearing." The baron marveled at the difference just a year could make. In the following month, that harshest of all critics—Washington himself—assured John Jay: "Our Army is better organized, disciplined, and clothed than it has been, at any period since the commencement of the war."[81]

At long last Washington had the well-tempered weapon he had always wanted; ironically, with the war winding down, there was now little prospect of wielding it against the Republic's red-coated enemies. In the summer of 1782, however, there were hints that a reliable, regular army might soon be needed elsewhere, on the western frontier. Washington received disturbing tidings from the Ohio Country, where militiamen sent against his old enemies the Delawares and Shawnees had met with catastrophic defeat at Sandusky. The slain included Washington's boyhood friend and later business partner Colonel William Crawford, a man for whom he "had a very great regard." The utter failure of the expedition was bad enough, but the manner of Crawford's death was worse still: taken captive, he had been subjected to a grisly and protracted ordeal by torture, a fate ordained in reprisal for the recent unprovoked massacre by drunken militia of ninety-six peaceful Delawares—men, women, and children—at the Moravian mission at Gnadenhütten. As Washington recognized, given their mood of exasperation, "no other than the extremest tortures which could be inflicted by savages" were to be expected by their captives. "For this reason," he warned, "no person should at this time, suffer himself to fall alive into the hands of the Indians."[82]

Kept sheathed against the Republic's external enemies, as peace looked ever more likely, the Continental Army remained a weapon that might be brandished elsewhere, at a Congress that continued to ignore its long-standing grievances. By October 1782, for all their smart looks and crisp drill, Washington sensed that his soldiers' simmering frustrations and anxieties for the future were coming to the boil. In a letter to Benjamin Lincoln, now secretary at war, he warned that the army's patience was almost exhausted, its "spirit of discontent" higher than ever before. Unpaid, all ranks faced a "prospect of poverty and misery." Even generals could offer their guests no better fare than "a bit of beef without vegetable," washed down with "stinking whiskey." Washington dreaded the consequences for civilian society of disbanding an army in which so many veterans were "soured by penury and what they call the ingratitude of the public."[83]

The anticipated unrest erupted in 1783 in a fashion that fed the most lurid fears of standing armies. Its flashpoint was the Continental Army's final winter quarters, around the quiet village of

Newburgh, just north of West Point.[84] As ever, the rank and file were clamoring for their back pay, but it was the officers' concerns that now drove events. Back in 1780, amid anxiety that Benedict Arnold's treason might trigger a wave of copycat defections, Congress had upgraded the officers' half-pay pensions from seven years to life. Since then, however, nothing had been done about them, fueling rumors that the anticipated peace and vociferous civilian opposition would persuade Congress to break its word. In December 1782, a group of officers led by General Alexander McDougall drew up a petition for Congress, offering to accept lump-sum severance payments in lieu of half pay. Further delays would have "fatal effects," it warned, implying that the army would mutiny to secure its goals.

The officers' petition was swiftly identified as a valuable weapon by those members of Congress, known as the "nationalists," who wanted a far stronger central government than that established under the Articles of Confederation ratified in 1781, one with the power to impose the taxation necessary to satisfy the officers. Even though it was just two years since angry, mutinous soldiers had marched on Philadelphia, Congress refused to be intimidated and rejected the petition. News of that development reached Newburgh on about March 8. Colonel Walter Stewart, who delivered the tidings, poured fuel on the flames by adding that Congress aimed to disband the army without settling its accounts. Stewart began seeking the assistance of a high-ranking officer capable of increasing pressure on the politicians. Such a role had already been suggested to Washington by his former aide, the brilliant, ambitious Alexander Hamilton, now a Congressman and vocal nationalist. On February 13, Hamilton wrote: "It appears to be a prevailing opinion in the army that the disposition to recompense their services will cease with the necessity for them, and that if they once lay down their arms, they will part with the means of obtaining justice." Hamilton, himself a veteran of the fighting from Long Island to Yorktown, regretted "that appearances afford too much ground for their distrust." While the army's unease might certainly prove useful in lending weight to Congress's drive to establish "general funds" capable of satisfying the Republic's creditors (not least, its soldiers), it would be difficult to keep "a complaining and suffering army within the bounds of moderation," he added. Washington's influence must be employed to "guide the torrent," channeling the pent-up anger for the greater good.[85]

But Washington shunned such a role. While sympathetic to his officers' plight, he considered the army "a dangerous instrument to play with." His second in command at Newburgh, Major General Horatio Gates, was more amenable to calls for concerted action against Congress. Gates had no liking for the nationalists, who numbered several old enemies, but he was badly in debt and believed in an effective protest campaign. Whether Gates was merely a "tool" of the politicians or followed his own agenda is a debatable point, but Washington swiftly came to believe that his former rival was behind the growing disaffection. In a clear reference to the "Conway Cabal," he wrote to Hamilton on March 4: "The source, may be easily traced as the old leaven, it is said, for I have no proof of it, is again, beginning to work, under the mask of the most perfect dissimulation, and apparent cordiality."[86]

While there is no hard evidence that Gates aimed to usurp Washington's position or was planning a coup d'état to overthrow Congress, he undoubtedly took a prominent role in the agitation. Acting without Washington's authorization and against military regulations, he seemed heedless that his actions might go beyond the settling of legitimate scores and ignite a full-blown military revolt against civilian authority. With Gates's approval, his close friend and aide, John Armstrong junior, issued anonymous addresses to the officers, implying that the time was ripe to take matters into their own hands; these were copied and distributed by another of Gates's associates, Captain Christopher Richmond.[87]

The first of the "Newburgh Addresses," which surfaced on March 10, called for a meeting of general and field officers the next day to secure "redress of grievances." It urged them to resent "the slightest mark of indignity from Congress." After all, whatever the "political event the army has an alternative": if peace came, only death could disband it without a just settlement; should the war drag on, the army could seek the direction of its "illustrious leader," Washington, then "retire to some unsettled country" in the west, leaving America helpless to its fate.[88]

Armstrong's wording implied that Washington backed the address. In fact, he was appalled, concluding that it was "not only planned, but also digested and matured in Philadelphia." He responded swiftly and decisively, using official General Orders of March 11 to deplore "such an irregular invitation" and to announce a meeting of his own on March 15 "to hear the report of the committee of the army to Congress" and to draw up a plan of action "best calculated to attain the just and important object in view." This move not only wrested the initiative from Armstrong and his supporters but also bought time, both for his own response and to allow emotions to cool, giving his officers "leisure to view the matter more calmly and seriously." Nothing daunted, Armstrong reacted with a second address, approving this change of plan and once again attempting to convince his readers that Washington approved of the steps already taken.[89]

Ironically, given his own role in stirring up the unrest, it was Gates, as senior ranking officer under Washington, who chaired the assembly on March 15. When it opened, in a newly constructed building called the "Temple of Virtue," Washington made a lengthy address of his own. This emphasized his consistent advocacy of the army's interests and warned against rash actions that would not only "sully the glory" they had won but "open the flood gates of civil discord, and deluge our rising empire in blood." In counterpoint to this horrifying scenario, Washington was convinced that Congress held "exalted sentiments" of the army's services, merits, and sufferings and would render it justice. But the workings of Congress were slow, he cautioned, and the men must be patient.[90]

At the close of his speech, which met with a stony silence, Washington delved into his pocket, unfolded a supporting letter from Congressman Joseph Jones, and started to read it. Then he hesitated, rummaged in his pocket again, and produced a pair of glasses. Washington's officers had no idea that he needed them. "Gentleman, you will permit me to put on my spectacles," he apologized, "for I have not only grown gray but almost blind in the service of my country." Washington's simple gesture and words achieved what the droning phrases of his carefully written speech had failed to do. The mood of the officers changed immediately. Men who had been surly, cynical and resentful were now choking back sobs and wiping away tears as they recalled the dangers and hardships they had shared under Washington's unwavering leadership. Whether his action was spontaneous or calculated is unclear, but beyond doubt he had played a masterstroke; it has been characterized as a "virtuoso performance," even his "finest hour."[91]

When Washington quit the "Temple of Virtue," his officers adopted a memorial affirming their "unshaken confidence" in Congress and condemning the anonymous addresses. The crisis was over. Having persuaded his officers to put their faith in Congress despite so many disappointments, Washington immediately resumed his campaign to ensure that his own trust hadn't been misplaced. Three days after the decisive meeting, he wrote to Elias Boudinot, the latest president of Congress, "entreating the most speedy decision" to settle the officers' grievances. Washington left no doubt of what his own feelings would be if the sufferings and sacrifices of his officers were not properly rewarded: "Then shall I have learned what ingratitude is, then shall I have realized a tale which will embitter every moment of my future life," he grimly pronounced. In a letter that same day to Congressman Jones, he warned that, while the "storm which seemed to be gathering" had "dispersed," there was no room for complacency. Those who now assumed that the danger of mutiny had passed should be wary, as men who believed themselves dealt with "ungratefully, and unjustly" were capable of anything, especially as "characters are not wanting, to foment every passion which leads to discord."[92] Congress didn't need Washington's prompting: shaken by the escalating threats and unaware of the dramatic turnaround at

Newburgh, it enacted a plan commuting half pay for life into full pay for five years.

By personally taking control of the situation rather than surrendering the initiative to militants bent upon confrontation, Washington ensured that he would continue to champion the army's cause as he always had, by persistent, respectful lobbying. His strong leadership at Newburgh was expressed as a voice of moderation, not the bullying ranting of a military dictator. Despite his immense and, by 1780, unrivaled prestige, Washington never succumbed to the temptation of grasping supreme power—like Oliver Cromwell before him and Napoleon Bonaparte after—even though some officers fervently believed that he should. When Colonel Lewis Nicola wrote to Washington in May 1782, suggesting that it would be in America's best interests if he declared himself king, he received short shrift: "Banish these thoughts from your mind" came the uncompromising reply. Indeed, Washington had warned that Nicola's proposed American monarchy, with a new King George supplanting the old one in London, was "big with the greatest mischiefs that can befall my country." It was a notion that he felt obliged to regard "with abhorrence and reprehend with severity." For all his promotion of a reliable, standing army and his determination to keep it in being until it was no longer needed, Washington never deviated from his belief that the military should remain subordinate to the civil power: he had no more desire to become a dictator at Newburgh in March 1783 than at Trenton in December 1776.[93]

Had Washington failed to defuse the "Newburgh Conspiracy" and instead endorsed its objectives, a group of officers might have menaced Congress into meeting their demands, thereby establishing a precedent for military interference in American government. The more drastic scenario of a full-blown coup d'état seems highly unlikely, not least because of a clear lack of solidarity between the officers and the enlisted men, whose mass support would have been essential to any takeover bid. While both groups had grievances in common, they never acted together. The unbridgeable social gulf between them was clear in 1780 and 1781, when mutinying soldiers turned wrathfully upon unpopular superiors. On their part, officers had shown no hesitation in implementing the harsher floggings ordered by Washington from December 1779 to combat marauding, even though these exceeded the army's *Articles of War*. Hierarchy and punishment only reinforced the traditional antipathy between the ranks that runs through the recollections of Joseph Plumb Martin: while he and his comrades might admire individual officers for their bravery, many others, like his own captain, David Bushnell, were heartily disliked and considered fair game for potentially lethal pranks: it was only with difficulty that Sergeant Martin persuaded several "young hotheads" to abandon their plan to frighten "the old man" by igniting a wooden canteen packed with enough gunpowder to blow him sky high.[94] Significantly, this conspicuous absence of the kind of fellow feeling that might have generated and sustained a coup was itself a consequence of Washington's own vision of the Continental Army as a formation in which officers would be "gentlemen" like him, distinct in background and ethos from the humble rank and file.

The upheaval at Newburgh had scarcely subsided when news arrived that a treaty signed in January had ended hostilities between Great Britain and the United States; although the definitive Peace of Paris was not ratified until September, as Washington announced in his General Orders of April 18, the initial proclamation had closed a "long and doubtful contest" and promised "the approach of a brighter day than hath hitherto illuminated the Western Hemisphere." Having now accomplished their "glorious task," it only remained for the actors in the drama to exit the stage with applause. Washington was confident that the men who had enlisted for the war—"who ought to be considered as the pride and boast of the American Army"—would be honorably discharged as soon as possible.[95]

Because the British still garrisoned Charleston, Savannah, and New York City, Congress decided that its troops should be put on "furlough," for recall if required, and released in batches to minimize the impact upon civilian society. Each veteran received three

months' pay in the form of "final settlement certificates"; their furlough papers could also be used to claim warrants for the 100 acres
of bounty land that every "three-year or the duration" enlistee had
been promised. Desperate for food and clothing to see them home,
many men swiftly sold their papers for a fraction of their face value.
As Joseph Plumb Martin recalled in old age, while there was talk of
bounty lands, nothing was done to help the soldiers secure them:
the only interest came from speculators "driving about the country
like so many evil spirits," who promptly fleeced the veterans. He
added bitterly: "When the country had drained the last drop of service it could screw out of the poor soldiers, they were turned adrift
like old worn-out horses, and nothing said about land to pasture
them upon."[96]

Like Sergeant Martin, George Washington had signed up "for the
duration." Despite their vastly different prospects, he, too, faced the
challenge of adjusting to peace. That process began with Washington's farewell address to his army, delivered in his General Orders
of November 2. Preparing "to take his ultimate leave . . . of the military character," he thanked all of his men, from the generals, "for
their counsel on many interesting occasions, as for their ardor in
promoting the success of the plans he had adopted," to the noncom-
missioned officers and privates, "for their extraordinary patience in
suffering, as well as their invincible fortitude in action." What this
"band of brothers" had achieved during eight long years of conflict,
Washington maintained, "was little short of a standing miracle."[97]

A month later, there was a more intimate parting scene in New
York City. The last redcoats were finally evacuated on November
25, 1783; Washington rode in that same afternoon to a hero's welcome from cheering crowds. On December 4, at Fraunces Tavern
on Pearl Street, Washington bid farewell to his general officers
and staff. Of his closest companions, only Henry Knox, Baron
Steuben, and a few others were present, but it was an emotionally
charged occasion for all that, with Washington embracing each
man in turn. The last links were severed on December 23, when
Washington broke his homeward journey to Mount Vernon and

paused at Annapolis, Maryland, where Congress had convened. Having completed the task entrusted to him back in 1775, Washington delivered his formal resignation, taking his "leave of all the employments of public life."[98]

Of course, Washington's retirement from what he had styled "the great theater of action" was temporary. Given his standing as the man who had done more than anyone else to win American independence, it was inevitable that there would be further calls upon his guidance and leadership as the young Republic struggled to stamp its credentials and construct a strong national government. In spring 1787, Washington was unanimously elected to chair the convention that hammered out the US Constitution; on April 30, 1789, he was inaugurated first president of the United States; reelected, he would hold the post until 1797. His retirement was all too short, and he died on December 14, 1799, aged sixty-seven, from an inflammation of the throat contracted while inspecting his farms on horseback during a snowstorm.

Detailed examination of these years falls beyond the scope of this study, but a brief overview makes it possible to revisit key themes from Washington's long military career. As president, Washington showed no more inclination to don the mantle of military dictator than he had when commander in chief of the Continental Army. Yet neither did he lose his faith in the kind of professional standing army that had been crucial to achieving American independence, but which remained anathema to many of his countrymen.

At the close of the Revolutionary War, the Republic's permanent military establishment had been axed. By January 1784 America's regular army amounted to a small unit of artillery and a single regiment of infantry: just 600 men guarding stores at West Point and Springfield, Massachusetts, and supervising the reoccupation of New York City. Mindful of civilian fears of a strong military, but aware of the need for national security, Washington had put forward his "Sentiments on a Peace Establishment" while his veterans were still disbanding: this scheme, which reflected his own experience and the advice of his general officers, envisaged a small regular force of just 2,600 troops, backed up by a properly trained and regulated militia, subject to Congress rather than to the individual states; a cohort of the youngest militiamen, aged eighteen to twenty-five, would drill more intensively, forming elite units like the minutemen companies of 1775. Washington had promoted a compromise solution in which some militia would be shaped to resemble regulars, but Congress rejected his plan. Instead, the tiny remnant of the old Continental Army was slashed further, to just eighty men.[99]

The same Republican suspicions that scotched Washington's "Sentiments" fueled the furor that followed the foundation of the Society of the Cincinnati in 1783. Promoted by Henry Knox and Baron Steuben, this was an exclusive fraternity for senior Continental Army officers, intended to commemorate and perpetuate the brotherhood forged during the hardships and dangers of the Revolutionary War. Its title was inspired by the Roman citizen-soldier Lucius Quinctius Cincinnatus, who had famously left his plow to serve the republic in its hour of need, only to relinquish power and return to farming once the crisis was over; the obvious parallels with Washington's own experience would earn him the title of the "American Cincinnatus"; with his liking for agriculture, it was a tag he did nothing to discourage. Despite such symbolism, given its elitist, martial character, it was scarcely surprising that the society immediately provoked howls of outrage from civilians who detected sinister purposes behind its worthy facade: membership was hereditary, descending through eldest sons, which hinted at the establishment of an American "nobility," while the payment of contributions into a fund for needy members suggested a war chest that might be tapped for other, less charitable purposes, perhaps even to topple the confederation. Washington's acceptance of the society's presidency offered evidence that his own motives were harmless, not least because he had no son to inherit his membership, but the public criticism of what looked like a militaristic organization, steeped in the traditions of standing armies, was unabated.[100]

Such entrenched attitudes ensured that in the years following the Peace of Paris the burden of national defense would fall upon the state militias, the same feckless amateurs who had frequently driven Washington to distraction during two wars. After 1789, the president's enduring belief in the superiority of regulars, which was shared by Alexander Hamilton and other leading nationalists, was only reinforced by events on the western frontier. There, the festering troubles with the fiercely independent nations of the "Old Northwest" beyond the Ohio River finally erupted in a bloody war.

This new conflict opened badly for the young republic, reflecting both the feebleness of its truncated military establishment and the emergence of a powerful pan-Indian confederacy galvanized by fear of American encroachment and the growing influence of spiritual leaders preaching a return to native values. During 1790–91, two expeditions met with humiliating defeat. The first, led by Brigadier General Josiah Harmar, escaped relatively lightly. It involved about 1,500 men; just 300 were regulars, the balance poor-quality Kentucky and Pennsylvania militia. Sent to "chastise" the Miamis and Shawnees along the Maumee and Wabash Rivers, they were themselves roughly handled by tribal warriors under the skillful Miami leader Little Turtle. Harmar's debacle merely served notice of a greater disaster to come.

In 1791, a second force was sent, this time to establish a fort in the heart of hostile territory. It was commanded by the revolutionary war veteran Major General Arthur St. Clair, now aging and gout ridden. St. Clair's campaign revealed no hint of strategic flair: poorly organized and supplied and lacking intelligence of its enemy, his undisciplined army blindly blundered its way into Indian country. On November 4, 1791, near the Wabash River, it was expertly ambushed by a tribal force embracing Shawnees, Delawares, Mingos, Wyandots, Ottawas, Miamis, Chippewas, and Cherokees and virtually annihilated. In scenes that recalled Braddock's defeat in 1755, some 650 of St. Clair's 1,400-strong command were slaughtered and hundreds more wounded; it was the bloodiest reverse ever suffered by the United States at the hands of Indians. The victors' spoils included 1,200 muskets and eight cannon, two of them howitzers reputedly captured from Cornwallis at Yorktown. During both expeditions the small contingents of regulars had fought bravely before being overwhelmed; but the militia fled in shameful panic, just as they had done at Kip's Bay in 1776 and Camden in 1780.[101]

The shocking carnage of "St. Clair's Defeat" and the unchecked frontier raiding that followed strengthened Washington's renewed calls for a larger regular army capable of tackling the tribes and restoring the Republic's dented martial reputation. Congress swiftly agreed to increase the size of the military establishment from two to five regiments of infantry, a total of 5,168 rank and file. Soon after, Washington realized another goal, a reformed and federally controlled militia. To pay for these new forces, Congress introduced a heavy and extremely unpopular tax on spirits.[102]

There remained the vexing question of who should inherit St. Clair's frontier command. Like the president himself, most of the surviving generals who had fought and won the Revolutionary War were past their prime; yet if passed over for a younger, more vigorous man of lower rank, like Colonel "Light Horse Harry" Lee for example, they could be counted upon to object on grounds of seniority. The selection process showed Washington at his most grudging; old comrades were summarily dismissed for real or perceived faults: rifleman Daniel Morgan was "intemperate," "illiterate," and often incapacitated by palpitations; Charles Scott and George Weedon were both overly fond of a drink; Steuben was competent enough, and both "sober and brave," but sadly a foreigner. After fifteen candidates were eliminated, the choice finally fell upon Major General "Mad Anthony" Wayne, although he, too, scarcely received a hearty endorsement from his former commander, being "open to flattery—vain—easily imposed upon—and liable to be drawn into scrapes." As for Wayne's drinking habits, Washington was unsure whether he was sober "or a little addicted to the bottle."[103]

Picked as the best of a bad bunch, Wayne was an excellent choice, proving himself an energetic trainer, firm disciplinarian, and resolute combat commander. Instead of filling five regiments, his 5,000 men were formed into the "Legion of the United States." This reorganization was approved by Washington and his secretary at war, Henry Knox, on the advice of Steuben. Besides conjuring up the spirit of Julius Caesar, it followed the recommendations of French military theorists like Maurice de Saxe and Turpin de Crissé and also the example of the highly effective legions led by men like Banastre Tarleton, John Graves Simcoe, and "Light Horse Harry" Lee during the Revolutionary War. Wayne's force was split into four "sublegions": each of them was a flexible, self-contained formation fielding infantry armed with muskets and bayonets, and also riflemen, cavalry, and field artillery.[104]

Over the next two years, while fitful efforts were made to negotiate with the Indians, Wayne recruited and trained his legionaries. Those who still favored a peaceful settlement with the tribes were dissuaded by the outbreak of war between Great Britain and France in 1793. Britain's policy of boarding American vessels and pressing their crews to man the Royal Navy sparked fresh resentment against the old enemy; it was only intensified by the revelation that a continued British presence in the Old Northwest, which flouted the terms of the 1783 peace, was inciting the Republic's Indian enemies.

When Wayne's offensive finally opened in the summer of 1794, he belied his reputation for rashness, leaving nothing to chance. Like John Forbes in 1758, Wayne anchored his advance on fortified camps. His regulars were screened by effective scouts—allied Chickasaw and Choctaw warriors, and also highly mobile mounted riflemen from Kentucky, the same type of fighters who had ruthlessly eliminated Major Ferguson's command on King's Mountain in 1780. At Fallen Timbers on August 20, Wayne's disciplined regulars proved their worth, routing their opponents under Shawnee war leader Blue Jacket with a close-range volley and bayonet charge that recalled Bouquet's tactics at Bushy Run. One Ottawa chief remembered how he and his warriors "were driven by the sharp ends of the guns of the Long Knives," while Wayne assured Henry Knox that the enemy had been "taught to *dread*, and our soldiery to *believe* in, the bayonet."[105] He consolidated his battlefield success with another tried and tested element of frontier warfare, the deliberate devastation of Indian crops. Wayne's victorious campaign and the marked reluctance of the British to intervene on behalf of their allies shattered the Indian confederacy.

Its mission fulfilled, the Legion was swiftly dismantled. Once again, the Republic would put its faith in a citizen militia. In fact, at the very time Wayne was leading his legionaries against Blue Jacket's warriors, no fewer than 15,000 militiamen from four states had been summoned to deal with a grave internal security issue in western Pennsylvania. The insurrection was dubbed the Whiskey Rebellion after the farmers who refused to pay the steep federal tax on the liquor they distilled to maximize profits from their grain. Part of the huge militia army was camped near Fort Cumberland, Maryland, a spot familiar to Washington from his first military career as a soldier of the king. Escorted by three troops of leather-capped light dragoons, Washington arrived on October 16, 1794 to find every regiment "drawn up in excellent order to receive him." According to Dr. Robert Wellford of Fredericksburg, as Washington reviewed the long line of infantry "he deliberately bowed to every officer individually."[106] Prepared to lead the militiamen in person, the sixty-two-year-old president was immaculate once more in a fashionably cut version of his old blue-and-buff Continental Army uniform and spurring another impressive white steed. Daunted by the sheer numbers mobilized against them and the awesome reputation of the man at their head, the whiskey rebels wisely dispersed without a fight.

Events across the Atlantic raised the prospect that Washington might be obliged to buckle on his sword again, this time in conflict with his former enemies and allies, the French. By 1794, the revolution that dethroned Louis XVI was already into its fifth year and had long since degenerated into the bloody terror that made the Americans' rejection of George III seem mild and restrained. The crippling debts incurred by France in helping to strip Britain of her North American colonies had done much to cause the upheavals; before they had run their course, most of Europe had been dragged into a cycle of wars that would last for decades, only ending in 1815 with Emperor Napoleon's defeat at Waterloo. Many Frenchmen who had fought alongside Washington's Continentals played prominent roles in their own country's revolution. For example, veterans of the sieges of Savannah and Yorktown led the storming of another strongpoint, the notorious Bastille; Lafayette was carried along on the tumult, experiencing its unpredictable currents; at the outset, his military fame gained him command of the Republican National Guard, and he achieved immense popularity before being forced into flight by the rise of the Jacobin extremists. Many others were less fortunate: unlucky as ever, the Comte d'Estaing went to the guillotine in 1794, marked down for death by his loyalty to Marie-Antoinette.[107]

That November, the Jay Treaty between Great Britain and America, which sought to iron out disputes and prevent fresh hostilities, only exasperated France. In what amounted to an undeclared war, the French preyed upon American merchant shipping. By the time John Adams succeeded Washington as president in March 1797, the old allies were on the cusp of open conflict. Anti-French sentiment was only stoked by the Paris government's contemptuous reception of a commission sent by Adams to repair relations. Washington was among those angered by Gallic affronts to America's commerce and dignity; old as he was, his warrior spirit still burned within him. Visitors to Mount Vernon heard him call upon his countrymen to arm themselves "with a strength and zeal, equal to the dangers with which we are threatened"; as for Washington himself, he was prepared to "pour out the last drop" of his blood in America's cause.[108] He heartily approved when Congress canceled the historic alliance cemented in 1778 and gave American privateers free rein to retaliate against French merchantmen, even though the move might provoke the dispatch of another formidable expeditionary force across the Atlantic, this time bent on conquest.

For all of Washington's fulminations against France, in July 1798, when Adams sent him a lieutenant general's commission as commander in chief of all United States forces, he accepted only reluctantly and on condition of staying at Mount Vernon unless a French invasion was imminent. That month, and once again in the teeth of necessity, Congress voted to raise a "New Army," strengthening the existing 3,000-strong "Old Army" on the western frontier with twelve more regiments totaling about 10,000 men. That reinforcement could be doubled, if war actually erupted, by another "Provisional Army." As commander in chief, Washington was obliged to appoint his staff, headed by a trio of major generals. Their selection embroiled him in an unseemly and hurtful dispute involving the faithful Henry Knox: although the most experienced of the three nominees, Washington ranked him behind the other two, Alexander Hamilton and Charles Cotesworth Pinckney; as the most senior, Hamilton would also serve as the army's inspector general—in practical terms, the man responsible for building and running the new force. The bulky but vigorous Knox was mortified, not least because Hamilton had never risen higher than colonel during the Revolutionary War. When he complained to Adams, the president overruled Washington's ranking and made Knox senior major general, with Hamilton relegated to the third. Increasingly curmudgeonly, Washington bridled at this affront to his authority and threatened resignation if Adams failed to reverse his decision. Under mounting pressure, Adams finally caved in: Knox, who struggled to comprehend Washington's apparent disregard for his long and loyal services, rejected his commission.

For all his reservations about his command, Washington showed some interest in building the New Army, meeting with Hamilton and Pinckney in Philadelphia to compile a list of politically reliable officers; given the heightened animosities between the Federalists and their Republican opponents, this was no easy task. At the prospect of taking the field once more, his thoughts turned again to the kind of figure he would cut at the head of his troops. While no dandy, Washington had always appreciated fine clothing; in 1798, however, he was determined to be more ostentatious, perhaps because he wanted no repetition of 1781, when Rochambeau's gaudy troops had outshone his ragged Continentals. In specifying his own uniform, Washington reverted to his habitual blue and buff but modified the austere elegance of his Revolutionary War outfit by suggesting embroidery "on the cape, cuffs and pockets," plus a white plume in the hat as "a further distinction." Washington was even pickier when it came to horseflesh. His preference was for "a *perfect* white," followed in descending order by "a dapple grey, a deep bay, a chestnut, [and] a black." But it was not just a question of looks, particularly as Washington was not as nimble as he used to be: long legs and height alone were "no recommendation," adding "nothing to strength, but a good deal to the inconvenience in mounting."[109]

Happy to act as little more than a dignified military figurehead, Washington offloaded increasing responsibility upon Hamilton: the former captain of artillery who shared his commander's strict honor code and who had once told Adams and Thomas Jefferson that Julius Caesar was "the greatest man that ever lived," welcomed the chance to create an efficient, modern standing army, capable of defending the Republic and even attacking Spain's American possessions.[110]

But Hamilton's martial dream was never realized. During 1799, as renewed talks with France lessened the likelihood of fighting, so the "New Army" was deemed a costly irrelevance and ultimately voted out of existence. In the opening decades of the new century, as Joseph Plumb Martin could testify, not only did the traditional preference for a citizen militia dominate America's current military establishment, it distorted perceptions of the war in which he had fought as a youngster. In 1818, when legislation promoted by President James Monroe, himself a Revolutionary War veteran who had been wounded at Trenton, authorized pensions for hard-up survivors of the Continental Army, Martin encountered resentment at his "good fortune." What hurt most was the prevailing sentiment that long-service regulars like Martin had been unnecessary and "that the militia were competent for all that the crisis required." Martin, like Washington, knew better.[111]

At the end of his own life, Washington looked back wistfully to the years that had set him on his path to international fame. In 1798, he wrote a remarkable, and revealing, letter to Sally Fairfax, still living in England and long widowed. From Mount Vernon, Washington could see the bleak shell of Belvoir, gutted by fire in 1783. He never looked upon it without regretting that the "former inhabitants, with whom we lived in such harmony and friendship," were gone. Now the ruins of the mansion which Washington had first entered as an impressionable teenager were no more than "the memento of former pleasures." Although his wife, Martha, would peruse what he had written and add a contribution of her own, Washington made a telling admission: despite all that had happened to him since, he assured Sally, nothing had "been able to eradicate from my mind, the recollection of those happy moments, the happiest in my life, which I have enjoyed in your company." Underpinning his decision to make his mark as a soldier, those cherished hours in Sally's company had exerted a crucial influence upon Washington's destiny, and that of his country.[112]

When he wrote to Sally Fairfax, Washington's attitude toward war had changed; his hunger for glory had been satisfied long before. In a letter to his good friend the Chevalier de Chastellux, written in 1788 as ominous storm clouds gathered in Europe, Washington had shunned the "waste of war and the rage of conquest." In what was surely a reference to his own youthful motivations, he had observed: "It is time for the age of knight-errantry and mad-heroism to be at an end." It is perhaps significant that in his final years Washington acquired not one, but two copies of the engraving taken from Joseph Wright of Derby's poignant 1789 painting *The Dead Soldier*, to decorate Mount Vernon's "New Room." Depicting a young mother with baby in arms, keening over the body of her husband, it was a dramatic depiction of the real cost of war.[113]

Yet there is no denying the centrality of warfare to Washington's towering reputation among his contemporaries. Washington knew this himself. It was as a soldier above all that he expected, and hoped, to be remembered. Why else, when on his deathbed and convinced that his "disorder would prove fatal," would he instruct his personal secretary Tobias Lear to "arrange and record all my late military letters and papers"?[114]

Washington not only witnessed his country's transformation from royal colonies into an independent republic but experienced the process at a starkly human and visceral level; by his frontline leadership of the Continental Army, a weapon forged to his own specifications, he did more than anyone to achieve it. Hence it was to Washington—rather than to the more intellectual John Adams or Thomas Jefferson—that Americans first turned for national leadership once their independence had been won. It was apt that Washington's final hours should be shared by Dr. James Craik, who had been with him at so many critical moments in his military career: Fort Necessity in 1754, Valley Forge in 1778, and Yorktown in 1781. Now the faithful doctor and his lancet achieved what the Indians, French, and British had all failed to accomplish: his remorseless medicinal bleedings slowly but steadily drained Washington's great frame of its strength until his pallor prefigured the "marble man" he would soon become.

As "Light Horse Harry" Lee phrased it in his famous eulogy, George Washington had been "first in war, first in peace, first in the hearts of his countrymen." Lee's careful ordering of these qualifications is revealing. Without his youthful hankering after military fame, kindled by his half brother Lawrence at Mount Vernon and the Fairfaxes at Belvoir, Washington would, in all probability, have remained a footnote in history: a respectable, if unremarkable, surveyor and planter. For Washington, war truly paved the way to everything else. The influences he absorbed as a youngster on the Potomac likewise contributed that other essential strand to his character—the conduct, bearing, and outlook that led his contemporaries to perceive him as a "complete gentleman."[115]

Writing in 1903, the British Army's historian, Sir John Fortescue, believed that all Englishmen should readily acknowledge Washington's bravery and determination, adding an explanation for his "remarkable" leadership qualities: "Washington had the advantage of being a gentleman," Sir John wrote. He continued rather stiffly:

"I am aware that this is now supposed to be no advantage; but Washington considered it to be essential to a good officer, and I am content to abide by his opinion."[116] While Fortescue was also commenting upon the blurring of social distinctions within his own society, his observation is no less valid: Washington's gentlemanly persona went beyond a veneer of polite manners; it shaped his whole approach to soldiering and was instrumental in his successful conduct of the American War of Independence. George Washington's extraordinary reputation as one of the most celebrated men of his own age, or of any other, can be traced back unerringly to his ambition to become both a gentleman *and* a warrior: it was the gradual fusion of those traits that ultimately forged such a formidably balanced fighter.

Notes

Abbreviations used in notes:

Diaries   Donald Jackson and Dorothy Twohig, eds., *The Diaries of George Washington*, 6 vols. (Charlottesville, Virginia, 1976–79)

GW   George Washington

JCC   Worthington C. Ford et al., eds., *The Journals of the Continental Congress, 1774–1789*, 34 vols. (Washington, D.C., 1904–37)

PMHB   *Pennsylvania Magazine of History and Biography*

PWCW   W. W. Abbot, Dorothy Twohig, and Philander D. Chase, eds., *The Papers of George Washington: Colonial Series*, 10 vols. (Charlottesville, Virginia, 1983)

PWRW   W. W. Abbot, Dorothy Twohig, and Philander D. Chase, eds., *The Papers of George Washington: Revolutionary War Series*, 20 vols. to date (Charlottesville, Virginia, 1985–)

WMQ   *William and Mary Quarterly* (3rd Series)

WW   John C. Fitzpatrick, ed., *The Writings of George Washington*, 39 vols. (Washington, D.C., 1931–39)

Note: After the first full citation, all other titles are given in shortened form.

Introduction

1. *The Annual Register . . . for 1776*, p. 148.

2. Patrick Ferguson to Dr. Adam Ferguson [?],January 31, 1778, in Howard H. Peckham, ed., *Sources of American Independence: Selected Manuscripts from the Collections of the William L. Clements Library* (Chicago, 1978), p. 300.

3. Message to the Delaware Nation, May 12, 1779, in *PWRW*, 20, pp. 447–48.

4. *London Chronicle*, January 5, 1782, quoted in Troy O. Bickham, "Sympathizing with Sedition? George Washington, the British Press, and British Attitudes During the American War of Independence," *WMQ*, 59 (2002), pp. 101–22: 120.

5. "Particulars of the Life and Character of General Washington . . . Signed an OLD SOLDIER," *Gentleman's Magazine*, August 1778, pp. 368–70: 370. This first appeared in two newspapers, *Lloyd's Evening Post* and *Public Advertiser*, on August 17, 1778.

6. *The Annual Register . . . for 1777*, p. 20.

7. See, for example, Dave Richard Palmer, *The Way of the Fox: American Strategy in the War for America, 1775–1783* (Westport, Connecticut, 1975), p. 143; John Ferling, *Almost a Miracle: The American Victory in the War of Independence* (New York, 2007), p. 100; Joseph J. Ellis, *His Excellency George Washington* (New York, 2004), pp. 74, 100–101; Edward G. Lengel, *General George Washington: A Military Life* (New York, 2005), p. 366.

8. For a discussion of these two paintings that reaches a different verdict on their effectiveness, see David Hackett Fischer, *Washington's Crossing* (New York, 2004), pp. 429–31.

9. On West, Copley, Peale, and Trumbull see Chapter 2, "Transatlantic Journeys," in Holger Hoock, *Empires of the Imagination: Politics, War, and the Arts in the British World, 1750–1850* (London, 2010), pp. 83–116.

10. Isaac J. Greenwood, "Remarks on the Portraiture of Washington," in *The Magazine of American History, with Notes and Queries*, 2 (1878), pp. 30–38: 38. The author of the article was the grandson of the dentist John Greenwood.

11. Ibid., p. 31.

12. GW to Greenwood, January 6, 1799, in *WW*, 37, p. 83.

13. Greenwood, "Remarks on the Portraiture of Washington," *Magazine of American History* (1878), p. 38. For Houdon's bust and statue, see William M. S. Rasmussen and Robert S. Tilton, *George Washington: The Man Behind the Myths* (Charlottesville, Virginia, 1999), pp. 155–58, 164.

14. Ibid., pp. 165, 205, 215–16, 222–25.

15. Stuart's portrait of "Washington at Dorchester Heights" in 1776, which was painted in 1806, is in Boston's Museum of Fine Arts. See Richard McLanathan, *Gilbert Stuart* (New York, 1986), pp. 127–31.

16. This memoir is given and discussed in Fred Anderson, ed., *George Washington Remembers: Reflections on the French and Indian War* (Lanham, Maryland, 2004).

17. For Washington's revision of the genesis of the Yorktown campaign, see below, p. 393.

18. William S. Powell, ed., "A Connecticut Soldier Under Washington: Elisha Bostwick's Memoirs of the First Years of the Revolution," *WMQ*, 6 (1949), pp. 94–107: 95, 101, 103–104.

1: Finding a Path

1. David Hackett Fischer, *Albion's Seed: Four British Folkways in America* (New York, 1989), p. 214.

2. "The American Ancestry of Mary Ball," Appendix 1 of Douglas Southall Freeman, *George Washington: A Biography*, 7 vols. (New York, 1948–57), 1, p. 530.

3. Ibid., p. 15.

4. Alan Taylor, *American Colonies: The Settlement of North America to 1800* (New York, 2001), p. 142.

5. See J. Frederick Fausz, "'Engaged in Enterprises Pregnant with Terror': George Washington's Formative Years among the Indians," in Warren R. Hofstra, ed., *George Washington and the Virginia Backcountry* (Madison, Wisconsin, 1998), pp. 115–55: 118.

6. James Thomas Flexner, *George Washington: The Forge of Experience (1732–1775)* (Boston, 1965), p. 11.

7. A. Roger Ekirch, *Bound for America: The Transportation of British Convicts to the Colonies, 1718–1775* (Oxford, 1987), pp. 17, 26–27.

8. See Franklin's editorials in the *Pennsylvania Gazette*, April 11 and May 9, 1751.

9. On the rise of Virginian slavery, see especially Edmund S. Morgan, *American Slavery, American Freedom: The Ordeal of Colonial Virginia* (New York, 1975).

10. For the Vernon phenomenon, see Kathleen Wilson, *The Sense of the People: Politics, Culture and Imperialism in England, 1715–1785* (Cambridge, 1995), pp. 140–48.

11. David Syrett, "The Raising of American Troops During the War of the Austrian Succession," in *Historical Research*, 73 (2000), pp. 20–32: 21–25.

12. Dated June 9, 1740, and delivered to him on July 10, 1740, Lawrence Washington's commission is preserved at Mount Vernon (Record no. 6236/W–734).

13. D. E. Leach, *Roots of Conflict: British Armed Forces and Colonial Americans, 1677–1763* (Chapel Hill, North Carolina, 1986), pp. 51–52.

14. Richard Harding, *Amphibious Warfare in the Eighteenth Century: The British Expedition to the West Indies, 1740–1742* (Woodbridge, Suffolk, 1991), p. 149.

15. Lawrence Washington to Augustine Washington, May 30, 1741, in *The Magazine of American History, with Notes and Queries*, 2 (1878), pp. 435–37: 437.

16. Ibid.

17. Smollett's "An Account of the Expedition Against Carthagena in the West Indies" first appeared in *A Compendium of Authentic and Entertaining Voyages* (1756). The citation here is from *The Miscellaneous Works of Tobias Smollett . . .* 6 vols. (2nd ed., Edinburgh, 1800), 4, p. 444.

18. Ibid., p. 432.

19. See Vernon to General Wentworth and to the Governor of Jamaica, both from aboard *Princess Carolina*, at anchor off Terra Bomba, March 20, 1741, in B. McL Ranft, ed., *The Vernon Papers* (Navy Records Society, 1958), pp. 193–95.

20. [Charles Knowles] *An Account of the Expedition to Carthagena* (Dublin, 1743), pp. 11, 33n, 46–47.

21. *Miscellaneous Works of Smollett*, 4, pp. 440, 442–43.

22. "George Washington's 'Remarks,'" in Anderson, ed., *George Washington Remembers*, p. 15.

23. For the "cherry tree story," see Rasmussen and Tilton, *George Washington: The Man Behind the Myths*, pp. 13–14.

24. I am extremely grateful to Dr. R. Scott Stephenson, director of Collections and Interpretation at the American Revolution Center, Philadelphia, for bringing this intriguing relic at Mount Vernon to my attention.

25. On the significance of the *Rules of Civility*, see especially Paul K. Longmore, *The Invention of George Washington* (Charlottesville, Virginia, 1988), p. 7; Rasmussen and Tilton, *George Washington: The Man Behind the Myths*, pp. 11–12.

26. Don Higginbotham, "George Washington and Revolutionary Asceticism: The Localist as Nationalist," in Hofstra, ed., *Washington and the Virginia Backcountry*, pp. 223–50: 229; C. R. Markham, *Life of Robert Fairfax of Steeton* (London, 1885), pp. 187–88.

27. On this point, and the extent to which English-built and occupied Belvoir was "exceptional" among Virginia's Georgian mansions, see Rasmussen and Tilton, *George Washington: The Man Behind the Myths*, pp. 20–21.

28. See Washington's "Journal of my Journey over the Mountains . . . ," in *Diaries*, 1, pp. 6–23.

29. This is the consistent verdict of two influential Washington biographers writing half a century apart. See Flexner, *Washington: The Forge of Experience*, p. 39; Ellis, *His Excellency George Washington*, p. 37.

30. *Diaries*, 1, p. 73.

31. Ibid., p. 81.

32. Ibid., p. 82; Max Farrand, ed., *The Autobiography of Benjamin Franklin: A Restoration of a "Fair Copy"* (Berkeley and Los Angeles, 1949), p. 123: Franklin wrote his account in 1784, adding: "This I mention for the sake of parents who omit that operation on the supposition that they should never forgive themselves if a child died under it—my example

showing that the regret may be the same either way, and that therefore the safer should be chosen."

33. Rhys Isaac, *The Transformation of Virginia, 1740–1790* (new ed., Chapel Hill, North Carolina, 1999), pp. 104–10.

34. Daniel K. Richter, *Facing East from Indian Country: A Native History of Early America* (Cambridge, Massachusetts, 2001), p. 168.

35. See Donald H. Kent, *The French Invasion of Western Pennsylvania* (Harrisburg, Pennsylvania, 1954).

36. Earl of Holderness, Secretary-of-State, to Dinwiddie, London, August 28, 1753, in National Archives, Kew, CO [Colonial Office], 5/211, fols. 11–15.

37. Instructions from Robert Dinwiddie, October 30, 1753, in *PWC*, 1, pp. 60–61.

38. The letter credited to Mercer, and believed to describe Washington's appearance in 1759, is cited in Freeman, *Washington*, 3, p. 6.

39. For Washington's journal of his "Journey to the French Commandant, October 31, 1753–January 16, 1754," see *Diaries*, 1, pp. 130–61.

40. See "Remarks," in Anderson, ed., *George Washington Remembers*, p. 16. That Washington may have "prompted" the Half-King to invoke Colonel John Washington's Indian name is suggested by Professor Fred Anderson. See his "Speculations on George Washington's Autobiographical 'Remarks' of 1787," in ibid., pp. 137–78, note 21. Interestingly, although Washington certainly used the name "Caunotocarious" (or "Caunotaucarious" etc.) from 1754 onward, it does not appear in the Indian speeches included in his journal of the 1753 Ohio expedition.

41. On these tattoos, see "The Journal of Robert Cholmley's Batman," in Charles Hamilton, ed., *Braddock's Defeat* (Norman, Oklahoma, 1959), p. 26 note.

42. For Saint-Pierre's distinguished career, see F. G. Halpenny, ed., *Dictionary of Canadian Biography*, 13 vols. (Toronto, 1966–94), 3, pp. 374–76.

43. Kent, *French Invasion of Western Pennsylvania*, pp. 75–76.

44. For example, the *Maryland Gazette* carried the journal in its editions of March 21 and 28, 1754, with the *Boston Gazette* printing it between April 16 and May 21, 1754.

2: Hearing the Bullets Whistle

1. GW to Augustine Washington, August 2, 1755, in *PWC*, 1, p. 352.
2. "Instructions to be observed by Major George Washington on the expedition to the Ohio [Jan. 1754]," in *PWC*, 1, p. 65.
3. GW to Dinwiddie, March 7 and 9, 1754, in *PWC*, 1, pp. 72, 73.
4. *Diaries*, 1, pp. 174–75.
5. GW to James Hamilton,. ca. April 24, 1754, in *PWC*, 1, p. 83.
6. GW to Dinwiddie, April 25, 1754, in *PWC*, 1, pp. 88–89.
7. GW to Horatio Sharpe, April 24, 1754, in *PWC*, 1, p. 86.
8. GW to Dinwiddie, May 18, 1754, in *PWC*, 1, pp. 99–100.
9. *Diaries*, 1, pp. 191–92.
10. GW to Dinwiddie, May 27, 1754, in *PWC*, 1, p. 105.
11. Ibid.; *Diaries*, 1, pp. 193–95. See "The Ohio Expedition of 1754. By Adam Stephen," *PMHB*, 18 (1894), pp. 43–50: 46.
12. This account of the Jumonville episode draws on the following sources: *Diaries*, 1, pp. 194–95; *Maryland Gazette*, June 13, 1754 (this, and other issues of the *Maryland Gazette* cited in these notes, were accessed via the Archives of Maryland online); GW to Dinwiddie, May 29 (two letters), May 31, and June 3, in *PWC*, 1, pp. 110–13, 116, 124; also GW to John Augustine Washington, May 31, 1754, in ibid., p. 118.
13. See Richard White, *The Middle Ground: Indians, Empires, and Republics in the Great Lakes Region, 1650–1815* (Cambridge and New York, 1991), p. 241; Fred Anderson, *Crucible of War: The Seven Years' War and the Fate of Empire in British North America, 1754–1766* (New York, 2000), pp. 5–6, 52–59. For the grisly detail of the Half-King handling Jumonville's brains, Professor Anderson cites the testimony of Private John Shaw. Although not present during the Jumonville skirmish, Shaw served during Washington's 1754 Ohio campaign and must have spoken with eyewitnesses. His description certainly squares with the convincing account in the *Maryland Gazette* of June 13, 1754, which reported that Ensign Jumonville was tomahawked by the Half-King.
14. *Diaries*, 1, p. 197; Washington to Dinwiddie, May 29, 1754, in *PWC*, 1, p. 111.

15. Holderness to Dinwiddie, August 28, 1753 (National Archives, CO 5/211, fol. 12).

16. *Virginia Gazette*, June 13, 1754 (digital reproductions of this, and other issues of the *Virginia Gazette* cited here, are available online via the Colonial Williamsburg Foundation).

17. Dinwiddie to the Board of Trade, June 18, 1754 (National Archives, CO 5/1328, fol. 117).

18. Francis Parkman, *Montcalm and Wolfe*, 2 vols. (Boston, 1884), 1, p. 156.

19. GW to John Augustine Washington, May 31, 1754, in *PWC*, 1, p. 118.

20. Jeremy Black, *George II: Puppet of the Politicians?* (Exeter, 2007), p. 38; Horace Walpole, *Memoirs of King George the Second*, ed. John Brooke, 3 vols. (New Haven and London, 1985), 2, p. 18.

21. The Half-King's speech as reported in Weiser's journal, in Paul. A. W. Wallace, *Conrad Weiser, 1696–1760: Friend of Colonist and Mohawk* (Philadelphia, 1945), p. 367.

22. See Fox to Demeré, August 25, 1754, National Archives, CO 5/211, fol. 69; "Draught of orders for settling the rank of the officers of His Majesty's Forces, when joined or serving with the Provincial Forces in North America," November 12, 1754, ibid., fol. 115.

23. *Diaries*, 1, pp. 202–207.

24. Wallace, *Conrad Weiser*, p. 367.

25. Dinwiddie to GW, June 1 and June 27, 1754, in *PWC*, 1, pp. 119, 150.

26. Major Adam Stephen's report, in *Maryland Gazette*, August 29, 1754. For the "siege" of Fort Necessity, see also Washington and Mackay's report, published in the *Virginia Gazette*, July 19, 1754, and George Washington's later "Remarks," in Anderson, ed., *George Washington Remembers*, pp. 17–18.

27. Reporting gossip circulating in Williamsburg, Landon Carter noted Muse's alleged misbehavior in his diary for August 22, 1754. See Jack P. Greene, ed., *The Diary of Colonel Landon Carter of Sabine Hall, 1752–1778*, 2 vols. (Charlottesville, Virginia, 1965), 1, pp. 110–11.

28. John Robinson to GW, September 15, 1754, in *PWC*, 1, p. 209.

29. La Péronie to GW, September 5, 1754, in *PWC*, 1, p. 194.

30. Despite some minor editorial tinkering, the published French translation was essentially the same as Washington's manuscript. See the discussion in *Diaries*, 1, pp. 171–73.

31. Donald H. Kent, ed., *Contrecoeur's Copy of George Washington's Journal for 1754* (first published in *Pennsylvania History*, January 1952; repr. Eastern National Park & Monument Association, 1989), pp. 3–4.

32. Dinwiddie expressed this opinion to both Maryland's lieutenant governor Sharpe and Horace Walpole in London. See Freeman, *Washington*, 1, p. 416.

33. Sir Thomas Robinson to Sharpe, July 5, 1754, National Archives, CO 5/211, fol. 33.

34. British Library, Add. MS [Additional Manuscripts] 32850, fol. 289: Albemarle to the Duke of Newcastle, September 11, 1754.

35. "Sketch for the Operations in North America, November 16, 1754," in Stanley Pargellis, ed., *Military Affairs in North America 1748–1765: Selected Documents from the Cumberland Papers in Windsor Castle* (New Haven, Connecticut, 1936), pp. 45–48.

36. GW to Colonel Fitzhugh, November 15, 1754, in *PWC*, 1, pp. 225–26.

37. Orme to GW, March 2, 1755, in *PWC*, 1, p. 241.

38. GW to Orme, March 15, 1755, in *PWC*, 1, pp. 243–44.

39. GW to William Byrd, Carter Burwell, and John Robinson, all April 20, 1755, in *PWC*, 1, pp. 249–57.

40. GW to Sarah Cary Fairfax, April 30, 1755, in *PWC*, 1, p. 261.

41. "Orme's Journal," in Winthrop Sargent, ed., *The History of an Expedition Against Fort Du Quesne in 1755* (Philadelphia, 1855), pp. 287, 309, 314–15. See also Adam Stephen to GW, November 7, 1755, in *PWC*, 2, p. 159.

42. "Journal of Cholmley's Batman," in Hamilton, ed., *Braddock's Defeat*, p. 12.

43. For a detailed and thoughtful examination of the 1755 expedition against Fort Duquesne, see Paul E. Kopperman, *Braddock at the Monongahela* (Pittsburgh, 1977). On the composition of Braddock's army, see the returns enclosed with Braddock to Robert Napier, in Pargellis, ed., *Military Affairs in North America*, pp. 86–89.

44. See "Return of Ordnance," Little Bear Camp, July 18, 1755, in ibid., pp. 96–97. For Wood's testimony, see Rex Whitworth, ed., *Gunner at Large: The Diary of James Wood, R.A. 1746–1765* (London, 1988), pp. 40, 53. For an overview of smoothbore artillery and its capabilities, see B. P. Hughes, *Firepower: Weapons Effectiveness on the Battlefield, 1630–1850* (London, 1974), pp. 13–18, 29–35.

45. Braddock to GW, May 15, 1755, in *PWC*, 1, p. 281.

46. See "Memorandum," in *PWC*, 1, pp. 282–83.

47. GW to William Fairfax, June 7, 1755, in *PWC*, 1, pp. 298–99.

48. "Remarks," in Anderson, ed., *George Washington Remembers*, p. 21.

49. Ibid, pp. 18–19.

50. See "Orme's Journal," in Sargent, ed., *History of the Expedition*, pp. 293–98, 318.

51. See Beverley W. Bond Jr., ed., "The Captivity of Charles Stuart," in *Mississippi Valley Historical Review*, 13 (1926), p. 63; also, "A Journal of the Proceedings of the Seamen," in Sargent, ed., *History of an Expedition*, pp. 378, 380.

52. "Journal of Cholmley's Batman," in Hamilton, ed., *Braddock's Defeat*, pp. 17–19.

53. GW to William Fairfax, June 7, 1755, in *PWC*, 1, pp. 299–300.

54. GW to Sarah Cary Fairfax, June 7, 1755, in *PWC*, 1, pp. 308–309.

55. Ellis, *His Excellency George Washington*, p. 36.

56. "Memorandum," May 30–June 11, 1755, in *PWC*, 1, pp. 293–94.

57. GW to John Augustine Washington, June 28 –July 2, 1755, in *PWC*, 1, pp. 319–21.

58. "Journal of a British Officer," in Hamilton, ed., *Braddock's Defeat*, p. 45; "Orme's Journal," in Sargent, ed., *History of an Expedition*, p. 341.

59. Roger Morris to GW, June 23, 1755, GW to John Augustine Washington, June 28–July 2, 1755, and to Orme, June 30, 1755, in *PWC*, 1, pp. 315, 319–24, 329.

60. "Orme's Journal," in Sargent, ed., *History of an Expedition*, p. 350.

61. GW to Dinwiddie, July 18, 1755, in *PWC*, 1, p. 339.

62. Duncan Cameron, *The Life, Adventures, and Surprizing Deliverances of Duncan Cameron, Private Soldier in the Regiment of Foot, Late Sir Peter Halket's* (3rd ed., Philadelphia, 1756), p. 13.

63. GW to Dinwiddie, July 18, 1755, in *PWC*, 1, p. 339.
64. "Orme's Journal," in Hamilton, ed., *Braddock's Defeat*, pp. 356–57.
65. Ibid; "Remarks," in Anderson, ed., *George Washington Remembers*, p. 20.
66. James Smith, *An Account of the Remarkable Occurrences in the Life and Travels of Col. James Smith* (Lexington, Kentucky, 1799), p. 9.
67. "Remarks," in Anderson, ed., *George Washington Remembers*, p. 20.
68. Ibid, p. 21.
69. Cited in Longmore, *Invention of George Washington*, p. 30.

3: Defending the Frontier

1. Letter of July 26, 1755, in *PWC*, 1, p. 346.
2. "Remarks," in Anderson, ed., *George Washington Remembers*, p. 21.
3. GW to Mary Ball Washington, and to Warner Lewis, August 14, 1755, in *PWC*, 1, pp. 359, 362.
4. Commission and Instructions from Robert Dinwiddie, August 14, 1755, in *PWC*, 2, 3–5.
5. GW to Andrew Lewis, September 6, 1755, in *PWC*, 2, pp. 23–4.
6. Orders, Fort Cumberland, September 17, 1755, in *PWC*, 2, pp. 40–41.
7. GW to Joshua Lewis, September 18, 1755, in *PWC*, 2, p. 48.
8. Stephen to GW, September 25 and October 4, 1755, in *PWC*, 2, pp. 62, 72.
9. Warren Hofstra notes that while the backcountry settlers were often reluctant to answer the calls of Washington and other officers for the "common" defense, they fought tenaciously to protect their own communities. See Hofstra, "'A Parcel of Barbarian's and an Uncooth Set of People': Settlers and Settlements of the Shenandoah Valley," in Hofstra, ed., *George Washington and the Virginia Backcountry*, pp. 87–114: 104.
10. GW to Dinwiddie, October 11–12, 1755, in *PWC*, 2, pp. 102–4.
11. On the need for Indian allies, see especially Washington's letters to Dinwiddie and John Robinson from Winchester on April 7, 1756, in *PWC*, 2, pp. 333, 338.
12. GW to Andrew Montour and Christopher Gist, October 10, 1755, in *PWC*, 2, pp. 97–99.

13. See GW to Lieutenant John Bacon, October 26, 1755, in *PWC*, 2, p. 137.

14. On the Dagworthy dispute, see Longmore, *Invention of George Washington*, pp. 37–38; also GW to Dinwiddie, December 5, 1755, and Dinwiddie to GW, December 14, 1755 and January 22, 1756, in *PWC*, 2, pp. 200, 213, 291–92.

15. GW to Stephen, November 18, 1755, in *PWC*, 2, pp. 172–73. See also James Titus, *The Old Dominion at War: Society, Politics and Warfare in Late Colonial Virginia* (Columbia, South Carolina, 1991), pp. 91–92.

16. For the New England provincials, see Fred Anderson, *A People's Army: Massachusetts Soldiers and Society in the Seven Years War* (Chapel Hill, North Carolina, 1984), pp. 123–25. The limit of thirty-nine lashes followed the teachings of the Old and New Testaments: Deuteronomy 25: 3 specified that punishment floggings must not exceed forty strokes; if they did, the recipient would be "degraded." To avoid this, it became customary for one lash to be withheld. Describing his sufferings, the apostle Paul boasted that he had five times "received from the Jews the forty lashes minus one"(II Corinthians 11: 24).

17. GW to Stephen, November 28, 1755, and GW to Dinwiddie, December 5, 1755, in *PWC*, 2, pp. 185, 201–202.

18. See Hog to GW, November 29, 1755, and GW to Hog, December 27, 1755, in *PWC*, 2, pp. 188, 236.

19. Titus, *Old Dominion at War*, p. 78.

20. GW to Dinwiddie, January 13, 1756, in *PWC*, 2, p. 278.

21. See Lester J. Cappon, ed., *Atlas of Early American History: The Revolutionary Era, 1760–1790* (Princeton, New Jersey, 1976), p. 97.

22. *Boston Gazette*, March 1, 1756.

23. Shirley to GW, March 5, 1756, in *PWC*, 2, p. 323.

24. Freeman, *Washington*, 2, pp. 165–67.

25. See "Memorandum," January 7, 1756, and note 1 giving the court proceedings, in *PWC*, 2, pp. 254–56.

26. "Address," Winchester, January 8, 1756, in *PWC*, 2, pp. 256–57. On the popularity of Bland's *Treatise*, see J. A. Houlding, *Fit for Service: The Training of the British Army 1715–1795* (Oxford, 1981), pp. 182–84. See also O. L. Spaulding, "The Military Studies of George Washington," in *American Historical Review*, 29 (1924), pp. 675–80.

27. Stephen to GW, March 29, 1756, in *PWC*, 2, p. 325; GW to Dinwiddie, April 18, 1756, in *PWC*, 3, p. 14.

28. Robinson to GW, ca. March 31–April 2, 1756, in *PWC*, 2, p. 329; GW to Robinson, April 18, 1756, in *PWC*, 3, pp. 15–16.

29. Carter to GW, April 21, 1756, in *PWC*, 3, pp. 30–31.

30. Dinwiddie to GW, April 15, 1756, in *PWC*, 2, pp. 355–56; GW to Dinwiddie, April 16, 1756, and Robinson to GW, April 17, 1756, in *PWC*, 3, pp. 1, 12.

31. See Lieutenant William Stark to GW, "Sunday Night [April 18, 1756] 8 Oclock"; GW to Dinwiddie, April 19, 1756, in *PWC*, 3, pp. 17–18, 20.

32. *Pennsylvania Gazette*, May 13, 1756.

33. For a perceptive analysis of the devastating impact of captive taking upon frontier communities, see Fred Anderson, *The War That Made America: A Short History of the French and Indian War* (New York, 2005), pp. 153–55.

34. GW to Dinwiddie, April 22, 1756, in *PWC*, 3, pp. 33–34.

35. Orders, Winchester, May 1, 1756: "Memorandum Respecting the Militia," May 8, 1756, in *PWC*, 3, pp. 70, 99.

36. William Fairfax to GW, May 13–14, 1756, in *PWC*, 3, p. 125.

37. Orders for the militia, Winchester, May 15, 1756, Dinwiddie to GW, May 27 and August 19, 1756, and GW to Dinwiddie, June 25 and August 4, 1756, in *PWC*, 3, pp. 136–37, 179, 224, 313, 359; Muster for July 13, 1756, cited in *PWC*, 3, p. 263, note 1. See also Titus, *Old Dominion at War*, pp. 79–80.

38. Roll of Washington's Company, August 28, 1757, in *PWC*, 4, pp. 389–92. Details for one man are missing. For the overall statistics for Virginia and Massachusetts provincials, see Matthew C. Ward, *Breaking the Backcountry: The Seven Years' War in Virginia and Pennsylvania, 1754–1765* (Pittsburgh, 2003), p. 264, table 1. On the backgrounds of the men of the Virginia Regiment in 1756–57, see also Titus, *Old Dominion at War*, pp. 81–88.

39. GW to Dinwiddie, April 27, 1756, in *PWC*, 3, pp. 59–60.

40. Orders, Fort Cumberland, July 6–8, 1756, in *PWC*, 3, pp. 239–41.

41. Stephen to GW, July 25, 1756, in *PWC*, 3, p. 294.

42. *PWC*, 3, p. 354.

43. GW to Dinwiddie, August 14, 1756, in *PWC*, 3, p. 350.

44. The *Virginia Gazette* of September 3, 1756 is one of only two issues of the newspaper surviving from that year. The "Virginia-Centinel" article was reprinted in the *Maryland Gazette* of November 25, 1756.

45. Kirkpatrick and Ramsay to GW, both September 22, 1756, in *PWC*, 3, pp. 410, 413.

46. Brian Leigh Dunnighan, ed., Pierre Pouchot, *Memoirs on the Late War in North America Between France and England* (Youngstown, New York, 1994), p. 88.

47. See Stanley Pargellis, *Lord Loudoun in North America* (New Haven, Connecticut, 1933).

48. GW to Dinwiddie, October 10, 1756, and GW to Stephen, October 23, 1756, in *PWC*, 3, pp. 431–32: 440; "Remarks," in Anderson, ed., *George Washington Remembers*, p. 22. For Washington and religion, see Ellis, *His Excellency George Washington*, p. 45; Longmore, *Invention of George Washington*, p. 169.

49. GW to Dinwiddie, November 9, 1756, in *PWC*, 4, pp. 1–5.

50. Dinwiddie to GW, November 16, 1756, in *PWC*, 4, pp. 25–26.

51. Dinwiddie to GW, December 10, 1756, GW to Captain William Bronaugh, December 17, 1756, in *PWC*, 4, pp. 50, 59.

52. Loudoun's comments were enclosed in Dinwiddie to GW, December 10, 1756, in *PWC*, 4, p. 51.

53. GW to Dinwiddie, December 19, 1756, in *PWC*, 4, p. 65.

54. GW to Loudoun, January 10, 1757, in *PWC*, 4, pp. 79–90.

55. *PWC*, 4, p. 92, note 29.

56. GW to Cunningham, January 28, 1757, in *PWC*, 4, p. 106.

57. GW to Dinwiddie, March 10, 1757, in *PWC*, 4, pp. 112–15. For his shorter, edited "Memorial" to Loudoun, dated Philadelphia, March 23, 1757, see *PWC*, 4, pp. 120–21.

58. Longmore, *Invention of George Washington*, pp. 43–44.

59. See the discussion in *Diaries*, 1, pp. 166–71.

60. Lawrence Henry Gipson, *The British Empire Before the American Revolution, Vol. 7: The Great War for the Empire: The Victorious Years, 1758–1760* (New York, 1949) pp. 98–99.

61. While "Billy" was awaiting a vacancy in the regulars, Colonel Fairfax lobbied Washington to find him a place in the Virginia Regiment. Although commissioned in the Virginia Regiment, he never served in it, instead taking the first opportunity to purchase a regular commission. See William Fairfax to GW, July 17, 1757 in *PWC*, 4, p. 310; and William Henry Fairfax to GW, December 9, 1757, in *PWC*, 5, pp. 71–72.

62. Longmore, *Invention of George Washington*, p. 54.

63. GW to Richard Washington, April 15, 1757, in *PWC*, 4, pp. 132–33. Despite their shared surname, the two men were not related.

64. GW to Stanwix, May 28, 1757, in *PWC*, 4, p. 169.

65. Dinwiddie to GW, May 16, 1757, in *PWC*, 4, pp. 153–54.

66. Mercer to GW, April 24, 1757, in *PWC*, 4, pp. 139–40.

67. GW to Dinwiddie, July 11, 1757; GW to Stanwix, July 15, 1757, in *PWC*, 4, pp. 295, 306.

68. General court-martial, Fort Loudoun, July 25–26, 1757; GW to Dinwiddie, August 3, 1757, in *PWC*, 4, pp. 329–34, 360.

69. "Particulars of the Life and Character of General Washington," in *Gentleman's Magazine, 1778*, p. 369. The anonymous veteran who authored this sketch served alongside Washington during the 1758 campaign against Fort Duquesne.

70. See Ian K. Steele, *Betrayals: Fort William Henry and the "Massacre"* (New York, 1990).

71. Stanwix to GW, June 18, 1757, and GW to Stanwix, July 15, 1757, in *PWC*, 4, pp. 228, 306.

72. Instructions to Company Captains, Fort Loudoun, July 29, 1757, in *PWC*, 4, pp. 341–45.

73. Baker to GW, June 10, 1757, and GW to Dinwiddie, June 12, 1757, in *PWC*, 4, pp. 200, 208–209; *Maryland Gazette*, July 7, 1757, giving extract of a letter from Fort Loudoun, June 12, 1757.

74. Atkin to GW, June 19, 1757, Captain Thomas Waggener et al. to GW, June 19, 1757, in *PWC*, 4, pp. 232–34, 239.

75. GW to Stanwix, July 15 and 30, 1757, in *PWC*, 4, pp. 306–307, 353.

76. GW to Dinwiddie, October 5, 1757, in *PWC*, 5, pp. 2–3.

77. See William Peachey to GW, August 22, 1757, and GW to Dinwiddie, September 17, 1757, in *PWC*, 4, pp. 381–83, 411–12.

78. Dinwiddie to GW, September 24, 1757, in *PWC*, 4, p. 422.

79. Stewart to Dinwiddie, November 9, 1757, in *PWC*, 5, p. 46.

4: Tarnished Victory

1. GW to Sarah Cary Fairfax, November 15, 1757, and February 13, 1758, in *PWC*, 5, pp. 56, 93.

2. GW to Stanwix, March 4, 1758, in *PWC*, 5, pp. 101–102.

3. Mercer to GW, August 17, 1757, in *PWC*, 4, pp. 370–71.

4. Rasmussen and Tilton, *George Washington: The Man Behind the Myths*, pp. 43–44, 80; G. M. Trevelyan, *England Under Queen Anne: Blenheim* (London, 1930), pp. 405, 409–410.

5. GW to Richard Washington, April 5, 1758, in *PWC*, 5, p. 112.

6. For Loudoun's plan for 1758, see copy of a letter to "Duke of B–d [Bedford]," New York, unsigned and undated but in the hand of John Forbes and written in February 1758, in National Archives of Scotland, Edinburgh, Microfilm RH 4/86/1: "Military Papers of Brig-Gen John Forbes in North America" (no piece reference).

7. Pitt to General James Abercromby, December 30, 1757, in G. S. Kimball, ed., *The Correspondence of William Pitt, When Secretary of State, with Colonial Governors and Military and Naval Commissioners in America*, 2 vols. (London, 1906; repr. New York, 1969), 1, pp. 143–46.

8. Pitt to the governors of Pennsylvania, Maryland, Virginia, South Carolina, and North Carolina, December 30, 1757, ibid., pp. 141–42.

9. GW to Stanwix, April 10, 1758, and to Gage, April 12, 1758, in *PWC*, 5, pp. 117, 126.

10. Anderson, *The War That Made America*, pp. 120–21.

11. GW to Stanwix, April 10, 1758, in *PWC*, 5, p. 117.

12. GW to Forbes, April 23, 1758, in *PWC*, 5, pp. 138–39, and note 1; St. Clair to Forbes, May 19, 1758, cited in *PWC*, 5, p. 198, note 1.

13. Mercer to GW, August 17, 1757, and Stephen to GW, August 20, 1757, in *PWC*, 4, pp. 372–73, 375.

14. GW to St. Clair, April 18, 1758, in *PWC*, 5, p. 131; Gipson, *The Victorious Years*, pp. 261–62.

15. Forbes to Pitt, October 20, 1758, in Alfred Proctor James, ed., *Writings of General John Forbes, Relating to His Service in North America* (Menasha, Wisconsin, 1938), p. 240.

16. Forbes to Bouquet, June 27, 1758, in ibid., p. 125.

17. William A. Hunter, ed., "Thomas Barton and the Forbes Expedition," *PMHB*, 95 (1971), pp. 431–83: 449–50; Bouquet to Forbes, Raystown Camp, August 20, 1758, in S. K. Stevens, Donald H. Kent, and Autumn L. Leonard, eds., *The Papers of Henry Bouquet, Volume II, The Forbes Expedition* (Harrisburg, Pennsylvania), 1951, p. 397.

18. Forbes to Pitt, July 10, 1758, in James, ed., *Writings of Forbes*, p. 141.

19. GW to Bouquet, July 21, 1758, in *PWC*, 5, p. 311. On this point, and the Frederick County election in general, see Longmore, *Invention of George Washington*, pp. 58–60.

20. See Bouquet to GW, July 24, 1758, and Bouquet to Forbes, July 26 and 31, 1758, in Stevens, Kent and Leonard, ed., *Bouquet Papers, II*, pp. 269, 277–78, 290–93; Bouquet to GW, July 27, 1758, in *PWC*, 5, pp. 344–45.

21. GW to Halkett, August 2, 1758, in *PWC*, 5, pp. 360–61.

22. GW to Bouquet, August 2, 1758, in *PWC*, 5, pp. 353–60; Forbes to Bouquet, August 9, 1758, and to Abercromby, August 11, 1758, in James, ed., *Writings of Forbes*, pp. 171, 173.

23. Forbes to Bouquet, September 4, 1758, in ibid., p. 199.

24. GW to Robinson, September 1, 1758, also John Kirkpatrick to GW, August 23, 1758, in *PWC*, 5, pp. 432–33, 413.

25. On the impact of Lord Howe and his brothers Richard and William, see Stephen Brumwell, "Band of Brothers," *History Today*, 58, no. 6 (June 2008), pp. 25–31; Washington to Bouquet, July 21, 1758, in *PWC*, 5, p. 311.

26. Forbes to Pitt, Philadelphia, June 17, 1758, in James, ed., *Writings of Forbes*, p. 118.

27. West, *War for Empire in Western Pennsylvania*, pp. 55–56; Forbes to Bouquet, August 9, 1758, in James, ed., *Writings of Forbes*, p. 171.

28. Hunter, ed., "Thomas Barton and the Forbes Expedition," *PMHB* (1971), pp. 458–59; GW to Bouquet, August 24, 1758, in *PWC*, 5, p. 417.

29. Stephen to GW, August 2, 1758, in *PWC*, 5, pp. 363 and 364, note 4.

30. Bouquet to Forbes, July 31, 1758, in Stevens, Kent, and Leonard, eds., *Bouquet Papers, II*, p. 293; Hunter, ed., "Thomas Barton and the Forbes Expedition," *PMHB* (1971), p. 445.

31. Ibid., pp. 468, 470.

32. GW to Sarah Cary Fairfax, September 12, 1758, in *PWC*, 6, p. 11.

33. GW to Sarah Cary Fairfax, September 25, 1758, in *PWC*, 6, pp. 41–42. Washington's admiration for *Cato* supports the interpretation that his own martial ambition was partially driven by a desire for Sally's acclaim. For example, at one point Juba announces that Marcia's declaration of love for him " . . . will give new vigor to my Arms / Add strength and weight to my descending sword, / And drive it in a tempest on the foe."

34. Hunter, ed., "Thomas Barton and the Forbes Expedition," *PMHB* (1971), p. 473.

35. Bouquet to Forbes, September 11, 1758, in Stevens, Kent, and Leonard, eds., *Bouquet Papers, II*, p. 493.

36. Howard H. Peckham, ed., "Thomas Gist's Indian Captivity 1758–1759," in *PMHB*, 80 (1956), pp. 285–311: 291.

37. Grant to Forbes, ca. September 14, 1758, Bouquet to Forbes, September 17, 1758; Joseph Shippen to Edward Shippen, September 19, 1758, in Stevens, Kent, and Leonard, eds., *Bouquet Papers, II*, pp. 499–504, 519–20, 527–28. For a detailed analysis of "Grant's Defeat," see Douglas R. Cubbison, *The British Defeat of the French in Pennsylvania 1758: A Military History of the Forbes Campaign Against Fort Duquesne* (Jefferson, North Carolina, 2010), pp. 122–40.

38. Ian McCulloch and Timothy Todish, eds., *Through So Many Dangers: The Memoirs and Adventures of Robert Kirk, Late of the Royal Highland Regiment* (Fleischmanns, New York, 2004), p. 42. The author's real surname was Kirkwood. See also "Extract of a Letter from Pittsburgh (Lately Fort Duquesne)," in *Pennsylvania Gazette*, December 14, 1758.

39. GW to George William Fairfax, September 25, 1758, in *PWC*, 6, pp. 38–39.

40. Forbes to Bouquet, September 23, 1758, in James, ed., *Writings of Forbes*, pp. 218–21.

41. GW to Fauquier, September 25, 1758, in *PWC*, 6, p. 45.

42. Orderly Book, Raystown, 24–25 September 1758, in *PWC*, 6, pp. 36–38; for Hanna, see p. 37 note 3.

43. Hunter, ed., "Thomas Barton and the Forbes Expedition," *PMHB* (1971), p. 482.

44. Orderly Book, Raystown, September 28, 1758, in *PWC*, 6, p. 50.

45. GW to Forbes, with enclosed plans, October 8, 1758, in *PWC*, 6, pp. 66–68.

46. West, *War for Empire in Western Pennsylvania*, p. 55.

47. GW to Fauquier, October 30 and November 5, 1758, in *PWC*, 6, pp. 99–100, 113–14.

48. GW to Bouquet, November 6, 1758, in *PWC*, 6, pp. 115–16.

49. Stevens, Kent, and Leonard, eds., *Bouquet Papers, II*, pp. 600–601.

50. *Pennsylvania Gazette*, November 30, 1758; Forbes to Abercromby, November 17, 1758, in James, ed., *Writings of Forbes*, p. 255; "Remarks," in Anderson, ed., *George Washington Remembers*, p. 23; Lengel, *General George Washington*, p. 75.

51. Peckham, ed., "Thomas Gist's Indian Captivity," *PMHB* (1956), pp. 295–8.

52. Chew to Washington, September 11, 1758, in *PWC*, 6, p. 9.

53. Bouquet to William Allen, Fort Duquesne, November 25, 1758, in Stevens, Kent, and Leonard, eds., *Bouquet Papers, II*, p. 610; "A Letter from an Officer who attended Brigadier Gen. Forbes" (dated February 25, 1759), in *Gentleman's Magazine, 1759*, pp. 173–74; Orderly Book, "Camp at Loyal Hannon," November 14, 1758, in *PWC*, 6, p. 125.

54. GW to Forbes, November 16, 1758, in *PWC*, 6, p. 131.

55. GW to Forbes, November 17, 1758, in *PWC*, 6, p. 135.

56. See General Court Martial, "Camp at Loyal Hannon," November 11, 1758, in National Archives, WO [War Office] 71/67, pp. 18–22, 28.

57. Forbes to Bouquet, October 21, 1758, in James, ed., *Writings of Forbes*, p. 241.

58. Orderly Book, "Bouquet's Camp," November 24, 1758, in *PWC*, 6, p. 156; "Letter from an Officer," *Gentleman's Magazine, 1759*, pp. 173–74; National Archives of Scotland, Edinburgh, Dalhousie Papers, GD 45/2/102/3: "American and other papers of Lieutenant-Colonel (later

Brigadier-General) John Forbes," undated pencil sketch of an order of battle. This is reproduced in Cubbison, *British Defeat of the French in Pennsylvania*, p. 164.

59. Bouquet to William Allen, November 25, 1758, in Stevens, Kent, and Leonard, eds., *Bouquet Papers, II*, p. 610.

60. See "Extract of a Letter from Pittsburgh (Lately Fort Duquesne)," and "Letter from General Forbes' Army, Pittsburgh (formerly Fort Duquesne), Nov. 28, 1758" both in *Pennsylvania Gazette*, December 14, 1758.

61. Bouquet to Anne Willing and William Allen, November 25, 1758, in Stevens, Kent, and Leonard, eds., *Bouquet Papers, II*, pp. 608, 610–11; GW to Fauquier, November 28, 1758, in *PWC*, 6, p. 158; "Remarks," in Anderson, ed., *George Washington Remembers*, p. 22.

62. See E. E. Curtis, "Mercer, Hugh," in Allen Johnson and Dumas Malone, eds., *Dictionary of American Biography*, 20 vols. (New York, 1929), 6, pp. 541–42.

63. "Remarks," in Anderson, ed., *George Washington Remembers*, p. 23.

64. "Address from the Officers of the Virginia Regiment," December 31, 1758, in *PWC*, 6, pp. 178–81.

65. GW to the Officers of the Virginia Regiment, January 10, 1759, in *PWC*, 6, p. 186.

66. GW to Richard Washington, May 7, 1759, in *PWC*, 6, p. 319.

5: Between the Wars

1. "Resolution of the House of Burgesses," February 26, 1759, in *PWC*, 6, p. 192.

2. Longmore, *Invention of George Washington*, p. 60.

3. Marriage among Washington's peers is discussed in Emory G. Evans, *"A Topping People": The Rise and Decline of Virginia's Old Political Elite, 1680–1790* (Charlottesville, Virginia, 2009), pp. 121–27. On Washington's relationship with his wife, see especially, Ellis, *His Excellency George Washington*, p. 42. For the declaration of "unalterable affection," see GW to Martha Washington, Philadelphia, June 23, 1775, in *PWRW*, 1, p. 27.

4. Esmond Wright, *Washington and the American Revolution* (New York, 1962), pp. 42–43.

5. Freeman, *Washington*, 2, p. 383. Rogers would achieve an even higher profile that autumn after leading a daring raid against the Abenaki village of St. Francis. See Stephen Brumwell, *White Devil: A True Story of War, Savagery, and Vengeance in Colonial America* (London, 2004; Cambridge, Massachusetts, 2005).

6. For the following overview, two essays were especially useful: Don Higginbotham, "Young Washington: Ambition, Accomplishment and Acclaim," in Anderson, ed., *George Washington Remembers*, pp. 66–87; and John E. Ferling, "School for Command: Young George Washington and the Virginia Regiment," in Hofstra, ed., *George Washington and the Virginia Backcountry*, pp. 195–222.

7. Wright, *Washington and the American Revolution*, p. 43.

8. See Gipson, *The Victorious Years*, pp. 336–38.

9. Mercer to GW, September 16, 1759, in *PWC*, 6, p. 343.

10. Stewart to GW, September 28, 1759, in *PWC*, 6, p. 361.

11. Forbes to Amherst, February 7, 1759, in James, ed., *Writings of Forbes*, pp. 289–90; Huntington Library, San Marino, California, LO [Loudoun Papers] 6043: Richard Huck-Saunders to Loudoun, February 20, 1759. Forbes died on March 11, 1759.

12. On the 48th Foot, see Stephen Brumwell, *Redcoats: The British Soldier and War in the Americas, 1755–1763* (Cambridge and New York, 2002), pp. 75, 318, table 5; for Alexander Stephen's service, see his obituary in *Pennsylvania Gazette*, May 19, 1768.

13. GW to William Henry Fairfax, April 23, 1758, in *PWC*, 5, p. 137; "A list of the killed and wounded at the Plains of Abraham, near Quebec, 13th Sept. 1759," in *Boston News-Letter*, October 26, 1759; Brigadier-General George Townshend to Pitt, September 20, 1759, in Kimball, ed., *Correspondence of Pitt*, 2, p. 166.

14. Anderson, *The War that Made America*, pp. 206–210.

15. On Lord Howe's monument, see Brumwell, "Band of Brothers," *History Today* (June 2008), pp. 25–31.

16. Invoice to Robert Cary & Co, September 20, 1759; and invoice from Robert Cary & Co, March 15, 1760, in *PWC*, 6, pp. 353, 358, note 77,

400. See also Rasmussen and Tilton, *George Washington: The Man Behind the Myths*, pp. 88–89.

17. See GW's reports to the House of Burgesses, November 10 and 14, 1760, in *PWC*, 6, pp. 371–72.

18. Stewart to GW, June 3, 1760, in *PWC*, 6, p. 431.

19. GW to Richard Washington, August 10, 1760, in *PWC*, 6, p. 453.

20. See Paul David Nelson, *General James Grant: Scottish Soldier and Royal Governor of East Florida* (Gainesville, Florida, 1993), p. 31.

21. David H. Corkran, *The Cherokee Frontier: Conflict and Survival, 1740– 62* (Norman, Oklahoma, 1962), p. 246.

22. See "Journal of an Expedition to South Carolina," by Captain Christopher French, 22nd Foot, *Journal of Cherokee Studies*, Summer 1977, pp. 275–301: 279; Ensign John Carden, 17th Foot, to William Johnson, February 8, 1762, and Richard Shuckburgh to Johnson, April 12, 1762, in J. Sullivan and A. C. Flick, eds., *The Papers of Sir William Johnson*, 14 vols. (Albany, New York, 1921–65), 3, pp. 625, 682.

23. Barré to Major-General Amherst, October 22, 1760, in Richard Middleton, ed., *Amherst and the Conquest of Canada* (Stroud, Gloucestershire, 2003), p. 239.

24. National Library of Scotland, Edinburgh, Fletcher of Saulton Papers, MS. 16523, fols. 178–79: Fletcher to his sister, July 16, 1762.

25. See Brumwell, *Redcoats*, pp. 225, 262; National Library of Scotland, MS 16523, fol. 172: Fletcher to his sister, February 28, 1762.

26. This synthesis follows Colin G. Calloway, *The Scratch of a Pen: 1763 and the Transformation of North America* (New York, 2006), pp. 10–14.

27. For the origins and course of this Indian war, see Gregory Evans Dowd, *War Under Heaven: Pontiac, the Indian Nations and the British Empire* (Baltimore, 2002), and David Dixon, *Never Come to Peace Again: Pontiac's Uprising and the Fate of the British Empire in North America* (Norman, Oklahoma, 2005).

28. McCulloch and Todish, eds., *Through So Many Dangers*, pp. 92–94.

29. Letter from New York in *Pennsylvania Gazette*, September 1, 1763; British Library, Add. MSS. 21,649, fol. 369: Gordon to Bouquet, Philadelphia, September 4, 1763.

30. *Diaries*, 2, pp. 120–21, 226. Appropriately enough, the rise of Virginian fox hunting in the early 1730s coincided with Washington's birth; it resulted from an increase in the amount of cleared land. See Evans, "A Topping People," pp. 152–53.

31. *Diaries*, 1, pp. 321–26.

32. Woody Holton, *Forced Founders: Indians, Debtors, Slaves and the Making of the American Revolution in Virginia* (Chapel Hill, North Carolina, 1999), pp. 7–8.

33. GW to Crawford, September 17, 1767, in *PWC*, 8, p. 28; Charles H. Ambler, *George Washington and the West* (Chapel Hill, North Carolina, 1936), p. 7.

34. See Holton, *Forced Founders*, pp. 10–11; Colin G. Calloway, *The Shawnees and the War for America* (New York, 2007), pp. 44–48.

35. Longmore, *Invention of George Washington*, p. 104.

36. *Diaries*, 2, p. 289.

37. *Diaries*, 2, p. 304. On the role of Guyasuta (Kiashuta) as an advocate of Indian unity, see Richard Middleton, *Pontiac's War: Its Causes, Course and Consequences* (New York, 2007), pp. 35–38, 41–42; Calloway, *The Shawnees and the War for America*, p. 32.

38. Wright, *Washington and the American Revolution*, p. 49; Longmore, *Invention of George Washington*, pp. 104–105.

39. GW to Muse, January 29, 1774, in *PWC*, 9, pp. 460–62.

40. Charles Coleman Sellers, *Charles Willson Peale: Early Life, I* (Philadelphia, 1947), p. 109.

41. Rasmussen and Tilton, *George Washington: The Man Behind the Myths*, p. 37; Longmore, *Invention of George Washington*, p. 100.

42. Anderson, *Crucible of War*, pp. 643–44.

43. GW to Dandridge, September 20, 1765, in *WW*, 2, pp. 425–26.

44. GW to George Mason, April 5, 1769, in *PWC*, 8, pp. 177–81.

45. Longmore, *Invention of George Washington*, pp. 112–13.

46. GW to Bryan Fairfax, July 4, 1774, in *PWC*, 10, pp. 109–11.

47. For this brief overview, see especially Longmore, *Invention of George Washington*, pp. 5, 119–21, 172–73.

48. *Annual Register for 1766*, cited in Sheila O'Connell, *London 1753* (London, 2003), p. 177.

49. See Alan Axelrod, *Patton: A Biography* (New York, 2006), p. 10.

50. *London Gazette Extraordinary*, March 23, 1762; Paul David Nelson, *General Horatio Gates: A Biography* (Baton Rouge, Louisiana, 1976), pp. 34–35.

51. See "American Strategy: Charles Lee and the Radical Alternative," in John Shy, *A People Numerous and Armed: Reflections on the Military Struggle for American Independence* (New York, 1976), pp. 137–38.

52. "Strictures on a Pamphlet Entitled a 'Friendly Address to All Reasonable Americans,'" in *Collections of the New-York Historical Society: The Papers of Charles Lee*, 4 vols. (New York, 1872–75) 1, pp. 151–66: 161–62; John Richard Alden, *General Charles Lee: Traitor or Patriot?* (Baton Rouge, Louisiana, 1951), pp. 51–53, 62–65.

53. GW to Thomas Lewis, February 17, 1774, and to James Wood, February 20, 1774, in *PWC*, 9, pp. 481–83, 490.

54. The Continental Association of October 20, 1774 is given in Peter D. G. Thomas, *Revolution in America: Britain and the Colonies 1763–1776* (Cardiff, 1992), pp. 76–78.

55. Mackenzie to GW, September 13, 1774, in *PWC*, 10, pp. 151–62; also McKenzie to GW, August 12, 1760, in *PWC*, 6, p. 454; GW to McKenzie, November 20, 1760, in *PWC*, 6, pp. 479–80; National Archives, WO 1/5, fols. 309–310: "State of the 58th Regiment of Foot When Captured by the French, July 21st 1762."

56. GW to Mackenzie, October 9, 1774, in *PWC*, 10, pp. 171–172.

57. William Milnor to GW, November 29, 1774, in *PWC*, 10, pp. 189–98.

58. GW to George William Fairfax, May 31, 1775, in *PWC*, 10, pp. 367–68.

6: His Excellency General Washington

1. L. H. Butterfield, ed., *Diary and Autobiography of John Adams*, 4 vols. (Cambridge, Massachusetts, 1961), 3, pp. 322–23. This is the only account of the debate over Washington's appointment to command the Continental Army.

2. Longmore, *Invention of George Washington*, pp. 160–62.

3. The "Olive Branch Petition" was formally adopted by Congress on 8 July 1775. It is reprinted in Thomas, *Revolution in America*, pp. 83–4.

4. Although it has been suggested that Washington attended Congress wearing his old Virginia Regiment uniform, as depicted in Peale's 1772 portrait, the one he had recently worn as head of the Fairfax Independent Company is more likely. This outfit—dark blue, with buff breeches, waistcoat, and facings—became the model for general officers' uniforms in the Continental Army.

5. Rush to Thomas Ruston, October 29, 1775, in L. H. Butterfield, ed., *Letters of Benjamin Rush*, 2 vols. (Princeton, New Jersey, 1951), 1, p. 92; Abigail Adams to John Adams, July 16, 1775, in L. H. Butterfield, ed. *Adams Family Correspondence*, 4 vols. (Cambridge, Massachusetts, 1963–65), 1, p. 246.

6. Address to the Continental Congress, June 16, 1775, in *PWRW*, 1, p. 1.

7. Cited in George W. Corner, ed., *The Autobiography of Benjamin Rush* (Princeton, New Jersey, 1948), p. 113; GW to Martha Washington, June 18, 1775, in *PWRW*, 1, pp. 3–4.

8. Instructions from the Continental Congress, June 22, 1775, in *PWRW*, 1, pp. 21–22.

9. Don Higginbotham, *The War of American Independence: Military Attitudes, Policies, and Practice, 1763–1789* (New York, 1971), p. 211; see also the same author's *George Washington and the American Military Tradition* (Athens, Georgia, 1985), pp. 76–77. On Wolfe's rejection of his brigadiers' plan at Quebec, see Stephen Brumwell, *Paths of Glory: The Life and Death of General James Wolfe* (London, 2007), pp. 249–51, 260–62.

10. Address from the New York Provincial Congress, June 26, 1775, in *PWRW*, 1, p. 40.

11. GW to New York Provincial Congress, June 26, 1775, in *PWRW*, 1, p. 41.

12. Charles K. Bolton, ed., *The Letters of Hugh Earl Percy from Boston and New York, 1774–1776* (Boston, 1902), pp. 52–53.

13. John C. Dann, ed., *The Revolution Remembered: Eyewitness Accounts of the War for Independence* (Chicago, 1980), pp. 2–4. Both men gave their testimony in old age to support their pension applications.

14. Houlding, *Fit for Service*, pp. 214–15.

15. Loftus's medal is illustrated in *1776: The British Story of the American Revolution* (London, 1976), p. 50.

16. GW to John Augustine Washington, July 27, 1775, in *PWRW*, 1, p. 183.

17. General Orders, Cambridge, July 4, 1775, in *PWRW*, 1, p. 54.

18. GW to Lund Washington, August 20, and to Richard Henry Lee, August 29, 1775, in *PWRW*, 1, pp. 372–73.

19. General Orders, Cambridge, July 7, 1775, in *PWRW*, 1, pp. 71–72, 74, note 1.

20. Petition from Captain Spaulding's company, August 10, 1775, in *PWRW*, 1, p. 285.

21. GW to Hancock, August 31, 1775, in *PWRW*, 1, pp. 390–91.

22. General Orders, Cambridge, July 17 and August 1 and 28, 1775, in *PWRW*, 1, pp. 114, 207, 371.

23. General Orders, Cambridge, July 17 and 23, 1775, in *PWRW*, 1, pp. 114–15, 158.

24. James Thacher, *Military Journal of the American Revolution* (Boston, 1827), p. 33.

25. GW to John Hancock, July 10–11, 1775, in *PWRW*, 1, pp. 88–89.

26. Thacher, *Military Journal*, pp. 33–34.

27. GW to Samuel Washington, September 30, 1775, in *PWRW*, 2, p. 73. For Washington's ownership of a rifle in the Fort Necessity campaign, see James Mackay to Washington, August 27, 1754, in *PWC*, 1, p. 194.

28. Greene to GW, September 10, 1775, in *PWRW*, 1, p. 445, and note 1, pp. 445–46; also Aaron Norcross Diary, September 10, 1775, cited in John A. Ruddiman, "'A record in the hands of thousands': Power and Negotiation in the Orderly Books of the Continental Army," *WMQ*, 67 (2010), pp. 747–74: 755–56.

29. General Orders, Cambridge, September 11 and 13, 1775, in *PWRW*, 1, pp. 449, 454–55; Proceedings of the Committee of Conference, Cambridge, October 18–24, 1775, in *PWRW*, 2, p. 195.

30. See Trask's testimony in Dann, ed., *The Revolution Remembered*, pp. 408–409. This recollection is accepted as genuine by Ron Chernow, *Washington: A Life* (New York, 2010), pp. 197–98. David McCullough, *1776* (New York, 2005), p. 61, notes that while Trask's story "may or may not be entirely reliable" it "portrays vividly the level of frustration and tension among the troops and Washington's own pent-up anger and exasperation."

31. GW to John Hancock, August 4–5, 1775, and to Nicholas Cooke, August 4, 1775, in *PWRW*, 1, pp. 227, 221.

32. GW to Gage, August 11, 1775, in *PWRW*, 1, pp. 289–90.

33. Gage to GW, August 13, 1775, in *PWRW*, 1, pp. 301–302.

34. "Royal Proclamation of Rebellion, August 23, 1775," in Thomas, *Revolution in America*, pp. 86–87.

35. See French to GW, August 15, 1775, in *PWRW*, 1, p. 311; and September 18, 1775, in *PWRW*, 2, p. 10; Thomas Seymour, Chairman, Hartford Committee of Safety, to GW, September 18, 1775, and GW to French, September 26, 1775, in *PWRW*, 2, pp. 13, 47–48.

36. GW to Hancock, September 21, 1775, in *PWRW*, 2, pp. 24–30. The enlistments of the Connecticut troops actually expired on December 10. See General Orders, Cambridge, December 3, 1775, in *PWRW*, 2, p. 475.

37. Circular to General Officers, Cambridge, September 8, 1775, and Council-of-War, Cambridge, September 11, 1775, in *PWRW*, 1, pp. 432–44, 450–51.

38. Council-of-War, Cambridge, October 18, 1775, in *PWRW*, 2, p. 184; *JCC*, 3, p. 270.

39. General Orders, Cambridge, September 5, 1775, in *PWRW*, 1, p. 415.

40. See Stephen Conway, "Britain and the Revolutionary Crisis, 1763–1791," in P. J. Marshall, ed., *The Oxford History of the British Empire, Volume II: The Eighteenth Century* (Oxford, 1998), pp. 325–46: 338–39.

41. James Wilkinson, *Memoirs of My Own Times*, 3 vols. (Philadelphia, 1816), 1, p. 29.

42. Council-of-War, Cambridge, October 8, 1775, in *PWRW*, 2, pp. 123–25; General Orders, Cambridge, November 12, 1775, in *PWRW*, 2, pp. 353–55. On the question of whether the "new army," like the old one, should utilize black manpower, it was agreed unanimously "to reject all slaves, and by a great majority to reject negroes altogether," in *PWRW*, 2, p. 125.

43. Reuben Fogg to GW, October 20, 1775, in *PWRW*, 2, p. 208; GW to the Falmouth Committee of Safety, October 24, 1775, in *PWRW*, 2, pp. 225–26.

44. GW to Reed, November 30, 1775, and to Arnold, December 5, 1775, in *PWRW*, 2, pp. 463, 494.

45. GW to Hancock, December 4 ,1775, in *PWRW*, 2, p. 486.

46. Instructions to Col. Henry Knox, November 16, 1775, in *PWRW*, 2, pp. 384–85.

47. GW to Reed, November 28, 1775, in *PWRW*, 2, pp. 448–49.

48. Jonathan Trumbull Snr to GW, December 7, 1775, in *PWRW*, 2, p. 511.

49. Lund Washington to GW, December 10, 1775, in *PWRW*, 2, pp. 526–28.

50. GW to Hancock, December 18, 1775, in *PWRW*, 2, p. 574.

51. GW to Arnold, December 5, 1775, in *PWRW*, 2, p. 493.

52. GW to Schuyler, December 5, 1775, in *PWRW*, 2, p. 498.

53. GW to Reed, January 4, 1776, in *PWRW*, 3, p. 24; General Orders, Cambridge, December 30, 1775, in *PWRW*, 2, p. 620.

54. General Orders, Cambridge, January 1, 1776, in *PWRW*, 3, p. 3; GW to Reed, January 4, 1776, in *PWRW*, 3, p. 24.

55. GW to Woodford, November 10, 1775, in *PWRW*, 2, pp. 346–47.

56. See Robert K. Wright, Jr., "'Nor Is Their Standing Army to Be Despised': The Emergence of the Continental Army as a Military Institution" in R. Hoffman and P. J. Albert, eds., *Arms and Independence: The Military Character of the American Revolution* (Charlottesville, Virginia, 1984), pp. 50–74: 66.

57. Quebec veteran Captain William DeLaune noted this point inside a copy of the 6th edition of Bland's book that Wolfe gave him in the early 1750s. See John Clarence Webster, ed., *Wolfiana: A Potpourri of Facts and Fantasies, Culled from the Literature Relating to the Life of James Wolfe* (privately printed, 1927), pp. 16–17. For the relevant coverage in Bland's *Treatise of Military Discipline*, see pp. 133–34 of the 6th edition (London, 1746). On Bland and Washington's other recommended titles for Woodford, see Spaulding, "Military Studies of Washington," in *American Historical Review* (1924), pp. 678–79.

58. See, for example, GW to Major General Philip Schuyler, August 20, 1775, in *PWRW*, 1, p. 332.

59. Freeman, *Washington*, 4, p. 6.

60. GW to Hancock, February 18, 1776, in *PWRW*, 3, p. 335.

61. GW to Reed, February 26–March 9, 1776, in *PWRW*, 3, p. 373.

62. Powell, ed., "Elisha Bostwick's Memoirs," *WMQ* (1949), pp. 98–99.

63. GW to Hancock, March 7–9, 1776, in *PWRW*, 3, pp. 422–24.

64. See Matthew H. Spring, *With Zeal and with Bayonets Only: The British Army on Campaign in North America, 1775–1783* (Norman, Oklahoma, 2008), pp. 141, 217.

65. GW to Hancock, March 19, 1776, in *PWRW*, 3, pp. 489–90.

7: The Times that Try Men's Souls

1. Lee to GW, February 19, 1776, in *PWRW*, 3, p. 340.

2. GW to Lee, March 14, 1776, in *PWRW*, 3, p. 468.

3. Piers Mackesy, *The War for America, 1775–1783* (1964; repr. Lincoln, Nebraska, 1993), pp. 39–40, 61–62.

4. GW to John Augustine Washington, May 31–June 4, 1776, in *PWRW*, 4, p. 412.

5. Wright, *Washington and the American Revolution*, p. 104; GW to Howe, in *PWRW*, 2, p. 576.

6. Lee to Rush, June 29, 1776, *Lee Papers*, 2, p. 95. On the siege of Charleston, see David K. Wilson, *The Southern Strategy: Britain's Conquest of South Carolina and Georgia, 1775–1780* (Columbia, South Carolina, 2005), pp. 36–58.

7. Butterfield, ed. *Letters of Rush*, 1, p. 103.

8. General Orders, New York, July 9, 1776, in *PWRW*, 5, p. 246.

9. General Orders, New York, July 10, 1776, in *PWRW*, 5, pp. 256–57.

10. GW to Hancock, July 10, 1776, in *PWRW*, 5, p. 260.

11. Nathan Schaner, ed., "Alexander Hamilton Viewed by His Friends: The Narratives of Robert Troup and Hercules Mulligan," *WMQ*, 4 (1947), pp. 203–25: 210.

12. See Franklin's "Journal of Negotiations in London," in a letter to his son William Franklin, March 22, 1775, in Leonard W. Labaree and William B. Willcox, eds., *The Papers of Benjamin Franklin*, 36 vols to date. (New Haven, Connecticut, 1959–), 21, pp. 565–74.

13. GW to Hancock, July 14, 1776, in *PWRW*, 5, pp. 305–306.

14. Edward H. Tatum, Jr., ed., *The American Journal of Ambrose Serle, Secretary to Lord Howe, 1776–1778* (San Marino, California, 1940), p. 35.

15. Ira D. Gruber, *The Howe Brothers and the American Revolution* (New York, 1972), pp. 94–95.

16. GW to Stephen, July 20, 1776, in *PWRW*, 5, pp. 408–409.

17. General Orders, Head Quarters, New York, August 1, 1776, in *PWRW*, 5, p. 534.

18. General Orders, Head Quarters, New York, August 13, 1776, in *PWRW*, 6, pp. 1–2.

19. GW to Jonathan Trumbull, Snr, August 24, 1776, and to Lund Washington, August 26, 1776, in *PWRW*, 6, pp. 123, 136.

20. W. B. Wilcox, *Portrait of a General: Sir Henry Clinton in the War of Independence* (New York, 1964), p. 105.

21. Nelson, *General James Grant*, pp. 85–87.

22. "Extract of a letter from New-York, dated Sept. 1," in *Maryland Gazette*, September 12, 1776.

23. Grant to Edward Harvey, September 2, 1776, cited in McCullough, *1776*, p. 179.

24. Henry Clinton, *The American Rebellion: Sir Henry Clinton's Narrative of his Campaigns, 1775–1782, with an Appendix of Original Documents*, ed. William B. Willcox (New Haven, Connecticut, 1954), p. 44.

25. Charles Stedman, *The History of the Origin, Progress and Termination of the American War*, 2 vols. (London, 1794), 1, pp. 198–99.

26. GW to Hancock, August 31, 1776, in *PWRW*, 6, pp. 177–78.

27. GW to Hancock, September 2, 1776, in *PWRW*, 6, pp. 199–200.

28. Tatum, ed., *Journal of Serle*, p. 91.

29. Greene to GW, September 5, 1776, in Richard K. Showman, ed., *The Papers of General Nathanael Greene*, 13 vols. (Chapel Hill, North Carolina, 1976–2005), 1, pp. 294–95.

30. GW to John Hancock, September 8, 1776, in *PWRW*, 6, pp. 248–52.

31. "From Certain General Officers" to GW, September 11, 1776, GW to Hancock, September 11, 1776, and Council-of-War, New York, September 12, 1776, in *PWRW*, 6, pp. 279, 280–81, 288–89.

32. Butterfield, ed., *Diary and Autobiography of Adams*, 3, p. 422. Adams's recollection on this point is corroborated by the minutes of the meeting made by the peace commission's secretary, Henry Strachey, and given in Labaree and Willcox, eds., *Papers of Franklin*, 22, p. 599.

33. Rush to Mrs. Rush, Philadelphia, September 14, 1776, in Butterfield, ed., *Letters of Rush*, 1, p. 109.

34. See Gruber, *Howe Brothers*; also Brumwell, "Band of Brothers," *History Today* (June 2008), pp. 25–31.

35. Rawdon to Lord Huntington, September 23, 1776, cited in Paul David Nelson, *Francis Rawdon-Hastings, Marquess of Hastings: Soldier, Peer of the Realm, Governor-General of India* (Cranbury, New Jersey, 2005), p. 47.

36. GW to Hancock, September 16, 1776, in *PWRW*, 6, p. 313; Weedon to John Page, President of the Virginia Council, September 20, 1776, in Henry Steele Commager and Richard B. Morris, eds., *The Spirit of 'Seventy Six: The Story of the American Revolution as Told by Participants* (New York, 1975), p. 467; Greene to Governor Cooke of Rhode Island, September 17, 1776, in Showman, ed., *Papers of Greene*, 1, p. 300.

37. GW to Hancock, September 16, 1776, in *PWRW*, 6, p. 314.

38. Joseph Reed to his wife, September 17, 1776, cited in Commager and Morris, eds., *The Spirit of 'Seventy-Six*, pp. 468–69.

39. Greene to Governor Cooke, September 17, and to William Ellery [?],October 4, 1776, in Showman, ed., *Papers of Greene*, 1, pp. 300, 307.

40. *JCC*, 5, p. 762–63; *JCC*, 6, pp. 944–45, 971. See also GW to Hancock, September 2 and October 4, 1776, in *PWRW*, 6, pp. 200, 463.

41. GW to Hancock, September 25, 1776, in *PWRW*, 6, pp. 393–400.

42. GW to Patrick Henry, October 5, 1776, in *PWRW*, 6, p. 482.

43. GW to Hancock, October 4, 1776, in *PWRW*, 6, p. 464.

44. William Tudor to John Adams, New York, September 6, 1776, and John Adams to James Warren, September 25, 1776, in Robert J. Taylor, ed., *The Papers of John Adams*, 8 vols. (Cambridge, Massachusetts, 1979), 5, pp. 13, 38, and pp. 39–40, notes; Butterfield, ed., *Autobiography of John Adams*, 3, pp. 409–410.

45. "Howe's Orders, 1776," in *Collections of the New-York Historical Society: The Kemble Papers, Volume 1, 1773–1789* (New York, 1883), pp. 287–88.

46. See Charles Patrick Neimeyer, *America Goes to War: A Social History of the Continental Army* (New York, 1996), pp. 134–35; Caroline Cox, *A Proper Sense of Honor: Service and Sacrifice in George Washington's Army* (Chapel Hill, North Carolina, 2004), pp. 94–96.

47. GW to Lund Washington, September 30, 1776, in *PWRW*, 6, p. 441–42.

48. Tatum, ed., *Journal of Serle*, p. 107.

49. Ibid., pp. 107–108.

50. Mackesy, *War for America*, pp. 95–96.

51. Gruber, *Howe Brothers*, pp. 124–26.

52. See Council-of-War, October 16, 1776, in *PWRW*, 6, p. 576; also Freeman, *Washington*, 4, pp. 217–20.

53. General Orders, Head Quarters, Harlem Heights, October 21, 1776, in *PWRW*, 7, p. 1.

54. Rawdon to Lord Huntingdon, November 3, 1776, cited in Nelson, *Francis Rawdon-Hastings*, p. 51.

55. Gruber, *Howe Brothers*, p. 133.

56. Howe to Germain, New York, November 30, 1776, in K. G. Davies, ed., *Documents of the American Revolution*, 21 vols. (Shannon, 1972–81), 12, p. 259.

57. Council-of-War, White Plains, November 6, 1776; GW to Hancock, November 6, 1776, in *PWRW*, 7, pp. 92, 96–98.

58. GW to Greene, November 8, 1776, and Greene to GW, November 9, 1776, in *PWRW*, 7, pp. 115–16, 120.

59. Instructions to Major General Charles Lee, White Plains, November 10, 1776, in *PWRW*, 7, pp. 133–35.

60. GW to Hancock, November 14, 1776, in *PWRW*, 7, p. 154.

61. See Colonel Magaw to Greene, November 15, 1776, and Greene to GW, "4 o'clock," November 15, 1776, in Showman, ed., *Papers of Greene*, 1, pp. 350–51.

62. Greene to Henry Knox, November 17, 1776, in ibid., p. 352.

63. Grant to Edward Harvey, November 22, 1776, cited in McCullough, *1776*, p. 244.

64. GW to John Augustine Washington, November 19, 1776, in *PWRW*, 7, pp. 103–104.

65. Ira D. Gruber, ed., *John Peebles' American War, 1776–1782* (Stroud, Gloucestershire, 1998), p. 63.

66. See National Archives, WO/34/41, fol. 122: Amherst to Bouquet, New York, August 25, 1763.

67. A. French, ed., *The Diary of Frederick Mackenzie*, 2 vols. (Cambridge, Massachusetts, 1930), 1, pp. 111–12.

68. Tatum, ed., *Journal of Serle*, pp. 88, 106.

69. GW to Hancock, November 19–21, 1776, in *PWRW*, 7, pp. 182–83.

70. GW to Lee, November 21, 1776, in *PWRW*, 7, pp. 193–94.

71. Reed to Lee, November 21, 1776, in *Lee Papers*, 2, pp. 293–94.

72. GW to Hancock, November 23, 1776, in *PWRW*, 7, pp. 196 and 197, note 2.

73. Heath to GW, November 24, 1776, in *PWRW*, 7, pp. 205–206.

74. GW to Hancock, November 30, 1776, in *PWRW*, 7, p. 233.

75. Lee to Reed, November 24, 1776, in *Lee Papers*, 2, pp. 305–306; GW to Reed, November 30, 1776, in *PWRW*, 7, p. 237.

76. Mackesy, *War for America*, p. 97.

77. GW to Hancock, "Decr 1st 1776 ½ after 7. P. M.," and to Colonel Richard Humpton, December 1, 1776, in *PWRW*, 7, pp. 245, 248.

78. Lee to GW, November 30, 1776, and GW to Lee, December 1, 1776, in *PWRW*, 7, pp. 235, 249.

79. Howe to Germain, December 20, 1776, in Davies, ed. *Documents of the American Revolution*, 12, p. 266; Captain Johann Ewald, *Diary of the American War*, trans. and ed. Joseph P. Tustin (New Haven, Connecticut, 1979), pp. 24–25.

80. GW to Hancock, December 5, 8, and 9, 1776, in *PWRW*, 7, pp. 262–64, 273, 283; and to Brigadier-General William Maxwell, December 8, 1776, in *PWRW*, 7, p. 278–79.

81. Lee to GW (two letters), December 8, 1776, in *PWRW*, 7, pp. 276–77.

82. GW to Lee, December 10, 1776; GW to Lund Washington, December 17, 1776, in *PWRW*, 7, pp. 288, 290.

83. Alden, *General Charles Lee*, pp. 158–61.

84. Lee to Gates, December 13, 1776, in *Lee Papers*, 2, p. 348.

85. *JCC*, 6, p. 1027.

86. GW to Hancock, December 20, 1776, in *PWRW*, 7, pp. 382–83; Greene to Hancock, December 21, in Showman, ed., *Papers of Greene*, 1, 372–74.

87. GW to Samuel Washington, December 18, 1776, in *PWRW*, 7, pp. 370–71.

88. Rush to Congressman Richard Henry Lee, December 21, 1776, in Butterfield, ed., *Letters of Rush*, 1, p. 121.

89. GW to Lund Washington, December 17, in *PWRW*, 7, p. 291.

8: Victory or Death

1. Mackesy, *War for America*, pp. 109–12.
2. R. Atwood, *The Hessians: Mercenaries from Hessen-Kassel in the American Revolution* (Cambridge, 1980), pp. 88–89.
3. GW to Major General Gates, December 14, 1776, and Robert Morris to GW, December 21, 1776, in *PWRW*, 7, pp. 333, 404.
4. Nelson, *General James Grant*, p. 108.
5. Reed to GW, December 22, 1776, in *PWRW*, 7, pp. 415–16.
6. GW to Reed, December 23, 1776, in *PWRW*, 7, pp. 423–24.
7. Ewald, *Diary of the American War*, pp. 42, 44.
8. Ibid., p. 39.
9. See Jac Weller, "Guns of Destiny: Field Artillery in the Trenton-Princeton Campaign, December 25, 1776 to January 3, 1777," in *Military Affairs*, 20 (1956), pp. 1–15: 7.
10. General Orders, December 25, 1776, in *PWRW*, 7, pp. 434–36. For the plan of attack and Washington's most detailed account of the entire Trenton operation, see GW to Hancock, December 27, 1776, in *PWRW*, 7, pp. 454–56.
11. See GW to Cadwalader, December 24 and 25, 1776, in *PWRW*, 7, pp. 425, 439.
12. David Hackett Fischer, *Washington's Crossing* (New York, 2004), pp. 203–205.
13. "General Joseph Reed's Narrative of the Movements of the American Army in the neighborhood of Trenton in the winter of 1776–1777," in *PMHB*, 8 (1884), pp. 391–402: 393; Corner, ed., *Autobiography of Rush*, p. 125.
14. GW to Hancock, December 27, 1776, in *PWRW*, 7, p. 454.
15. Corner, ed., *Autobiography of Rush*, pp. 124–25.
16. "Elisha Bostwick's Memoirs," in *WMQ* (1949), p. 102.
17. "Joseph Reed's Narrative," in *PMHB* (1884), p. 398. On this episode see also McCullough, *1776*, p. 279; and Fischer, *Washington's Crossing*, pp. 231–33.
18. "Elisha Bostwick's Memoirs," in *WMQ* (1949), p. 102.

19. See Monroe's "Autobiography," extracted in Daniel Preston, ed., *The Papers of James Monroe, Volume II: Selected Correspondence and Papers, 1776–1794* (Westport, Connecticut, 2006), p. 2.

20. Weller, "Guns of Destiny," *Military Affairs* (1956), p. 1.

21. Greene to Catherine Greene, December 30, 1776, in Showman, ed., *Papers of Greene*, 1, p. 377.

22. Tatum, ed., *Journal of Serle*, p. 163; Ewald, *Diary of the American War*, p. 44.

23. General Orders, Head Quarters, Newtown, Pennsylvania, December 27, 1776, in *PWRW*, 7, p. 448.

24. "The Battle of Princeton, by 'Sergeant R,'" in *PMHB*, 20 (1896), pp. 515–19: 515–16. This account was originally published on March 24, 1832 in *The Phoenix*, Wellsborough, Pennsylvania. The identification of the author as Sergeant Nathaniel Root rests upon very close similarities in the account of "Sergeant R" and Root's Revolutionary War pension application of August 1832. These are established in *The Battle of Princeton Mapping Project: Report of Military Terrain Analysis and Battle Narrative* (West Chester, Pennsylvania, 2010), Appendix I: Items 111–12, pp. 1–6. I am greatly indebted to Dr. Will Tatum of the David Library at Washington's Crossing, Pennsylvania, for alerting me to this important research project, which sheds fresh light on several aspects of the battle.

25. Isaac J. Greenwood, ed., *The Revolutionary Services of John Greenwood of Boston and New York, 1775–1783* (New York, 1922), pp. 43–45, 48.

26. Greene to Christopher Greene, January 20, 1777, in Showman, ed., *Papers of Greene*, 2, p. 9; *JCC*, 6, pp. 1043–46; GW to Executive Committee of Congress, and to Hancock, January 1, 1777, in *PWRW*, 7, pp. 500, 503–504.

27. "Joseph Reed's Narrative," in *PMHB* (1884), pp. 400–401; Corner, ed., *Autobiography of Rush*, pp. 126–27.

28. Washington to Hancock, January 5, 1777, in *PWRW*, 7, pp. 519–21.

29. Fischer, *Washington's Crossing*, pp. 281–83; Ewald, *Diary of the American War*, p. 48.

30. Wilkinson, *Memoirs*, 1, p. 138; "Extract of a letter from an officer of distinction [John Cadwalader] in General Washington's Army, dated Pluckemin, Jan 5, 1777" in *PMHB* (1884), pp. 310–12: 310.

31. Alfred Hoyt Bill, *The Campaign of Princeton 1776–1777* (Princeton, New Jersey, 1948), p. 88.

32. St. Clair's recollection is contained within an account of his disastrous defeat by the Ohio Indians in 1791. See *A Narrative of the manner in which the Campaign against the Indians . . . was conducted, under the command of Major-General St. Clair* (Philadelphia, 1812), p. 242; see also Wilkinson, *Memoirs*, 1, pp. 139–40.

33. Bill, *Campaign of Princeton*, pp. 90–92; GW to Hancock, January 5, 1777, in *PWRW*, 7, p. 521.

34. Ewald, *Diary of the American War*, p. 49.

35. Caesar Rodney, ed., *The Diary of Captain Thomas Rodney, 1776–1777* (Wilmington, Delaware, 1888), p. 32.

36. Ibid.

37. "The Good Soldier White," in *American Heritage*, 7, no. 4 (June 1956), pp. 73–79: 78; see also Robert E. Lee, *Blackbeard the Pirate: A Reappraisal of His Life and Times* (Winston-Salem, North Carolina, 1974), p. 12.

38. Wilkinson, *Memoirs*, 1, p. 142.

39. See especially *Battle of Princeton Mapping Project*, tables 2–3, pp. 38–42, giving detailed orders of battle.

40. "Battle of Princeton, by 'Sergeant R,'" *PMHB* (1896), p. 517; "George Inman's Narrative of the Revolution," in *PMHB*, 7 (1883), pp. 237–48: 240.

41. "Battle of Princeton, 'By Sergeant R,'" *PMHB* (1896), p. 517; "Letter from an officer of distinction," *PMHB* (1884), p. 311; Wilkinson, *Memoirs*, 1, pp. 145–46.

42. Ibid., pp. 148–49.

43. For British criticism of the 55th and 40th Foot, see especially the information supplied by an eyewitness, Andrew Wardrop (the surgeon of the 17th Foot) and reported by John Belsches to Lord Leven, Edinburgh, May 21, 1777, in Marianne M. Gilchrist, ed., "Captain Hon. William Leslie (1751–77). His Life, Letters and Commemoration," in David G. Chandler, ed., *Military Miscellany II: Manuscripts from Marlborough's Wars, the American War of Independence and the Boer War* (Stroud, Gloucestershire, 2005), pp. 133–96: 172.

44. Greene to Paine, January 9, 1777, in Showman, ed., *Papers of Greene*, 2, p. 3.

45. See "Letter of James Read, of Philadelphia, 1777," in *PMHB*, 16 (1892), pp. 456–66: 466; and letter of Shaw, from Morristown, New Jersey, cited in William S. Stryker, *The Battles of Princeton and Trenton* (Boston, 1898), p. 481.

46. Greene to Paine, January 9, 1777, and to Christopher Greene, January 20, 1777, in Showman, ed., *Papers of Greene*, 2, pp. 3, 8.

47. "An Officer of the Army [Captain William Hall, 28th Foot]," *The History of the Civil War in America* (London, 1780), 1, pp. 245–46, cited in *Battle of Princeton Mapping Project*, Appendix II, Item 2, p. 2; J. W. Fortescue, *A History of the British Army: Volume III, 1763–1793* (London, 1903), p. 205; Gruber, *Howe Brothers*, pp. 154, 157.

48. For the implications of Howe's "fixation" upon Washington and Pennsylvania, see especially Conway, *War of American Independence*, pp. 88–89.

49. "Battle of Princeton, By 'Sergeant R,'" *PMHB* (1896), p. 519; GW to the New York Convention, February 10, 1777, in *PWRW*, 8, pp. 299–300.

50. Gruber, ed., *Peebles' American War*, pp. 95–98, 102.

51. John Adams to Nathanael Greene, May 9, 1777, in Showman, ed., *Papers of Greene*, 2, pp. 74–75.

52. GW to Hancock, Morristown, May 12, 1777, in *PWRW*, 9, pp. 396–97.

53. Samuel Adams to Greene, May 12, 1777; and Greene to Adams, May 28, 1777, in Showman, ed., *Papers of Greene*, 2, pp. 77–78, 100.

54. Council-of-War, Basking Ridge, New Jersey, May 2, 1777, in *PWRW*, 9, p. 324.

55. GW to John Hancock; Stephen to GW; and GW to Stephen, all May 12, 1777, in *PWRW*, 9, pp. 396, 404–406.

56. GW to Heath, February 3, 1777, in *PWRW*, 8, p. 229.

57. GW to Pennsylvania Supreme Executive Council, July 9, 1777, in *PWRW*, 10, p. 233.

58. GW to John Augustine Washington, August 5–9, 1777, in *PWRW*, 10, pp. 514–15.

59. GW to Israel Putnam, August 22, 1777, in *PWRW*, 11, p. 46.

60. General Orders, headquarters, Wilmington, September 5. 1777, in *PWRW*, 11, pp. 147–48.

61. See Lieutenant Colonel James Ross to GW, "Sept 11, '77, Great Valley Road, Eleven O'clock A.M."; and Major General Sullivan to GW, Brintons Ford, September 11, 1777, in *PWRW*, 11, pp. 196–97. In following the confusing sequence of events at Brandywine, the detailed Editorial Note (ibid., pp. 187–95) is most helpful.

62. "The Actions at Brandywine and Paoli described by a British Officer," in *PMHB*, 29 (1905), pp. 368–69: 368.

63. GW to Hancock, "12 o'Clock at Night," September 11, 1777, in *PWRW*, 11, p. 200.

64. Greene's role is briefly described in a letter written ten months later. See Greene to Henry Marchant, July 25, 1778, in Showman, ed., *Papers of Greene*, 2, p. 471.

65. "George Inman's Narrative," in *PMHB* (1883), p. 241.

66. GW to Hancock, September 23, 1777, in *PWRW*, 11, p. 301.

67. "The Actions at Brandywine and Paoli," in *PMHB* (1905), p. 369. For a thoughtful analysis of this controversial episode, see Armstrong Starkey, "Paoli to Stony Point: Military Ethics and Weaponry during the American Revolution," in *Journal of Military History*, 58 (1994), pp. 7–27.

68. GW to Hancock September 23, 1777, in *PWRW*, 11, pp. 301–302.

69. Proceedings of a Council of General Officers, headquarters at Pennibeckers Mills, September 28, 1777, in Showman, ed., *Papers of Greene*, 2, pp. 167–69; GW to Hancock, October 5, 1777, *PWRW*, 11, p. 393.

70. General Orders for attacking Germantown, October 3, 1777, in *PWRW*, 11, pp. 375–76.

71. GW to Howe, October 6, 1777, in *PWRW*, 11, p. 410. If Howe acknowledged the return of his dog, which was identified as his property by its collar, his letter has not been found.

72. GW to Hancock, October 5 and 7, 1777, in *PWRW*, 11, pp. 393–95, 416–17. My brief account of Germantown draws heavily upon the excellent editorial notes in Showman, ed., *Papers of Greene*, 2, pp. 171–77.

73. Gruber, ed., *Peebles' American War*, p. 140.

74. *JCC*, 9, p. 785.

75. *Major André's Journal: Operations of the British Army under Lieutenant-Generals Sir William Howe and Sir Henry Clinton, June 1777 to November 1778* (Tarrytown, New York, 1930), p. 57.

76. In February 1781, Peebles noted that heavy drinking was "constantly the custom": at dinner "above two bottles of Madeira or port is generally the quantity that most people carry off." See Gruber, ed., *Peebles' American War*, p. 429; Corner, ed., *Autobiography of Rush*, p. 157; Rush to John Adams, October 31, 1777, in Butterfield, ed., *Letters of Rush*, 1, p. 164.

77. For the court of inquiry on Stephen, see General Orders, headquarters, Whitpain Township, October 25, 1777, in *PWRW*, 11, pp. 605–606; for his court-martial and dismissal, see General Orders, HQ, White Marsh, November 20, 1777, in *PWRW*, 12, pp. 327–28.

78. Ewald, *Diary of the American War*, p. 96.

79. See E. C. Joslin, A. R. Litherland, and B. T. Simpkin, *British Battles and Medals* (London, 1988), p. 16.

80. Clinton, *American Rebellion*, pp. 80–81.

81 GW to John Augustine Washington, August 5, 1777, in *PWRW*, 10, p. 515.

82. Washington to Benjamin Harrison, August 19, 1777, in *PWRW*, 11, p. 4. For the French cannon captured at Brandywine, see *Major André's Journal*, p. 47.

83. "Memoir of 1776" in Stanley J. Idzerda, ed., *Lafayette in the Age of the American Revolution: Selected Letters and Papers, 1776–1790*, 5 vols. (Ithaca, New York, 1977–83), 1, pp. 8–9, 11, 90, 100. On the relationship between Washington and Lafayette, see especially Rasmussen and Tilton, *George Washington: The Man Behind the Myths*, pp. 138–39.

84. General Orders, headquarters, "Towamensing," October 15, 1777, in *PWRW*, 11, pp. 512–13.

85. GW to Carter, October 27, 1777, in *PWRW*, 12, p. 27.

86. GW to Gates, October 30, 1777, in *PWRW*, 12, pp. 59–60.

87. Circular to the General Officers, October 26, 1777, and Council-of-War, October 29, 1777, in *PWRW*, 12, pp. 2–3, 46–48.

88. See Brigadier General John Cadwalader's Plan for Attacking Philadelphia (ca. November 24, 1777) and the opinions on it sent to

Washington by Generals Greene (November 24), Armstrong, Dupor-
tail, Irvine, Kalb, Maxwell, Paterson, Poor, Scott, Smallwood, Stirling,
Sullivan, Wayne, and Woodford (November 25) and Knox (November 26), in *PWRW*, 12, pp. 371–73, 379–80, 383–84, 387–88, 391–94,
396–404, 414–17.

89. Ewald, *Diary of the American War*, p. 108; Armstrong Starkey, "War
and Culture, a Case Study: The Enlightenment and the Conduct of
the British Army in America, 1755–1781," in *War and Society*, 8 (1990),
pp. 1–28: 13–14.

90. *Major André's Journal*, pp. 67–70.

91. General Orders, headquarters at the Gulph, December 17, 1777, in
PWRW, 12, pp. 620–21.

9: Treason of the Blackest Dye

1. GW to Henry Laurens, December 23, 1777, in *PWRW*, 12, pp. 683–85.

2. Joseph Plumb Martin, *A Narrative of a Revolutionary Soldier: Some of
the Adventures, Dangers, and Sufferings of Joseph Plumb Martin* (new
ed., New York, 2001), p. 88; "Memoir of 1779" in Idzerda, ed., *Lafayette
in the Age of the American Revolution*, 1, p. 170.

3. GW to the Board of War, January 2–3, 1778, in *PWRW*, 13, p. 112.

4. See GW to Lieutenant Colonel James Innes, January 2, and GW to a
Continental Congress Camp Committee, January 29, 1778, in *PWRW*,
13, pp. 116 and 116–17 (note 1), 379–80; Martin, *Narrative of a Revolutionary Soldier*, pp. 53–54; GW to Lund Washington, February 28, 1778,
in *PWRW*, 13, p. 699; Martin and Lender, *A Respectable Army*, pp. 88–
92. For a revealing regional case study of recruitment, see Michael A.
McDonnell, "'Fit for Common Service?' Class, Race, and Recruitment
in Revolutionary Virginia," in John Resch and Walter Sargent, eds.,
*War and Society in the American Revolution: Mobilization and Home
Fronts* (DeKalb, Illinois, 2007), pp. 103–131.

5. Scholarship on the composition of the Continental Army is extensive
and ongoing, but for useful overviews see Charles Patrick Neimeyer,
America Goes to War: A Social History of the Continental Army (New

York, 1996), and Martin and Lender, *A Respectable Army*, especially pp. 69–77, 87–99. Another study, which places greater emphasis upon ideology as a motivator for the rank and file, is Charles Royster, *A Revolutionary People at War: The Continental Army and the American Character, 1775–1783* (Chapel Hill, North Carolina, 1979), especially pp. 373–78.

6. For Bragg and Ingram, see Chelsea Boards of May 12 and June 18, 1787, in National Archives, WO 121/1, and for Haymer, Board of May 3, 1790, WO 121/8.

7. Stephen Conway, *The British Isles and the War of American Independence* (Oxford, 2000), pp. 34–35.

8. See the discussion in Spring, *Zeal and Bayonets*, pp. 28–29.

9. This overview follows Martin and Lender, *A Respectable Army*, pp. 100–103.

10. Paul David Nelson, *Anthony Wayne: Soldier of the Early Republic* (Bloomington, Indiana, 1985), p. 66; General Johann de Kalb to Count Charles Francis de Broglie, Valley Forge, December 25, 1777, in Commager and Morris, eds., *Spirit of 'Seventy-Six*, p. 646; *JCC*, 7, pp. 196–97 (March 24, 1777); see also Higginbotham, *War of American Independence*, p. 211.

11. John Adams to Abigail Adams, October 26, 1777, in P. H. Smith. ed., *Letters of Delegates to Congress, 1774–1789*, 26 vols. (Washington, D.C., 1976–2000), 8, p. 187. For widespread public praise of Washington, and the extent to which American propagandists depicted him as a virtuous replacement for the "tyrant" George III, see Longmore, *Invention of George Washington*, pp. 202–11.

12. Rush to John Adams, October 21, 1777, in Butterfield, ed., *Letters of Rush*, 1, p. 161.

13. Wilkinson, *Memoirs*, 1, pp. 331–32.

14. Stirling to GW, November 3, 1777, in *PWRW*, 12, p. 111.

15. GW to Conway, ca. November 5, 1777; Conway to GW, November 5, 1777, in *PWRW*, 12, pp. 129–30. A paraphrased extract from Conway's original letter to Gates was copied by Henry Laurens, who passed it to Washington's aide-de-camp, Lieutenant Col. John Fitzgerald; he in

turn enclosed it in a letter to Washington of February 16, 1778 (*PWRW*, 13, pp. 555–56).

16. Conway to GW, January 10, 1778, in *PWRW*, 13, p. 195.

17. See H. James Henderson, *Party Politics in the Continental Congress* (New York, 1974), p. 119. The notion of a "cabal" was comprehensively debunked by Bernhard Knollenberg in *Washington and the Revolution: A Reappraisal* (New York, 1940), pp. 65–77.

18. Craik to GW, January 6, 1778, in *PWRW*, 13, p. 160; Lafayette to Henry Laurens, ca. January 5, 1778, and Laurens to Lafayette, January 12, 1778, in Idzerda, ed., *Lafayette in the Age of the American Revolution*, 1, pp. 213, 231–32.

19. Lovell to Adams, January 20, 1778, in Smith, ed., *Letters of Delegates to Congress*, 8, p. 618.

20. See Rush to Patrick Henry, January 12, 1778, in Butterfield, ed., *Letters of Rush*, 1, p. 183.

21. GW to Conway, December 30, 1777; Conway to GW, December 31, 1777, in *PWRW*, 13, pp. 66–67, 78.

22. Lafayette to GW, December 30, 1777, in *PWRW*, 13, p. 69.

23. See "Conway, Thomas," in Johnson and Malone, eds., *Dictionary of American Biography*, 2, pp. 365–66. While most accounts assume that Cadwalader "called out" Conway, Freeman suggested that Conway was the challenger (*Washington*, 5, p. 39). For Conway's letter to Washington from Philadelphia (misdated to February 23, instead of July 23, 1778), see Thacher, *Military Journal*, p. 129 note.

24. Gates to GW, December 8, 1777, and February 19, 1778, in *PWRW*, 12, pp. 576–77, and *PWRW*, 13, p. 590; and GW to Gates, January 4 and February 24, 1778, in *PWRW*, 13, pp. 138–39, 654–55.

25. For the "witch hunt" comparison and a thoughtful overview of the "Conway Cabal," see Higginbotham, *War of American Independence*, pp. 216–22.

26. GW to Continental Congress Camp Committee, January 29, 1778, in *PWRW*, 13, pp. 377–78; Henderson, *Party Politics in the Continental Congress*, p. 124.

27. See Royster, *A Revolutionary People at War*, pp. 208–10.

28. Ewald, *Diary of the American War*, Introduction, pp. xxv–xxvi.

29. Thacher, *Military Journal*, p. 205 (mispaged as p. 189).

30. Joseph J. Ellis argues that Valley Forge was the "honor-driven place where dueling first became a fixture in national politics." See *His Excellency George Washington*, p. 295, note 9.

31. See Mark Evans Bryan, "'Slideing into Monarchical extravagance': *Cato* at Valley Forge and the Testimony of William Bradford Jr.," *WMQ*, 67 (2010), pp. 123–44.

32. Gruber, ed., *Peebles' American War*, pp. 181–83; Tatum, ed. *Journal of Serle*, p. 294. For a detailed account of the "Mischianza" written by one of the organizers, Captain John André, dated Philadelphia, May 23, 1778, see the *Annual Register* for 1778, pp. 267–70. On the event's "Gothic" dimension, see Starkey, "War and Culture: a Case Study," in *War and Society* (1990), pp. 17–18.

33. GW to Henry Laurens, April 30, 1778, in *PWRW*, 14, pp. 681–83.

34. Baron von Steuben to Franklin, September 28, 1779, in Labaree and Willcox, eds., *Papers of Franklin*, 30, p. 412; Clinton, *American Rebellion*, p. 95, note 16.

35. See Paul Lockhart, *The Drillmaster of Valley Forge: The Baron de Steuben and the Making of the American Army* (New York, 2008), pp. 193–94.

36. General Orders, headquarters, Valley Forge, May 5, 1778, in *PWRW*, 15, pp. 38–40, 41, note 6.

37. Gruber, ed., *Peebles' American War*, p. 188.

38. See William B. Wilcox, "Sir Henry Clinton: Paralysis of Command," in George A. Billias, ed., *George Washington's Opponents: British Generals and Admirals in the American Revolution* (New York, 1969), pp. 73–102: 74.

39. Lee to GW, April 13, 1778, enclosing his "Plan of an Army, Etc" in *Lee Papers*, 2, pp. 382–89: 388; and June 15, 1778, in *PWRW*, 15, p. 404.

40. Council-of-War, Hopewell Township, New Jersey, June 24, 1778, in *PWRW*, 15, pp. 520–21; Hamilton to Elias Boudinot, July 5, 1778, in Harold C. Syrett, ed., *The Papers of Alexander Hamilton*, 27 vols. (New York, 1961–87), 1, p. 510.

41. See Greene, Lafayette, and Wayne to GW, June 24, 1778, and Hamilton to GW, June 26, 1778 in *PWRW*, 15, pp. 525–26, 528–29, 535. and 547.

42. Lee to GW, June 25, 1778, in *PWRW*, 15, p. 541.

43. Martin, *Narrative of a Revolutionary Soldier*, pp. 110–11.

44. Despite much colorful speculation, exactly what was said is unclear from the evidence, although Lee maintained that Washington made use of "very singular expressions." Washington denied doing so and could only recall using language "dictated by duty and warranted by the occasion." See Lee to GW, and GW to Lee, both June 30, 1778, in *PWRW*, 15, pp. 594–95; also, the discussion of the episode in James Thomas Flexner, *George Washington in the American Revolution, 1775–1783* (Boston, 1967), p. 305.

45. Hamilton to Boudinot, July 5, 1778, in Syrett, ed., *Papers of Hamilton*, 2, p. 512; Nathanael Greene to [his brother] Jacob Greene, July 2, 1778, in Showman, ed., *Papers of Greene*, 2, p. 451.

46. Ewald, *Diary of the American War*, p. 136.

47. General Orders, headquarters, Freehold, and GW to Laurens, both June 29, 1778, in *PWRW*, 15, pp. 583, 587.

48. See Lee to GW, June 30, 1778 (three letters), and GW to Lee, June 30 (two letters) in *PWRW*, 15, pp. 594–97.

49. For the charges, see *Lee Papers*, 3, p. 2, with the verdict at p. 208. The voluminous court testimony fills the intervening pages.

50. Shy, *A People Numerous and Armed*, p. 159.

51. Clinton, *American Rebellion*, p. 96.

52. See the "Account" of the duel prepared by the "seconds," Alexander Hamilton and Major Evan Edwards, in Syrett, ed., *Papers of Hamilton*, 1, pp. 602–604.

53. Rush to John Adams, October 13, 1777, in Butterfield, ed., *Letters of Rush*, 1, p. 158. A leading modern historian of the war concludes that Lee "would have been a disaster as the army's commander." See Ferling, *Almost a Miracle*, p. 573.

54. On the war at sea, see especially William M. Fowler, *Rebels Under Sail: the American Navy During the American Revolution* (New York, 1976); David Syrett, *The Royal Navy in American Waters, 1775–1783*

(Aldershot, 1989); and Daniel A. Baugh, "Why Did Britain Lose Command of the Sea During the War for America?," in Jeremy Black and Philip Woodfine, eds., *The British Navy and the Use of Naval Power in the Eighteenth Century* (Leicester, 1988), pp. 149–69.

55. GW to d'Estaing, July 17, 1778, in *PWRW*, 16, p. 88.

56. Washington to Nathanael Greene, September 1, 1778, in *PWRW*, 16, pp. 458–59.

57. For the diverging views of British officers, see Stephen Conway, "To Subdue America: British Army Officers and the Conduct of the Revolutionary War," in *WMQ*, 43 (1986), pp. 381–407.

58. Freeman, *Washington*, 5, p. 87.

59. Washington to Henry Laurens, November 14, 1778, in *PWRW*, 18, pp. 149–51.

60. See Mackesy, *War for America*, p. 232; Fortescue, *History of the British Army*, 3, pp. 268–71; Spring, *Zeal and Bayonets*, p. 192; Mark Urban, *Fusiliers: Eight Years with the Redcoats in America* (London, 2007), p. 306.

61. Gruber, ed., *Peebles' American War*, p. 271.

62. See GW to Wayne, July 10, 1779, in *WW*, 15, pp. 396–97; also, Nelson, *Anthony Wayne*, pp. 94–101; and Starkey, "Paoli to Stony Point," *Journal of Military History* (1994), pp. 20–27.

63. Washington to Major General Lord Stirling, August 21, 1779, and to Lafayette, September 12, 1779, in *WW*, 16, pp. 145–46, 267–68.

64. Ewald, *Diary of the American War*, pp. 166–67.

65. On this episode, known as the "Indian Field" skirmish, see Ewald, *Diary of the American War*, pp. 144–45, and Brigadier General Charles Scott to GW, August 31, 1778, in *PWRW*, 16, p. 448; also Colin G. Calloway, *The American Revolution in Indian Country: Crisis and Diversity in Native American Communities* (Cambridge and New York, 1995), pp. 96–97.

66. Instructions to Major General John Sullivan, May 31, 1779, in *PWRW*, 20, pp. 717–18. For an analysis of Sullivan's expedition that emphasizes the different "rules" governing war against Indians, see Wayne E. Lee, *Barbarians and Brothers: Anglo-American Warfare, 1500–1865* (New York, 2011), pp. 209–31.

67. See Isabel Thompson Kelsay, *Joseph Brant, 1743-1807: Man of Two Worlds* (Syracuse, New York, 1984), pp. 62, 161–74, 182–83.

68. Tatum, ed., *Journal of Serle*, p. 55.

69. GW to Lafayette, September 12 and 30, 1779, in *WW*, 16, pp. 268, 375. For the extent to which this wholesale destruction conformed to a well-established pattern of targeting Indians' food resources, see John Grenier, *The First Way of War: American War Making on the Frontier* (Cambridge and New York, 2005), especially pp. 166–67.

70. See Fausz, "'Engaged in Enterprises Pregnant with Terror': George Washington's Formative Years Among the Indians," in Hofstra, ed., *George Washington and the Virginia Backcountry*, p. 137.

71. Circular to Governors of the States, headquarters, Morristown, December 16, 1779, in *WW*, 17, pp. 273–74.

72. Thacher, *Military Journal*, pp. 181–82.

73. General Orders, January 28, 1780, in *WW*, 17, pp. 459–60.

74. Thacher, *Military Journal*, p. 182.

75. Martin, *Narrative of a Revolutionary Soldier*, p. 157.

76. Gruber, ed., *Peebles' American War*, pp. 372–73.

77. Lee Kennett, *The French Forces in America, 1780-1783* (Westport, Connecticut, 1977), pp. 29–30.

78. GW to Rochambeau, July 16 ,1780, and General Orders, Head Quarters, "Pracaness [New Jersey]," July 20, 1780, in *WW*, 19, pp. 186, 220–21.

79. Williams to Alexander Hamilton, August 30, 1780; Hamilton to James Duane, September 6, 1780, in Syrett, ed., *Papers of Hamilton*, 2, pp. 385, 420–21.

80. GW to Samuel Huntington, September 15, 1780, in *WW*, 20, pp. 49–50.

81. See Anthony J. Scotti, Jr., *Brutal Virtue: The Myth and Reality of Banastre Tarleton* (Bowie, Maryland, 2002), p. 134. While focused on Tarleton and his British Legion, Scotti's book also provides a nuanced analysis of the factors behind the brutality of warfare in the Carolinas.

82. See Washington's "Answers to Queries by the Comte de Rochambeau and the Chevalier de Ternay," and "Conference at Hartford," Hartford, September 22, 1780, in Syrett, ed., *Papers of Hamilton*, 2, pp. 435–38. See also Kennett, *French Forces in America*, pp. 59–61.

83. Clinton to Germain, October 11, 1780 in Clinton, *American Rebellion*, pp. 462–65.

84. See Robert E. Cray Jr., "Major John André and the Three Captors: Class Dynamics and Revolutionary Memory Wars in the Early Republic, 1780–1831," in *Journal of the Early Republic*, 17 (1997), pp. 371–97: 375–76.

85. General Orders, headquarters, Orangetown, September 26, 1780, in *WW*, 20, p. 95.

86. GW to Clinton, September 30, 1780, in *WW*, 20, pp. 103–104.

87. Robertson to Clinton, October 1, 1780, in Carl Van Doren, *Secret History of the American Revolution* (New York, 1941), pp. 488–89.

88. Ibid., p. 475.

89. André to GW, October 1, 1780, in *Major André's Journal*, p. 9; Hamilton to Lt. Col. John Laurens, October 11, 1780, in Syrett, ed., *Papers of Hamilton*, 2, p. 468.

90. Thacher, *Military Journal*, pp. 222–23; Gibbs's account is reproduced in *Major André's Journal*, p. 112.

91. Ewald, *Diary of the American War*, p. 250.

92. Rasmussen and Tilton, *George Washington: The Man Behind the Myths*, p. 140.

93. Given in Commager and Morris, eds., *The Spirit of 'Seventy Six*, p. 763.

94. Clinton, *American Rebellion*, p. 217.

95. Washington to Laurens, October 13, 1780, in *WW*, 20, p. 173.

96. Thacher, *Military Journal*, pp. 224–5; Martin and Lender, *A Respectable Army*, p. 161.

97. Arnold to GW, "On Board the *Vulture*," September 25, 1780, enclosed in Alexander Hamilton to GW, September 25, 1780, in Syrett, ed., *Papers of Hamilton*, 2, pp. 439–40.

10: The World Turned Upside Down

1. See Royster, *A Revolutionary People at War*, pp. 302–303.

2. James Kirby Martin, "A 'Most Undisciplined Profligate Crew': Protest and Defiance in the Continental Ranks, 1776–1783," in Hoffman, ed., *Arms and Independence*, pp. 119–40: 134.

3. Kennett, *French Forces in America*, pp. 83–84.

4. GW to Wayne, January 3–4, 1781, in *WW*, 21, pp. 55–58.

5. GW to the President of Congress, January 23, 1781, in *WW*, 21, pp. 135–36.

6. Thacher, *Military Journal*, pp. 244–46.

7. Kennett, *French Forces in America*, pp. 96–97.

8. GW to Lafayette, February 20, 1781, in *WW*, 21, pp. 253–55; Ewald, *Diary of the American War*, p. 295.

9. See Berthier's "Journal" in Howard C. Rice Jr. and Anne S. K. Brown, eds., *The American Campaigns of Rochambeau's Army, 1780, 1781, 1782, 1783*, 2 vols. (Princeton, New Jersey, and Providence, Rhode Island, 1972), 1, p. 241.

10. Evelyn M. Acomb, ed., *The Revolutionary Journal of Baron Von Closen* (Chapel Hill, North Carolina, 1958), p. 64.

11. See "Diary of a French Officer, 1781, presumed to be that of Baron Cromot du Bourg, Aid to Rochambeau, Part 2," in *The Magazine of American History*, 4 (1880), pp. 293–308: 296.

12. For Washington's reception, see Kennett, *French Forces in America*, p. 98.

13. Ibid, pp. 98–100.

14. *Diaries*, 3, p. 356.

15. See Lawrence E. Babits, *The Devil of a Whipping: The Battle of Cowpens* (Chapel Hill, North Carolina, 1998).

16. GW to Greene, April 18, 1781, in *WW*, 21, pp. 471–72.

17. See Allan R. Millett and Peter Maslowski, *For the Common Defense: A Military History of the United States of America* (New York, 1984), p. 54.

18. This synthesis draws especially on Martin and Lender, *A Respectable Army*, pp. 198–200; Conway, *The War of American Independence*, p. 30; and Howard H. Peckham, ed., *The Toll of Independence: Engagements and Battle Casualties of the American Revolution* (Chicago, 1974), pp. 132–33. Since 1818, half-pay pensions had been available to all Continental officers and men, along with members of the US Navy and Marines, who were in financial distress. By contrast, applicants under the 1832 law didn't have to prove disability or hardship. The many

thousands of testimonies taken to support pension applications have been described as "a remarkable body of historical data" amounting to "one of the largest oral history projects ever undertaken." See Dann, ed., *The Revolution Remembered*, pp. xv–xvii.

19. On Hobkirk's Hill, see Nelson, *Francis Rawdon-Hastings*, pp. 94–96; Terry Golway, *Washington's General: Nathanael Greene and the Triumph of the American Revolution* (New York, 2006), pp. 267–69.

20. Acomb, ed. *Journal of Closen*, p. 78; Kennett, *French Forces in America*, pp. 104–105.

21. Marquis de Chastellux, *Travels in North America*, trans. and ed. Howard C. Rice Jr., 2 vols. (Chapel Hill, North Carolina), 1, pp. 106–14.

22. See Kennett, *French Forces in America*, p. 105.

23. "Conference with Comte de Rochambeau," Wethersfield, May 23 [actually 22], 1781, in *WW*, 22, pp. 105–107; GW to Sullivan, May 29, 1781, in *WW*, 22, pp. 131–32.

24. This interpretation follows Kennett, *French Forces in America*, pp. 107–109; also Jonathan R. Dull, *The French Navy and American Independence: A Study of Arms and Diplomacy, 1774–1787* (Princeton, New Jersey, 1975), pp. 242–43. See also GW to Rochambeau, June 13, 1781, in *WW*, 22, p. 208.

25. See Rice and Brown, eds., *American Campaigns of Rochambeau's Army*, 1, p. 33; Acomb, ed., *Journal of Closen*, pp. 89–92.

26. For a detailed examination of the controversial issue of the black contribution to the Continental Army, see Neimeyer, *America Goes to War*, pp. 65–88.

27. *Diaries*, 3, p. 397.

28. See John Austin Stevens, "The Operations of the Allied Armies before New York, 1781," in *Magazine of American History*, 4 (1880), pp. 1–31.

29. *Diaries*, 3, pp. 403–405.

30. Nelson, *Anthony Wayne*, pp. 128–33.

31. See Clinton to Cornwallis, June 11 and June 15 (extract) in Clinton, *American Rebellion*, Appendix, pp. 529–32; Ewald, *Diary of the American War*, p. 315.

32. On Green Spring, see F. and M. Wickwire, *Cornwallis*, pp. 342–47; Nelson, *Anthony Wayne*, pp. 135–37.

33. See extracts of letters from Clinton to Cornwallis, June 28 and July 11, 1781 (extracts of two letters), in Clinton, *American Rebellion*, pp. 534, 543–54.

34. Ewald, *Diary of the American War*, p. 319.

35. *Diaries*, 3, pp. 409–10.

36. *Diaries*, 3, p. 411.

37. GW and Rochambeau to de Grasse, August 17, 1781, in *WW*, 23, pp. 7–10.

38. Acomb, ed., *Journal of Closen*, p. 115.

39. "Diary of a French Officer, 1781: Part 3," *Magazine of American History*, 4 (1880), pp. 376–85: 377–79.

40. Thacher, *Military Journal*, p. 263.

41. Acomb, ed. *Journal of Closen*, pp. 120–21.

42. See GW to Lafayette, August 27 and September 2, 1781, and to Greene, September 4, 1781, in *WW*, 23, pp. 52–53, 75–78, 84–86.

43. Acomb, ed., *Journal of Closen*, p. 123; "Diary of a French Officer, 1781: Part 3," *Magazine of American History* (1880), p. 384.

44. GW to Noah Webster, July 31, 1788, in *WW*, 30, pp. 26–28.

45. GW to the Superintendent of Finance, September 6–7, 1781, in *WW*, 23, pp. 89, 95; Acomb, ed., *Journal of Closen*, p. 124.

46. *Diaries*, 3, p. 419, and note 1; Acomb, ed., *Journal of Closen*, p. 129.

47. For a balanced discussion of this controversial episode, see M. M. Boatner, *Encyclopedia of the American Revolution* (New York, 1958), pp. 787–88.

48. Edward M. Riley, ed., "St. George Tucker's Journal of the Siege of Yorktown, 1781," in *WMQ*, 5 (1948), pp. 375–95: 377.

49. Kennett, *French Forces in America*, pp. 143–44.

50. GW to de Grasse, September 25, 1781, in *WW*, 23, p. 136.

51. Thacher, *Military Journal*, pp. 269–70.

52. For Cromwell's story and a reproduction of his discharge certificate, see Sidney Kaplan, *The Black Presence in the Era of the American Revolution 1770–1800* (Washington, D.C., 1973), pp. 47–48.

53. General Orders, headquarters, Williamsburg, September 27, 1781, *WW*, 23, pp. 147–48; Martin, *Narrative of a Revolutionary Soldier*, p. 197.

54. Steuben to Franklin, September 28, 1779, in Willcox, ed., *Papers of Franklin*, 30, p. 413.

55. See Harold L. Peterson, *Arms and Armor in Colonial America* (New York, 1956), pp. 286–89. See also General Orders: Valley Forge, December 22, 1777, in *PWRW*, 12, p. 663; Morristown, April 4, 1780, in *WW*, 18, pp. 214–15; Newburgh, August 9, 1782, in *WW*, 24, pp. 491–92. For the incident at White Plains, see Clinton, *American Rebellion*, pp. 51–52, and note 27.

56. Golway, *Washington's General*, pp. 280–84.

57. F. and M. Wickwire, *Cornwallis*, pp. 369–70.

58. *Diaries*, 3, p. 423.

59. Martin, *Narrative of a Revolutionary Soldier*, p. 199.

60. Thacher, *Military Journal*, p. 274.

61. *Diaries*, 3, p. 425; Acomb, ed., *Journal of Closen*, pp. 152, 156.

62. Thacher, *Military Journal*, pp. 274–75.

63. Dann, ed., *The Revolution Remembered*, pp. 244–45. Sarah Osborn's story survives in the testimony she provided in 1837, when aged eighty-one, to secure her dead husband's military pension.

64. Freeman, *Washington*, 5, p. 369.

65. GW to the President of Congress, October 16, 1781, in *WW*, 23, p. 228.

66. Thacher, *Military Journal*, pp. 275–76.

67. See Hamilton to Lafayette, October 15, 1781, and to Elizabeth Hamilton, October 16, 1781, in Syrett, ed., *Papers of Hamilton*, 2, pp. 679–82.

68. Suddarth's testimony was included in the narrative he submitted in 1839 to support his successful application for a revolutionary war pension. See Dann, ed., *The Revolution Remembered*, pp. 239–40.

69. See the terms in GW to Cornwallis, October 18, 1781, in *WW*, 23, pp. 237–38.

70. Griffiths's story emerges from a testimonial that Simcoe wrote on his behalf in 1789 to support his belated application for a Chelsea pension. See National Archives, WO/121/6, Chelsea Board of August 5, 1789. The registers of Royal Hospital Chelsea for the same date (in WO/116/9) show that Griffiths, who was then aged twenty-six, was appointed to a company of invalid soldiers as an alternative to being placed upon the "out-pension." Although appointed to the invalids at Chester Castle, he was discharged on Christmas Eve, 1790 (see WO/12/11600: Musters of the Invalids, Chester, 1783–1802).

71. Gruber, ed., *Peebles' American War*, pp. 480, 483–4.

72. This follows Count Mathieu Dumas, *Memoirs of His Own Time*, 2 vols. (Philadelphia, 1839), 1, 52n–53n, cited in George F. Scheer and Hugh F. Rankin, *Rebels and Redcoats: The American Revolution Through the Eyes of Those Who Fought and Lived It* (New York, 1957), p. 494, supplemented by Thacher, *Military Journal*, p. 279. See also the balanced account in Freeman, *Washington*, 5, pp. 388–90.

73. Dann, ed., *The Revolution Remembered*, p. 245. Lieutenant O'Hara was described as "a spirited young officer." See Lieutenant Colonel Banastre Tarleton, *A History of the Campaigns of 1780 and 1781, in the Southern Provinces of North America* (London, 1787), p. 280.

74. The evidence is discussed in Freeman, *Washington*, 5, p. 388, note 47.

75. See National Archives, Kew, WO/121/8 (Chelsea Board of June 8, 1790). Both men must have served in the 2nd Battalion of the 71st, as the 1st/71st was captured at Cowpens in January 1781.

76. See Greene to GW, May 31, 1779, in Showman, ed., *Papers of Greene*, 4, p. 108; Millett and Maslowski, *For the Common Defense*, p. 55.

77. GW to the President of Congress, November 5, 1780, in *WW*, 20, p. 293.

78. Ewald, *Diary of the American War*, pp. 339–41.

79. Conway, "Britain and the Revolutionary Crisis," in Marshall, ed., *Oxford History of the British Empire: The Eighteenth Century*, pp. 342–43.

80. See F. and M. Wickwire, *Cornwallis*, p. 978, citing Bill, *Campaign of Princeton*, p. 121.

81. Acomb, ed., *Journal of Closen*, pp. 239–40; GW to John Jay, October 18, 1782, in *WW*, 25, p. 275.

82. GW to Brigadier General William Irvine, July 10 and August 6, 1782, in *WW*, 24, pp. 417, 474. See also Calloway, *The Shawnees and the War for America*, p. 72.

83. GW to Lincoln, October 2, 1782, in *WW*, 25, pp. 226–28.

84. On this episode, see especially, Richard H. Kohn, "The Inside Story of the Newburgh Conspiracy: America and the Coup d'Etat," in *WMQ*, 27 (1970), pp. 187–220; and the same author's *Eagle and Sword: The Federalists and the Creation of the Military Establishment in America, 1783–1802* (New York, 1975), pp. 17–39; also Royster, *A Revolutionary People at War*, pp. 333–38.

85. Hamilton to GW, February 13, 1783 in Syrett, ed., *Papers of Hamilton*, 3, pp. 253–55.

86. GW to Hamilton, March 4, 1783, in *WW*, 26, p. 186; also Freeman, *Washington*, 5, p. 429.

87. Nelson, *General Horatio Gates*, pp. 271–73.

88. *JCC*, 24, pp. 295–97.

89. GW to Joseph Jones, March 12, 1783, in *WW*, 26, pp. 213–14; General Orders, headquarters, Newburgh, March 11, 1783, in *WW*, 26, p. 208; *JCC*, 24, pp. 297–99.

90. GW to the Officers of the Army, headquarters, Newburgh, March 15, 1783, in *WW*, 26, pp. 224–27.

91. See Freeman, *Washington*, 5, p. 435, and note 39; also Flexner, *Washington in the American Revolution*, p. 507. For "virtuoso performance," see Millett and Maslowski, *For the Common Defense*, p. 83; for "finest hour," see Higginbotham, *George Washington and the American Military Tradition*, p. 99. Paul Longmore observes that Washington increasingly saw himself as an actor "playing the primary role in a great historical drama," capable of delivering restrained, but highly effective performances. See Longmore, *Invention of George Washington*, pp. 182–83.

92. See GW to Boudinot and Jones, March 18, 1783, in *WW*, 26, pp. 230–34.

93. See Richard H. Kohn, "American Generals of the Revolution: Subordination and Restraint," in Don Higginbotham, ed., *Reconsiderations on the Revolutionary War* (Westport, Connecticut, 1978), pp. 104–23: 117; GW to Colonel Nicola, May 22, 1780, in *WW*, 24, pp. 272–73; Freeman, *Washington*, 5, p. 416.

94. On divisions between the Continental Army's officers and men and the implications for any attempted coup, see Martin, "'A Most Undisciplined Profligate Crew,'" in Hoffman and Albert, eds., *Arms and Independence*, pp. 137–39; also Royster, *A Revolutionary People at War*, pp. 335–36; Martin, *Narrative of a Revolutionary Soldier*, pp. 218, 226.

95. See General Orders, headquarters, Newburgh, March 29 and April 18, 1783, in *WW*, 26, pp. 268–69, 334–36.

96. Martin, *Narrative of a Revolutionary Soldier*, pp. 243–44.

97. Orders to the Armies of the United States, November 2, 1783, in *WW*, 27, pp. 223–27.

98. GW's "Address to the Continental Congress on Resigning his Commission," December 23, 1783, *WW*, 27, pp. 284–85.

99. See Martin and Lender, *A Respectable Army*, pp. 201–203.

100. Kohn, *Eagle and Sword*, p. 13

101. This overview of Harmar's and St. Clair's defeats follows Armstrong Starkey, *European and Native American Warfare, 1675–1815* (Norman, Oklahoma, 1998), pp. 141–47. For Cornwallis's guns, see Wiley Sword, *President Washington's Indian War: The Struggle for the Old Northwest, 1790–1795* (Norman, Oklahoma), p. 188.

102. Ibid., pp. 204–205.

103. See "Opinion of the General Officers," March 9, 1792, in *WW*, 31, pp. 509–15.

104. Starkey, *European and Native American Warfare*, p. 150; Kohn, *Eagle and Sword*, p. 124.

105. Quoted in Nelson, *Anthony Wayne*, pp. 266–67.

106. *Diaries*, 6, p. 192 and note.

107. On French veterans at the Bastille, see Kennett, *French Forces in America*, xii–xiii; for Lafayette and d'Estaing, see Boatner, *Encyclopedia of the American Revolution*, pp. 350, 593.

108. Lengel, *General George Washington*, pp. 359–60.

109. GW to the secretary at war, December 13, 1798, and to William Fitzhugh, August 5, 1798, cited and discussed in Rasmussen and Tilton, *George Washington: The Man Behind the Myths*, pp. 113–14.

110. See Kohn, *Eagle and Sword*, p. 253; Ellis, *His Excellency, George Washington*, pp. 158–60; Longmore, *Invention of George Washington*, p. 297, note 25.

111. Martin, *Narrative of a Revolutionary Soldier*, pp. 249–52. Martin published his memoir anonymously in 1830, two years before the introduction of pensions for all eligible Revolutionary War veterans, including militiamen.

112. GW to Sarah Cary Fairfax, May 16, 1798, in *WW*, 36, pp. 262–64.

113. GW to Chastellux, April 25–May 1, 1788, in *WW*, 29, pp. 484–85. The engraving of Wright's painting was issued in 1797. See Robert

Rosenblum, "Sources of Two Paintings by Joseph Wright of Derby," in *Journal of the Warburg and Courtauld Institute*, 25 (1962), pp. 135–36: 136.

114. See James Thomas Flexner, *George Washington: Anguish and Farewell (1793–1799)* (Boston, 1969), p. 459.

115. For this description, see Congressman Thomas Cushing to James Bowdoin Snr., June 21, 1775, in Smith, ed., *Letters of Delegates to Congress*, 1, p. 530.

116. Fortescue, *History of the British Army*, 3, pp. 409–10.

Acknowledgments

This book goes back to the summer of 2004, when I was invited to speak at Fort Necessity, Pennsylvania, as part of a weekend of events to commemorate the 250th anniversary of the young George Washington's defeat there. By that time I had already had the pleasure of meeting Robert and Mary Matzen of Paladin Communications, who asked me to participate, as an on-screen commentator, in what would become a trilogy of award-winning dramatized documentaries examining Washington's career before the Revolutionary War. Interviews conducted for the third of their films, *Pursuit of Honor: the Rise of George Washington*, prompted me to begin exploring themes that ultimately became central to *George Washington: Gentleman Warrior*. These were shot in 2005 during the 17th Annual French and Indian War History Seminar, organized by the Braddock Road Preservation Association at Jumonville, Pennsylvania, just a short hike from the rocky glen where Washington helped to trigger a war that changed the course of North America's history.

Since then, the opportunity to speak at other conferences in both Great Britain and the United States has proved extremely helpful in shaping my ideas. While actually writing my book I was fortunate to have the chance to talk about the wars that made Washington's reputation, and his relationship with the British Army, at Fort Loudoun, Vonore, Tennessee, in August 2010 and at the University of Leeds, Yorkshire, in July 2011. Both of these very lively and stimulating gatherings provided me with useful and timely feedback as I finalized my arguments. Thanks also go to Kurt A. Bodling, of the library at George Washington's Mount Vernon Estate and Gardens, for his courteous response to my inquiries. It is likewise a pleasure to acknowledge the help I've received from Tony Morris and John Houlding.

Through my research interests in Colonial and Revolutionary America I have been lucky enough to strike up some enduring transatlantic friendships. For their continuing fellowship and hospitality I'm especially grateful to Walt and Sue Powell, Martin and Penny West, Jeff and Diane Wells, Nick Westbrook, Tom Hatley, David Miller, Ian McCulloch, John-Eric Nelson, Anthony Hatch, and Tom Fink. Two other American friends, R. Scott Stephenson and Will Tatum, generously helped to confirm sources for me. On several trips to western Pennsylvania I also enjoyed meeting the late David Dixon, a fine scholar and a good companion who is greatly missed.

In Amsterdam, where the extensive American history collection in the University humanities library was an invaluable resource, I have much appreciated the company of Ray Barlow and Alex Thirlwall. Neither of them is a historian, but both have listened to my ramblings in the city's hostelries without complaint and maintained a keen interest in the project's progress. Another friend and drinking companion, Andy Robb, kindly read one of my draft chapters while recovering in hospital following surgery. I'm also obliged to Dick Visser, whose expertise saved the day when my aged computer crashed at a critical moment.

From the outset, all at my London publisher, Quercus, have shown professionalism, enthusiasm, and consideration. Crucially, nonfiction publishing director Richard Milner allowed me scope to refocus the book along new lines. I also owe special thanks to my editor, Joshua Ireland, for all his patience, encouragement, and close attention to the manuscript. His thoughtful comments have resulted in a much-improved book. In addition, I wish to thank picture researcher Elaine Willis for her indefatigable efforts in tracking down the precise images that I wanted, Bill Donohoe for transforming my rough sketches into clear and attractive maps, and David Watson for his thorough copy editing of the original British text. The North American edition has benefited enormously from the diligence of Nathaniel Marunas and his colleagues at the Quercus Publishing offices in New York, especially copy editor Mary Anne Stewart and managing editor Theresa Deal.

Finally, I have always valued the interest shown in my work by all of my family, and especially the unstinting support and understanding of my wife, Laura, and our children, Milly and Ivan. This book is dedicated to them with affection and gratitude.

Index